THE CHANNEL ISLANDS IN
ANGLO-FRENCH RELATIONS, 1689–1918

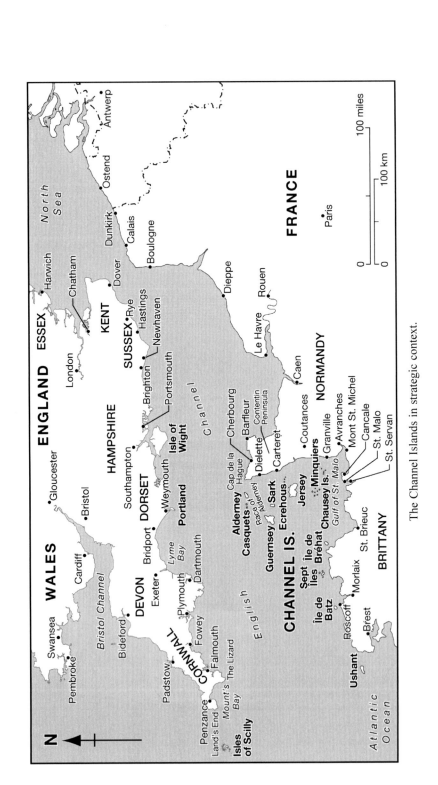

The Channel Islands in strategic context.

THE CHANNEL ISLANDS IN ANGLO-FRENCH RELATIONS 1689–1918

Edited by
Colin Partridge, Jean de Préneuf and Andrew Lambert

THE BOYDELL PRESS

First published 2024
The Boydell Press, Woodbridge

ISBN 978 1 78327 655 4

The Boydell Press is an imprint of Boydell & Brewer Ltd
PO Box 9, Woodbridge, Suffolk IP12 3DF, UK
and of Boydell & Brewer Inc.
668 Mt Hope Avenue, Rochester, NY 14620–2731, USA
website: www.boydellandbrewer.com

A CIP catalogue record for this book is available
from the British Library

The publisher has no responsibility for the continued existence or accuracy
of URLs for external or third-party internet websites referred to in this book,
and does not guarantee that any content on such websites is, or will remain,
accurate or appropriate

This publication is printed on acid-free paper

In memory of our dear friend Marc Michel, tireless advocate of the Channel Islands he loved so much, enthusiastic promoter of the Entente Cordiale.
This book owes him so much.

A la mémoire de notre cher ami Marc Michel, avocat infatigable des Îles anglo-normandes qu'il aimait tant, promoteur enthousiaste de l'Entente cordiale.
Ce livre lui doit tant.

CONTENTS

ILLUSTRATIONS

Frontispiece: The Channel Islands in strategic context

Full credit details are provided in the captions to the images in the text. The editors, contributors and publisher are grateful to all the institutions and persons for permission to reproduce the materials in which they hold copyright. Every effort has been made to trace the copyright holders; apologies are offered for any omission, and the publisher will be pleased to add any necessary acknowledgement in subsequent editions.

CONTRIBUTORS

William Allsop founded his own consulting practice in 2017 having worked at HR Wallingford (previously the Hydraulics Research Station) for 48 years. As Technical Director for Maritime Structures, he was responsible for consultancy and research studies on breakwaters, sea walls and a wide range of shoreline, estuarial and coastal structures, as well as performance and certification of temporary flood prevention devices. He devised the UK's first laboratory tsunami simulators. He has cooperated on research projects to advance design methods for breakwaters and coastal structures in the UK, Europe and the USA, and is an Honorary Professor at University College London. He is uniquely equipped to assess the engineering background and performance of the Alderney breakwater as one of the Channel 'harbours of refuge', and the problems faced with its continuing maintenance.

Michel Aumont was elected Chairman of the Société Française d'histoire maritime (SFHM) in 2017, under the patronage of UNESCO. He obtained a PhD in June 2010 from the University of Caen Basse-Normandie with a doctoral thesis on the privateers of the French harbour of Granville in Normandy (1688–1815). He has since broadened his research into new areas and topics concerning maritime history generally (fishing, economy, populations, life on board, etc.). He is frequently invited to present lectures, and regularly publishes articles and books on these subjects. He recently retired from the University of Caen in Normandy as *chargé de cours*, where he qualified as a university lecturer in 2012. He is still a member of the working teams HISTEMÉ and *Espaces maritimes, sociétés littorales et interfaces portuaires* at Caen University, specialising in French and Channel privateering and European maritime history. He is currently working on a collaborative study of European privateer captains for a critical survey of French sea power from the 1540s to 1815 and is writing a book about the Channel Islands' privateers.

Captain Michael Barritt, a past president of The Hakluyt Society and the recipient of the second Alexander Dalrymple Award for outstanding work in world hydrography, served as Hydrographer of the Navy from 2001 to 2003. His publications include *Eyes of the Admiralty* (2008) describing hydrographic activity of the Royal Navy during the blockade of the French Channel coast in 1799–1800. He commanded the surveying ship HMS *Bulldog* in the SW Approaches to the English Channel in the 1980s, and his experiences of the challenges are used to confirm the achievement and deserved reputation of his precursor, Captain Martin White – a towering figure in the early history of the RN Surveying Service which was launched in the aftermath of the Napoleonic Wars. Martin White's devotion to duty, superior skills, meticulous attention to detail, and fine draughtsmanship first came to note during front-line wartime service in the testing waters of the Channel Islands.

Anna Brinkman-Schwartz is a lecturer in the Defence Studies Department at King's College London. She was awarded her PhD from the Department of War Studies at King's in 2017, focussing on eighteenth-century prize law as an instrument of British foreign policy towards Spain and Holland. After her PhD she was a Post-Doctoral Research Fellow in the Department of Hispanic Studies at the University of Warwick, working on the AHRC funded project 'Imperial Entanglements: Transoceanic Basque Networks in British and Spanish Colonialism and their Legacy'. Her research now focuses on the history of maritime strategic thinking and international law in the eighteenth and nineteenth centuries.

Isabelle Delumeau teaches history at the French Naval Academy in Brest. She holds a PhD in history from the University of Western Brittany at Brest, with a dissertation on the history of French hydrography in the 19th century, in which the Dépôt des cartes et plans was responsible for collecting geographical data for producing nautical charts and providing the fleet and merchant seamen with nautical publications. Surveys were conducted by engineers and also by naval officers in a strategy aimed at defending the coasts in the event of a naval war against Great Britain. The difficult waters between the Channel Islands and the coasts of France hold a very special place in these plans. She is a member of the Fédération de recherche, histoire et archéologie maritime, Université Paris-Sorbonne, and has contributed articles to the Revue d'histoire maritime (25), *Le navire à la mer* with Olivier Chaline, and the Revue Maritime (495), *Usages et représentations de la carte nautique du XVIIe au XIXe siècle*.

Richard Harding is a Fellow of the Royal Historical Society and Professor Emeritus at the University of Westminster, where he was head of the Department of Leadership and Professional Development from 2009 to 2016. His research specialisms are amphibious operations, naval leadership and the organisational development of navies. He is the author of numerous books including *Seapower and Naval Warfare, 1650–1850* (UCL Press, 1999); *The Emergence of Britain's Global Naval Supremacy* (Boydell, 2010); and *Modern Naval History: Debates and Prospects* (Bloomsbury, 2016). He is co-editor of *Naval Leadership and Management, 1650–1950* (Boydell, 2013).

Alexander Howlett received his PhD from the Defence Studies Department of King's College London in January 2019. His dissertation on the Royal Naval Air Service has been published by Routledge as *The Development of British Naval Aviation, 1914–1918*. Dr Howlett has presented papers on the RNAS at the McMullen Naval History Symposium, US Naval Academy, Annapolis, and at the National Maritime Museum, Greenwich. He is currently researching the origins of the Canadian Surface Combatant programme, and the history of Canadian naval policy since 1964. His paper examines the Royal Navy's combined arms approach to trade protection and anti-submarine warfare in the English Channel, including the Channel Islands, between 1914 and 1918.

Alan James is a Reader in International History in the Department of War Studies at King's College London. He began his studies at the University of Alberta, Canada, before receiving his PhD at the University of Manchester. He is a trustee of the British Commission for Maritime History, on the council of the Navy Records Society, and an active member of the Society for Nautical Research and of the Société française d'histoire maritime. In addition to a number of essays and articles, he is the author of *The Navy and Government in Early Modern France, 1572–1661* (Boydell, 2004) and *The Origins of French Absolutism, 1588–1661* (Pearson, 2006). One of his most recent collaborations is as co-author with Carlos Alfaro Zaforteza and Malcolm Murfett, of *European Navies and the Conduct of War* (Routledge, 2019).

Andrew Lambert is Laughton Professor of Naval History in the Department of War Studies at King's College London. After completing his early research in the department, he went on to teach at the Royal Naval Staff College, Greenwich, and the Royal Military Academy, Sandhurst. He is Director of the Laughton Naval History Unit at King's, and a Fellow of the Royal Historical Society. He is the author of many books beginning with *Battleships in Transition: The Creation of the Steam Battlefleet: 1815–1860* (Conway, 1984), through *The Crimean War: British Grand Strategy Against Russia, 1853–1856* (Manchester, 1990) to *The Challenge: Britain Against America in the Naval War of 1812* (Faber, 2012) for which he was awarded the Anderson Medal, and *Seapower States; Maritime Culture, Continental Empires, and the Conflict That Made the Modern World* (Yale, 2018).

Colin Partridge lives in Alderney where he runs an architectural practice, is a founder trustee of The Henry Euler Memorial Trust and former consultant to the States of Guernsey's 'Fortress Guernsey' programme for the restoration and interpretation of that island's fortifications of all periods. He holds a degree from the Open University in comparative British and American history, is a past president and honorary life member of the Channel Islands Occupation Society (Guernsey) and was one of only three UK speakers invited to address the Vauban Tercentenary colloque at Cherbourg. Appointed OBE for 22 years' voluntary service to the Court of Alderney, sixteen as chairman, he is the author of *Hitler's Atlantic Wall* (DI Pub., 1976), and co-author of *Mirus: The Making of a Battery* (Ampersand, 1983) and *The Fortifications of Alderney* (AFC, 1993). He is currently compiling the maritime archive database for The Henry Euler Memorial Trust.

Jean de Préneuf is a Senior Lecturer at the University of Lille and directs the projet HIMARIAN (Histoire maritime des îles anglo-normandes) within the research unit IRHiS of which he is a member. He is also Head of the Research, Teaching and Studies Unit at the Historical Branch of the French Ministry of Defence (Service historique de la Défense) at Vincennes, as well as being a Lieutenant de vaisseau de reserve in the Marine nationale. He has participated in many international service and academic conferences on naval history and current affairs. Amongst a number of publications, he is the joint author of *La Marine française sur les mers du monde 1860–1939* (2012) with Philippe Vial, and he has been co-editor of *Entre terre et mer: l'occupation militaire des espaces maritimes et littoraux* (2014) with Eric Grove and Andrew Lambert.

Frédéric Saffroy is a practising Avocat à la Cour working in Paris, specialising in regulatory and compliance matters in innovative defence, aerospace and life science industries, and is a member of IRHiS (where he co-directs project HIMARIAN) and GIS d'histoire et sciences de la mer. Since completing his PhD in history and the publication of his thesis under the title *Le bouclier de Neptune* (2015), his research has concentrated on the naval and maritime aspects of French defence policy during the Third Republic (1875–1940). His recent papers relate to innovation during two World Wars and the naval-industrial complex, the evolution of littoral warfare, cartography from Gallipoli (1915) to the Provence landing (1944), and the future challenge of Geographic Intelligence (GeoInt). Frédéric Saffroy is one of the contributors to the *Dictionnaire Clemenceau* (2018), and is a member of the Institut de stratégie comparée (ISC).

Thomas Vaisset is an Assistant Professor at Le Havre Normandie University and a member of UMR CNRS-IDEES 6266. His areas of research have concentrated on the history of the French navy between 1870 and 1945, investigating the role played by the navy in a global dimension including politics, international relations, social and cultural matters. He has contributed to numerous conferences and publications on the French navy during the First World War. His PhD, published in 2017 as *L'amiral d 'Argenlieu: le moine soldat de gaullisme*, was awarded the French military history prize. His most recent published work is *Militaires en résistance en France et en Europe* (with Claire Miot and Guillaume Piketty), Presses universitaires du Septentrion, Villeneuve d'Ascq, 2020.

PREFACE

When the idea for an international maritime history symposium in the Channel Islands was first mooted some twenty years ago, it received the enthusiastic support of the late Marc Michel. It was fitting, therefore, that he should live to see his dream realised in Alderney in September 2019, and that he should play such a prominent role in the organisation and recording of the event which proved to be such a popular and resounding success. All of this was made possible by the foresight and generosity of Mary Euler, who set up The Henry Euler Memorial Trust in commemoration of her husband, Henry Euler, a direct descendant of the celebrated Swiss mathematician, who had served as an RNVR torpedo officer in HMS *Illustrious* from her date of commission, through the Mediterranean campaign and including the raid on the Italian fleet at Taranto.

As the Trust's patron, His Excellency, the Lieutenant Governor of Guernsey, Vice Admiral Sir Ian Corder, KCB stated in his opening address at the 2019 Symposium that one of the Trust's principal objectives is 'to inform, develop and maintain the interest of the inhabitants of Alderney and others in the maritime heritage of Alderney'. By placing Alderney in its Channel Islands' setting, thence within the wider context of Anglo-French relations between 1689 and 1918, the Symposium enabled leading British and French historians to complement existing scholarship which has tended to treat the Islands as a place apart. Their strategic location was of immense importance in Anglo-French relations – the Islands shaped national strategies in war and peace, and strategy shaped the Islands in equal measure.

The Trustees have expressed their warm gratitude for the unreserved support received from Andrew Lambert and Jean de Préneuf in the organisation of the 2019 Symposium, and for the agreements reached with their respective academic institutions – King's College London, the Université de Lille and the Service Historique de la Défense, Paris. The close working relationship thus established, and the outstanding contributions of all those speakers who participated in the 2019 Symposium, have laid a solid foundation for future cooperation and research into the maritime history of Alderney and the Channel Islands throughout all periods of history.

Colin Partridge: Alderney, December 2020

INTRODUCTION:
'THE EHRENBREITSTEIN OF THE ENGLISH CHANNEL'

ANDREW LAMBERT

In the mid-nineteenth century the complex relationship between Britain, France and the Channel Islands acquired a new urgency, as the British state launched a massive project to create an artificial harbour on the Island of Alderney, the lynchpin of a system of maritime security that would ensure the safety of British merchant shipping in wartime, countering the threat posed by the rapidly advancing naval base and fortified harbour at Cherbourg. In the event of war Braye Harbour would be critical to Britain's global system, the physical manifestation of a distinctive maritime culture and the strategic methods of a unique seapower state.[1] Together with a second new harbour at Portland, 60 miles north, it would enable the Royal Navy to control the western entrance of the English Channel, isolating Cherbourg from the French naval bases on the Atlantic and Mediterranean coasts. This massive, costly project, the product of an era of heightened Anglo-French tension, exploited the latest engineering expertise to address the strategic problem of commanding the seas with short-ranged steam ships. But Braye was only the latest in a long line of developments that linked the Channel Islands into the British strategic system and, like those that had gone before, it changed the relationship between Britain, France and the Islands, and the Islands themselves. How should we understand the interlocking relationships between great powers and small islands, terrestrial identities and maritime realities? The conflicted history of Braye Harbour suggests an ambitious cultural reading could offer a way forward.

Early in 1862, as the British House of Commons prepared to decide whether to continue funding the massive naval harbour project at Braye, geologist,

---

[1] Lambert, Andrew *Seapower States; Maritime Culture, Continental Empires and the Conflict That Made the Modern World.* London, Yale UP 2018, pp. 1–16 for a discussion of these concepts.

mining engineer and author David Thomas Ansted (1814–80) elevated a humdrum issue of expenditure and engineering onto an altogether higher plane. Ansted presented the harbour and fortress complex as the key to naval dominion, and a totem of national culture. His article 'England's "Broad Stone of Honour"' linked the great Prussian fortress of Ehrenbreitstein, looming over Coblenz at the confluence of the Moselle and the Rhine, the key to the defence of Germany, with the new bastion that secured command of the English Channel: they were the representative bulwarks of their respective countries.[2]

Ansted's word play linked his argument with familiar cultural artefacts: Lord Byron's poetry, J. M. W. Turner's striking images of the German fortress, allegories of power and control, and Sir Kenelm Digby's romantic revival of chivalry, *The Broad Stone of Honour* of 1822. Digby's impressive drawings of the Prussian fortress were the visual core of a lament for a lost age of nobility and deference, a scarcely veiled attack on the rising middle class. Digby had chosen this German castle because it had been the prison of Richard Coeur de Lion, the ultimate English chivalric hero; that he had been the last 'good' English King of Normandy added another twist to the allegory. *The Broad Stone of Honour* had many readers, exerting a powerful influence on mid-nineteenth century British culture: Wordsworth dedicated a poem to the author, cultural critic John Ruskin was overwhelmed by Digby's agenda, while William Morris and Edward Burne-Jones were profoundly affected by his vision of a better past shaping a superior future. Progressive liberal thinkers were predictably unimpressed.[3] Ironically while Digby, an Anglo-Irish landowner, looked back to a lost golden age, his Cambridge friend, scientist William Whewell, achieved fame by mastering the theoretical basis of tidal prediction in the Channel.[4] The Islands were critical to British policy and strategy and attracted a significant level of defence spending. It is telling that the only French 'invasion' in this period occurred during the one war when France was not engaged in European continental operations.

While Ansted belonged to the generation that consumed Digby's book, his revival of the title may have been prompted by Charles Kingsley, who used it as a chapter title in his 1857 novel *Two Years Ago*. Kingsley had fallen under Digby's spell view as a young man, and his hero drew similar inspiration from

[2] Ansted, D. T. and Latham, R. G. *The Channel Islands.* London, W. H. Allen 1862, 2nd edn 1865, p. 19. Ansted wrote this section. He had lived on Guernsey for four years and visited the other islands. His chosen frontispiece was a view of the Casquets Lighthouse off Alderney. Both authors were Fellows of the Royal Society.

[3] Girouard M. *The Return to Camelot: Chivalry and the English Gentleman.* London, Yale UP 1981, pp. 62–5.

[4] Girouard describes Digby as a man out of his time, besotted by an imagined past: Girouard, pp. 58 & 63. For Turner and the German fortress: Celia Powell *Turner in Germany.* London, Tate Gallery 1995, pp. 24, 35, 65, 103–4, 188–91.

a visit to the German castle, holding up Digby's agenda as a response to the national anxieties prompted by the Crimean War. Kingsley's book inspired 'Muscular Christianity', and the Rifle Volunteer movement of 1859.[5] Sparked into life by Lord Tennyson's powerful, poetic call to arms the Rifle Volunteers were a response to the naval challenge of the French Second Empire, and anxiety about a cross-Channel invasion.[6]

Those issues retained their power in 1862. Ansted's heroic references did not end with the title: he credited Wellington for the decision to secure Alderney and the Channel Islands, lamenting the slow pace at which the work had been carried out, However, 'our Ehrenbreitstein is also on the French side of the Channel, and we are by its means enabled most effectually to command both shores of our Rhine'.[7] Ansted's study of the Channel Islands, published alongside the essay, made the point explicit. Alderney: 'corresponds, however, to what Ehrenbreitstein would be, if in the hands of the French, and held against Germany, rather than to the value of that fortress in the hands of Prussia'.[8] Braye was an offensive bridgehead on the French coast, a base from which to project power.

Ansted lamented the failure to enclose a far larger area of water, leaving the harbour, despite modifications, with unsatisfactory accommodation. Even so, it would be a national disgrace to leave it unfinished. The Channel Islands were badly served by communication links with the mainland; he condemned the broken telegraph as 'a mere thread, exposed to the constant rubbing on sharp rocks'. Yet 'there is but one Alderney in the Channel'; it was the key to keeping the Channel Islands, without which command of the Channel would be lost, 'and now that Cherbourg and Brest both are available, France only requires these islands to concentrate so large a fleet in the Channel, that England, with its numerous colonies in all parts of the world, could not hope to remain mistress of this important sea'. The issue was too clear and urgent for any doubt. It would be 'insane' not to complete the project, including an eastern arm to the breakwater, and clearing the rocks inside the breakwater.

Controlling the Channel gave Britain status in Europe, while the security of the entire global empire structure relied on prestige and perception, rather

---

[5] Girouard, pp. 58, 63, 142.

[6] Beckett, I. F. W. *Riflemen Form! A Study of the Rifle Volunteer Movement, 1859–1908.* Aldershot, Ogilby Trust 1982, pp. 7–38.

[7] 'England's "Broad Stone of Honour" ' *Temple Bar*, February 1862 (no. 4), pp. 427–38, quotes from pp. 428, 437 & 439. *Temple Bar* (1860–3) targeted the growing middle class market for monthly reading. The essay promoted Ansted and Latham's massive book about the Islands, published in 1862, and again in 1865. The attribution is from the online edition of the *Wellesley Index of Victorian Publications*.

[8] Ansted and Latham, *The Channel Islands*, 2nd edn 1865, p. 19.

than power. The peroration, clearly directed at Members of Parliament who might be reluctant to foot the bill, was compelling:

> So far as home defences are concerned, there would seem to be nothing that more truly represents the honour of England than the continued possession of Alderney; and it is quite certain that Alderney will only then begin to be useful when its harbour is completed.[9]

In 1865 everything changed. As the French ironclad battlefleet challenge, another bloodless contest waged with words and images, ebbed Britain recovered battlefleet dominance. French strategy focussed on the rising military challenge of Prussia-Germany. With that the Channel and the Islands slowly drifted out of the official mind, and questions were asked about the headline project at Alderney. Cost overruns and the irrelevance of the harbour for commercial purposes opened a long-running, if small-scale, Parliamentary debate, pressure to complete the works eased, and the garrison was left at a low level. Now that the threat of an invasion, or even a war with France ceased to trouble the House of Commons radical members attacked the project. Something that had once seemed all-important, a cultural icon of security to compare with Dover Castle and the Rock of Gibraltar, suddenly become a minor embarrassment, an unwanted gift to be passed between Government departments. It was easy to forget what Peter Heylyn had noted in 1656, that the Islands were 'seated purposely for the command and Empire of the Ocean'.[10] Heylyn's description had appeared in print between two great maritime conflicts, with the Dutch and then the Spanish.

There remains something curiously apposite in Alderney's moment of glory, and the overwrought paean that David Ansted compiled to mark its ebb. That a man of hard science, a friend of Darwin, chose to make his case in the language of chivalry is suggestive. The Victorians did not read the world as a matter of fact; they had ample room for intangibles, for deeper meanings and extended allegories. They understood the value of prestige, image and illusion in the maintenance of power. The contemporary Royal Navy was dominated by names that connected the present with battles won, classical allegories and a litany of captured enemy warships. Turner's immortal *Fighting Temeraire* was doubly powerful because the name of the ship was a testament to naval glory long before Trafalgar. As Ansted published, the

---

⁹ 'England's "Broad Stone of Honour" ' *Temple Bar*, February 1862 (no. 4), pp. 427–38, quotes from pp. 428, 437 & 439.

¹⁰ Peter Heylyn *A Full Relation of Two Journeys: The One into the Main-land of France: The Other into some of the Adjacent Islands.* London 1656, p. 299 cited in Thornton, Tim *The Channel Islands 1370–1640; Between England and Normandy.* Woodbridge, Boydell 2012, p. 153.

latest ironclads HMS *Black Prince* and *Agincourt* made obvious points, but naming another *Northumberland*, to honour the ship that had taken Napoleon to St Helena, made an altogether more specific reference, one directed at the Emperor who had presided over the ceremonial opening of Cherbourg a few years earlier. In sum the great project on Alderney was not a matter of cost or need, but of asserting cultural dominion over a space defined by the sea; a question of 'honour'. That was why the British state poured millions into Braye Harbour, and why, when the challenge had passed, those outside the decision-making process condemned such profligate expenditure on an asset of limited utility.

The Harbour of Refuge at Alderney was only the latest and largest example of a project driven by the Islands' strategic role. Their unique relationship with the United Kingdom, including separate legal systems and customs status, had been shaped by the interests of a maritime community that readily swapped legitimate commerce, fishing and smuggling in peace for privateering and smuggling in war. Those wartime roles, which included intelligence gathering, became increasingly important to the British war effort across the long cycle of Anglo-French conflicts. The limits placed on Channel Island privateers in the 1750s were conspicuous by their absence in the 1800s, when they became 'ubiquitous' elements in the attack and defence of trade, primarily through re-captures of French prizes, the resulting detention of French seafarers and the rapid movement of intelligence in a global maritime conflict. As Sir Julian Corbett observed, one of the 'ubiquitous Guernsey privateers' played a critical role in the climactic campaign of 1805 that ended at Trafalgar.[11]

The islanders had long recognised that they were well served by their unique status within an English/British state that recognised their 'lasting strategic value' and was prepared to accommodate local interests across a range of issues, including language, law and religion.[12] Remaining distinct had many advantages. Local connections would have left them in no doubt that French sovereignty would see the application of the Inscription Maritime, set up between 1668 and 1673, to the seafaring population, the costly presence of powerful garrisons and new, less favourable arrangements for trade and customs. These considerations encouraged loyalty. While islanders continued to use Norman French, they happily assumed an English identity.

The aim of this volume, and of the conference at which these contributions were originally presented, has been to examine the role of Alderney and the Channel Islands in an era of Anglo-French conflicts and competition, from William III's abrogation of their neutral status between the two Kingdoms,

---

[11] Corbett, J. S. *The Campaign of Trafalgar.* London, Longman 1910, p. 330.
[12] Thornton, pp. 1–8, 150–3, 158 for the survival of island particularism, Norman links and English identity.

through the 125-year cycle of wars that followed, the uneasy peace of the nineteenth century and the First World War, when the two powers were allied against Imperial Germany, using each other's bases and facilities in a joint effort to defend the oceanic and short-sea shipping that fuelled their combined war efforts. An era that began with Louis XIV's threat to seize the Islands ended with a French seaplane squadron operating from Guernsey, flying over a sea area that legally belonged to Britain, but had been placed under French control. Furthermore. that same area had, only twenty years before, been a prospective battleground in an imperial war sparked by rivalry in central Africa.

As the first links in a global chain of insular locations from which Britannia would ultimately rule the world, the ocean assured their place in a national identity. As a maritime empire and a seapower state, Britain privileged such places as an alternative to continental expansion and military power. The cultural power of the Islands in the British worldview became obvious whenever they were thought to be at risk. It would be a 'disgrace' to lose them... their loss would undermine a global system built on confidence, prestige and capital ships rather than bayonets, calling into question the legitimacy of the wider empire, and with that Britain's status as a Great Power.

The Islands were far more important to Britain, as observation posts off French harbours, bases for extensive privateer fleets, intelligence gathering centres and smuggling and blockade depots to attack the French economy in peace and war, than they could possibly be to France. The islanders exploited that reality to shape a profitable relationship with the state, one that emphasised local rights and customary law over national practice. At the same time their proximity to France, and vulnerability to invasion, made them among the most highly militarised territories under the British crown, with substantial fixed defences, regular garrisons and highly trained local militia units. New defensive bastions were constructed on the two largest islands in the Revolutionary and Napoleonic era, to ensure they could be held until relief came by sea, even if the French manged to establish a beachhead.

The Islands' peculiar financial status ensured they remained profitable commercial centres, with adequate capital to fund a dynamic privateer industry. Economic and cultural links between the Norman-speaking Islands and the adjacent coast of France remained strong, even in wartime. But between 1815 and 1914 enhanced maritime connectivity shifted the linguistic link to England, as new maritime connections brought them closer to the mainland. Proximity and presence anglicised this cultural outlier.

In strategic terms French threats against the Islands were, Sir Julian Corbett observed, a useful diversion. He noted how in 1757 France lacked the naval power to threaten an invasion of Britain, but 'kept up the distraction by organising a scheme for seizing the Channel Islands, and this, in the demoralisation of the Ministerial crisis, was enough to immobilise a large Channel fleet'.[13] In 1779 the risk of a mainland invasion was exacerbated by the presence of a superior Franco-Spanish Fleet at Brest, while troops assembled at Cherbourg and le Havre. In response 'two cruiser squadrons and flotillas were at once formed at the Downs and Channel Islands to watch the French coasts and prevent the concentration of transports'. If the transports sailed, they would be attacked, while stationing the main fleet twenty leagues WSW of the Scilly Islands protected inbound merchant shipping and controlled the Channel approaches.[14]

In the Revolutionary and Napoleonic conflicts the British controlled the Channel by concentrating major fleets in the Downs and off Ushant, with strategic connection through the 'minor cruiser centre at the Channel Islands'.[15] This squadron was also critical to the defence of floating trade in the Western Approaches. Along with a second stationed off le Havre, its key role was to prevent French cruisers and privateers sailing to attack British coastwise and ocean-going trade, with the blockading forces linked by cruising patrols: 'naval defence was supplemented by defended ports of refuge, the principal ones being on the coasts of Ireland to shelter ocean trade, but others in great numbers were provided within the defended areas against the operations of privateers, and the ruins of batteries all round the British shores testify how complete was the organisation'.[16] This concept was revived in the 1840s for a series of 'Harbours of Refuge', including in the Channel Islands, to shelter merchant shipping in distress.

Once British command of the sea was secure 'the Channel Islands began to be regarded as a base from which the British would operate offensively against the French coast. Consequently, French strategy in this area was devoted to defence... One of our precautions was to scize the Islands of Marcou or St. Marcouf, on the eastern side of the Cotentin or Cherbourg peninsula, as an anchorage from which Havre could be watched.'[17] When this time-honoured method was revived and remodelled in the 1840s, with steam warships taking the place of sailing cruisers, regional infrastructure had to be overhauled, but the directing principles were unchanged. Across the era Britain managed to keep the strategic initiative at and from the sea, with rare exceptions like 1779, obliging France to protect harbours and naval bases on an exceptional scale.

Ownership of the Channel Islands, when combined with the Scillies, the south coast of England and a superior naval force, gave the British state control

---

[13] Corbett, J. S. *England in the Seven Years War: A Study in Combined Strategy.* London, Longman 1907 vol. I, p. 164.

[14] Corbett, J. S. *Some Principles of Maritime Strategy.* London, Longman 1911, pp. 255–7.

[15] Ibid., p. 140.

[16] Ibid., p. 266.

[17] Corbett, J. S. ed. *The Spencer Papers Vol. I.* London, Navy Records Society 1912, p. 4.

of the Western Approaches to what would become the English Channel. In wartime that control translated into the ability to dominate the French coast between St Malo and Cherbourg; nor was it any accident that in wartime the British sought to extend that control and did so between 1793 and 1815 by seizing the Iles Marcouf and the Chaussys, pushing their sea control into French coastal waters and tightening the economic blockade.

The Anglo-French wars were wars of the Exchequer, waged with costly navies that emphasised the need to raise long-term loans. Britain depended on maritime commerce for trade, increasingly for food and always for naval stores. In Britain those long-term loans were provided by the City of London, if it had confidence in the conduct and competence of the war effort. In exchange, the City expected the state to use the Navy to secure its shipping and judged the success of the Navy on the commercial insurance rate. The fiscal/military state structure enabled Britain to maintain and increase the Navy in wartime, while *Ancien Regime* France normally found the naval war a costly distraction from continental theatres of war. French attacks on British trade were most significant in the Western Approaches and the Channel, where small, cheap craft could be used to attack isolated merchant vessels. This opening for private enterprise at the local level informed post-1688 strategic choices, with privateers taking the place of national warships, or even borrowing them, to conduct a war of profit. The need to control this threat shaped the British response, including the development of naval infrastructure. After 1688 Plymouth moved from a useful place to assemble merchant shipping to a major naval base supporting British squadrons in the Western Approaches and holding station off Brest, the primary French naval base outside the Mediterranean. In the nineteenth century Cobh, Portland and Alderney were added to support cruisers, the main fleet and finally the steam gunboats for a projected bombardment of the new French base at Cherbourg. These were costly investments, only possible after the 1688 Revolution had shaped a new governing system and economic structure. For Britain, the threat to merchant shipping was too serious to be ignored.

Command of the sea enabled Britain to secure the Islands and to use them – their loss would have ripped open the system of trade defence that sustained long wars of economic exhaustion between 1688 and 1815, releasing the privateer fleets of St Malo, Granville, and the newly French islands into the Western Approaches. The Islands' land defences were designed to deter raids by small forces and bought time for a naval force to drive off the shipping of a serious invasion. In wartime small cruisers stationed at the larger islands maintained contact with the Channel or Grand Fleet, usually at sea off Brest, and the major bases at Portsmouth and Plymouth. Locally based cruisers and privateers effectively cut French coastal shipping routes along the north coast of Brittany and west coast of Normandy. They blockaded or observed the privateer harbours at St Malo, Granville and St Servan, recapturing French prizes returning to port.

The introduction of steam propulsion, iron hulls and the screw propeller created new navigational issues for France, Britain and the Islands. While technology did not change the Islands' consequence as bases from which to counter French commerce raiding, gather intelligence and dominate the adjacent coastal routes, the Islands lacked deep water or floating harbours, essential for the safe operation of wooden-hulled steam ships. If these vessels were beached they risked hull deformation, which could derange their fragile machinery. Extending piers and jetties at St Peter Port and St Helier enabled steamers to disembark passengers and mail, but they remained exposed to bad weather. Effective bases for steam warships needed an enclosed area of sheltered water as an anchorage and coaling depot.

Island shipping had limited military value in the age of iron steamships, but the Islands remained a critical front line for the seemingly inevitable resumption of Anglo-French conflict. After 1830 the changing character of war at sea rapidly reduced the utility of Island shipping for privateering. Privateers, including sailing vessels, remained the primary wartime threat to merchant shipping into the 1850s, and the experience of combatting French and American privateers between 1793 and 1815 was not forgotten. However, the solution lay in steam-powered warships, both regular and auxiliary armed merchant vessels, escorting convoys and blockading privateer bases. It was in Britain's interests to remove this threat: in 1856 Britain and France agreed to outlaw privateering, in the Declaration of Paris, which codified Maritime International Law. Consequently, the maritime threat shifted to armed commercial steam vessels, commissioned as national warships.

Steam power and larger ships meant that the entire Channel region, including British, French and Island coastal waters, required new charts, based on the latest land surveys, and new pilots. Local knowledge gained in fishing craft and coasters was replaced by state-trained expertise, working off new charts, and improved navigational markers. The increased size and speed of steamships informed a major new survey of the Islands, the entire Western Approaches, and the training of regional specialist naval pilots, using the Survey and Fishery protection vessels, a process that had echoes in France. Local navigation had always been difficult, but once mastered it offered major advantages for attack and defence. That the leading hydrographers of Britain and France often co-operated only emphasised the difficulty and dangers of the area, and their shared scientific agenda, but both were preparing for a future war.

While the States of Jersey and Guernsey considered creating a wet harbour, for which they hoped to secure Government support, much of the local alarmism about defence was inflected by commercial concerns. London accepted the need to fund an artificial harbour to support steam-powered naval operations between the Islands and the French coast, while watching the ports of St Malo, Granville and Cherbourg, to prevent hostile cruisers from reaching the exposed shipping lanes of the Channel and the Western Approaches. These concerns were emphasised by the dramatic deterioration of Anglo-French relations over the Syrian Crisis in 1840 and the Spanish Marriages affair of 1846–8. Yet when the Government decided to create suitable steamship harbours it followed the strategic dynamic, building at St Catherine's in Jersey, and Braye in Alderney, locations with little or no commercial value. When St Catherine's 'strategic' location proved highly unsatisfactory the project was abandoned. A costly Guernsey harbour project was never started, leaving the larger islands to develop their existing harbours.

Although publicly described as a 'Harbour of Refuge' for distressed merchant shipping the major new defended harbour created at Alderney in the 1850s was essentially offensive, designed to watch Cherbourg, which had become a major cruiser and invasion base, and support sustained naval offensive operations to neutralise the threat. Little wonder France reacted.

By the time the works at Alderney were ready the development of screw propulsion, telegraph cables and long-range artillery had reduced the pressing need of the 1840s, while the downfall of the Second Empire in 1870–1 ended two decades of heightened tension, created by divergent approaches to wider European and imperial issues, and made manifest in successive naval arms races, imposing infrastructure upgrades and alarmist rhetoric. Without a French naval challenge Alderney, no longer 'England's Broad Stone of Honour' was discounted, condemned as a failure and largely forgotten. It returned to front-line service at the end of the century, as renewed imperial tensions fuelled strategic developments: French torpedo boats would be countered by British torpedo-boat destroyers, based at Alderney.

Costly French harbour projects at Cherbourg, St Malo and Granville proved long-drawn-out, and never came close to breaking Britain's geo-strategic grip on the region. Instead, steamships and new harbours changed the Islands linguistically. They were anglicised by tourism, trade and the influx of workmen, with the new harbour-building population of Alderney the most dramatic example.

Ultimately this collection examines how maritime regions are at once connected and divided by the sea. Living within view of France, and sharing a language, did not encourage the islanders to see themselves as French, while in wartime the sea facilitated illicit and illegal exchanges, invariably for profit. Local knowledge informed fishery disputes, privateer operations and intelligence gathering. French craftsmen helped build the harbour and forts at Alderney, a process that resulted in the island becoming linguistically English. When Queen Victoria embraced steam power to become the first British monarch to visit the Islands, she helped shift cultural perceptions on both sides of the Channel. The Islands became a tourist destination, the new visitors replacing French exiles and impoverished English gentlemen, who, after 1815, included several unemployed naval officers.

Historiography

While all aspects of this symposium, from Anglo-French relations, war and hydrography to harbour engineering have already produced significant bodies of literature, the purpose of the event and this book has been to bring them together and find fresh perspectives. British literature invariably represented the Channel as a barrier, the primary bulwark against a threatening foreign other, be it Philip II, Louis XIV or two Napoleons. This cultural construct, most obvious in connection with the events of 1588, which became the foundation myth of English (not British) identity, shaped every debate about war and peace, friends and enemies and the role of the Islands in national policy. The walls of the House of Lords debating chamber were completely covered with a fabulous cycle of tapestries recording the defeat of the Spanish in 1588 between 1660 and 1832. These images prompted frequent allusions to past greatness and present prospects, notably in the final speech of William Pitt the Elder, Earl of Chatham.

As late as 1959, James Williamson's *The English Channel: a History* related this national view of the adjacent seas as separating, defining and defending national identity. Not only did Williamson's Channel set England apart, but the only index entry for the other side was 'France, wars with', which harked back to another epoch. Williamson's statist focus and adversarial ocean can be traced to his academic debut in the Edwardian era, as a historian of Tudor oceanic enterprise, and the experience of living through two world wars, the events of 1940 providing a fitting bookend to the Armada.[18] Furthermore his Channel is narrow: Alderney, Guernsey and Jersey are not mentioned in the index, not even as 'Channel Islands'. They only appear, somewhat outsize, on a map in the end papers. Williamson was not the only historian to leave the Islands out of the Channel. This volume emphasises maritime connection over terrestrial limits. The Channel has always been a major sea route, since the Roman era, flowing east to west and west to east, linking the world's oceans to the North Sea and the Baltic, the ports of Flanders, Holland and Germany, Scandinavia and Russia, rather than the occasional focus of English anxieties about invasion from the near continent. The original three towers of the Caskets Lighthouse marked the southern limits of safe navigation, linked to the single light on the Scillies and the Lizard's double tower, marking the western and northern landfalls.[19] Control of the Caskets light was a strategic prize, which may explain why it featured on the title page of David Ansted's

---

[18] James A. Williamson (1886–1964) *The English Channel: A History*. London, Collins 1959.

[19] Tarrant, M. *Cornwall's Lighthouse Heritage*. Truro, Twelveheads Press 2007. Captain Michael Tarrant of Trinity House was an expert on navigational issues on the Cornish coast before the development of electronic navigational aids.

1862 account of the Islands.[20] During the Anglo-French wars lighthouses were excluded from acts of war, enabling the Royal Navy to use French lights as navigational markers when blockading Brest.[21] It should not be forgotten that the Islands were critical to the effective defence of merchant shipping in the Western Approaches and the English Channel, in peace as well as war.

These national and regional approaches encouraged the idea that the sea was unimportant; even Island history has focussed on terrestrial issues, and as Williamson's old standard text demonstrated, the Islands have often been ignored, not really part of the 'Channel' at all. In 1986 Alan Jamieson's excellent collection *A People of the Sea* brought the Islands' maritime history into focus, addressing the local, national and international elements of a complex watery engagement.[22]

The latest text to consider the watery space between France and England, Renaud Morieux's important book *The Channel: England, France and the Construction of a Maritime Border in the Eighteenth Century*, was first published in French, and later in English. It shifts the debate away from nation-states and borders.[23] Morieux emphasises the remarkable fluidity of the maritime world; how the waters between the two countries enabled men to avoid customs dues, and national obligations. These relationships revise older ideas of constant Anglo-French hostility throughout the long eighteenth century. Morieux's Channel mediated the many and varied connections between the two countries and the Anglo-Norman Islands, where cartography, law and politics shaped the Channel and steadily hardened its role as a boundary that was a response to the growing maritime rivalry between the two powers. In the 1760s France gave up the claim to a share of Channel sovereignty, a feature of the reign of Louis XIV, preferring to redouble their attack on Britain's maritime hegemony through legal means. Naming the Channel as English was a cartographic victory, one that followed naval success. At the same time France developed ideas about the 'Freedom of the Seas', attempting to disarm Britain's chosen strategic instrument, the economic blockade, and promoting smuggling through the Islands to attack its economy. The contest was asymmetric, highlighting divergent continental

[20] Ansted *The Channel Islands* title page.

[21] Woodman, R. *View from the Sea*. London, Century Publishing 1985, p. 93; Barritt, M. K. *Eyes of the Admiralty: J.T. Serres An Artist in the Channel Fleet, 1799–1800*. London, National Maritime Museum 2008, p. 40.

[22] Jamieson, Alan. *A People of the Sea. The Maritime History of the Channel Islands* London, Routledge 1986.

[23] Morieux, Renaud. *The Channel: England, France and the Construction of a Maritime Border in the Eighteenth Century.* Cambridge, Cambridge University Press 2016. Originally in French: *Une mer pour deux royaumes: La Manche, frontiers franco-anglaise XVIIe–XVIIIe siècles*. Universitaires de Rennes, 2008.

and maritime concepts of law, power and identity, with distinctive political systems. By the late eighteenth century the French rhetoric of state rivalry had adopted Montesquieu's classical analogy, positioning France and Britain as the incarnations of Rome and Carthage. This language of annihilation became more visceral when Republican France adopted the style and ambition of the Roman Republic that had destroyed the Punic city. France began to harden its maritime borders in the era of Louis XIV, Marshal Vauban erecting fortresses to secure critical towns and harbours.[24] Vauban's forts were located just above the high-water mark that the British took as their frontier.[25] They conceded command of the Channel, denying French armies the opportunity to invade the Islands or the mainland, while British armies occasionally attacked French bases. French commerce raiding, by warships and privateers, was countered by convoys, patrols, shore-based signalling systems, a powerful marine insurance market with access to the Admiralty and a City of London collectively committed to the state and the defence of merchant shipping. The City was a consequence of Britain's maritime culture.[26]

In 1806 Napoleon, the master of western and central Europe, imposed an economic counter-blockade of Britain, the Continental System blocking British access to European markets. The British responded with the Orders in Council, tightening the existing economic blockade. These attempts at economic total war were constantly undermined by local actors who made their living by ignoring such measures, in peace and war. The development of state control during the wars between 1793 and 1815 did much to harden borders, reducing opportunities for smuggling and other illicit practices. Thereafter, states on both sides imposed new systems of control. However, reducing or harmonising customs tariffs proved more effective in combatting the practice. The French left the cross-Channel connection to the English, who dominated shipping between Dover and Calais. In wartime, communications were maintained through Belgium and Holland, just like those of business, legitimate and otherwise.

Yet for much of the period the idea of a nation remained fluid, and relatively unimportant to local actors. Rivalry between towns on the same side of the Channel could be significant, while co-operation with others across the water was excellent. Patriotism rarely impinged upon the everyday seafaring activities of trade and fishing, while localism did exert real influence.

---

[24] Morieux, p. 326.

[25] Meyer-Sable, N. *Les Fortresses Maritime de Vauban.* St Étienne, Le Télégramme 2013; Bloomfield, R. *Sebastian le Prestre de Vauban 1633–1707.* London, Methuen 1938.

[26] Lambert, Andrew *Seapower States: Maritime Culture, Continental Empires and the Conflict That Made the Modern World.* London, Yale 2018, pp. 272–91. See also the role of Amsterdam in shaping Dutch Culture at pp. 182–5.

Merchants used the Channel to build ambiguous positions, as Adam Smith observed, switching their tax base, for economic or strategic reasons, without compunction. War often prompted men to seek neutral ports, where they were welcome, to reduce the risk of predation, and impressment. Smugglers, the ultimate exponents of this maritime fluidity, carried many flags and different sets of papers, to traverse the watery boundaries. The connection between fishing and smuggling was strong, legitimate activity providing ideal cover for illegitimate commerce. Little wonder fishermen were closely policed. The Channel Islands and Dunkirk, located at the margins of their respective states, dominated the redistribution of smuggled goods, eroding the maritime border.[27] Their unique status was secured by local political activity and the willingness of central authorities to tolerate their behaviour to secure other advantages. Dunkirk's free port status was carefully contrived to damage British interests – including smuggling tea. When the new Republic abolished that privilege most of the merchants moved to Holland. The Channel Islands mobilised a powerful privateering force in war, from the smuggling trade, which crushed French coastal trade, and helped secure British shipping in the Western Approaches at no cost to the state. Smugglers moved secret agents and propaganda across the water, in both directions, and featured in every significant attempt to operate large naval forces in the Channel's complex coastal zones. They were the experts on local navigation. Research on tides ended uncertainty about the rise and fall of water, just as steamboats reduced the crossing to a timetabled journey.

After 1815 both states took control of that information, using Hydrographic bureaus to chart and record the ever-shifting sea floor and the motion of tides and currents, matters of growing strategic significance. These projects echoed the tidal research of Edmund Halley in 1701, a rare year of peace in this period, and often served the same strategic reconnaissance function.[28] Knowing an enemy's coast, and its defences had always been important. The emergence of surveillance states brought control to the maritime frontiers, and Government message services. Commercial links using steam packets rapidly enhanced the Islands' connectivity to the British mainland, creating a tourist industry. Telegraph cables, laid with considerable naval assistance, linked the Islands back to the mainland, through Weymouth and Southampton, the ports that handled Island steamship services, with telegraph links to London. This reduced the opportunity for strategic surprise in the face of a dominant Navy. The cable system also enhanced commercial activity, while by 1905 wireless had reduced the time lag to a few minutes.

Renaud Morieux's Channel is anything but the self-evident, bounded geographical entity discussed in older literature: across the long eighteenth

---

[27] Morieux, pp. 328, 335.
[28] Morieux, p. 93.

century it remained a fluid space, used by different actors, in peace and war, to connect and separate. He concluded it was more dynamic than the mountainous Franco-Spanish Pyrenean border. Ironically, his conclusions hint at a closer European identity that would return the Channel to an older fluidity, only for Brexit to shift the direction of travel back towards separation and barrier. It is likely that Britain and Europe will find a way to create a functional border that permits trade and movement, with the Islands remaining resolutely different, for compelling reasons.

Ultimately, as Morieux recognises, the distinctly different roles the Channel plays in English, French and Island culture have evolved over time, reflecting historical experience rather than geography. While France has long seen itself as a continental state, extending west and south, and facing military threats, Shakespeare coined the term Channel in 1593, and defined its place in English culture in 1595. He did so shortly after the greatest naval battle in the Channel, the defeat of the Spanish Armada in 1588, which became the foundation myth of the English nation. The importance of the event in shaping eighteenth-century culture suggests it deserved discussion. Tapestries depicting the Armada formed the backdrop, quite literally, to discussions in the House of Lords throughout the long eighteenth century and can be seen to advantage in John Singleton Copley's brilliant *Death of the Earl of Chatham* of 1781. Two years later Copley produced *The Death of Major Peirson, 6 January 1781*, commemorating the successful defence of Jersey. Both pictures were created for public display, and reproduction in print by London print dealer John Boydell, as part of a dynamic London-based print culture focussed on identity, war and power.

Morieux may have underestimated just how powerfully the idea of the Channel as a barrier resonated in English culture, how these ideas predisposed Englishmen to view the naval power of Louis XIV as an existential threat, and why J. M. W. Turner created more images of Dover Castle than any other subject.[29] The modern English/British state was created in the 1690s to fund the fleet needed to secure control of the Channel – and did so at Barfleur-la Hogue in 1692. France had other borders, with other great powers, but after 1707 England had no land borders. The new British state could focus its identity on a single maritime frontier, one that included the Anglo-Norman Islands. Briefly the great naval base at Braye became an emblem of British

---

[29] Morieux used Turner's *Fishing boats becalmed off Le Havre* on the dust-jacket of the English edition without mentioning him in the text, asking why an Englishman was creating such striking images of a French beach, or addressing Turner's astonishing output of English Channel views in print form, images that spread the sense of the coast as the boundary and bastion throughout Britain. Shanes, Eric *Turner's Rivers, Harbours and Coasts*. London, Chatto & Windus 1981 is the best guide to these images.

identity, a touchstone of power to rival Dover Castle and the Rock of Gibraltar. Turner used artistic languages of power from the preceding five centuries to shape a richly allegorical art of Britishness. Images of Tyre, Carthage, Venice and the Dutch Republic, Britain's seapower precursors, hung alongside contemporary landscapes, coastal views and battle scenes focussed on Nelson and Trafalgar. In 1806 his triptych transformed HMS *Victory* into a religious icon, echoing medieval altarpieces, and proclaimed the divinity of Nelson in *Trafalgar as seen from the Mizzen Top*. His major picture of 1810 featured Hannibal, a fitting subject for the modern Punic Wars.[30] Out in the Channel the Islands developed identities that relied on an assumed Britishness, which was constantly subverted in the pursuit of local interests.

The space this book addresses, of short seas, coasts and islands, has been variously defined and represented, subject to endless reconstruction across time, as contexts shifted. It is unlikely that process will stop, as new generations seek to understand their own history, and the connections that it makes.

[30] Shanes, E. *Young Mr Turner – 1815*. New Haven, Yale UP 2017, p. 375.

PART 1

CORSAIRS – THE ANCIEN RÉGIME AND FRENCH WARS FROM 1689

1

Granville's Privateers and Anglo-French Conflict in the Seventeenth and Eighteenth Centuries

MICHEL AUMONT

Saint-Malo and Dunkirk were mainland France's most important privateering centres, and are referred to constantly by historians in France and elsewhere in discussions of privateering. Their reputation often obscures the activity of other ports, which are unfairly left in the shadows despite having also engaged in such warfare, with varying degrees of participation and success. The Norman port of Granville is one such example. It was heavily involved in privateering throughout the Second Hundred Years War, but is rarely mentioned as one of the major privateer towns.[1] Its population was small and its port cramped, but Granville's location in the Channel, along with its history, maritime wealth, naval potential and entrepreneurial spirit, encouraged its inhabitants to take up privateering. What were the driving forces behind this decision? What were the characteristics of this activity? What were the results?

Granville's cod fishing and privateering within a distinctive geopolitical context

According to tradition, Granville was founded by the English during the wars of the Middle Ages, on the west coast of what is now the Cotentin Peninsula in Normandy, when they were planning to invade France. Mont-Saint-Michel blocked their way to Brittany and hindered their progress towards the centre of the kingdom. Unable to capture it, in 1439 the English bought the almost uninhabited cliff of Cap Lihou.[2] This rocky promontory, jutting out westwards into the sea only a few kilometres from Mont-Saint-Michel,

---

[1] Michel Aumont, *Les corsaires granvillais. Une culture du risque maritime, 1688–1815* (Rennes, 2013).
[2] Archives Nationales, Paris (hereafter AN), Marine, C⁴ 159, item 29, C, '*Memoir of Granville by Mr. Sicard*', 1731.

offered an easily defendable position and a firm base for future operations. In 1440, they reinforced an enclosure on top of the cliff. To protect themselves from the possibility of the French returning, a deep trench was dug across the isthmus to the east that connected the peninsula to the mainland. Finally, they forced many in the surrounding area into the new enclosure (frontispiece). The English thereby created Granville, both as a stronghold and a town. The occupation did not last, however, and the town was taken three years later by the knights of Mont-Saint-Michel.

Thereafter, the town and its port grew in importance. Its inhabitants engaged in coastal shipping and oyster, freshwater and cod fishing. At the end of the seventeenth century, it seems its population was small. The commissioner general of fortifications, Vauban,[3] stated in a report drawn up in 1686 following an inspection that 'the total number in the town and its suburbs amounts to 3,768 persons of all ages and sexes, among whom are some twenty families of merchants of some standing, who provide a living for all the others; the rest are sailors, with very few craftsmen'.[4] In 1771, we read, 'there are nine to ten thousand inhabitants, including those in the suburbs'.[5] Despite its small population and meagre port,[6] Granville was the only important port in Normandy between Saint-Malo and Honfleur until the French Revolution of 1789.

The town's prosperity became evident in 1720–30, during the reign of Louis XV, when it came to be recognised alongside Saint-Malo as a major port for cod fishing. Shortly before the French Revolution, more than a hundred ships of between seventy and 350 tons were sent to Newfoundland for wet fishing up and down the banks, or dry fishing off the coast of Newfoundland and in the Gulf of Saint Lawrence. At the end of each voyage, the ships would unload their cargo in French ports, mainly Marseille and Bordeaux, and collect another load to transport elsewhere. On these voyages, Granville ships took in a circuit of three or four stations. In the eighteenth century, Granville and neighbouring Saint-Malo were friendly rivals, vying for primacy in the French ports of Newfoundland. Granville's seafaring population had become the

---

³   Michèle Virol, *Vauban: De la gloire du roi au service de l'État* (Paris, 2003).

⁴   Service Historique de la Défense (hereafter SHD), Vincennes, Armée de terre, V 4, art.8, section 1, Granville, box 1, art. 31. As a comparison, there were already 20,000 people living in Saint-Malo at the end of the seventeenth century. André Lespagnol, *Messieurs de Saint-Malo: Une élite négociante au temps de Louis XIV* (Rennes, 1997), p. 37. Translator's note: Our translation. Unless otherwise stated, all translations of cited foreign language material in this article are our own.

⁵   Robert de Hesseln, *Dictionnaire universel de la France* (Paris, 1771), vol. 3, p. 247.

⁶   The port was drying up, poorly protected from the wind and tides, and comprised a single, badly constructed stone jetty. In spite of this, it was used heavily.

largest in Normandy, accustomed to crossing the Atlantic to spend months in North America in difficult conditions, doing work that required many hands.[7] These men were professional seafarers, under the class system developed by Colbert.[8] Granville was also recognised as a training ground for particularly experienced seamen.[9]

The complicated relationship with England was the only real shadow hanging over Granville's prosperity between the late seventeenth century and 1815. The involvement of the Channel Islands, alarmingly close by, made the situation particularly tense. In periods of hostility, the Islands represented the enemy, just a stone's throw away from the town and the western coast of the Cotentin Peninsula: Guernsey was only fifty-five miles from Granville, and Jersey only thirty. Slightly further north, Alderney lay only a few miles from Cap de la Hague. The smaller island played less of a role in local history, although not in local smuggling. This proximity to the Channel Islands meant that Granville had long been in the immediate vicinity of England. Up until the Second World War, the inhabitants of the Channel Islands primarily spoke French, or, more precisely, Norman – a fact that encouraged close relations, trade, espionage and very active smuggling. The authorities in Granville, and in Normandy and France more generally, were unhappy about such closeness: 'the islands of Jersey and Guernsey [are] perfidious neighbours, in peace as well as war; the principles of their moral code are fraud and piracy'.[10] The Channel Islanders, too, were cod fishermen, and Granville sailors encountered them working alongside the English in Newfoundland.[11] This proximity, and this rivalry, led the people of Granville to engage in privateering.

Early successes and the lure of profit motivated shipowners and captains to become involved in privateering during the Nine Years War. The frustration and anger caused by a series of treaties which reduced their Newfoundland fishing grounds, to the benefit of the English,[12] encouraged them to pursue

---

[7] AN, Marine, C⁴ 138, unnumbered page.

[8] This class system was laid out by the edict of Nancy, between 22 September 1668 and 13 September 1673, to replace the press system. Beginning in 1665–70, every seaman in France with a civil maritime role was registered and assigned to yearly classes or contingents, so that they could work on the king's ships in alternating years.

[9] AN, Marine, G144, n° 25, 'Réflexions sur les encouragements de la course'. André Lespagnol also emphasises the importance of this in *Messieurs de Saint-Malo*, p. 87.

[10] Granville, Médiathèque, Fonds du Patrimoine, Transcription of Charles de la Morandière, 'Mémoire général sur Granville présenté à la commission de l'organisation et du mouvement des armées par la commission mixte de Granville, le 5 prairial de l'an III'.

[11] On fishing in Newfoundland, see Charles de La Morandière, *Histoire de la pêche française de la morue dans l'Amérique septentrionale* (Paris, 1962–4).

[12] The treaties of Utrecht (1713) and Paris (1763).

this activity under Louis XV.[13] So too did the desire to avenge the violence and humiliation inflicted in North America during peacetime by the English, who, the Granville sailors claimed, made it clear that they wanted to expel the French for good. They had to make up for the loss of twenty-nine of Granville's Newfoundland cod fishing vessels, captured when they returned from the voyage of 1744.[14] Similarly, they needed to respond to the raid by Boscawen and Hawke in 1755,[15] which deprived Granville of its ships and its best men, dashing its hopes of asserting itself as a major port at a time when it could proudly challenge Saint-Malo's supremacy in cod fishing. Finally, they wanted revenge for their powerlessness during the Seven Years War, when the English navy had imposed an effective, humiliating blockade on the town. Granville thus found itself involved in the Anglo-French conflicts which stretched from the Nine Years War to the end of the First Empire. As early as 1688, the town was involved in privateering. For shipowners and captains, this was a risky undertaking, where daring could bring fame and fortune.

Granville at war

Research shows that the inhabitants of Granville were consistently involved in privateering over the period, although only at a modest level.[16] Strictly speaking, this was not a compensatory activity, as only a small number of shipowners (20%) were involved. These were large traders, dreaming of making their fortunes, or, at least, of significantly increasing their assets. Also involved were more modest operators, with smaller boats used for coastal

---

[13] AN, Marine, B³ 383, f° 52–3. Letter from Philibert Orry, general comptroller of finances (29 January 1737).

[14] AN, Marine, B³ 428, f° 310. In the autumn of 1744, the English captured 29 of the 69 cod fishing vessels which Granville shipowners had sent to Newfoundland before the declaration of war, and which were subsequently returning to France. The port lost around a third of its fleet, as well as its cargo. Of the crew, 782 were sent to English prisons.

[15] André Zysberg, *La monarchie des Lumières* (Paris, 2002), p. 246. In 1755, between them, the admirals Boscawen and Hawke captured 300 French ships and 6,000 sailors and officers, who they held in English prisons for long periods even before the official declaration of war on 10 January 1756. Granville lost 34 ships, with a value of 773,000 livres, according to insurance estimates, and 1,093 sailors (AN, Marine, B³ 526, f° 221–3) – more than a tenth of all French ships captured, and a sixth of all French seamen in English prisons.

[16] The detailed study of Granville privateering in my doctoral thesis described this frequent participation, the ships outfitted for it and its intensity. See Aumont, *Les corsaires granvillais*.

shipping and freshwater fishing, who saw a way to improve their day-to-day existence, to rise in the social hierarchy and to join the elite of the port.[17]

Until 1746, privateering was carried out using specifically designated raiding ships, or else using craft outfitted en guerre et marchandise – that is, authorised to trade and potentially to use force against the enemy. Not all ships with this second type of commission were privateers, since the majority engaged primarily in trade. They did everything they could to avoid the enemy. Others took the same approach but succumbed to temptation when they came across easy prey. A few, the number of which is difficult to assess, were more active: they used the aggressive possibilities these mixed commissions provided to deliberately attack enemy ships. For our purposes, we will only consider as privateers those ships outfitted en guerre et marchandise which carried out one or more successful raids. After 1746, Granville's inhabitants practised privateering using specially armed ships.

Ship sizes varied significantly over the period, depending on the availability of capital and individual shipowners' strategies. During the Nine Years War, the vessels used in Granville averaged 100–200 tons, typical for Newfoundland cod fishing vessels. The tonnage dropped significantly in the next war due to lack of funds. During the three wars which took place between 1744 and 1783, the gap between large and small vessels widened. Some shipowners outfitted very small boats for small-scale local raiding; others opted for ever larger privateers, better able, they believed, to bring in rich catches. The second category included a few particularly impressive craft: the *Granville* (530 tons); the *Monsieur* (475 tons); and the *Aimable Grenot*, the *Madame* and the *Patriote* (all 390 tons). During the Revolutionary and Napoleonic wars (1793–1815), the gap narrowed considerably, with ships weighing between three and 151 tons. Only smaller ships of less than 100 tons were used for privateering, primarily luggers.

The two sizes of ship used in Granville privateering during the period reflected the two contrasting strategies used by shipowners: offshore raiding used large ships, and local raiding used smaller boats. Frigates were used for operations on the high seas. They generally sailed to the entrance of the Channel, between Ireland, the Scilly Isles and Ushant. Under Louis XIV they sometimes went further afield, to Morocco or Newfoundland. Constructing, arming and crewing such ships was expensive, and they were only used by large shipowners involved in the Newfoundland trade, who hoped to capture high-value enemy shipments destined for mainland Europe.

To carry out local raids along the English coast and neighbouring archipelagos – the Channel Islands, or the French archipelago of Chausey, where

---

[17] Michel Aumont, 'Les armateurs granvillais et la guerre de course: d'une activité de compensation à la tentation du risque', *Annales de Normandie*, 2 (July–December 2011), pp. 81–99.

many small enemy vessels harvested kelp – coastal shipping and freshwater fishing operators preferred small vessels like luggers and cutters. They often owned them. Such raids required smaller investments, and they found they could make attractive profits by attacking smaller ships – even Jersey or Guernsey privateers, who also used small vessels – even though such targets were less lucrative than large merchant ships. In both cases, frigates and luggers were fast, manoeuvrable ships with many sails, perfectly suited to attacking or quickly retreating from a superior enemy.

Granville raiding was characterised primarily by the imposing frigates used, which sometimes surpassed 300 tons. During the reign of Louis XV, these included the *Grand Grenot* (300 tons) in 1746, the *Aimable Grenot* (390 tons) in 1747 and the *Mesny* and the *Machault* (both 300 tons) in 1756–8. The peak was reached in 1757 with the *Granville*, at 530 tons, with 36 cannons and a crew of 316 – a genuine small warship, and one that met with an unfortunate end, exploding in an accident during its first mission before it had even made a single capture. During the American War of Independence, the ships that sailed from Granville included the *Américaine* (340 tons) in 1778–81, the *Patriote* (390 tons) in 1780, the *Duc de Coigny* (325 tons) in 1780, the *Daguesseau* (340 tons) in 1780 and the *Madame* (390 tons) and the *Monsieur* (475 tons), both in 1780–2. Very few other ports outfitted such large privateer vessels: Saint-Malo could,[18] but things were entirely different at Dunkirk, where all the privateers were below 150 tons.[19] Few private individuals dared take such financial risks, for fear of 'going under' if the ship was captured or sunk.

Impressive results

The destruction of the Granville archives has made compiling a comprehensive list of seizures impossible.[20] However, cross-referencing the information scattered across archives in western France offers substantial insight. Of the 238 seizures for which we know the precise circumstances, only thirty-two (13.4%) occurred following combat. In 86.5% of cases, intimidation was enough for the opposing crew to conclude that it was better to surrender without resistance. Contrary to the legend spread by Hollywood, it was extremely rare for ships to be boarded: only two instances are recorded, one of which occurred without resistance. The rarity of violence is explained by the shipowners' strategy: for a campaign to be fully profitable, privateers

---

[18] Annick Martin-Deidier, 'La guerre de course à Saint-Malo de 1681 à 1814' (Unpublished PhD thesis, Sorbonne University, 1976).

[19] Patrick Villiers, *Marine royale, corsaires et trafics dans l'Atlantique de Louis XIV à Louis XVI* (Dunkirk, 1991), 2 vols.

[20] The Granville archives were almost completely destroyed when Saint-Lô was bombed on 6 June 1944.

had to behave like predators, not soldiers. As a result, they were asked to avoid combat as much as possible so as not to damage their own ship or their target, harming its market value.

Looking beyond the numbers, a few remarkable local players gave a particular lustre to privateering in Granville. During the reign of Louis XIV, the *Jeune Homme*, a frigate, made at least twenty-five seizures and five ransoms in seven operations, without being captured. This was an exceptional achievement, as most privateers usually made only a single voyage, and the best managed only three or four. The credit goes primarily to the Lévesque brothers, Jean Beaubriand-Lévesque and André La Souctière-Lévesque, who were part-proprietors, shipowners and captains during a series of successful campaigns between Ireland and Morocco. Also responsible was the ship's famous Honfleur captain, Jean Doublet, as well as its other, less well-known commanders.

The success of these men and their comrades was celebrated in France and beyond. Thanks to their exploits, the Lévesque brothers became the king's privateers on much larger warships.[21] This period was one of the greatest moments in Granville's privateering. The American War of Independence was another prosperous period, thanks to successful campaigns by frigates like the *Monsieur* and the *Madame*, outfitted by the highly enterprising Nicolas Deslandes. In all likelihood, he was supported financially by the brother of King Louis XVI – the future Louis XVIII – and his wife. Between 1779 and 1782, these ships carried out so many remarkable raids that Granville ranked third among metropolitan ports in terms of the number of ships outfitted and the value of seizures and ransoms.[22]

Clashes with the Channel Islanders

Once again, the destruction of the local archives complicates the task of understanding the raids carried out by Granville's inhabitants. Still, we have records of 204 seizures between 1688 and 1815 for which the port of origin is known. Of this number, 151 of the ships raided (74%) came under the jurisdiction of the Kingdom of Great Britain and Ireland, as is to be expected: London had been at war with France since 1688 and was Granville's closest enemy. The number of Channel Island seizures, however, was small: thirteen (nine from Jersey, three from Guernsey and one from Alderney, accounting for only 6.4%

---

[21] Michel Aumont, 'Jean Lévesque, sieur de Beaubriand, dit "Beaubriand-Lévesque", bourgeois granvillais et corsaire de Sa Majesté Louis XIV', in ADCC (ed.), *Capitaines corsaires. Audaces, fortunes et infortunes* (Saint-Malo, 2014), pp. 139–50.

[22] Mainland ports by the value of seizures and ransoms are ranked in an unnumbered record in the Archives Nationales, Marine, F² 74. For a comparison in terms of number of ships, see Aumont, *Les corsaires granvillais*, p. 188.

of the 204 seizures). Given the tense geopolitical situation, the long period under consideration, and these islands' proximity to Granville, such a low number is remarkable. Eight of these operations occurred between 1694 and 1710, under the reign of Louis XIV, and three others between 1797 and 1811, under the Consulate and the Empire. They included two small privateers: the *Seloupe* (sloop?), from Jersey, captured after a genuine battle at Cape Fréhel in 1697,[23] and the *Elisabeth of Guernsey* (8 tons) in 1746.[24] Note also that in 1781 the *Duc d'Harcourt* (28 tons), commanded by Nicolas Saint-Lô, helmsman, captured the *Paquet*, from Aurigny.[25] Unfortunately, the register, which only lists successful operations by the French in 1781, does not give any further information.

A survey of the National Archives in Kew gives an idea of British naval efforts against Granville raiders,[26] despite the available information being imprecise and incomplete. Searching for 'Grandville' – as it was once spelled – revealed several useful facts about operations against ships from the French port. Many were made by Her Majesty's Ships (HMS), i.e. warships, but eleven were carried out by privateers from the Channel Islands, eight from Guernsey and three from Jersey – a very small number. Eight of these occurred during the War of the Spanish Succession between 1704 and 1709, and three during the War of the Austrian Succession. Why did most of these operations take place in the first decade of the eighteenth century? The Channel Island privateers surely did not think themselves too weak to attack Granville's ships – something made clear by their exploits in Brittany. Why were such a low number of ships seized on either side? It may have been that privateers from Granville and the Channel Islands, especially Jersey, avoided each other. Smuggling was frequent and well known in the seventeenth and eighteenth centuries, often passing through Chausey.[27] It is tempting to conclude that the two groups avoided each other in times of war, with a view to the coming peace and the renewal of their illicit activities.

Smuggling did take place, as proven by a report of François Leguay from Néville, captain of Granville corsair *Gaye*. On 28 February 1710, having captured the *Gesme* on its way to Chausey, he wrote that 'the Gesme, from Jersey, was loaded with prohibited goods including tobacco, stockings, and

23 AN, G5/231 f° 444 et G5/233 f° 84. 'Registres des minutes de jugements du conseil des prises' (1697) and 'Dépouillement des jugements des prises' (1695–1701).

24 Archives of Ille and Vilaine, Rennes, 9 B 589, f° 11. 'Enregistrement du Conseil des prises' (1746).

25 AN, G5/264, n° 1182. 'Dépouillement des procédures de prises au greffe du Conseil' (1778–82).

26 https://discovery.nationalarchives.gov.uk/results/r?_q=Grandville.

27 Renaud Morieux, *Une mer pour deux royaumes: La Manche, frontière franco-anglaise (XVIIe–XVIIIe siècles)* (Rennes, 2008).

linen from France,[28] and took it to Granville', adding that 'various fishermen on leave had taken up this trade of which he had been informed several times'. The captain of the Jersey ship, when questioned, replied:

> I have gone out from Jersey with six men and a governor's passport to fish for fresh fish; but that, on the embankment he encountered several merchants who begged him to put some goods in his boat, and brought him tobacco, linen, stockings, camisoles, and culottes, having neither nets nor traps to fish with, but only iron hooks, as was usual …[29]

Was this an avoidance strategy? Since the world of smuggling is by its nature secretive, there is no evidence in the archives. Nonetheless this theory deserves to be examined, even if doing so is extremely difficult.

Profits, success, and disappointments

Once at sea, the privateers found themselves in the hands of fate. The possibility of shipwreck, of being captured or of returning empty-handed brought with it fear and disappointment − as well as violence, death, injury, imprisonment and illness. A study of the fates of the eighty-six privateer ships which sailed from Granville between 1744 and 1815 shows that most voyages ended badly (fig. 3). The fate of eleven of these ships (12.7%) is unknown. Of the remainder, fifty-nine (61.6%) disappeared, exploded, sank, or were captured. Only sixteen (18.6%) emerged unscathed. Other ports faced similar results. An anonymous report, written around 1781 by someone who knew Granville well, complained about the risks:

> But they object, privateers were almost always caught in the end, giving the enemy many prisoners, the King was obliged to buy back. Privateers were in great danger of being caught…. Examining the results of Granville's privateering, mentioned above, we find that, of the five ships which sailed from that port − the Monsieur, the Duc de Coigny, the Prince de Montbarrey, the Américaine, and the Madame − the first three were captured, giving the enemy 780 prisoners.[30]

A survey of the careers of 1,350 men (captains, officers, and sailors) selected at random from Granville privateer crews confirms this view: nearly 60%

---

[28] According to the report, the cargo included 250 livres of tobacco, 7 bales of linen, and 75 pairs of stockings made in Jersey.

[29] AN, G5/249 f° 272. 'Registres des minutes de jugements du conseil des prises' (1710).

[30] AN, Marine, G144, n° 25, 'Réflexions sur les encouragements de la course'. This report is undated, but its tone and some of the events mentioned enable us to estimate that it was written in the late 1780s.

were captured between 1706 and 1811.[31] The duration of their captivity varied considerably from one war to another, depending on the military circumstances in which their release was negotiated. Periods of imprisonment rarely exceeded a few weeks in the late seventeenth century, but gradually increased to several years after 1747, reaching a decade under the Empire. The English had understood that the weakness of the French Navy was the small pool of sailors it could draw on. This could be exploited by keeping French seamen in prison for long periods of time to hinder the recruitment of crews for the navy and privateering. But what happened to these men's families during these long periods of imprisonment? No academic work has been done on the subject.[32] We must assume, however, that without income from their husbands or any state support, the women, children and the elderly had to labour to provide for their most basic needs. Oyster fishing flourished in Granville, and the coastline was suited to fishing by hand; we can assume that these activities provided them with food.

Given the risks and their consequences, everyone waited anxiously for news of the privateers. Each announcement of a successful operation raised hopes at home. A small vessel captured was typically a disappointment, but the shipowners were happy if they could break even on the voyage. Ransoms had the same effect. The capture of a large vessel, by contrast, created high hopes. If its cargo was valuable, one large ship alone could make a voyage profitable, as in the case of the *Aimable Flore*, a 151-ton three-master outfitted for raiding by Deslandes. It left Granville in December 1809, outfitted with fourteen six-pounder cannons and eighty-six crewmen, each of whom had received 1,324 francs in advance. It made three seizures, but the last two were recovered by the English. Only the first, made the same day that it set out in the company of three gunboats from the Imperial Navy which had been attached to Granville, was successful. This was a 342-ton three-master, the *Governor Carlton*,[33] travelling from Suriname to London and loaded with coffee, rum, cocoa, sugar, cotton and other goods, and with sixteen cannons and a crew of nineteen men.[34] It found itself close to Granville as the result of an error by its captain, who, after sixty days at sea, had lost his way, mistaking Jersey for the Isle of Wight and thinking, incorrectly, that he had made landfall in England. The sale of this unique catch brought in 206,789.60 francs. Even when shared

[31] Aumont, *Les corsaires de Granville*, pp. 452–77.

[32] Emmanuelle Charpentier, 'Incertitude et stratégies de survie: le quotidien des femmes de "partis en voyage sur mer" des côtes nord de la Bretagne au xviiie siècle', *Annales de Bretagne et des Pays de l'Ouest*, 117 (2010/3), pp. 39–54, and *Le peuple du rivage: Le littoral nord de la Bretagne au xviiie siècle* (Rennes, 2013).

[33] Brest SHD, uncatalogued archives, dossier of seizures, *Governor Carlton*.

[34] Granville, Médiathèque, Fonds Patrimoine Ancien, transcriptions of La Morandière, *Aimable Flore*, 1810.

with the three gunboats, it was enough to make the voyage profitable, despite the loss of the other two ships.

The *Governor Carlton* ultimately yielded a profit of 185,361.15 francs. In accordance with the law of the time, two-thirds (123,574.10 francs) was divided among the stockholders, and the remaining third (61,787.05 francs) was reserved for the crew. After an obligatory levy for the Invalides fund[35] – five centimes on each franc of profit – the amount to be shared among the crew was 58,697.70 francs. The officers divided this into 156.25 shares, with each share worth 375.70 francs.[36] The captain received twelve shares, the chief mate ten, and the lieutenants between six and eight. The senior officers received four, the petty officers between one and four, and the soldiers and sailors between one and one and a half. Novices received only three-quarters of a share, and apprentices only half a share. There were also the proceeds from the sale of eight bales of silk taken from one of the two ships captured before they were recovered by the English – 10,208.93 francs, after the Invalides levy. Expenses were deducted, and the rest split between the shareholders and crew. The proceeds were divided into 160.75 shares, at 19.39 francs per share.

Both sums combined, an ordinary seaman in the crew who received only one share made a profit of 395.09 francs. Of course, the shipowner claimed back the advances they had received before embarking. As the records for the outfitting of the *Aimable Flore* have not survived, it is difficult to tell what advances its crew received, and therefore how much they received at the end of the voyage. Comparing them with other privateer crews that year, however, we can estimate that an ordinary sailor received 200 francs in advances, and an apprentice sixty francs.[37] The sailor received 195.09 francs on decommissioning. The captain, who never received advances, earned 4,741.08 francs from his twelve shares.

To understand the scale of these profits, we should compare them to the earnings of others in the period. Based on estimates by Vauban,[38] as well as those of Jean-Pierre Poussou in his study of Bordeaux and south-west France in the eighteenth century,[39] at the end of the eighteenth century a labourer could

---

[35] François-Nicolas Dufriches-Foulaines, *Code des prises et du commerce de terre et de mer* (Paris, 1804), vol. 2, p. 854. The Invalides fund (*Caisse des Invalides*) was created in 1673, during the Franco-Dutch War, to care for soldiers and seamen injured while serving the king.

[36] It was the captain and officers who decided retrospectively on the number of shares to allocate to each member of the crew, based on what they had achieved during the voyage.

[37] Cherbourg SHD, 12P4 109, n° 36, 'Rôle d'armement de l'Embuscade' (1808).

[38] Sébastien Le Prestre de Vauban, *Projet d'une dixme royale* (Rouen, 1707), pp. 75–6.

[39] Jean-Pierre Poussou, *Bordeaux et le Sud-Ouest au XVIIIe siècle: croissance*

earn between 150 and 300 livres a year in the countryside around Granville, and a small-scale farmer between 350 and 400 livres. The fishermen who went to Newfoundland, of course, earned more. A study of the topic was conducted in 1788 by Mauduit, commissioner of classes in Granville, for the Secretary of State for the Navy.[40] It gives precise details of the income for a Newfoundland dry fishery crew from Granville. A good fisherman could earn 400 to 600 livres in seven to eight months[41] – far more than farm labourers, who could earn between 150 and 300 livres each year. This difference led many to abandon farming for cod fishing, leading to the expansion of Granville's maritime district.

With 395.09 francs in earnings after four months at sea,[42] the privateer crew of the *Aimable Flore* were in an enviable position compared to the peasants and Newfoundland fishermen who remained ashore, leaving aside, of course, the risks involved. Fortune fuelled these men's dreams.[43] And, indeed, it could smile on some lucky ones, like the crew of the *Argus*, a 24-ton lugger with four small, 2-pound cannons, 4 pierriers, and a crew of 27 men commanded by a captain Daguenet. It sailed from Granville on 4 March 1807. On 11 March, it captured a 290-ton British ship, the *Montegobey*, loaded with coffee, sugar, logwood and salt. Unfortunately, the *Argus* was captured by the British on 19 October.[44] Despite this, proceeds from the sale of its only successful raid meant the voyage was largely profitable. The sale of the *Montegobey* and its cargo brought in 560,231.54 francs.[45] After subtracting expenses, the sum stood at 532,697.55 francs. Two-thirds of this went to the shareholders (355,131.67 francs), and one third to the crew (177,565.84 francs). Once expenses and the Invalides levy had been deducted, the crew was left with 168,666.03 francs. This was divided into 64.75 shares by the officers, each valued at 2,604.88 francs. It was an incredible stroke of luck.

The distribution record has been preserved at Granville's Musée d'Art et d'Histoire, and we can estimate the fortunes earned by the crew through the example of one quite ordinary sailor. François Blouet had received an advance

---

économique et attraction urbaine (Paris, 1983).

[40] AN, Marine, C⁵ 59, 'Mémoire sur les façons de rémunérer à Granville et à Saint-Malo'.

[41] Aumont, *Les corsaires de Granville*, p. 93.

[42] The law of 28 Thermidor Year III (15 August 1795) established a new currency, the franc. Eight months later, the law of 25 Germinal Year IV (14 April 1796) established the equivalence between the franc and the livre.

[43] On the motivations behind privateering, the way such journeys were undertaken, and the risks involved, see Aumont, *Les corsaires de Granville*.

[44] Cherbourg SHD, 12P⁷ 3 and Brest SHD, 2Q 84, 'États de corsaires'.

[45] Musée d'Art et d'Histoire de Granville, dossier on the *Argus*, distribution report for the *Montegobey* seizure, 1807.

of 306 francs on shares from any ships seized. After the liquidation, the officers decided to give him a single share, valued at 2,604.88 francs. His advances were deducted from this. From his time on the *Argus*, Blouet earned five or six times what a Newfoundland fisherman earned in a good fishing season during the 1780s, and ten to fifteen times the salary of a farm labourer. The captain, Daguenet, pocketed the tidy sum of 31,258.56 francs – a genuine fortune. But how many sailors could boast of such good luck? Very few, it is likely: fewer and fewer sailors engaged in privateering between 1793 and 1815, for the risks were high and the profit increasingly uncertain.

Some shipowners amassed substantial wealth through privateering, including Léonor Couraye du Parc, who outfitted four privateers during the War of the Austrian Succession. The *Charles Grenot* – an old 150-ton Newfoundland frigate with eighteen cannons – made five successful raids over the course of two voyages, finally being shipwrecked on the island of Batz. The *Grand Grenot* – a new 300-ton frigate with forty cannons – only carried out a single voyage, during which it captured eleven enemy ships, ultimately sinking at the entrance to Granville's port. The *Aimable Grenot* – another new 390-ton frigate with forty cannons, some of them recovered from the *Grand Grenot* – carried out two voyages. It made ten successful attacks in the first, and seven in the second. A fourth raiding vessel made only a single modest operation before being captured. Arming the three *Grenots* cost 506,323 livres, 6 sols, and 7 deniers, but brought in 1,843,034 livres, 17 sols, and 7 deniers, less the six deniers per livre for the Invalides fund, the tenth paid to the admiral of France, decommissioning costs, and other expenses – in other words, three and a half times the initial investment.[46] This financial power immediately enabled the shipowner to buy land close to Granville, where he built a manor. Upon his death, his son was granted a title as a reward for the success of his father's enterprises.

During the American War of Independence, Deslandes won for himself a title and a substantial fortune: 'He had six privateers built ... the Monsieur captured nineteen ships, including twelve privateers ... the Madame captured thirty-two ships, including nine privateers ... both were outfitted five times',[47] These two frigates earned vast profits: the *Madame* alone made 1,171,450 livres by the end of her three voyages. Their success was enough that, in a survey of raiding during the war conducted by the Ministry of the Navy, Granville ranked third among mainland privateer ports for the total value of its catches, behind Dunkirk and Saint-Malo, but ahead of Le Havre, Calais, Marseille and Boulogne.[48] Deslandes' success was clearly a determining factor in this

---

[46] AN, Marine, C⁷ 85, Request for letters of nobility, Deslandes dossier (1782).

[47] AN, Marine, C⁷ 85, Request for letters of nobility, Deslandes dossier (1782).

[48] AN, Marine, F² 74, 'Récapitulation générale du montant des prises dont les répartitions ont été faites aux équipages des corsaires et de celles qui ne sont point réparties dont les liquidations particulières sont arrêtées' (1783).

assessment. With his new fortune, he too built a manor a few kilometres from the port.

Couraye du Parc and Deslandes served as models for those who followed in their wake, and who dreamed of imitating them. With their exceptional success, they made others believe there was a chance – slim but real – of making a fortune, or, at least, of significantly increasing their assets. However, not everyone let themselves be carried away. They knew the risks were real; everyone remembered the misfortunes of Anquetil Brutière, a shipowner who had quickly gone under when the large privateer he had placed his fortune and his hopes in, the *Daguesseau* (340 tons), was captured fifty-two hours after setting sail without having made a single capture.[49] Quinette de la Hogue was remembered for having accidentally lost the equally unsuccessful *Granville* (530 tons) in 1757. There were any number of disappointments: fruitless voyages, captured ships and bankrupt shipowners. Among the crews, countless men were taken prisoner and held in notorious jails for ever longer periods of time. Potential players knew the risks, even if they did not know the precise figures. Everyone followed their own character, temperament and interests.

It was the proximity of England and the Channel Islands, and the desire for revenge on a power they considered too arrogant and too invasive on their fishing grounds, which convinced those in Granville to take up privateering. There was no lack of skill, entrepreneurship, capital, ships or manpower. But the real motivation apparently lay elsewhere. An in-depth study of Granville shipowners between 1680 and 1815 shows that only a few became privateers.[50] The vast majority preferred to stay in port and wait for peace to return. Only 20% of shipowners in Granville turned to privateering, and half of those abandoned it after the first attempt.

Historians have argued that privateering served as a substitute during a period of war: it was a necessity for sailors condemned to inactivity and financial insecurity, a compensation 'for the losses resulting from the total or partial cessation of peacetime trade'.[51] But this argument, defended by André Lespagnol,[52] does not seem to fit Granville, where the vast majority of shipowners (around 80%) deliberately chose to remain outside the conflict – unlike Saint-Malo and Dunkirk, where many began to outfit their ships for privateering.[53]

---

[49] AN, Marine, F2 80, 'État des prises faites sur les Français par les ennemis de l'État, depuis le commencement des hostilités'. The *Daguesseau* is valued at 216,000 livres (1779).

[50] Aumont, *Les corsaires de Granville*, pp. 211–74.

[51] Jean Meyer, 'La course: romantisme, exutoire social, réalité économique. Essai de méthodologie', *Annales de Bretagne* (June 1971), 312–13.

[52] Lespagnol, *Messieurs de Saint-Malo*, vol. 1, p. 378.

[53] This is clear from the work of Janine Lemay, André Lespagnol, Annick

Conclusion

It becomes clear that there were two categories of decision-makers in Granville privateering: large shipowners, involved in Newfoundland fishing, and smaller operators who made their money from coastal shipping and small-scale fishing. The former typically outfitted vessels of between 200 and 530 tons. Their personal finances meant they could wait for peace to return. If they really needed to, they could turn temporarily to small-scale coastal shipping, which was less affected by the war. But such work did not interest them. For their part, coastal shipping operators could have continued their activity normally, carefully following the coastline without much fear of the enemy. Nonetheless, some decided to take up the risky business of privateering. For these men, too, privateering was by no means a source of compensation forced on them by necessity. They had other motivations. The war opened a window of opportunity, an opportunity that even the most enterprising did not want to miss − a way of forcing fate's hand. With luck, fortune would smile on the bold. A handful of proactive men carried in their wake the entire population of the coast, ready to do their utmost to prepare ships, to embark on them and to take in captured ships. Each hoped to obtain his share of the loot, directly or indirectly.

It is pointless to reduce their motivations to purely economic considerations. Enterprise was these men's habit, but they seemed here to succumb to a different sort of temptation: playing with fate. Such risk-taking might appeal to some during wartime. How else can we explain the difference in behaviour between the 80% of Granville shipowners who turned away from privateering and waited for peace, and the 20% who embraced it? In the seventeenth century, the chances of success in privateering drew comparisons with a lottery. But such a comparison silently glosses over the disappointments many shipowners experienced, and the distress of those who found themselves ruined. A better comparison is with poker: players could win, or lose, a fortune. Knowing the risks run by previous generations, some shipowners consciously accepted the exhilarations of this life-size game. Patriotism was never mentioned: they saw privateering as a way to combine their appetite for risk with their habit of enterprise.

Martin-Deydier and Anne Morel on Saint-Malo, and the work of Henri Malo and Patrick Villiers on Dunkirk.

2

'Fire No Guns, Shed No Tears': Channel Island Privateers, British Strategic Thinking and the Politics of Neutrality During the Seven Years War

ANNA BRINKMAN-SCHWARTZ

The phrase 'fire no guns, shed no tears' is part of the chorus from a song called 'Barret's Privateers', which tells the story of a man who signed up to be part of the crew of a British privateer called *The Antelope* during the American War of Independence. The protagonist of the song deems himself deceived by the promise that the crew would have to fire no guns and shed no tears and that American ships would simply surrender themselves to *The Antelope* as prizes. As a whole the song evokes a darkly romanticized version of eighteenth-century privateers as poor sailors duped into joining leaky old ships with bad-tempered captains. These privateers would then ply the seas with abandon looking for gold-laden prizes with the blessing and non-intervention of the British state. It is the second part of this romantic outlook on privateers that this chapter seeks to address. Far from being a benign overseer of legalised piracy, British wartime governments in the eighteenth century were deeply concerned about the effect that the actions of privateers could have on British maritime strategy. Privateering as a concept and as a reality was deeply embedded in British strategic thinking and in British diplomacy with neutral nations. Far from operating as a remote arm of the British wartime mercantile sector, privateers played a key role in the delicate negotiations over neutral rights. This was certainly the case during the first four years of the Seven Years War when Anglo-Dutch relations were focused on Dutch neutral rights and the taking of Dutch prizes by British privateers.

From a strategic perspective, the ideal role for privateers in the first few years of the Seven Years War was to destroy French seaborne trade without needlessly molesting or antagonizing neutral shipping. This ideal role was consistently complicated by two factors. Firstly, neutral nations like the Dutch Republic often carried French goods in their ships in order to profit from wartime relaxations of mercantilist-inspired trade restrictions. Secondly, privateers were hard to control at sea and often captured neutral vessels indiscriminately. Much political effort was therefore expended in trying to contain the political damage done by privateers and in trying to get neutral nations to both remain neutral and to stop carrying French trade. The main architects of British negotiations with the Dutch Republic on the subject of neutrality and privateering were William Pitt (Secretary of State for the Southern Department for most of the war), Lord Holdernesse (Secretary of State for the Northern Department), the Duke of Newcastle (Secretary of the Treasury), Lord Hardwicke (ex-Chancellor and judge in the Court of Prize Appeal) and Charles Yorke (British Representative in the Hague). Together, these men were able to successfully maintain Dutch neutrality throughout the war whilst protecting Britain's ability to aggressively pursue the destruction of French seaborne commerce. Their method was to engender Dutch trust in the British prize system and, particularly, the Court of Prize Appeal, as the institution that would defend Dutch neutral rights.[1] On the privateering side, efforts were made to convince privateers that unwarranted aggression toward neutral Dutch ships not carrying French trade would be punished in the prize courts, but warranted aggression would be rewarded.

Privateers and the extent of their 'rights' to capture neutral shipping were used as political pawns in Britain's negotiations with the Dutch in the first four years of the war. Privateers, in general, may not have been aware of the extent to which they featured in Anglo-Dutch negotiations, but they also did not sit idly by as the government sought to control their actions. Throughout the first years of Anglo-Dutch negotiations, the five men in charge of securing Dutch neutrality were aware that privateers, when banded together, could create a troublesome lobbying group that had political influence because they were a vital part of British maritime strategy and because they had the support of politically influential characters like William Beckford and William Pitt himself.[2] The active privateering lobby was largely made up of privateering interests from Bristol, Liverpool and London, the biggest privateering ports during the Seven Years War.[3] When Anglo-Dutch negotiations were being

---

[1]   See the wider argument made by the author in: Anna Brinkman, 'The Court of Prize Appeal as an Agent of British Wartime Foreign Policy: The Maintenance of Dutch and Spanish Neutrality During the Seven Years War' (King's College London DPhil thesis, 2017).

[2]   William Beckford was a wealthy West Indian planter and future mayor of London. See Perry Gauci, *William Beckford: First Prime Minister of the London Empire* (New Haven: Yale University Press, 2013).

[3]   David Starkey, *British Privateering Enterprise in the Eighteenth Century* (Liverpool: Liverpool University Press, 1990), 42. See also Sheryllynne Haggerty, 'Risk, Networks and Privateering in Liverpool During the Seven Years War, 1756–1763', *The International Journal of Maritime History* 30(1) (2018): 30–51.

carried out and concessions made, it was the interests of the wealthier privateer investors from these three main ports that were being protected. The privateers who were used as scapegoats in Anglo-Dutch negotiations were the smaller, less connected, privateers of the Channel and the Channel Islands.

Channel Island privateers have, so far, been a neglected sub-group in the historiography of British strategic thinking and wartime negotiations over neutral rights. This is partly because this particular historiography is fairly small, but it is also because it is mainly a history of neglect where the absence of primary sources is the most common type of evidence.[4] The architects of British maritime strategy in the Seven Years War did not concern themselves with Channel Island privateers unless it was to point to them as the perpetrators of the worst abuses of neutral shipping: an accusation that does not necessarily hold up to scrutiny. However, their neglect and castigation of Channel Island privateers was rooted in sound strategic thinking.

The purpose of this chapter is to analyse and explain how Channel Island privateering fitted into British strategic thinking about neutrality and Anglo-Dutch negotiations in the first years of the war. The analysis will look specifically at two strands of Anglo-Dutch negotiations. First, the negotiations over prohibiting the Dutch to carry French colonial trade but allowing them to carry European trade will be examined in the context of the disproportional effect on Channel Island privateers, which tended to be of smaller tonnage and focused on capturing more local trade. Secondly, the analysis will then move on to examine the Privateers Act of 1759, which was designed as a political concession to the Dutch and a demonstration that Britain was cracking down on privateers who did not respect Dutch neutrality. The act also had a disproportionate effect on Channel Island privateers because it was aimed at privateers of less than 100 tons. Together, these two branches of Anglo-Dutch negotiations show that not all privateers were considered equal in British strategic thinking and that Channel Island privateers in particular were seen

---

4   Daniel Baugh, *The Global Seven Years War, 1754–1763* (London: Pearson, 2011); Lauren Benton and Lisa Ford, *Rage for Order: The British Empire and the Origins of International Law 1800–1850* (Cambridge: Harvard University Press, 2016); Lauren Benton and Richard J. Ross eds, *Legal Pluralism and Empires, 1500–1850* (New York: New York University Press, 2014); Alice Clare Carter, *Neutrality or Commitment: The Evolution of Dutch Foreign Policy 1667–1795* (Bath: The Pitman Press, 1975); Julian Stafford Corbett, *England in the Seven Years War a Study in Combined Strategy* Vol. I (London: Longmans, Green, 1907); Sarah Kinkel, *Disciplining the Empire: Politics, Governance, and the Rise of the British Navy* (Cambridge: Harvard University Press, 2018); Carl Kulsrud, *Maritime Neutrality to 1780* (Boston: Little Brown, 1936); Richard Pares, *Colonial Blockade and Neutral Rights 1739–1763* (Philadelphia: Porcupine Press, 1975).

as strategically dispensable in the grander pursuit of securing Dutch neutrality and destroying French colonial trade.

Neutrality, strategy and privateering

Neutrality was not a static state of inaction and disengagement; rather, it was a very dynamic position from which concessions, liberties and privileges might be won from belligerent powers who were keen not to see a neutral nation become allied with an enemy. By the same token, however, the dynamism of neutrality could plunge neutral actors into uncertainty over the safety of their trade and the rights of their citizens. Neutral nations were able to wield power during times of war because trade in maritime empires was largely based on mercantilist thinking. France, Spain and Britain prohibited their colonial trade from being carried in foreign ships, and foreign traders were mostly confined to operating in European ports by measures prohibiting them from trading directly with colonies overseas. Empires whose approach to trade was governed by such mercantilist principles rendered themselves particularly vulnerable to economic warfare, because merchant ships carrying their flag became legal targets for enemy warships in wartime. The most obvious means of avoiding capture by enemy warships was to allow trade to be carried in neutral bottoms, as neutral shipping was not universally acknowledged as a legitimate target in wartime. The legitimacy of targeting neutral shipping would depend on existing bilateral treaties between belligerent and neutral states. Neutral maritime nations could thus profit from wars between maritime empires, and they became crucial factors in deciding the viability of a maritime strategy based on economic warfare.

As in many previous wars, it was paramount for Britain to keep France from obtaining a foothold in the Netherlands and setting up naval bases next to the Strait of Dover (the shortest crossing to England and a direct trade route into the Baltic).[5] As a maritime power without a particularly powerful army, Britain's best mode of securing the Netherlands against France was through diplomacy, and by making sure that the Dutch played the role of a neutral nation. At sea, Britain enjoyed superiority over France, which meant that when fighting in the colonies or at sea, where commerce predation was a key factor, Britain had the upper hand. However, if Spain (with its large colonial presence in the Americas), or the Dutch Republic, became an ally of France, Britain's maritime superiority would be threatened.

For diplomacy to succeed in Europe, and for maritime supremacy to be maintained, Britain tried to ensure that other European maritime nations remained neutral or became allies during its war with France. Dutch neutrality,

---

[5]   Julian Stafford Corbett, *England in the Seven Years War: a Study in Combined Strategy* Vol. I (London: Longmans, Green, 1907), 18.

like that of most nations, was not necessarily a given when colonial hostilities began between Britain and France in 1754. The Dutch, who were, in many respects, culturally closer to Britain than to France, did not wish for either country to emerge as the hegemonic victor.[6] If Britain had been perceived by other European powers as the aggressor in the conflict, it very well could have pushed the Dutch Republic and other maritime powers into an alliance with France. Such alliances would have changed the balance of power at sea and, in the case of the Dutch, given the French access to the Netherlands.[7] Once war was declared in 1756, the Dutch Republic proclaimed its neutrality and signed an agreement with France that kept the French out of the Low Countries and ensured that the Dutch would carry French trade in return.[8] The Dutch also secured a promise from the French that the Austrian Netherlands would not be invaded. The inviolability of the Austrian Netherlands was also strategically valuable to Britain because it checked France's ability to launch an invasion from the Scheldt.[9] With Dutch neutrality declared, Britain focused on defeating the French at sea and, through her Prussian ally, neutralising France on land in Europe. However, Britain's maritime strategy of commerce predation would be plagued throughout the first four years of the war by the constant need to maintain Dutch neutrality and protect Dutch neutral rights from perceived violations by British privateers. This task was made increasingly difficult by what Julian Corbett called the 'law of maritime warfare' – the direct correlation between a country's increasing command of the sea and the likelihood of neutral powers becoming enemies.[10]

The 'law of maritime warfare' and commerce predation

The growth of British maritime hegemony in the eighteenth century meant that British prize law – which adjudicated the legality of the prizes taken at sea by British privateers and warships – increasingly became the international norm by which neutral maritime rights were governed. It was not, however, only the power of Britain's navies that caused concern. During times of war,

---

6   Alice Clare Carter, *The Dutch Republic in Europe in the Seven Years War* (London: MacMillan, 1971), xvi.

7   Ibid., 83.

8   Carter, *Dutch Republic*, 34.

9   Daniel Baugh, *The Global Seven Years War 1754–1763* (London: Pearson, 2011), 149 and 176.

10   Julian Stafford Corbett, *England and the Seven Years War a Study in Combined Strategy* Vol. II (London: Longmans, Green, 1907), 5. In 1907 Corbett was working on the contemporary relevance of these issues in a war against Germany. See his essay: 'The Capture of Private Property at Sea: The Nineteenth Century and After', in Alfred T. Mahan, *Some Neglected Aspects of War* (London: Sampson, Law, 1907), 115–54.

the actions of British privateers were likely to cause friction between Britain and neutral maritime nations.[11] If the British prize court system was to be an arbiter in disagreements over maritime neutral rights and the rights of British privateers, then the neutral nations had to trust that the system was fair and would protect the rights of their seaborne citizens. If this trust were lost, if the prize courts failed to uphold neutral rights and were seen rather to favour the rights of British privateers, then Corbett's law of maritime warfare would come to its natural conclusion, and neutral nations in Britain's wars would become belligerents. Such an eventuality would run counter to Britain's strategy in its maritime wars against France.

The first year of the Seven Years War was not a resounding success for Britain in the maritime sphere but, by the end of 1759, France's colonial commerce had been all but eradicated; French Canada was under British control; France's navy was defeated, if not eliminated, in the battle of Quiberon Bay; and the French West India islands were falling prey to British invasion. Britain's increasing dominance over France at sea and in the colonies directly affected the relationship between Britain and neutral maritime countries such as the Dutch Republic. The behaviour of Britain's privateers, when inter-acting with neutral Dutch ships was, ostensibly, governed by the Anglo-Dutch treaty of 1674. However, it was ultimately impossible to control or police the actions of Britain's representatives at sea. Events between ships at sea were often completely isolated, and the only witnesses were those involved in the encounter. News of an encounter could take weeks to reach authorities in Europe or London, by which time there was little that could be done to deter any diplomatic damage which the actions of British or neutral citizens might have sparked during a seaborne encounter. As a result, Britain's negotiations with the Dutch about upholding maritime neutral rights and the treaties that defined them were always reactive. By the same token, any system that was put in place to contain the fall-out of seaborne incidents involving neutral nations, such as prize courts, was also necessarily reactive. Such systems were not particularly put in place to change the behaviour of the privateers but rather to allow Dutch grievances to be aired and restitution made. Contentious incidents that occurred between British and Dutch ships that ended up in the prize courts were not to be treated as isolated incidents. Rather, they became an integral part of the negotiations over neutrality and of Anglo-Dutch relations in general. This meant that privateers formed a critical component of British strategic thinking during the Seven Years War and were at the forefront of negotiations over neutrality with the Dutch Republic.

---

[11] Sophus Reinert, 'Rivalry: Greatness in Early Modern Political Economy', in *Mercantilism Reimagined: Political Economy in Early Modern Britain and its Empire*, ed. Philip J. Stern and Carl Wennerlind (Oxford: Oxford University Press, 2014), 352.

Anglo-Dutch negotiations

Disputes between the two countries arose during the Seven Years War, soon after the Dutch declared their neutrality and British privateers began to take Dutch merchant ships as prizes. The various interpretations and disputes over the rights granted by the treaty of 1674 were played out in the British prize courts. The sentences passed on Dutch ships in these courts mainly focused on whether the cargo was being legally carried, i.e., whether the Dutch ships were violating the treaty and their neutrality by aiding the French, or whether the cargo being shipped was legal under the circumstances prescribed by the treaty.[12] As the war progressed, the factions of the Dutch government that were anti-British, and the Dutch merchant interests, mostly concentrated in Amsterdam and Rotterdam, became increasingly frustrated by the treatment of Dutch ships in the British prize courts. They began to lose faith that the British prize system could protect their neutral rights.

By 1758, Anglo-Dutch relations had reached what Richard Pares called the 'Anglo-Dutch crisis'.[13] The crisis, from 1758 to early spring of 1759, encompassed the straining of Anglo-Dutch relations due to the condemnation of Dutch ships in the British prize courts and the inability of the two countries to agree on the neutral rights to be enjoyed by the Dutch. With no agreement outside of the prize courts on what constituted Dutch neutral rights, and with sentencing throughout the prize court system seen as inconsistent and arbitrary, the justice and due process of the prize courts were regarded with suspicion and contested by the Dutch government. The crisis, which almost led to open hostilities, was eventually resolved when Dutch grievances over neutral rights and the behaviour of privateers were allayed, largely, by the opening of the Court of Prize Appeal to Dutch cases in March of 1759; the understanding that the Court of Prize Appeal would focus on stopping Dutch carriage of French colonial goods but not inter-European trade; and by the passing of the Privateers Act in June of the same year. These concessions were made with the understanding that they would most adversely affect the least influential sector of the privateering lobby, the Channel Island privateers.

Channel Island privateers and the privateering lobby

The men and women who had a vested interest in privateering were able to exert some political influence, because a successful privateering arm was an important component of Britain's maritime strategy. The ubiquity of

---

[12] Anna Brinkman, 'The Court of Prize Appeal as an Agent of British Wartime Foreign Policy: The Maintenance of Dutch and Spanish Neutrality During the Seven Years War' (King's College London DPhil thesis, 2017), chapters 1–3.

[13] Richard Pares, *Colonial Blockade and Neutral Rights*, 75.

newspapers and their accessibility through distribution in coffee houses gave privateers and their investors a wide-reaching platform.[14] Britain's maritime community could be stirred by the privateering lobby either to laud or condemn the government's actions when it came to neutral rights and the rights of privateers. It is extremely unlikely that the privateering lobby could pose a political threat to the government's stability and support in Parliament through public shows of discontent that stirred the maritime community.[15] Nonetheless, if privateers did not trust in the government and in prize courts to protect their interests, they could choose to not engage as actively in commerce predation, which would be detrimental to Britain's maritime strategy against France. It was in the government's interest to make sure that privateers had full confidence in the impartiality and fairness of prize law and the prize courts.

When Britain entered into a state of war, merchants could shift their money and focus to privateering from whatever peacetime trade they normally plied.[16] The privateering interest during wartime, therefore, was largely the same as the maritime commercial interest during peacetime, if slightly smaller. When these merchants chose to stand together as a political body, they could resist ministerial pressure and, sometimes, exert influence of their own. The political aims of the privateering lobby are not particularly difficult to discern because as members of a venture capital scheme they disliked legislation that attempted to impose rules or restrictions that hindered their chances of a high return on their investment. This generally meant that they opposed legislation that protected the rights of neutral ships.[17] It was, understandably, more difficult for Channel Island-based privateers to exert political influence due to their distance from the metropole. Nonetheless, some Island privateers were sensible to the importance of having the government's ear, such as Daniel Messervy who urged his fellow Jerseymen in London to make sure that the exploits and successes of Jersey privateers were known. Messervy ultimately hoped that the contribution of Jersey privateers to the war effort would lead to governmental aid in the form of warships to protect the island from the French.[18]

The ministry were not strangers to the privateer and merchant lobbies. William Pitt was often considered a favourite of the privateers because, as a Patriotic-Whig, he looked out for their interests. Many of the people who

---

[14] Anna Brinkman, 'The *Antigallican* Affair: Public and Ministerial Responses to Anglo-Spanish Maritime Conflict in the Seven Years War 1756–1758', *The English Historical Review* 135(576) (Dec. 2020).

[15] Jeremy Black, *Parliament and Foreign Policy in the Eighteenth Century* (Cambridge: Cambridge University Press, 2004), 7–9.

[16] Ibid., 67.

[17] Starkey, *British Privateering Enterprise*, 60.

[18] Alan G. Jamieson, *A People of the Sea: Maritime History of the Channel Islands* (London: Routledge, 1986), 152.

supported the Patriotic Whigs were drawn from the urban and commercial population; the same sort of demographic that would support privateering during times of war.[19] From Pitt's political and ideological perspective, it made sense to champion the privateers' cause. Though Pitt tried to keep the privateers happy and working for the interest of British strategy, he found it very difficult to influence or control them. Even when the political situation with the Dutch Republic was dire, Pitt was only able to threaten privateers with the due process of the law.[20] Part of the reason Pitt could only issue threats was that there were no legal sanctions that could be applied to privateers before a prize case went through the court system. The Prize Act of 1708 gave the captors a statutory right to their prizes and to all the proceeds gained from condemnation – in other words, prizes became a matter of private property. The act deprived the Crown of any control over the administrative or judicial procedures in prize affairs. Attempts to return powers of administration over prize affairs to the Crown in subsequent prize acts were shunned by administrations over fear that such a move would provide fodder for parliamentary opposition and accusations that the Crown was trying to erode Parliament's authority.[21]

The specific aims of the Channel Island privateers differed from those of their mainland counterparts in ports like Bristol, Liverpool and London. Fundamentally, Channel Island merchants wished to protect their legal and illicit trades with England, France and Spain. They also wished to protect themselves from possible French invasions.[22] Given the islands' proximity to France, this was no small concern. The Channel Island privateers were therefore heavily involved in intelligence gathering, trade with neutral nations, illicit trade with France and commerce predation.[23] The achievements of the Channel Island privateers were hardly negligible in terms of harassing France's maritime commerce. Early in the war, the commerce from St Malo was cut by a third. The tonnage coming in and out of Bordeaux was also cut by a third. Nantes' maritime trade was virtually destroyed by 1759 and other ports such as La Rochelle were equally affected.[24] When it came to disposing of prizes and prize goods, Channel Island privateers also appear to have operated a bit differently from those based in mainland ports. The selling of prize goods and prizes was, technically, regulated by prize courts and the Prize Act of 1708. The profits of prize sales were only given to privateers if the capture was

---

[19] Kinkel, *Disciplining the Empire*, 125 and 138.

[20] Pares, *Colonial Blockade*, 69–70.

[21] Ibid., 66–9.

[22] Peter Raban, 'Channel Island Privateering 1739–1763', *International Journal of Maritime Research* (December 1989): 287–8.

[23] Ibid.

[24] Jamieson, *A People of the Sea*, 152.

deemed to have been legal.[25] Prizes brought into the Channel Island ports, however, were under much less strict control particularly because customs controls in the Channel Islands were much less well-established than in the mainland. Channel Island privateers could, therefore, dispose of their prizes and prize goods without necessarily having to go through the British prize system at all.[26] Being physically removed from the mainland and operating under unique circumstances meant that Channel Island privateers did not play a large role in the privateering lobby, nor were their interests as well protected by men like William Pitt. As will be seen, this led to their interests being easily sacrificed to the needs of Anglo-Dutch negotiations.

Channel privateers and Anglo-Dutch negotiations

It is clear from the correspondence amongst British ministers involved in Anglo-Dutch relations that they were concerned about the behaviour of British privateers and the effect that the capture of Dutch prizes would have on Dutch neutrality. Lord Hardwicke, William Pitt and the Duke of Newcastle were also concerned about the amount of French trade that was carried in Dutch ships. These concerns were never couched in terms specifically relating to Channel Island privateers, but the solutions put forward by Lord Hardwicke and his colleagues make it clear that Channel Island-based privateering interests could be sacrificed to the greater strategic need.

By September 1756, a few months into the war, Lord Hardwicke had split Franco-Dutch trade into five categories which needed to be addressed by Anglo-Dutch negotiations and the British prize courts: contraband trade, the trade in naval stores, the coastal trade, trade to and from French colonies and the general carrying trade for France. The first three, Hardwicke considered, were adequately covered by the Anglo-Dutch treaty of 1674, though he advocated a wider definition of contraband. The fourth and fifth categories troubled Hardwicke the most. Of the colonial trade he wrote

> ...it can by no means be tolerated. All the European nations exclude foreigners from their American colonies, and so things stood at the time of making the Treaty of 1674. It is the general rule still, and cannot possibly be varied, except as a new invention fraudulently to screen French efforts from capture and the question is whether England shall suffer them to trade thither, in time of war, without seizure, when the French themselves will not suffer them to trade thither, in time of peace, without seizing them on most any account.[27]

[25] Starkey, *British Privateering Enterprise*, 25–7.
[26] Raban, 'Channel Island Privateering', 288.
[27] BL Add MS 32997 Newcastle Papers, Hardwicke's Notes Relating to the Dutch Trade with France. September 1756. ff. 48–51.

His objection to the French colonial trade would have repercussions for British privateers who preyed on colonial trade and more local European trade. If European nations did not allow foreigners to trade with their American colonies in times of peace then, Hardwicke considered, the British should not allow the trade to exist in times of war. Hardwicke's reasoning would eventually become the basis for his 'Rule of the War of 1756', a guiding principle employed by the Court of Prize Appeal and unofficially recognized by the Dutch.[28]

Hardwicke's thoughts on the fifth category of trade, the general carrying trade for France, were rooted in the Grotian concept that 'free ships make free goods'; in other words, enemy goods carried in a non-enemy ship were protected by the status of the non-enemy ship. Once again, Hardwicke's main worry was about the carriage of French colonial goods in Dutch ships but, in this case, he was concerned with French goods which had been landed in other neutral ports, such as Spain or Portugal, and then put on Dutch ships for the final leg of the voyage, expressly to avoid capture by British ships. Such fraudulent practices were considered by Hardwicke to be a '…continuation and completion of the original [French] voyage, and ought to be liable to the like capture although the vessel is collusively changed, and the goods transhipped. These ought to be subject to condemnation on proof that the goods are French property…'[29] One of the ways to justify British seizures of Dutch ships carrying French colonial goods out of neutral ports was to claim that the shipment of French colonial goods into any country other than France was illegal under French law during times of peace and should therefore be illegal in times of war. By the same token, any French colonial goods that were illegally imported into a neutral country could not legally be shipped out to France in a Dutch ship. Such reasoning, were it to be defended in the prize courts and by the ministry, would lend legitimacy to the smaller Channel privateers were they to pursue neutral coastal shipping to the north and south of France.

It would take two years for Lord Hardwicke's ideas to come to fruition due to on-going stagnation in Anglo-Dutch negotiations. On 7 September 1758, Hardwicke wrote to Lord Holdernesse (Secretary of State for the Northern

[28] For a full discussion of the Rule of the War of 1756 and its relation to debates over neutrality see Brinkman, 'The Court of Prize Appeal as an Agent of British Wartime Foreign Policy', 92–4. Recognition of Hardwicke's principle occurred after decisions were handed down by the Court of Prize Appeal in the cases of the captured Dutch ships *Maria Theresa* and *America.* The decisions in the cases, led by Hardwicke's legal reasoning, were designed to both uphold Dutch Neutrality and not anger the privateering lobby. They were also designed to support the Rule of the War of 1756 without making any firm decision based on the Anglo-Dutch treaty of 1674.

[29] BL Add MS 32997 Newcastle Papers, Hardwicke's Notes Relating to the Dutch Trade with France. September 1756. ff. 48–51.

Department), describing his distress over the lack of progress in the Dutch disputes. Hardwicke believed it was time for a solution, and that Britain should make overtures to the Dutch Republic.[30] Ever since 1756, Hardwicke wrote, he had been pushing for an amendment to prize law that would grant the Crown the power to release captured neutral ships without going through the usual legal motions of a trial. In other words, grant the Crown the power to take away neutral prizes from privateers without going through the prize system. He suggested to Holdernesse that recently taken Dutch ships should be released, and that this gesture of goodwill would cause the Dutch to give up carrying French trade to and from the West Indies. He claimed that had his proposal been enacted at the start of the war, 'Much of this mischief might then have been prevented.'[31] and he proposed that his amendment be considered once more. Hardwicke's solution to the Dutch disputes was threefold: first, the Crown should be given more power to release neutral ships; second, the Dutch would have to give up carrying French trade to and from the Americas, but as a token of friendship, Britain would be lenient and forgiving of Dutch trade with France within Europe; and third, restrictions would have to be placed on British privateers for 'otherwise they will put their kind at war with all the world.'[32] Hardwicke's approach would give the Crown more power, and would allow the ministry to alleviate tensions immediately by releasing Dutch ships when their seizure by British privateers caused an uproar in the Dutch Republic. However, giving the Crown the additional power to bypass laws put in place by Parliament would likely also cause an uproar in Parliament and amongst the privateers, as it would encroach on parliamentary authority and the rights of privateers granted by the 1708 Prize Act. Hardwicke's solution, which ensured that French colonial trade would continue to be destroyed by privateers, would disproportionately affect the Channel privateers who preyed on French coastal and inter-European trade. Hardwicke's suggestion to restrict the privateers would eventually lead to the Privateers Act of 1759. In the meantime, it convinced Holdernesse and others in the ministry to make overtures to the Dutch Republic in the winter of 1758–9.

Per Hardwicke's suggestion, a memorial was sent to the Dutch in the winter of 1758 that required the Dutch to give up the French trade to and from the Americas. If the Republic agreed, Britain would grant the Dutch the benefits of the treaty of 1674 – i.e. freedom to carry French inter-European trade. In terms of redressing potential wrongs done to Dutch merchants by British privateers, Holdernesse suggested and encouraged the Dutch merchants to appeal cases to the Court of Prize Appeal in order that the mistakes of privateers and the lower

---

[30] BL Add MS 3431 Leeds Papers, Letter from Hardwicke to Holdernesse, 7 September 1758.

[31] Ibid.

[32] Ibid.

courts could be rectified.[33] The proposal was perfectly in line with British strategic thinking. Destruction of French West India commerce was a necessary part of Britain's strategy to reduce French power and gain bargaining chips for future peace negotiations. Allowing the Dutch to carry French commerce within European waters, as defined by the treaty of 1674, would not have been detrimental, as Hardwicke had identified at the beginning of the war. The interests of Channel Island privateers were not explicitly sacrificed in negotiations over Dutch neutral rights, but the effect of focusing on destroying colonial trade essentially meant that the interests of Channel Island privateers were sidelined for the greater strategic good.

The Privateers Act of 1759

Unfortunately, by mid-December 1758, the situation between Britain and the Dutch Republic had not improved. Joseph Yorke (son of Lord Hardwicke and British representative to the Dutch Republic) wrote to the Duke of Newcastle (Secretary of the Treasury) on 12 December that, in order for the French carrying trade to the Americas to be given up by the Dutch, more concessions would need to be granted by the British ministers in terms of the Franco-Dutch trade that was not concerned with the Americas, and regarding British visitations of Dutch ships.[34] On 15 December, Newcastle wrote a letter to William Bentinck, a close advisor of the Dutch Regent. In his communication with Bentinck, Newcastle made it abundantly clear that if the Dutch agreed to renounce the French trade to the Americas, then the detained ships that did not participate in that trade could be released extra-judicially by getting the consent of the privateers.[35] In a letter to Yorke written on the same day, he enclosed a copy of his letter to Bentinck and added that, should the Dutch agree to the British terms, in the future, the release of captured ships not trading to the Americas could be arranged, and that an alteration to the Prize Act could be made. He concluded by writing that Pitt had introduced the idea of altering the Prize Act in the House of Commons that day and that it had gone well.[36] This was the genesis of the Privateers Bill of 1759. Pitt had agreed to support a new bill because he feared that the Dutch would join the French and launch an attack on Britain, an event that posed a much greater

---

[33] Ibid.

[34] BL Add MS 32886 Newcastle Papers, Letter from Yorke to Newcastle, 12 December 1758.

[35] BL Add MS 32886 Newcastle Papers, Letters from Newcastle to Yorke, 15 December 1758. ff. 319–20.

[36] Ibid.

threat than that of any political discontent that the new bill might foment amongst British privateers.[37]

The British ministry spent the early months of 1759 discussing, drafting and passing what would come to be known as the Privateers Act of 1759. The act was a collaborative effort between Pitt, Newcastle, Lord Holdernesse and Lord Hardwicke, aimed at curtailing the abuses that privateers committed against neutral shipping by imposing a variety of restrictions on the issuing of commissions and letters of marque. It was hoped that the bill would raise Dutch faith in the British legal system and in Britain's commitment to Dutch neutral rights. The bill, which became an act once it was passed in June, constrained the actions of privateers by prohibiting owners of privateering vessels to act as guarantors for their voyages and decreed that the commission of any vessel under 100 tons was null and void as of 1 June. Any further commission of a vessel under 100 tons was at the discretion of the Lords of the Admiralty.[38] This concession to the Dutch would, once again, have a large effect on Channel Island privateers. From the High Court of Admiralty records, which contain the Admiralty-issued and High Court of Admiralty-registered letters of marque, commissions were granted to a total of 129 Channel Island privateers during the war.[39] This number is likely incomplete, as these are records that explicitly name a ship as having a home port in the Channel Islands or being owned by Channel Island merchants. Of these 129 ships, 70 were under 100 tons and had been granted their commission before the 1759 Act came into effect. Thirty-nine of these ships were over 100 tons and were granted their commission before June 1759. After the Privateering Act came into effect, only 15 Channel Island privateers under 100 tons were commissioned and only 5 over 100 tons were commissioned.[40]

It is important to contextualize these numbers because the large drop in commissions after June 1759 was not entirely due to the new act. The act was largely a symbolic gesture by the British ministry. According to David Starkey's analysis, 'The 1759 Act, therefore, was a corrective measure designed to placate the neutral powers, by restricting the unbridled assault on their shipping. Its timing, however, suggests that it was little more than a gesture.'[41] According to Starkey, French seaborne commerce had been largely eradicated by early 1759 and, as a result, there was little incentive for new privateers

[37] BL Add MS 32886 Newcastle Papers, Memorandums for the King, 22 December 1758. f. 431.

[38] Starkey, *British Privateering*, 163.

[39] TNA HCA 26/5 – 12 High Court of Admiralty: Prize Court: Registers of Declarations for Letters of Marque.

[40] Ibid.

[41] Starkey, *British Privateering*, 163.

to seek a commission.[42] The Privateering Act, therefore, served mostly as a demonstration to the Dutch that Britain was serious about reforming the ill conduct of its privateers when it came to violations of Dutch neutrality. It is interesting, however, to delve into the possible strategic thinking behind the specific form given to the Act of 1759. As a concession to the Dutch, it was meant to ease concerns about the behaviour of British privateers, but since it only restricted the smaller portion of Britain's privateering arm, two assumptions can be made. Either it was assumed that smaller privateers were responsible for most of the abuses committed against Dutch neutral vessels or it was assumed by Pitt and his fellow ministers that an act which affected only the smaller portion of the privateering arm would not cause an uproar within the privateering lobby. It is also possible that both lines of reasoning were believed to be true.

According to Julian Corbett's brief treatment of the Privateers Act 'The resistance of the privateer owners was violent and formidable.'[43] However, the English newspapers of May and June 1759 contained almost no discussion of the Privateers Act and no reports of anger aimed at its passage. The only references to the act were found in two London newspapers. In the *Lloyd's Evening Post* edition of 28 May and on the 5 June edition of the *London Chronicle*.[44] Neither of these editions went into detail about the particulars of the act or the repercussions it would have on privateering ventures. If there was, as Corbett claimed, a large amount of opposition to the act, it did not play out very publicly in newsprint. In regard to the assumption that smaller privateers were the main perpetrators of depredations against neutral Dutch shipping, there is not a lot of evidence that corroborates Channel Island privateers as culprits. During the war, Channel Island privateers captured 48 neutral vessels in total.[45] Of these 48 vessels, seemingly none became the subject of a case in the Court of Prize Appeal.[46] Channel Island privateers, therefore, were unlikely to have been the main cause of Dutch anger over British abuse of Dutch neutrality. These findings suggest that the British ministry designed the

---

[42] Starkey, *British Privateering*, 167.

[43] Corbett, *England in the Seven Years War* V. II, 8.

[44] *Lloyd's Evening Post*, 28–30 May 1759, Numb. 291. and *The London Chronicle*, 2–5 June 1759, No. 380.

[45] Peter Raban, 'The Profits of Privateering: A Guernsey Fleet, 1756–1762' *The Mariner's Mirror*, 80(3) (1994): 306.

[46] This assertion was made through cross-referencing the Channel Island privateers found in HCA 26/5–12 and Lord Hardwicke's Court of Prize Appeal records found in BL Add MS 36208–36215. In order to verify this assertion more fully it would be necessary to also cross reference against the Court of Prize Appeal records found in TNA HCA/45. However, the closing of the National Archives due to the Covid-19 outbreak made this final verification impossible.

Privateers Act of 1759 to fit British strategic needs in regard to neutral nations rather than actually address concerns over illegal behaviour. Channel Island privateers served, ultimately, as a strategic scapegoat in Britain's negotiations over neutrality.

Conclusion

In the first years of the Seven Years War, British strategic thinking was partly guided by the necessity of ensuring that neutral nations did not become belligerents. In the case of Anglo-Dutch negotiations, it was vital that Britain be able to come to an agreement whereby the Dutch agreed that carrying French colonial goods in Dutch ships was a violation of Dutch neutrality. This concession would allow Britain to pursue an aggressive strategy of maritime predation against France's lucrative colonial trade. The political cost of such a valuable concession was largely foisted – not intentionally but almost carelessly – on the Channel Island privateers. In order to get the Dutch to agree to abandon the French colonial trade, British ministers offered to more stringently protect Dutch access to French inter-European trade. Channel Island privateers, however, often concentrated their predatory efforts on French and neutral inter-European trade because it was more accessible. Channel Island privateers were therefore the losers in strategic considerations over Dutch neutral rights.

As Anglo-Dutch relations improved towards the latter years of the war, British ministers assessed that a legal gesture in support of Dutch neutral rights would gain Britain some much-needed goodwill. Mindful of the gains that British maritime strategy had made in crippling France's seaborne trade by the summer of 1759, British ministers did not want to undertake any sort of change that might threaten the functionality of its privateering arm. The Privateers Act of 1759 was limited to affecting vessels under 100 tons because smaller privateer investors were considered less politically powerful and because smaller privateers could easily be accused of perpetrating a large number of offences against Dutch neutral vessels. And because they operated closer in, in the Channel and approaches, where the coastal inter-European shipping they wished to see unmolested was to be found.

Both the protection of Dutch access to French inter-European trade and the Privateers Act of 1759 demonstrate that not all elements of Britain's privateering arm were considered equal in British strategic thinking. When negotiating with neutral nations, the British needed concessions that did not damage Britain's overall maritime strategy. Unfortunately for the Channel Island privateers, they were often the perfect concession.

PART 2

THE ISLANDS – FRENCH AND BRITISH INTELLIGENCE FROM THE SEVEN YEARS WAR TO 1815

3

The Channel Islands in
Anglo-French Strategy, 1756–82

RICHARD HARDING

On 7 November 1739, the British declaration of war against Spain was solemnly proclaimed on Guernsey. War had long been expected and the Lieutenant Governor, John Graham, had already been pressing the government for support.[1] He had some success, but this had not reassured the civil authorities. In early November the States ordered Peter Cary, deputy to the States, to explain their concerns to the Secretary of State for the Southern Department, the Duke of Newcastle. From their perspective, Guernsey was hemmed in between St Malo and Cherbourg, so close to the French coast that an invasion force embarked on barques and shallops could be on the island within a few hours. All male inhabitants between the ages of sixteen and sixty, which might amount to 2,000 men, were required to turn out for the militia, but about a third of these men were likely to be employed on privateers. There were only two weak companies of regulars on the island, old soldiers known as invalids, to provide a professional backbone. A proper defence would need at least a regiment and twenty-five field cannon to prevent a landing. However, even this would not be enough. According to Cary, 'the natural defence of all the Islands' was effective naval support. If part of the Channel squadron were stationed at Guernsey, which had a good and safe anchorage, it would protect the island from invasion; protect British commerce; destroy French commerce and drive away their privateers. Cary reminded Newcastle of the importance of the Channel Islands. In the last wars with France (1689–98, 1702–13) they had thirty to forty privateers continually cruising along the French coast. Guernsey privateers alone employed 1,700 men (50% of whom were English, Irish and Dutch seamen). They took 1,500 prizes, including many valuable ships. They disrupted French coastal trade, and even penetrated up their rivers. They went where deep-drafted men of war could not venture. They retook prizes from the

---

[1] TNA, SP 47/4, unfolioed, Graham to Yonge, 22 Sept. 1739.

French and returned them to their owners. They brought frequent and valuable intelligence gleaned from contacts ashore and captured French documents on prizes. For example, Cary claimed that in 1703 intercepted letters, taken on a recaptured English vessel, prevented the 200 ships of the Virginia convoy from falling into the hands of a French squadron that was cruising for them.[2]

In a couple of pages, Cary had summed up the key strategic and tactical opportunities and the threats that faced Britain and the Channel Islands during the long eighteenth century. The essential consistency in the situation is well known. The great privateering endeavours of 1689 to 1713 were mirrored between 1793 and 1815. The famous intelligence-gathering operations of Commodore Philippe d'Auvergne, between 1794 and 1813, were a sophisticated development of a practice that had been in operation for decades.[3]

What is less often discussed is how changes in the overall strategic situation challenged the defence of the Islands. Those changes were slow, for most of the century, enabling measured and containable responses, but the crisis of 1778–83 forced the naval, military and civil authorities to accept permanent changes in their attitudes to ensure the defence of the Islands. The purpose of this paper is to highlight this process of change.

English policy in relation to the Channel Islands had been consistent ever since the loss of the Angevin lands in Europe in the early thirteenth century. They were outposts that the English Crown wanted in order to secure the western Channel approaches, but they were not sterile fortress barriers. Their value lay in the communities that lived, worked and interacted with other communities along the French and English coasts. Their distance from England and their proximity to the French coast presented difficulties of control and support. A great deal of care was taken over the centuries to encourage loyalty to the English Crown and to ensure that Crown rights over the Islands were not diluted by the demands of wider diplomatic or military events.[4] The Islands were considered neutral in Anglo-French conflicts from the mid-fifteenth century, but William III doubted this could be sustained in the desperate war that was beginning, and in December 1688 one of his first fleet dispositions was to send some small vessels to Guernsey to forestall a possible French occupation of the Channel Islands.[5] The neutrality was formally abandoned in 1689.

By the end of the War of Spanish Succession in 1713 the Islands had proven their value in war. The maritime economy lay at the core of this value. Although not wealthy, the Islands had a strong fishing and carrying

---

2   Ibid., Cary to Newcastle, 9 Nov. 1739.

3   For d'Auvergne's operations between 1794 and 1799, see TNA, Adm 1/221.

4   Thornton, Tim. *The Channel Islands, 1370–1640: Between England and Normandy.* Woodbridge: Boydell Press, 2012.

5   Ehrman, John. *The Navy in the War of William III, 1689–1697: Its State and Direction.* Cambridge: Cambridge University Press, 1953, 247.

trade. Islanders traded between the French and British coasts in various products including wine, spirits and coal. Jersey had a strong presence in the Newfoundland fisheries which also took their boats to Southern Europe and the West Indies.[6] This produced experienced and hardy seamen who were of great value to Britain in wartime, ideally placed to exploit the opportunities of privateering. They knew the French coast as far south as Bordeaux and had vessels suited to operating in those difficult waters. Their impact on French morale was far greater than the value of any prizes they took, and they did something to check the depredations of the Malouin privateers. The intelligence that they brought back was important, with contacts from Cherbourg to Morlaix providing valuable information on shipping and events inland.

The Islanders provided vital pilotage services for the Royal Navy. As Greenville Collins noted in *Great Britain's Coasting Pilot* (1686), once the navigator struck soundings in Western Approaches, his 'Art must now be laid aside and Pilotage taken in hand'.[7] The force of the Atlantic, driving northeast, funnelled into the narrowing Channel, produced strong currents as the waters divided around the Gulf of St Malo and the Bay of the Seine. Failure to notice drift or night-time navigation could be fatal. Royal Navy warships operating in these waters needed skilful local pilots. Working with these pilots and local privateers, who acted as scouts, enabled the Anglo-Dutch fleet under Admiral Russell to operate in these waters in 1692, and defeat the French at Barfleur-La Hogue.[8]

A further advantage of the Channel Islands to Britain was the pressure they put upon French naval power. By securing the Atlantic coastline and later by massively expanding his fleet, Louis XIV made France an Atlantic power, but lacked deep-water ports along the Atlantic coast north of Brest, while that port was isolated from the sources of naval stores, both French and foreign. The Channel Islands lay astride the route between Brest and the Baltic, the mouth of the Rhine and Cherbourg, the 'Hotel of the Channel, the anchorage of every convoy between Brest and Havre'. [9] Small Channel Island vessels could observe coastal movements and, if necessary, disrupt the supply of stores heading to the naval base. Furthermore, the possession of the Channel Isles made it impossible for the French to anchor large forces in the area without

[6]   Raban, Peter. 'Channel Island Privateering, 1739–1763'. *International Journal of Maritime History* 1, no. 2 (1989): 287–99.

[7]   Collins, G. *Great Britain's Coasting Pilot*. London: W. and J. Mount and T. Page, 1686, 9.

[8]   Le Pelley, John. 'Channel Island Seamen in the Wars of William III and Anne'. *Transactions of the Sociétié Guernesiase* 14, no. 1 (1946): 35–47. Channel Islands pilots were equally important to the expedition to St Malo in 1758.

[9]   Holland Rose, J., and A. M. Broadley. *Dumouriez and the Defence of England against Napoleon*. London: John Lane Bodley Head, 1908, 41.

being observed by British cruisers. Defeated at the Battle of Barfleur on 19 May 1692 Tourville determined to make his way back to Brest. The light winds and misty weather meant that the fleet could only progress westward on a strong current produced by the ebb tide, flowing out of the Channel. Perhaps in desperation, he decided to pass through the Alderney Race. The French fleet of thirty-four ships held together as it passed into the Race on the morning of 21 May and anchored as the flood tide began. However, the ground is poor and thirteen of the ships found their anchors dragging in the strong current. Eventually, they had to cut their cables and run with the flood tide. These vessels were caught by Russell at La Hogue and burned. The remaining twenty-one ships were able to hold their position until the ebb tide set and got clear to St Malo.[10] The English and Dutch under the command of Vice Admiral Sir John Ashby declined to follow the French, but decided, instead, to go around north of the Caskets. Although Russell criticised Ashby for that decision, he later understood the difficulty. Approaching Guernsey in July his pilots refused to take him through the Race owing to the poor visibility and poor anchoring ground for such a large squadron.

The advantages of the Channel Islands had to be protected and there is little evidence that the Crown ever doubted their importance. With Jersey only three hours' sailing from the French coast and Guernsey at least twelve hours from Portsmouth, in ideal conditions, invasion was never far from the thoughts of the Islands' authorities. Fears of a French invasion of the Islands persisted in the 1690s. Periodically, troops and ships were sent from Britain to reinforce the local militia.[11] In 1696 the threat of a 'Bloody Armada' from Boulogne being sent to the Channel Islands was countered by preparing to withdraw forces from Flanders and send them south, escorted by Admiral Russell's squadron, which would overwhelm any land or sea forces the French might land on the Islands[12].

On the other hand, the Islands were by no means an easy proposition for an invader. Although there were good landing beaches, wind and water conditions were hazardous. The Islands were small, and the defenders had interior lines. If a landing could not be prevented, holding out in fortified positions until the weather turned against the invader or a relieving force arrived was possible.[13]

   10 Aubrey, Philip. *The Defeat of James Stuart's Armada*. Leicester: Leicester University Press, 1979, 106–111; TNA, MPH 1/566 Channel Islands, 1781.

   11 Ehrman, J. *The Navy in the War of William III*, 392–3.

   12 Le Pelley, J. 'The Privateers of the Channel Islands, 1688–1713'. *The Mariner's Mirror* 30, no. 1 (1944): 37. Interestingly, there were few local plans to base an invasion of France in the islands. The only case appears to be a French émigré plan to exploit local distress in Normandy in 1710 by capturing La Hogue. See TNA, SP 47/3, unfolioed, Thomas Le Coq to ? 20 Aug. 1711, Auregny.

   13 Ronciere, Charles de la. *Histoire de la Marine Francaise VI : Le crépuscule du Grand Regne. L'apogée de la Guerre de la Corse*. Paris, 1932, 420–1.

The royalist deputy governor of Guernsey, Sir Peter Osborne, and his successors held Castle Cornet against the local population and Parliamentary reinforcements for nearly nine years (1643 to December 1651).[14] Sir George Carteret, commanding the royalist forces on Jersey, held Robert Blake at bay for two days in September 1651, although his inexperienced militia was no match for the Parliamentarian soldiers. Blake took a tremendous risk landing during the night of 22/23 October 1651, forcing Carteret to retreat into Elizabeth Castle, which surrendered on 19 December 1651.[15]

Geography, weather and the flexibility of British resources offered some reassurance. Nevertheless, the closeness of the French threat was difficult to ignore. One of the first modern histories of Jersey, by the Rev. Philip Falle, was published in 1694 and presented to William and Mary as a memorial of the importance of the island to Britain and the threat posed by France. Falle argued too many in England were indifferent to the island, but if Jersey fell to the French it would soon become a privateer base as dangerous as Dunkirk, in the Western Approaches.[16]

During the second quarter of the eighteenth century peace with France meant that affairs in the Channel Islands were quiet. Indeed, the small garrison on Guernsey was completely withdrawn in 1719 to reinforce the West Country in the face of a threatened Spanish invasion.[17] Despite the breakdown of the Anglo-French alliance in the early 1730s, which prompted Falle to produce a second edition of his history, there were no substantive threats to the working lives of the Islanders nor their relations with Britain. The main diplomatic problem for Britain was Spain and commerce with the West Indies. The crises in 1717–19 and 1727–9 had little impact on the Islands. No privateers were fitted out and the trade appears to have continued relatively undisturbed. In October 1739 war between Britain and Spain broke out again. However, the war did not induce Channel Islanders to apply for privateering commissions.[18] Trade had not been disturbed enough to force seafarers and merchants to look to privateering for economic survival, but a corollary was that enemy privateers quickly sought pickings in the Channel Islands waters and by 1740 Spanish privateers were appearing in the Western Approaches. On 4 August

[14] Tupper, Ferdinand Brock. *History of Guernsey and Its Bailiwick, with Occasional Notes of Jersey.* Guernsey: Stephen Barbet, 1854, 217–303.

[15] Baumber, M. *General-at-Sea: Robert Blake and the Seventeenth Century Revolution in Naval Warfare.* London: John Murray, 1989, 100–5.

[16] Falle, Philip. *An Account of the Island of Jersey.* Jersey: Richard Giffard, 1837 (4th ed.), xiv–xvii.

[17] De Guerin, T. W. M. 'The English Garrison of Guernsey from Early Times'. *Transactions of the Guernsey Society of Natural Science and Local Research*, 5 (1905): 79.

[18] Raban, Peter. 'Channel Island Privateering, 1739–1763', 289. Four letters of marque were taken by ships engaged in commercial voyages.

1740 the Deputy Baillie and jurats of Guernsey wrote to the Admiralty about the situation.

> The privateers my Lords which infest these coasts are for the most part double shallops carrying forty or fifty men with eight or ten oars of a side wch being shelter(ed) in French ports and in a manner publically countenanced as well as manned by that nation, do an infinite deal of damage to the commerce of these islands wch must remain in a manner block'd up if some speedy remedy be not apply'd.[19]

The Board ordered a small frigate to protect the trade. However, a larger ship was actually despatched. The *Panther* (50) was ordered from the Bristol Channel to Plymouth in order to cruise in the Soundings. The *Panther* returned to Plymouth in October and the *Argyle* (50) took up the station from May to July 1741. Thereafter, as more cruisers were commissioned and privateers took up cruising stations in the Western Approaches, from Cape Clear to Ushant, the seas were covered more consistently.[20] The absence of complaints suggests this policy had been effective.

In February 1744 war between Britain and France erupted, bringing the threat much closer to the Islands and raising their strategic importance for Britain. The Channel Islands began to play their traditional roles in an Anglo-French conflict. Although the Islands put far fewer privateers to sea than was the case in the War of Spanish Succession, their success rate exceeded any other region, albeit with small and low value prizes.[21] Invasion once again became a real possibility. Although French plans were more ambitious in 1745, rumours of troop concentrations in Normandy prompted urgent appeals to London for naval support.[22] It was at this point that local constitutional peculiarities began to impact on the operational effectiveness of defence. For example, petitions to the King had resulted in a decision to send small arms and cannon to Alderney, but not troops – the island would have to rely on its militia. This raised the question of who had the authority to call out the militia and organise the defence of the island. The Lt Governor of Guernsey claimed that authority, but it was not admitted by the civil authority on Alderney, which complained to London.[23]

The anxiety continued throughout the war, and it was fortunate that the French ships and troops in Brittany were aimed at America rather than the

---

[19] TNA, Adm 1/3817, unfolioed, J. Charlton to the Admiralty Board, 4 Aug. 1740.

[20] This paragraph is based on dispositions listed in TNA Adm 8/20 (1740) to Adm 8/26(1748).

[21] Starkey, David J. *British Privateering Enterprise in the Eighteenth Century.* Exeter: University of Exeter Press, 1990, 142.

[22] TNA, SP 47/4, unfolioed, Lt Gov. Strahan to Newcastle, 7 Sept. 1745.

[23] Ibid., memo of judge and chief magistrate of the court of Alderney on behalf of himself and others to the Duke of Newcastle (no date).

Islands. The Royal Navy cruising pattern gave some security to trade and the island, while the militia and independent invalid companies manning the fortifications and batteries were undisturbed.

When war broke out with France again in 1756, it resumed a familiar pattern. British attacks on French trade, including from the Channel Islands, accelerated during 1755–6. From the beginning the Channel Islanders were aware of the importance of their privateering activities and the reciprocal threats they seemed to be creating, but as they had in the Atlantic, the British effectively stole a march upon the French. In June 1756, Captain Richard Howe was given command of a small squadron to protect the Channel Islands and to disrupt French trade between Cherbourg and St Malo. Howe quickly captured Grand Ile, the largest of the iles Chausey, off Granville, which he had hoped to use as a base. It was found to be too large to defend, so Howe destroyed the fortifications and based his coastal blockade on Guernsey. Nevertheless, the blockade was effective throughout the summer until autumn weather led to his recall in October.[24] Howe's actions spread fear along the French coast and people fled Cherbourg, fearing an attack.[25] The success of the blockade and privateering proved a mixed blessing. In May 1757, the Baillie and Jurats of Guernsey alerted the Admiralty that there were 500 French prisoners on the island, without proper accommodation, risking an outbreak of disease, while consuming victuals the Islands could ill afford. Since Howe's withdrawal, there were no Royal Navy warships on station, so French privateers were venturing out from St Malo, Granville and Cherbourg, cutting communication with England. Ships dare not sail without convoy because of the threat posed by privateers, and the island would soon run out of corn. The military camps that had broken up after the capture of Grand Ile were re-appearing. A large military camp was established near Granville, while troops were seen practising embarking and disembarking from flat-bottomed boats. The island authorities feared an invasion would be soon attempted, unless ships were sent to protect them. The French were inspecting the island's defences under cover of cartel ships, which had ostensibly come to negotiate the prisoner exchanges. The land defences were in poor condition and many of the Guernsey militia, according to Lt Gov. John Mylne, had gone out on privateers. He estimated that a third of them, the best and most active, languished in French gaols. The solution, as in 1756, was a good squadron in local waters, to end the privateering problem, enable the re-provisioning of the island and deter any invasion.[26] Nothing happened, prompting further petitions by the States for a

---

[24] Syrett, D. *Admiral Lord Howe: A Biography*. Annapolis: Naval Institute Press, 2006, 13–14.

[25] TNA, SP 47/5, unfolioed, John Le Mesurier to ?, 9 June 1756.

[26] TNA, Adm 1/3818, f.32, Baillie and Jurats of Guernsey the Admiralty, 14 May 1757; f.41, Mylne to Clevland, 14 May 1757; f. 86, Mylne to Amherst, 19 May 1757.

permanent naval squadron in those waters.[27] As late the summer of 1761 the Islands were disturbed by news of preparations along the Brittany coast. There was a worrying report from captured privateer captain Charles Gallienne, held at Dinand and St Malo before being exchanged. Gallienne swore on oath that he had been asked to pilot an invasion force to Guernsey but had refused. He saw flat-bottomed boats being prepared in St Malo, apparently 150 of them, and troops were converging on the port. No invasion came. Instead by 1757 British warships and privateers dominated the Western Approaches and French Atlantic trade had collapsed by 1760. Once again regional naval power, not local defences, provided the security the Islanders demanded.[28]

When the war of American Independence broke out in 1775, local ships were attacked by American privateers, but the immediate threat to the Channel Islands was remote. However, that threat soon reached new heights. After 1763 France had focused on the Atlantic rather than central Europe.[29] Not only did this prompt important naval reforms and a major ship-building programme, but a closer examination of the French coast. The Duc de Choiseul and his successors considered several projects for invading Britain.[30] If Britain's domination of the Channel were to be challenged, the need for a deep-water port east of Brest had long been recognised. An examination of Channel ports was ordered by the Comte de St Germain, the new Minister of War, in 1776.[31] Cherbourg was an attractive option, but without a protected roadstead it remained a dangerous anchorage. In 1778, the governor of Cherbourg, Colonel Dumouriez, planned an invasion of the Isle of Wight, developing Cherbourg as the primary embarkation point.[32] His plan was abandoned in 1779, but work began at Cherbourg, continuing after the war, potentially creating a major new naval base at the mouth of the Channel.

The Channel Islands threatened this development and Dumouriez planned to invade Jersey from Granville to secure French coastal traffic. In the end, both invasions, of the Channel Islands and the Isle of Wight, were called

[27] TNA, SP 47/5, unfolioed, States of Jersey to William Pitt, 28 Feb. 1758.

[28] Starkey, David J. *British Privateering Enterprise in the Eighteenth Century*, 167–87.

[29] Scott, H. M. 'The Importance of Bourbon Naval Reconstruction to the Strategy of Choiseul after the Seven Years War'. *International History Review* 1, no. 17–35 (1979).

[30] Lacourt Gayet G. *La Marine Militaire de la France sous la Regne de Louis XV.* Paris: Honore Champion, 1902, 42–458.

[31] Dumouriez, Charles François Du Périer, François Barrière , and Saint-Albin Berville. *La Vie et les Mémoires du Général Dumouriez.* 3 vols. Vol. 1, Paris: Baudouin Frères, 1822, 318–22.

[32] Holland Rose, J., and A. M. Broadley. *Dumouriez and the Defence of England against Napoleon.* London: Bodley Head, 1908, 50–61.

off, but these and other projects suggested the Islands had become more important, and needed better defences. The subject was debated by General Lord Amherst, Commander-in-Chief of the army and governor of Guernsey (1770–97) and General Sir Henry Conway, governor of Jersey (1772–95); two of the most senior officers in the British Army. The Channel Island governors were usually resident in England, relying on local deputies. Although much of Amherst's correspondence with Conway and the lieutenant governors on the islands concerns the income that he might expect as governor from seizures of French shipping in local waters, it also demonstrated that the Islands were recognised as important military and maritime assets.

As was common in the eighteenth century, fortification improvements were only funded when the situation demanded. The idea of a prudential rolling maintenance programme was largely unknown. This meant that the threat of war with France in 1778, in the wake of Burgoyne's defeat at Saratoga, created considerable anxiety about defective defences. The Lieutenant Governor of Guernsey, Lieut. Col. Paulus Aemilius Irving, wrote to Amherst on 7 April describing the island's defences. Castle Cornet, which dominated St Peter Port, was in generally good repair and had a good boat to communicate with other parts of the island, but the garrison was weak, with limited stores. He advised building a temporary fort on high ground to the west that dominated Castle Cornet.[33] Throughout 1778 Irving worked to improve the Islands' defences, but he faced problems typical of the period. On 11 January 1779 Irving informed Amherst that he was having difficulty manning the two main forts, Castle Cornet and Fort Valle. The militia did not think that they were responsible for manning the fortifications. Irving agreed – he needed trained artillerymen, not militiamen. The Board of Ordnance had allowed a sergeant and twelve artillerymen in the previous war and Irving hoped for a similar establishment. Orders had also been given to build a series of towers around the coast, principally as fortified musketry points covering artillery batteries.[34] Irving only secured labour to build them by taking men from private building projects. However, the money rapidly ran out, but Irving kept the building works going by ordering the Storekeeper to draw money to pay the men.[35]

The Islands' well-established connections with Normandy continued to be important of for intelligence, as rumours in France suggested that an invasion could be mounted during 1779. Troops assembling in Brittany, near Brest, could be destined for anywhere, but the camps were a worrying prospect to the British.[36]

---

[33] TNA, WO 34/105, f.1, Irving to Amherst, 7 April 1778.
[34] Clements, Bill. *Martello Towers Worldwide*. Barnsley: Pen and Sword, 2011, 98–103.
[35] TNA, WO 34/105, f.5, Irving to Amherst, 11 Jan. 1779.
[36] Ibid., ff. 7–8, intelligence enclosed in Irving to Amherst, 11 Jan. 1779.

In the same month, Conway, governor of Jersey, considered the situation from his London home. He was deeply worried that France was now proportionately stronger than at any time in the recent past; the revived navy was much closer to parity with the Royal Navy. The reduction in building, the dispersal of the fleet and a limited mobilisation to meet the rebellion in America, left the British vulnerable to the expanded Bourbon navies in European waters.[37] Furthermore, peace in Europe meant that the French army 'has now much less employment than in any former war' enabling it to concentrate on the Atlantic coast. Conway had felt that the garrison, too weak in former wars, was far more so now. The weaknesses of his island command were becoming very apparent. The coastal towers were progressing slowly. The engineer ordered to Jersey had yet to leave England and no convoy had been allocated to bring over the stores. Conway regretted his lack of influence in these matters. He had also requested a large-scale map of the island, with soundings marked, from the Board of Ordnance, but had so far received no reply. He had no idea what the Admiralty's plans for the defence of the Islands were. Warships were usually withdrawn from the Islands when the winter weather set in, but the present calm, easterlies seemed good for any invasion attempt.

Of more direct concern to Amherst were Conway's worries about the troops sent to reinforce the militia. The 78th Regiment of Foot was a newly raised unit under the command of the Earl of Seaforth. Arriving in September 1778, five companies were stationed on Guernsey and five on Jersey. Reports from Lieutenant Governor Major Moses Corbett informed Conway that the troops were ill-disciplined and young, with raw officers who were unable to control them. Conway begged that this unit be replaced by one of the older regiments that might be prepared for overseas service in the coming year.[38]

Conway cannot have been reassured by Amherst's reply on the 14th. Amherst confessed that, like Conway, he had no idea of the Admiralty's plans for the defence of the Islands. Nor had he any knowledge of the wartime establishment of regular troops on the Islands, nor the availability of maps at the Board of Ordnance, but he would investigate the matter. He had enquired about an engineer for Guernsey: Captain Mulcaster had been ordered there as soon as his health permitted.[39]

Conway pressed again, sending Mulcaster to Amherst with details of the problems relating to the towers. Of the thirty towers ordered only two had been completed by the Ordnance. Another two had been completed by the

---

[37] Baugh, Daniel A. 'Why Did Britain Lose Command of the Sea During the War for America?'. Chap. 7 in *The British Navy and the Uses of Naval Power in the Eighteenth Century*, ed. by Jeremy Black and Philip Woodfine, 149–70. Leicester: Leicester University Press, 1988.

[38] TNA, WO 34/105, f.9, Conway to Amherst, 12 Jan. 1779.

[39] Ibid., f.11 Amherst to Conway, 14 Jan. 1779.

Jersey government and a further two had been begun. Money was not the only problem. Many of the masons were also farmers and could not be kept to their work. The government of Jersey had helped in prohibiting work on private buildings, but there were simply too few masons on the island. Again, he pressed Amherst who, as Commander-in-Chief, would have a broad view of the military and naval situation, to get some naval protection and send an old regiment to the Islands.[40]

At the same time Amherst was receiving similar alarms from his Lieutenant Governor, Irving, on Guernsey. The waters around the Islands were infested with French privateers; he could see a fourteen-gun snow anchored off the island. Merchants were refusing to send goods to England without a strong escort. At present only two cutters were available, too weak for convoy duty. News from St Malo was of flatboats being built, each armed with a cannon. Irving also had his doubts about the 78th. An old and experienced campaigner with a strong sense of social hierarchy, he was unimpressed by the new arrivals. The Earl of Seaforth, a young man with no experience, had been accompanied by his new wife, the daughter of an apothecary, and of dubious reputation. Irving blessed his luck that a cold would prevent him from having to wait upon the couple. The other officers were similarly unimpressive: one had been a sergeant in a Guards regiment and 'his wife keeps a public house and thought handsome. I wish there was a better way of providing for sergeants. I seldom see them do much good when they get the rank of a gentleman.'[41]

Invasion anxieties continued into the spring. Two spies were said to have been apprehended on Jersey. The Islands were overloaded with prisoners from French prizes: there was no secure accommodation, nor could they be sent to England. French privateers were seen in the offing every day, crippling trade.[42]

Conway was, by now, getting better information from Corbett on Jersey. Although thirty to forty vessels were still laid up at St Malo, about 10,000 troops encamped around the port could concentrate within twenty-four hours, with a similar number at Granville. Rumours were circulating that the people of Bordeaux and other towns were pressing the French court to act against the Islands, even offering to pay the costs. The invalid companies on Jersey were also in a very poor state. He pressed Amherst again to have the 78th replaced by another regiment.[43] Increasing pressure from the authorities on Jersey forced him to renew his appeal two weeks later. The 78th seemed to be as great a threat to the islanders as the French. The inexperienced officers seemed afraid of their men, few of whom had shown much familiarity with their muskets. All this was against a rising fear of invasion as the spring and

[40] Ibid., 12–13, Conway to Amherst, 19 Jan. 1779.
[41] Ibid., 19–20, Irving to Amherst, 31 Jan. 1779.
[42] Ibid., 21, Irving to Amherst, 4 Feb. 1779.
[43] Ibid., 24, Conway to Amherst, 7 Feb. 1779.

better weather was approaching. According to Conway, who had surveyed the island, there were fourteen possible landing places to be covered, which, if the French landed veteran troops under an experienced commander, required at least a full battalion to contain. However, more helpful still would be 'a considerable naval force, which should be sent immediately. Nothing would be so liable to deter any attempt than the appearance of such attention'.[44]

This anxious correspondence began to bear fruit during the spring of 1779. Two additional regiments were being prepared to sail for the Islands.[45] Although feeling the strain of his years and the disappointment of having missed out on promotion, Irving's letters show greater confidence. He reported the arrival of Major Stuart and several other officers of the 78th on Guernsey.[46] Fortuitously, Seaforth was too ill to command and Stuart took over. He found the regiment in better condition than he had been led to believe, and drill and discipline quickly improved.[47] Irving was soon entirely satisfied with the 78th. The defensive towers were nearly finished, but stores, artillery and victuals were still needed. Orders were sent to the Board of Ordnance for the items requested, but with French privateers hovering around the Islands any store ships would require a naval escort.[48] By early April, Irving could report that Castle Valle was now entirely defensible, and fifteen towers had been finished. As rumours of French preparations reached Britain, a concerned King ordered Weymouth to propose that Conway should proceed immediately to Jersey. He did not want a formal order, which might hint of panic and the affair might be over 'one way or the other' before he could get there.[49]

He was right. The day before Weymouth wrote to Amherst, the feared invasion force finally arrived off the coast of Jersey. Between fifty and sixty vessels, including three frigates, cutters and gunboats appeared in St Helier Bay on 1 May 1779. The French force moved west on seeing the prepared state of the defences, intending to land in St Ouens Bay. Troops were embarked into small boats while the cutters and prames came inshore to cover the landing with grape shot.[50] The defences had been quickly manned. The bulwarks and towers along the bay narrowed the practicable frontage for a landing. Batteries near the shore, reinforced by field artillery, began to fire into the shipping. Two companies of the 78th, supported by militia, deployed behind sand dunes,

44 Ibid., 34, Conway to Amherst, 26 Feb. 1779.

45 Ibid., 72, Conway to Jenkinson, April 1779. In the event only the 83rd was available at this time.

46 Ibid., 52, Irving to Amherst, 5 March 1779.

47 Ibid., 50, Stuart to Amherst, 12 March 1779.

48 Ibid., 55, Ordered for Guernsey, no date.

49 Ibid., 94, Weymouth to Amherst, 2 May 1779.

50 Ibid., 102, St James, 6 May 1779.

ready to move out on the French landing.[51] When an iron 24lb cannon, served by the militia, burst, discouraging the gunners, decisive leadership by militia Major Robins kept the men to their guns.[52] Realising the beach was effectively covered, the French slipped their cables and disappeared.[53]

Where they were going was unknown. The alarm was raised on Guernsey, but the French did not appear. When the waters around Guernsey remained undisturbed it was assumed that the force had returned to St Malo. There was a sense of dismay. Conway could not believe that an attempt had been made with such small forces and others agreed that it was ill-conceived and 'executed in the most dastardly manner'.[54]

Nevertheless, the alarm had been thoroughly raised. Irving was certain the French would return with a larger force gathered from Brest, and this time aimed at Guernsey.[55] During the attack on Jersey, he sent a lugsail privateer with an urgent report to Plymouth for naval support. The privateer was met by Captain Cosby, commander of *Robust* (74), part of Admiral Marriot Arbuthnot's small force which was then south of the Needles on its way to America with a convoy. Arbuthnot immediately sent the convoy into the shelter of Torbay and took his squadron to the Channel Islands.[56] The news also reached Admiral Pye, Commander-in-Chief at Portsmouth, who immediately despatched Captain Ford of the *Unicorn* with four sloops and an armed ship to Jersey.[57] Captain John Gidion of the *Richmond* was cruising with the *Pallas* out of Plymouth, when he met other ships out of Portsmouth and made directly for Guernsey.[58] En route he was joined by Sir James Wallace in the *Experiment* from Arbuthnot's squadron.

On the morning of 3 May, watchers on Guernsey could see a squadron through the haze off the northern side of the island. As no boats were seen putting off, Irving immediately put the island on a state of alert. Eventually, a boat with a letter from Captain Robinson of the *Guadeloupe* arrived. The force in the offing comprised eight ships under Ford. Ford was to track down the French and needed some pilots for his voyage to Jersey. By the 6th, Gidion, Ford and Wallace with a substantial force of small ships were at Guernsey. They proceeded to Jersey, which they reached on the 9th. Then they patrolled

[51] Ibid., 107, Irving to Amherst, 7 May 1779.
[52] Ibid., 90, Mulcaster to Amherst, 2 May 1779.
[53] Ibid., 105, Weymouth to Amherst, enclosure, 3 May 1779.
[54] Ibid., 98, Conway to Amherst, 3 May 1779.
[55] Ibid., 97, Irving to Amherst, 3 May 1779.
[56] Barnes, G. R. and J. H. Owen, eds (1936). *The Private Papers of John, Earl of Sandwich, First Lord of the Admiralty, 1771–1782.* London, Navy Records Society, 121, Arbuthnot to Sandwich, 2 May 1779.
[57] TNA, Adm 1/1790, f. 289, Pye to Ford, 2 May 1779.
[58] TNA, Adm 1/1898, unfolioed, Gidion to Stephens, 11 May 1779.

the bays of Jersey for signs of the French and on the 11th news arrived of a French force near Coutances. Gidion divided his force, ordering Wallace to the west of Jersey towards St Malo, while he took the rest of the ships directly towards the enemy. As soon as they saw Gidion's ships the French put on full sail. Light winds hindered the chase and by the morning of the 13th Gidion was forced to anchor between Granville and Iles Chaussee to wait for the winds to change. The French anchored in Cancale Bay, where Wallace caught up with them. In about 90 minutes the French ships were run aground and abandoned: a frigate, a brig and a cutter were taken, and two more frigates and a cutter were burned.[59]

The speed with which a capable naval force could be mobilised to support the Islands had been impressive. On the Islands the measures taken to secure them were taking effect. On the night of 25 May, the 83rd Foot (Glasgow Volunteers) arrived on Guernsey. This was another newly raised regiment and Conway had hoped for two regiments. Instead, the 83rd would be split in half and five companies sent on to Jersey.[60] Irving was nevertheless pleased by the bearing of the troops – all young but well disciplined 'and what is not common the rattan is never allowed to be made use of'.[61]

However, all was not well. With growing numbers of troops on the Islands, pressure on resources began to tell. There were no barracks nor straw for bedding. Food prices were rising, causing serious grumbling among the troops. The squadron that had covered the Islands in the immediate aftermath of the invasion threat had disappeared by early June, leaving only two frigates. Irving was also concerned about Alderney. He wanted to send some regulars to the island which was, in his words, an appendage of Guernsey, but one of the most prominent citizens, John Le Mesurier, had styled himself as governor and commander-in-chief, with his son as lieutenant governor. This was causing some confusion in the public service.[62]

Furthermore, the French threat had by no means disappeared. Very soon after the dramatic news of the attempt on Jersey had reached London, even more troubling news began to arrive that a large Franco-Spanish invasion fleet was assembling to attack Great Britain. The crisis lasted over the summer and it was not until mid-September that the ministry could breathe a sigh of relief that the threat had passed.[63] However, at Havre de Grace, over fifty transports and eighty flat-bottomed boats were available in a heavily defended

---

59 TNA, WO 34/105, 114, Irving to Amherst, 17 May 1779; Adm 1/1898, Wallace to Gidion, 13 May 1779.

60 Ibid., 122, Irving to Amherst, 26 May 1779.

61 Ibid., 138, Irving to Amherst, 5 June 1779.

62 Ibid., 149, Irving to Amherst, (private).

63 Temple Patterson, A. *The Other Armada: The Franco-Spanish Attempt to Invade Britain in 1779.* Manchester: Manchester University Press, 1960.

harbour.[64] Preparations continued at St Malo.[65] The King had intelligence that the French plans to attack the Islands remained active and Rear Admiral Sir John Lockhart Ross was detached with a small squadron to investigate the French ports. Ross had rejoined the main fleet by 25 September, but left the *Jupiter* (50) and smaller frigates at Guernsey.[66]

For Britain, 1779 had been a great shock. Overshadowing it all was the Franco-Spanish invasion force that had entered the Channel that summer. While the attempt on the Channel Islands had been poorly executed, it was still disturbing. As the pressure to defend the Islands became more intense, tensions that had long existed between the civil and military authorities increased.

More troops arrived in 1780: two newly raised regiments, the 95th and 96th, on Jersey and Guernsey respectively, but there was no bedding for them. Unfortunately, the 96th brought sickness to Guernsey and without proper accommodation this was likely to spread. Lt Governor Irving proposed ordering the men into winter quarters early to assist their recovery. However, the demand for labour to build lodgings for the troops proved highly unpopular and Irving continued to meet obstructions. Progress was reluctantly made throughout the autumn. Buildings were prepared and a new fort to protect Castle Cornet was completed, but in December 1780, local inhabitants came during the night to knock down the chimney arches constructed for the new barracks.[67] Victuals were also a serious problem as the garrison grew. Irving tried to enforce the royal order to prevent the export of provisions, but was openly challenged by the royal court as being responsible for 'the most tyrannical order that ever was issued'.[68]

Under Island law, justice was determined by a standing jury with no appeal for clemency to the Crown even for capital offences. This became a matter of major concern in the autumn of 1781. Captain Pole had brought in a captured French privateer, *L'éclair*, which it turned out was an ex-British ship, *Ranger.* A Robert May, a Folkestone man, had bought the vessel at Dunkirk and set out under French colours. May and other seamen were held captive, but the lack of secure buildings meant that containing them was difficult. Command of the guard was entrusted to Lieutenant Webber of the 96th Foot. He was a fractious man, who had already had a serious dispute with the son of one of the most powerful people on the island. Webber saw two men moving away from the group. He drew his bayonet and warned them that 'if they attempted to run off he would be under the disagreeable necessity of running one of them

[64] TNA, WO 34/105, 155, Henry Howlett (no date).
[65] Ibid., Militia colonels and lieutenant-colonels to Irving, Sept. 1779.
[66] Barnes and Owen, eds (1936). *Earl of Sandwich*, 100, Hardy to Sandwich, 14 Sept. 1779, 101, North to Sandwich, 12 Sept. 1779.
[67] TNA, WO 34/106, 216, Irving to Amherst, 28 Dec. 1780.
[68] TNA, WO 34/108, f. 69, Commissary of Provisions to Irving, 12 March 1782.

thro the body'. They ran, and in the pursuit, after many warnings, Webber accidentally ran one of them through. The danger of this situation seems to have been well understood by his brother officers, who spirited Webber off the island before the Lieutenant Governor was informed. Irving was sympathetic and the case was raised by officers of other corps stationed on the Islands. Unlike merchants and seamen, soldiers were not willing visitors to the Islands and to be deprived of the British birthright of royal mercy was unacceptable. Even the suspension of execution pending royal confirmation was questioned and the conduct of courts martial might be illegal. The question rumbled on into the spring of 1782. Amherst supported the officers, but the government's legal opinion favoured the island constitution. While the soldiers had to accept the judgement, they pointed out that they were the only British soldiers not to have access to royal clemency.[69]

The presence of the navy had also increased tensions. As Philip Stephens, the Secretary to the Admiralty Board, admitted, there had been many applications for a squadron stationed in the Islands, but this had been resisted on the grounds that there was no sheltered harbour in winter. Although most requests for ships were for frigates, the Board expected a significant invasion would be supported by a line of battleships, which the frigates could not resist. Line of battleships could not ride out the winter in the Channel Islands and, like frigates, could be quickly despatched from England in an emergency.[70] This argument was questioned in the Islands, where it was claimed Howe had sheltered successfully at Jersey in the Seven Years War.[71] Although by the beginning of 1781 the Admiralty had relented slightly, approving a small squadron, augmented by locally hired cutters, under Sir James Wallace, it confirmed the local commanders' views that the Islands would have to resist an invasion with the resources at hand – regulars, militia, fortifications and fieldworks – all contentious points with the civil authorities.[72] In the context of 1781 this was a serious issue. Jersey had defeated a small-scale invasion in January of that year. However, intelligence from France continued to indicate far larger and more powerful invasions could be in hand. If a foothold had been established, prolonged occupation and large-scale fighting were a worrying prospect. Nor was it entirely self-evident that naval power would eventually

---

[69] Ibid., f. 65, Petition of 82 officers on Jersey, no date. It is interesting that in March 1783 there was a serious mutiny among the 104th Foot, stationed at Fort George, Guernsey, but no punishments or courts martial were ordered. Whether doubts about the legality of the court martial was a factor in this needs to be established. See Tupper, Ferdinand Brock. *History of Guernsey and Its Bailiwick, with Occasional Notes of Jersey*. Guernsey: Stephen Barbet, 1854, 379–80.

[70] TNA, WO 34/107, f.118, Irving to Amherst, 25 March 1781.

[71] TNA, SP 47/8, unfolioed, Corbett to Weymouth, 12 March 1778.

[72] Barnes and Owen, eds (1936). *Earl of Sandwich*, 340._

restore the situation. The example of the sudden loss of St Eustatius in the West Indies, which was not recovered, had not passed unnoticed.[73] At this time the Royal Navy was not in undisputed command of the local seas. The decision to denude the Channel of warships in order to relieve Gibraltar probably put Britain at its weakest in those waters during the entire war. That there was to be a remarkable recovery in 1782 was not obvious to those watching the trajectory of events between 1778 and 1781. The naval balance shifted attention back to land-based defences.

The increased presence of the navy raised its own problems. The first was the provision of local cutters. The Admiralty had assumed local ship-owners would hire their cutters, but they demanded the authorities buy them. Far more contentious was the matter of pressing. The Islands' claim to exemption from the press had been upheld earlier in the war, when Lt Dumaresq pressed some men on Jersey. The order was sent for their immediate release.[74] The privilege of the Islands was well known and there was said to be a steady stream of small boats from Cawsand Bay and Brixham to the Islands with deserters from the ships at Plymouth and Torbay. As the urgency of naval expansion developed in 1778–9 and the presence of more warships in Channel Island waters increased, so tensions grew. Assuming command in the Channel Islands in the summer of 1781 Captain Charles Pole was infuriated by the insolence of seamen, some of whom he believed to be deserters and smugglers. His correspondence indicated a determination to secure seamen he believed were unjustifiably evading service.[75] Pole began pressing men from ships in local waters. This produced an immediate response from the Guernsey royal court, demanding the release of the men. Lieutenant Governor Irving tried to defuse the conflict, acknowledging the traditional usage, but asking the court to consider the critical circumstances and the ambiguity of the law. It was not clear if the charter intended that Guernsey should be a place of sanctuary for all seamen who were unwilling to serve the Crown, or if that right was restricted to native-born seamen. Irving conceded it was probably the former, but Pole would have none of this. He acknowledged the charter prevented him pressing on land, but denied this right extended to all waters within sight of the Islands. Nevertheless, he claimed that he had enough men for the present and would not prolong the dispute. Well aware that he could be arrested should he set foot on the Islands he was, no doubt, relieved to sail for England in the autumn of 1781.

At the heart of this conflict between the military and naval commanders and the local authorities between 1778 and 1783 lay the growing French threat. Traditional liberties were challenged by new realities of war. Nothing

---

[73] TNA, WO 34/108, f. 67, Mulcaster to Hillsbrough, 6 March 1782.

[74] TNA., SP 47/8, unbound, Weymouth to the Lt Gov. of Jersey, 20 Jan. 1778.

[75] See Pole's letters in TNA, Adm 1/2306.

demonstrated the new reality more than the surprise landing on Jersey on the night of 5th/6th January 1781 when around 900 French troops under the Marquis de Rullecourt landed.[76] They came during the long winter night in flat-bottomed boats, supported by cutters and sloops, surprising a small battery covering the beach at La Roque.[77] Once ashore the French moved quickly to St Helier, capturing Lieutenant Governor Moses Corbett. Corbett was induced to sign a capitulation of the island and all its fortified places, which was immediately taken to Elizabeth Castle, but the commander refused to negotiate. Meanwhile the garrison and militia had rallied under the command of Major Pierson of the 95th Foot. Most of the French ships retired to Normandy after the landing. The beach was retaken by noon, leaving the main French force trapped in St Helier. The militia and elements of the 78th and 95th advanced into the marketplace where the final battle took place. The firefight was unequal, the French losing far more men. Pierson was killed and Rullecourt mortally wounded. Surrounded, fired on from all sides and faced by an imminent bayonet charge, the French broke and took shelter in the houses. Soon after the whole force surrendered.[78]

The affair was over very quickly, but the shock reverberated to England. Once again, it was not believed that this invasion was so small and poorly executed. Many thought it must be the harbinger of something greater. Rumours of 6,000 troops being ready at Granville continued. Fears of traitors ready to assist them spread.[79] Conway was quickly on his way to the island while reinforcements, the 4th and 97th regiments with artillery, soon followed from Portsmouth. On the Islands the lack of naval support was regretted. Sir James Wallace only arrived on station on the 8th. Lieutenant Governors Irving and Corbett again urged the permanent stationing of frigates on the Islands.

Strengthening the Islands continued until the end of the war. The fortifications were completed during the peace and when war broke out again in 1793 there was no delay in reinforcing the Islands. In 1794 a separate squadron under Rear Admiral John McBride was appointed to secure the Islands and watch the Normandy coast.[80] The regular garrisons of the Islands, which had not exceeded 2,000 before 1781, stood at over 5,000 on Guernsey alone in 1798.[81]

---

[76] The best account is Mayne, Richard. *The Battle of Jersey*. London: Phillimore, 1981.

[77] TNA, WO 34/107, f.23, extract of letter from Pye to Stephens, 8 Jan. 1781. The initial force may have been about 1,200, but 200 drowned in the night landing, about 200 more never left the transports. See, ibid., f. 44–5, La Hogue barrack, no date.

[78] Ibid., f. 37, Copy of a letter from Jersey, 8 Jan. 1781.

[79] Ibid, f. 32, Corbett to Amherst, 12 Jan. 1781; f. 52, Corbett to Amherst, 17 Jan. 1781.

[80] Morriss, Roger, and David Saxby, eds *The Channel Fleet and the Blockade of Brest, 1793–1801*. London: Navy Records Society, 2001, 35, Admiralty to Howe, 17 April 1794.

[81] De Guerin, T. W. M. 'The English Garrison of Guernsey from Early Times'.

Clearly the events of 1779 to 1781 had shaken British confidence. British political opinion, which had long seen large armies and fortifications as marks of impending slavery and absolutist government, looked to the navy for protection. Channel Islanders shared this ideology, as far as it related to their own liberties. However, invasion threats in 1779 to 1781 forced a reconsideration of this position. In the early 1780s, the Master General of the Ordnance, George Townshend, ordered a review of the topography and defences of the South of England.[82] In 1785 a new Master General, the Duke of Richmond, proposed a major reconstruction of the defences around Plymouth and Portsmouth to permit a force of militia to withstand attack by substantial land forces. The fortifications would ensure the dockyards would be able to support the Royal Navy, restore local sea control and isolate the invaders. However, some members of Parliament saw it as a ministerial plan to reinforce the standing army and undermine British liberties. Fortress ports, which detached the soldiery from the civil population, provided 'seminaries for soldiers, and universities for Praetorian bands'.[83] They would saddle the taxpayer with permanent maintenance costs, depriving the Royal Navy of funds to maintain superiority over the resurgent Bourbon navies. The first debate in May 1785 ended with an agreement to submit the matter to a board of naval and military experts. A second debate in February 1786, following the submission of the report, rehearsed the same arguments, adding claims that Richmond had manipulated the membership of the board to secure the result he wanted. After a long, impassioned debate on 27 February the House divided equally, 169:169, with the casting vote of the Speaker against the motion. While the motion was lost the division of the House demonstrated how the events of 1779 had induced many to accept that it was necessary to invest in a deeper defensive system.

There were similar reflections on the Channel Islands. As in Britain, liberties were preserved, but there was a greater willingness to live with soldiers, forts and a naval presence. Compromises had to be made by all parties; soldiers, sailors and local authorities. The strategic role of the Channel Islands remained unchanged throughout the eighteenth century. It was a vital forward position to secure the Channel and Western Approaches, ideally placed for intelligence-gathering and commerce disruption. However, the revival of Bourbon naval power in the 1770s forced a change in the operational mode towards a more integrated defensive posture. Ultimately, the Royal Navy guaranteed their security, as it did for the British Isles as a whole, but the public had

---

Transactions of the Guernsey Society of Natural Science and Local Research, 5 (1905): 81.

[82] B.L., Add Ms 50008A (Townshend Papers), passim.

[83] Cobbett, W., *The Parliamentary History of England from the Earliest Period to the Year 1803* Vol. 25 (1 Feb. 1785–5 May 1786). Hansard, London, 1815, 375–90; 1096–1157. Quotation, 1114.

been given a vision of what was needed if that guarantee vanished. At the time no one knew that French naval power would collapse as a result of the French Revolution, but the changes which put both Britain and the Channel Islands in a stronger defensive position would have an important impact on British offensive, expeditionary capacity in the great conflicts of 1793–1802 and 1803–15.

PART 3

TERRITORIAL WATERS – THE LAND AND SEA INTERFACE FROM THE 17TH TO 20TH CENTURIES

4

Channel Islands Territorialisation: A Challenge Between Local, National, and International Law (XVII°–XIX°)

FRÉDÉRIC SAFFROY

On 23 July 2019, the territorial waters of the Bailiwick of Guernsey (Guernsey, Alderney and Sark) were increased from 3 to 12 nautical miles ('nm'). This unilateral decision taken by the Bailiwick of Guernsey[1] came after the United Kingdom extended its territorial waters from 3 to 12nm in 1987, the Isle of Man in 1991 and Jersey in 1997. However, the maritime boundaries between the Bailiwick of Guernsey and France are still to be agreed. Indeed, the lines to the south-west and east of the Bailiwick were defined in the 1992 Schole Bank Agreement,[2] but only for fishing purposes.

This decision is linked to the potential impact of Brexit on fishing for the Channel Islands, in order for the Bailiwick to be able to control and monitor fishing in its surrounding seas more efficiently than if they were not territorial waters. It does not only imply opening negotiations with France regarding the maritime boundaries between Normandy, Brittany and the Bailiwick, but also raises questions as to free navigation between the Islands of the Bailiwick, more particularly by French navy ships.

On Jersey's side, things are not necessarily simpler, but they were at least agreed between the Bailiwick of Jersey and France. In 2004, the Bay of

---

[1]   Extending the Bailiwick of Guernsey's Territorial Seas, P.2019/5, Billet d'Etat, II – 2019, Wednesday, 30th, 2019 <https://www.gov.gg/article/172632/Bailiwick-of-Guernseys-territorial-seas-will-be-extended-on-23-July-2019> [accessed 25 March 2020].

[2]   Exchange of notes constituting an agreement concerning the activities of fishermen in the vicinity of the Channel Islands and the French coast of the Cotentin Peninsula and, in particular, on the Schole Bank (with annex and lists), 10 July 1992 (entry into force: 10 July 1992; registration #: 30858; registration date: 28 March 1994).

Granville Treaty between France and the United Kingdom (4 July 2000)[3] entered into force to:

(i) define the maritime boundaries between Jersey and France, and
(ii) set the fishing rights of French and Jersey (but also Guernsey ...) fishermen.

It should be noted however that the treaty maintains a disconnection between territorial waters and the definition of fishing zones. The 2000 treaty is the latest in a long history of negotiations between Jersey and France regarding fishing rights in the Bay of Granville. It came back to the 'oyster war' that occurred at the beginning of the 19th century, which will be discussed later.

These two very recent examples show the complexity and fragmentation of the sea for economic and political reasons. It also demonstrates the complexity of dividing the sea in the Channel Islands area, given the particularities of the Islands' status in international law. The Islands are not part of the United Kingdom, but a dependency of the British Crown which supervises and signs off any decision of the two Bailiwicks. This legal complexity is not only an internal challenge for the United Kingdom, but also at international level for France, the negotiations involving not two states but three parties (the Channel Islands, the United Kingdom and France), if not even more, as the opinions of the States in each of the Guernsey Bailiwick Islands do not necessarily always converge.

Defining the sea as a 'territory', or a 'territory' at sea, remains therefore a sensitive topic at both internal and international levels. The word 'territorialisation' is itself an oxymoron. Territory comes from the Latin word '*terra*' which means earth. So how can rules set for the land apply to the sea? Defining a 'territory' at sea is also a question of lines and charts, given the fact that there are no natural boundaries, except the coast itself. It is therefore more complex than on land and relies on scientific surveying and mapping. As the scientific means of surveying and charting have developed, defining accurate lines raises even more questions.

On this question, it is worth quoting Carl Schmitt:

> The Earth is bound to law in three ways. She contains law within herself, as a <u>reward of labour</u>; she manifests law upon herself, as <u>fixed boundaries</u>; and she sustains law above herself, as a <u>public sign of order</u>. (...) Every new age and every new epoch in the coexistence of peoples, empires, and countries, of rulers and power formations of every sort, is founded on <u>new</u>

---

[3] Christian Fleury, 'Jersey and Guernsey: two distinct approaches to cross-border fishery management', *Shima: The International Journal of Research into Island Cultures*, vol. 5, n° 1–2011, 24–43.

spatial divisions, new enclosures (boundaries/delimitations), and a new spatial order of the Earth.[4]

Carl Schmitt's reflection on sea-appropriation will guide us through that presentation. The recent rediscovery of Schmitt is linked to the end of the Cold War and the growing translation of his works into English. His original thinking on the origin of law helps us to understand the origin of international law, and its connection to land and sea-appropriation as implemented by continental and maritime powers. However, his compromise with the Nazis and his role in defending Hitler's power in the 1930s should not be forgotten when referencing his works.

This paper will begin with an historical overview of sea-appropriation over the centuries, a 'battle of the books', and then examine how territorial waters and customs boundaries are linked to State sovereignty, and finally the Channel Islands, where they are linked to the 'reward of labour': fishing wars and fishing rights.

Sea-appropriation: *Mare Liberum vs Mare Clausum*

The sea has no character, in the original sense of the word, which comes from the Greek *charassein*, meaning to engrave, to scratch, to imprint. The sea is free.[5]

Is the sea really free? At the end of the 16th century, Queen Elizabeth I advocated that the sea was free. It was in her own interest, as the origin of the dispute was the actions of Sir Francis Drake in the Pacific Ocean against Spanish interests. Answering to the claim of the Spanish Ambassador Mendoza, Queen Elizabeth stated in 1580:

The use of the sea and the air is common to all, and that no title to the ocean can belong to any nation, since neither nature nor regard for the public use permit any possession of the ocean.

This vision of a free sea quickly changed twenty years later when King James took the British crown in 1603. The new King imported from Scotland a different concept of maritime law. The Scots have indeed a long tradition of struggling with Dutch fishermen to defend their fishing rights along the

---

[4] Carl Schmitt, *The Nomos of the Earth in the International Law of the Jus Publicum Europeanum*, trans. G. L. Ulmen [first German edition 1950] (New York, 2003), p. 42.
[5] Ibid., p. 43.

Scottish coast. For the King, the British Seas – i.e. the seas from Norway to Galicia (Spain) – included all the 'narrow seas' of the Channel, which was indeed called the 'British Channel'. Therefore, all foreign ships shall salute the British flag when navigating in the British seas. This principle was strictly enforced, as shown by the incident with the French vessel carrying the future Duc de Sully 'en route' to represent the King of France, Henri IV, at James I's coronation. As soon as it came off the French coast, the vessel was forced by two British frigates to lower its flag before continuing its course. The Duc de Sully had no choice but to salute the British flag.[6]

However, the key issue was fishing. At the beginning of the 17th century, the English were bitterly observing the prosperity of the United Provinces that was in part driven by Dutch fishing in English waters. As the King received numerous complaints concerning foreigners fishing in English waters, the Privy Council decided to appoint a special committee in 1606 to examine the issue. However, nothing came of that committee. The contemplated peace between Spain and the United Provinces, and a possible alliance between the latter and England and France, did not change anything in the fishing war. The situation became even worse in 1609 when King James received yet another petition from English fishermen, complaining that the Dutch drove them away from their fishing grounds, and sold some of their catch in English ports, contrary to the laws of England. Consequently, on 6 May 1609, James issued a royal proclamation demanding that all foreign fishermen purchase a licence from the English Crown before fishing in English or Scottish waters.[7]

This British proclamation came in the same year as the publication of Hugo Grotius's *Mare Liberum* (*The Free Sea*). *Mare Liberum* was part of a legal opinion financed by the Dutch East-India Company (*Verenigde Oost-Indische Compagnie* or VOC) to justify Dutch trade in the Spanish and Portuguese trading zones of the East Indies. It not only dealt with East Indies matters, but also with questions of fishing. Grotius or Huigh de Groot (1583–1645) was a brilliant young Dutch jurist and scholar, who would soon be regarded as a European statesman, and be called the 'father of international law'. In this seminal book, based on the *Corpus Iuris Civilis*,[8] he set out three principles which confirm the freedom of the seas:

---

6 Renaud Morieux, *Une mer pour deux royaumes. La Manche, frontière franco-anglaise (XVII°–XVIII° siècles)* (Rennes, 2008), p. 155. English edition *The Channel : England, France and the Construction of a Maritime Border in the Eighteenth Century* (Cambridge, 2016), pp. 157–8.

7 Joel D. Benson, 'England, Holland, and the fishing wars', *Philosophy Study*, September 2015, vol. 5, n°9, 447–52.

8 The *Corpus Iuris Civilis* was issued in three parts at the request of Emperor Justinian in 529–34. The first part was the *Codex Justinianus*, compiling the imperial *Constitutiones* from the time of Hadrian. The second part, the Digest (*Digesta*), was

(i) As stated by Celse (67–130), the sea is for the Common use of all men (*Maris commune usum omnibus hominibus, ut aeris*). Seas are therefore what the Roman jurists called *res communis* and *res publicae*;

(ii) Sovereignty (*dominium*) only exists where possession exists;

(iii) A difference between coastal waters (*diverticulum*), which may be occupied, and high seas (*pelagus*), which cannot be occupied nor appropriated, should be made.

As an answer to Grotius's *Mare Liberum*, William Welwod published in 1613 the *Abridgement of All Sea-Lawes*. Welwod (1578–1622) was a professor of civil law at the Scottish University of Saint Andrews. His work was dedicated to King James I. Based on the Bible (mainly on Genesis) and on the work of the Italian lawyer Bartolus de Saxoferrato (or Bartole – 1314–57), he attempted to justify the possession of seas by the British crown. He also stated three principles:

(i) Coastal waters are subject to possession by private or public persons as they belong to nobody (*res nullius*);

(ii) Such appropriation includes the coastal waters (*diverticulum*), and '*at the sea-side, and hundred miles of sea forth from their coasts, at least*';

(iii) The main sea or great ocean should be as free and as open as possible: '*Atque ita esto mare vastum liberrimum*'.

To justify the above statements, Welwod quotes Genesis when '*immediately after the creation, God saith to man,* Subdue the earth, and rule over the fish, *which could not be, but by a subduing of the waters also*'.[9] In a direct response to Grotius's arguments, he also referred to the Roman jurists to justify that the seashore may be subject to private or public appropriation if the Public Authority allows it:

> Moreover, albeit these and other Roman Lawyers pronounce so, concerning the community of the sea-shoar, and coast, that private men may build Houses within the flood-mark, and appropriate them to themselves, according to that which Neratius writes, *Quod in littore quis ædiftcat, ejus sit*: That is, what a man builds on shoar, it becometh his own; yet upon this condition, *Tamen decretum Prætoris adhibendum est ut id facere liceat*, saith Pomponius: That is, providing the Praetor his decree be interponed thereunto; or that the Prince give grant, as Ulpian writes;...[10]

issued in 533 and compiled the writings of great Roman jurists such as Ulpian. The third part, the Institutes (*Institutiones*), was intended as a legal textbook for law schools.

[9] William Welwod, An *Abridgement of All Sea-Lawes*, London, printed by Humfrey Louves, 1613, p. 62 (Title 27 of the Community and Propriety of the Seas), accessible on Gallica.bnf.fr.

[10] Ibid., p. 65.

The hundred miles theory is based on the works of Bartole:

> Which bounds Bartolus hardily extends and allows for Princes and People
> at the sea-side, an hundred miles of sea forth from their coasts, at least;
> and justly, if they exercise a protection and conservancie so far: And this
> reach is called by the Doctors, *Districtas maris*, & *territorium*. It is true,
> Baldus esteemeth *potestatem, jurisdictionem & districtum*, to be all one.[11]

The only concession to Grotius's argument was for the high sea, which
Welwod considered to be the only part of the ocean that is free.

Shortly after the publication of William Welwod's book, James I requested
the jurist and scholar John Selden (1584–1654) to write a comprehensive
counter-theory to Grotius's *Mare Liberum*. Selden's work was submitted to
King James in the summer of 1618, but the Court asked Selden to remove
the final chapter on British claims in the North Sea. The concern was that
the claim might offend James's brother-in-law, Christian IV of Denmark.[12]
However, the new version of Selden's work was not submitted to James I
before the King died, and it seems that Selden had problems in reaching the
Court, more particularly the Lord High Admiral, the Duke of Buckingham
(Selden was heavily involved in politics and, as a member of the House of
Commons, had been instrumental in the impeachment of Buckingham before
he was assassinated in 1628). It was only in the spring of 1635 that Selden
was approached by noblemen with Charles I's order to publish. The revised
manuscript was submitted to Charles I, approved in August 1635 and published
in November of that year.[13]

Selden's *Mare Clausum* refutes Grotius's thesis that by nature the high seas
cannot be occupied nor subject to dominion because, on the one hand, the
sea is in practice virtually as capable of appropriation as terrestrial territory,
and, on the other hand, the subsequent governments of England continuously
claimed dominion of the seas around England. The first argument is clearly
based on Welwod's argument of the *decretum praetoris* which goes back
to Ulpian's works. If, subject to the permission of public authorities, man
can erect buildings on the shore, then the sea is likely to be appropriated.
The second argument is the ancestor of currently applicable international
rules mentioning 'continued and permanent settlements and rulings over the

---

11 Ibid., p. 69.

12 Christian had created a powerful fleet: Martin Bellamy, *Christian IV and his
Navy: A Political and Administrative History of the Danish Navy1596–1648* (Leiden,
2006).

13 Mark Somos, 'Selden's Mare Clausum: the secularisation of international law
and the rise of soft imperialism', *Journal of the History of International Law*, 14
(2012), 287–330.

disputed areas'.[14] Selden's conclusion is therefore that the English Monarchy has a historic right to all seas around England (*dominium publicum*).

This battle of the books between two extreme theories was in a certain way settled at the beginning of the 18th century by another famous Dutch lawyer, Cornelius Bynkershoek (1673–1743). In 1702, he published *De Dominio Maris* in order to advocate a middle ground between the extremes of Grotius and Selden, which could be summarised in three principles:

(i) Sea-appropriation is only possible to the extent of actual domination of the area (*imperium*);
(ii) This domination is limited by the actual power of the coastal State (*dominium*) over the sea;
(iii) Practically that power is determined by the effective range of shore-based artillery.

This gave birth to the famous 'Cannon shot rule'. What is amazing in this rule is that the distance was set at three nautical miles, whereas at that time no gun, whatever its power, had such a range! At the end of a century of battle of the books, the emerging theory, as stated by Bynkershoek, was the freedom of States to navigate and exploit the resources of the high seas and a right of coastal States to assert wide-ranging rights on a limited territorial sea:[15] '*Potestatem terrae finiri ubi finitur armorum vis.*'

State sovereignty: territorial waters and customs

The question of sovereignty over the Channel Islands has a long history of complex relationships, both in peace and in war, between France and England.

In 933, the Islands were part of the *duché de Normandie*. In 1066, after William the Conqueror's conquest of England, the latter became part of the *duché de Normandie*. One and half centuries later, when Philippe Auguste conquered Normandie in 1204, he did not occupy the Islands. At the treaty of Paris in 1258, between Saint-Louis and Henry III, if the Islands were mentioned, it is not clear if they meant the Atlantic Ocean Islands and/or the Channel Islands or both of them. One century later, in 1360, the Treaty of Brétigny between Charles V and Edouard III confirmed English possession of the Channel Islands. During the 15th century, the French occupied Jersey, but the Islands, which used to belong to the *Diocèse* of Coutance, were attached to

---

[14] Renaud Morieux, *op. cit.*, pp. 155–62.

[15] Michael Widener, *Freedom of the Seas, 1609: Grotius and the Emergence of International Law. An exhibit marking the 400th anniversary of Hugo Grotius's Mare Liberum* (Part 8), October 2009, Lillian Goldman Law Library (Yale Law School) <https://library.law.yale.edu/news/freedom-seas-part-8> [accessed 25 March 2020].

the *Diocèse* of Salisbury in 1496. After a complex period, Jersey and Guernsey joined the English Church in 1620 and 1663.

When Welwod and Selden published their work at the beginning of the 17th century, the Channel Islands were considered British. Indeed, Guernsey is mentioned by Welwod as being one of these 'eminent and visible marks above water, for the designation of the bounds (…) of the divisible parts' of the sea. The possession of Guernsey thus justified sovereignty over the 'narrow seas' of the Channel: 'What more evident monuments for our King his right in the narrow seas, than these Isles of Guernsey etc.?'.[16] This is in fact the kind of self-justification that also works the other way round: as the Islands are British so is the sea. Nothing is mentioned nor justified as to the reason why the Channel Islands are British; they are closer to the French coast than to the British shore. The British concept of sovereignty over the seas was such that all of the Channel was considered to be British, including on the French shore.

Indeed, in France the maritime boundary is seen as a line. This line is drawn on the shore and defended by coastal fortifications as far as their guns are able to deter enemy ships from 'insulting the coasts'. In England the maritime boundary is a space, far beyond the English shore and on which the 'Wooden Walls' of the Navy defend the island and its dependencies like the Channel Islands:

> England is an Ifland, whofe Frontier is the Sea, whofe Forts and Caftles are the Ships of the Royal Navy, which bear Analogy and Proportion to the Frontier Towns, and Fortified Places of Inland Dominions; (…)[17]

Given the above diverging concepts of boundary, sovereignty on the Channel and its limits in the Channel Islands area was then not an issue between the two Kingdoms. However, from 1688 to 1815, six attempts at invasion of England were prepared by the French. Nevertheless, until 1755 (during the Seven Years War), the French maritime boundary was not a priority for the Kingdom. It is only from that date that defending the coast from Saint-Malo to Le Havre became a priority, especially on the coast facing the Channel Islands. Similarly, risks of French invasion of the Channel Islands became higher with the American War of Independence (as demonstrated by the Nassau attempt of 1779, and the Rullecourt attempt of 1781, discussed by Richard Harding[18]). Therefore, in the 1780s and the 1790s, the land defences

---

[16] William Welwod, *op. cit.*, p. 68.

[17] Sir Philip Meadows, *Observations concerning the dominion and sovereignty of the seas* (London, 1689).

[18] See Richard Harding's presentation: 'The Channel Islands in Anglo-French Strategy, 1756–82' – chapter 3.

of the Islands improved (with the building of Martello towers), more troops were sent, and more warships were dedicated to the Islands, creating a true 'militarisation of the islands'. However, given the existing rules, the limits of sovereignty in the Channel Islands area were still not an issue between the two Kingdoms.

This remained true during the 19th century, with the 'cannon-shot rule' and its 3nm range of the territorial waters becoming the international standard for coastal States, until recently. This limit of sovereignty was disconnected from the fishing areas issues – as we will see later – and it did not raise – per se – major issues as the Channel Islands are more than 6nm away from the French coast.

Despite this geographical status, sovereignty over the Channel waters became a more sensitive matter in the mid-19th century with the construction and fortification of a major naval base at Cherbourg (and the mirror facility built in response on Alderney), the development of the French navy, the new navy policy of the 1880s (the *Jeune Ecole*) and the crisis of Fashoda (1898). Queen Victoria inspected the fortification and harbour works of Alderney on three occasions, – in 1854, 1857 and 1859 – the last just one year before the French launched the first ironclad, *La Gloire*, designed by Dupuy de Lôme.[19]

If the limits of sovereignty between the two States were far enough from each other to avoid major difficulties, this did not mean that knowing and drawing these limits was not important. In fact, knowing and understanding the environment became key, more particularly in the Channel Islands area, for the safety of navigation. This is particularly well illustrated by the accurate survey of the islets and rocks of this part of the Channel, such as the Minquiers and the Ecrehous. As Captain Michael Barritt[20] and Isabelle Delumeau[21] demonstrated in their chapters, both navies surveyed and charted the area in the 1860s and the 1880s. This was mainly a scientific project organised to ensure the safety of navigation in the area, but it also became a test of sovereignty over the islets for the two States. Surveying is indeed regarded as an act of appropriation and sovereignty: 'appropriating land always is associated with an initial measurement'. *Landnahme* is 'the primeval act in founding law'.[22]

It was only in 1953 that the dispute between France and the United Kingdom over the sovereignty of the islets was settled by the International Court of

[19] See Jean de Préneuf's presentation: 'The Channel Islands in French Naval Strategy from 1815 to 1906' – chapter 7.

[20] See Michael Barritt's presentation: 'Surveying the Islands: Captain Martin White RN and the Hydrography of the Islands' – chapter 5.

[21] See Isabelle Delumeau's presentation: 'Hydrographic and Nautical Knowledge in French Coastal Defence Strategy: the Case of the Channel Islands Area' – chapter 9.

[22] Carl Schmitt, *op. cit.*, p. 45; Claudio Minca and Rory Rowan, *On Schmitt and Space* (Abingdon, 2016), pp. 216–17.

Justice, which decided that the Minquiers and the Ecrehous belonged to the United Kingdom.[23]

At the crossroads of sovereignty and finance are the customs. They demonstrate to the utmost the sovereignty of the State, not only inland, but also vis-à-vis the outside world, by imposing a payment when 'crossing the line'. As with the fishing areas, customs limits are not connected to, nor consistent with, the limits of territorial waters: they go beyond to ensure that a maximum of taxable items and activities are grasped and efficiently taxed. And, as for the territorial waters, there is no treaty between France and the United Kingdom during our period to define the range of their tax boundaries. They were only defined in national legislation.

In France, consistent with the concept of a boundary being a line, the customs limit remained set at 2 leagues (6nm) from the shore until the Revolution. At that date a decree extended that limit to 4 leagues (12nm). In England, things are quite different and more complex. Customs limits changed twenty-three times from 1699 to 1819:

- 1719 – 2 leagues
- 1736 – 4 leagues
- 1779 – 2 leagues
- 1784 & 1794 – 4 leagues (Independence War)
- 1802 – 8 leagues (French Revolution)
- 1805 – 'in the British Channel'

After the French Revolution, customs limits of the two States crossed each other in several areas, Alderney island being, for instance, within the French customs limits of 4 leagues! All these mixed or 'grey' zones fuelled smuggling and generated disputes between the two States. But these disputes were not as violent as the disputes between the fishermen of each country.

Reward of labour: fishing wars and fishing rights

As seen above, the origin of disputes about the use of the sea was Dutch fishing close to the British shores. Following these disputes, new ones appeared in the 18th century between France and England: there were French fishermen fishing in English waters, and English fishermen fishing in French waters. Things were particularly complex in the Channel Islands area, where the competition between fishermen from Guernsey and Alderney with fishermen from Carteret and Granville was serious. In addition, local fishing regulations differed, depending on the area (Normandy, Brittany, Channel Islands)

---

[23] 'The Minquiers and Ecrehos case', Judgment of 17 November 1953: *I.C.J. Reports 1953*, p. 47.

and on the product: fish, shells, crustaceans, etc. As there were no treaties on fisheries between France and England, it was difficult to define the French and British fishing areas.

One usual and customary limit was the territorial water (1 league from the shore). But the British authorities, as for sovereignty and customs, often went beyond that limit. In the 1730s, the British claimed against French fishermen using dredges that had been forbidden on the French coast since 1726. Similarly, in the 1790s, the French claimed against English fishermen using means that were forbidden in France for fishing oysters. This last claim started what was later to be called the 'oyster war'. In 1797, oysters were discovered on a bank in the Chaussey Islands vicinity, between France and Jersey. From 1815 to 1820, more particularly after the end of the war in 1814, the British regularly organised fishing from Mont-Orgueil (Jersey) to supply Kent and Sussex with oysters. This industry supported 300 fishing smacks, 2,000 British fishermen and 1,000 Jersiais fishermen.[24]

In March 1821, British fishermen were seen dredging on the Bout-du-Roc and Haguet Banks, just off Granville. This generated a violent reaction from French fishermen, leading to many skirmishes, hopefully without injury. The French navy intervened with the corvette *Lynx* and British smacks were seized and oysters confiscated. It is amazing to compare Ralph Mollet's story in the 1935 *Bulletin of la Société Jersiaise* and the 1821 report of the French Port Authority in Granville:

> In 1821 French armed vessels cruised in the vicinity of the oyster banks and exercised against the English and Jersey fishermen the most wanton and unwarrantable acts of violence. They seized several smacks and carried them into Granville, the crews were beaten, ill-treated and threatened with imprisonment and confiscation of their vessels if again they dared appear upon the banks.

> For several days, they [the English fishermen], around ten of them, keep on their depredation on the Haguais bank located one league from Granville rock. (…) the sworn guards went to talk to them and instructed them to leave, as they are not authorised to fish within our limits, which instructions were already given to them several times. Some of them left, but others refused to leave, insulting us, behaving disgustingly and even threatening us. Therefore, the sworn guards, assisted by ships that were around, seized three boats and took them to Granville. M. Hugon, fisheries inspector, brought the captains before me, I registered their name and those of their boats, I informed them of the limits that they shall not trespass, and after explaining the harm they

---

[24] Ralph Mollet, 'Jersey's oyster fishing industry', *Annual Bulletin of La Société Jersiaise*, 1935 <https://www.theislandwiki.org/index.php/Jersey%27s_oyster_fishing_industry> [accessed 25 March 2020].

cause to our fishermen, I made them promise that they will not return to our oyster banks and I let them go.[25]

In April of the same year 250 Jersey smacks went fishing again on the same banks and the *Lynx* then fired to warn them…[26] This situation became so serious that in 1822 a Franco-British commission was created to solve the dispute. The British Government decided not to cover or protect Jersey fishing within one league of the low water mark from the coast of France, which automatically became a French fishing area. In 1824, the distance increased to two leagues, but this did not stop the disputes between fishermen. In 1828 and 1834, new fights between fishermen of both countries occurred, with – this time – casualties on both sides. Between 1825 and 1836, 284 British boats were seized by the French authorities.

Consequently, the two countries decided to negotiate a treaty on the fishing rights in this area. In 1839, the first treaty between France and the United Kingdom on fishing areas in the Granville Bay was signed. It defined three zones with different fishing rights:

- An 'A to K' zone of 3nm from the French coast was reserved to the French fishermen,
- A 3nm zone around Jersey was reserved to the Jersey fishermen, and
- Between these two zones, a 'Common Sea' was reserved to French and Jersey fishermen.

It should be noted that this treaty did not involve Guernsey fishermen, who were therefore excluded from the three zones defined by the treaty.

---

[25] Depuis plusieurs jours, ceux-ci [the English fishermen], au nombre de dix, ont renouvelé leurs déprédations sur le banc Haguais situé à une lieue du roc de Granville. (…) les gardes-jurés ont été leur parler et leur ont signifié de se retirer, attendu qu'ils n'avaient pas le droit de pêcher en dedans de nos limites, ce dont ils ont déjà été prévenus plusieurs fois. Quelques-uns se sont retirés, mais plusieurs autres ont refusé de le faire en disant des injures, faisant des démonstrations malhonnêtes et même hostiles. Alors les gardes-jurés, appuyés des autres bateaux qui se tenaient à portée, en ont saisi trois qu'ils ont amenés ici. M. Hugon, inspecteur des pêches, ayant fait conduire devant moi les patrons, j'ai pris leurs noms et ceux de leurs bateaux, je leur ai donné connaissance des limites qu'ils ne doivent pas dépasser et, après leur avoir fait des représentations sur le tort qu'ils faisaient à nos pêcheurs, je leur fis promettre qu'ils ne reviendraient plus sur nos huîtrières et je les ai renvoyés. (quoted by Charles de la Morandière, 'Grandeur et décadence de la pêche des huîtres dans la région granvillaise', *Études Normandes*, n° 96, 1958, 95).

[26] Charles de la Morandière, *op. cit.*, 85–111.

Conclusion: from territorialisation to fragmentation

With the development of its use in many areas and activities, the sea becomes today more divided and fragmented than the earth. In addition, there are inconsistencies between limits, depending on the purpose of that limit: territorial waters, customs, fishing areas, etc. Even in one single activity, there are also inconsistencies between fishing regulations at local, national and international levels.

This growing use of the sea was backed by the coastal States who issued more and more claims over the sea after the First World War. After the Second World War, several disputes ended up before the International Court of Justice, among which the Channel Islands case was a particularly significant one, with the two International Court of Justice decisions of 1953 on the Minquiers & Ecrehous and that of 1977 on the Continental shelf between France and the United Kingdom.

Even if international regulation is now stabilised thanks to the United Nations Convention on the Law of the Sea (the so-called 'Montego Bay Convention') signed in 1982, which entered into force in 1994, there are still difficulties; not only regarding fishing areas, but also on the definition of the territorial waters of the Channel Islands and its impact, in view of the British decision to leave the European Union.

5

Surveying the Islands: Captain Martin White RN and the Hydrography of the Islands

MICHAEL BARRITT

The summer of 1812 was wet and cool, bringing some relief to the small staff of the Hydrographical Office on the often-stifling top floor of the Admiralty Building in Whitehall. Every space in the passageways was taken up by the boxes which they laboured to fill with charts destined for ships of the war-time Royal Navy deployed from the Baltic to the Cape of Good Hope, and from the East Indies to an unwelcome new theatre on the borders of the USA.[1] On Thursday 1 July, during a lull in superintendence of this work, the Hydrographer returned to his desk to consider a letter and a manuscript survey, one of over 30 which were rendered from the fleet during the year.

Captain Thomas Hurd examined these eagerly as they were passed up by the clerks to the Board of Admiralty. It was generally a mixed bag. Many were swift reconnaissance surveys made in the heat of operations, sometimes recorded as a sketch in the remark books which captains and masters were required to render. They might supply a few soundings which could be dropped into smaller-scale published charts. This inspection was, however, the only opening for Hurd to spot talent for the vision which he would represent repeatedly to the Board and eventually bring to fruition: ' an establishment [...] of officers and scientific young men [...] capable of making nautical surveys in whatever part of the world their future services may happen to place them in'.[2]

Hurd's vision had been shaped by his own experience in the front line. His reputation in the Admiralty had been made by a remarkable survey which enabled the creation of a naval base in the hazardous waters of the Bermudan archipelago. Consequently, he had been the immediate choice to undertake an

---

[1]   Webb, Adrian J. 'The Expansion of British Naval Hydrographic Administration, 1808–1829' (PhD thesis, University of Exeter, 2010), 276, 366, 427.

[2]   The National Archives, Admiralty Papers (henceforth TNA ADM) 1/1933 Cap H 310, dated 23 July 1807.

examination of another complex of islets and rocks in the approaches to the French naval base of Brest following the loss of a 74-gun ship of the Royal Navy's Inshore Squadron in 1804.[3]

When he came to reiterate his vision in 1814, he would stress 'the great deficiency of our nautical knowledge in almost every part of the world, but more particularly on the coastline of our own Dominions'.[4] This focus was particularly justified in the English Channel. It was the key theatre for home defence, naval and economic blockade of the enemy and amphibious intervention, all of which had to be delivered in a testing regime of weather and tides. The cost is clear in the record of those shipwrecks during the wars of 1793–1815, which can be attributed to navigational error or reliance on inadequate hydrographic information. There were nearly four times as many in Home Waters and English Channel as in the operating area of the Mediterranean Fleet, and twice as many as in the waters of North America and the West Indies.[5] The fleet lost four frigates, a gunboat and a cutter through these causes in the waters of the Channel Islands, including the 38-gun *Amethyst* off Alderney in 1795. An additional two frigates, two gun-vessels, a gun-brig and a cutter were lost in the same way off the nearby Atlantic coasts of France.

Now Hurd had before him a fine survey, and a letter from the man who had made it, volunteering to continue the work. He lost no time in writing to the First Secretary:

> A correct survey of the numberless distant dangers surrounding the Islands of Guernsey, Jersey etc. has long been wanted and as the mode here proposed will make it an easy one in point of expence (sic) I trust the Board will take it into consideration.
>
> Captain White seems to be very well qualified for such an employ and I send his own survey of St Aubyns Bay in Jersey [...] as a specimen of his abilities.[6]

Martin White

Hurd's correspondent was a 33-year-old veteran of the conflict with France. His father was a prosperous wine-merchant in Portsmouth who could pull strings. Martin White had been found a place afloat at the outbreak of war in 1793 and he was continuously employed, seeing plenty of action including the

---

[3] Fisher, S. 'Captain Thomas Hurd's Survey of the Bay of Brest during the Blockade in the Napoleonic Wars'. *The Mariner's Mirror*. 79:3 (1993).

[4] TNA ADM 1/3459, minute dated 7 May 1814.

[5] Analysis of the lists in Gosset, W. P. *The Lost Ships of the Royal Navy 1793–1900* (London, 1986).

[6] TNA ADM 1/3458, letter dated 1 July 1812.

expedition to Copenhagen in 1801. When the Portsmouth MP, John Markham, was appointed to the Board of Admiralty, White senior, now a burgess of the town, lost no time in working his interest.[7] Martin was given command of the cutter *Pigmy* in the winter of 1802, watching ports on the coast of Normandy and Brittany from Le Havre to the privateer base of St Malo. He would have three further small ship commands in the Channel and southern North Sea. One, the gun-brig *Manly*, was stranded in the Ems estuary by the negligence of a pilot and then seized illegally by the Dutch. After release from prison White was promoted to commander in September 1806. Once again, his father swung into action, lobbying Admiral Markham. A brief command of the store-ship *Weymouth* was followed by appointment in September 1808 to the Jersey guardship *Vulture*.[8]

In old age Martin White would be a revered local hero in Jersey. But what sort of man was he? Even allowing for the challenge of preserving discipline in a minor warship, the log of the *Pigmy* reveals a high incidence of floggings for its small complement. In his next command, the hired lugger *Sandwich*, the master and crew fell out with White and walked off, and the owner asked for the vessel to be discharged from naval service.[9] The Flag Officer in the Channel Islands would describe White as 'captious and irascible'. In September 1811 the Flag Captain in Portsmouth reported his investigation into a string of eight court martials and supersessions of subordinates and concluded that White should be superseded. The Board of Admiralty took up their Secretary's suggestion that: 'Possibly the best way to get rid of him would be to pay the ship off …'. To his dismay, White was directed to hand over command of *Vulture* and found himself on half pay.[10] It was an unhappy prospect coming just one month after his marriage to a Jersey girl. It was time to play another card.

In later life White would indicate that his interest in hydrographic matters had been sparked by experience in Gulf Stream waters during service as a midshipman on the North American station.[11] He had lost no time in making surveys on the enemy's coasts throughout his small ship commands. This is borne out by the log of the *Pigmy* whilst operating with vessels of the Channel Islands squadron watching the division of French gunboats in Granville at the height of the invasion scare in the autumn of 1803. White records a 'boat away sounding and reconnoitring' inshore of Îles Chausey,

---

7   National Maritime Museum (henceforth NMM) MRK/104/51–3.

8   TNA ADM 9/4, No. 993.

9   NMM ADM 354/216/19, 306 and 308.

10   TNA ADM 1/226 K408 letter dated 2 Sep. 1811; ADM 1/2709 Cap W 542 and 573 letters dated 24 Sep. and 26 Oct. 1811.

11   United Kingdom Hydrographic Office (henceforth UKHO) Surveyors Letters 1c, letter dated 21 Feb. 1840.

where one of his consorts, the gunboat *Grappler*, would run aground later that year and be destroyed by the enemy.[12] In charts arising from his later Channel survey he would use little vignettes of *Pigmy* to indicate 'good holding ground' in this patrol area. In another chart he inserted vignettes and soundings to show work in *Pigmy* off Le Havre and in *Manly* over the Bassure de Baas and other banks between Boulogne and Étaples.[13] All the original documents were lost in the *Manly* except one of the Weilingen Channel which had been sent to the Admiralty, where it had earned plaudits from Hurd and other officers.[14]

The product now on Hurd's desk bore out White's claim that, during the three years in *Vulture* in the Channel Islands, 'every opportunity was taken, and every exertion used to obtain correct soundings around them and also along the French coast in the ship's boats'. It was described as a 'Compass Survey', but the Hydrographer would note that the results had been corrected for errors in polarity caused by the 'magnetic qualities' identified in several of the rocks at Jersey.[15] His eye would also be caught by an expansive key to the detailed depiction of drying areas, tidal stream regime, recommended tracks and leading marks which characterise all White's work.

The manuscript was matched with an offer which was difficult to refuse. Almost as soon as he had taken office, Hurd had been urging the Board to adapt a gun-brig for survey work in the English Channel 'under the direction of a qualified person'.[16] He would have to wait another decade before any such allocation was made. Now, with a careful report of anticipated costs and timescale for the task, he secured the Board's approval to hire the pilot vessel *Fox* of Portsmouth, which White had identified through local contacts. It was 'a sloop [...] of a light draught of water and strongly put together [...] in every particular well adapted for the performance of that service'. White was summoned to the Hydrographer's office to be briefed on the extent of previous survey work by Mr Anthony Lockwood, another touchy man who had eventually fallen out with the naval authorities in the Channel Islands.[17] He returned to Portsmouth to equip the vessel, which was to be manned with three able seamen of the Royal Navy.[18]

12 TNA ADM 51/4032, 6 Oct. 1803.
13 UKHO 817 and 841 on 5k; D845 on 15e.
14 TNA ADM 1/3523, report dated 26 May 1808.
15 UKHO 820 on Ps.
16 TNA ADM 1/3523, letter dated 13 June 1809.
17 TNA ADM 1/3458, letter dated 6 July 1812.
18 TNA ADM 1/2711 Cap W191 dated 10 July, W221 dated 17 July and W222 dated 24 July 1812.

Channel Islands survey

Most of Hurd's own work in the Channel had been conducted in vessels of opportunity or in boats loaned from warships when other duties permitted, and he would view sympathetically the challenges which lay ahead. It was necessary to inform the senior officer on station of the significance of the operations of the officer now importuning for cordage and replacement of worn lead-lines. White had little need to point out that return to Portsmouth or Plymouth for stores 'during the present fine weather will throw me greatly behind hand'. *Fox* was always short-handed since seamen had to be sent back to base port to receive their pay and collect slops.[19]

In January 1813 White's first fair sheet, of Jersey, reached the Hydrographical Office.[20] It was followed in July by one covering Guernsey and Sark.[21] They were described, like many of the sheets and accompanying remark books which he produced, as 'rough'. Yet they reflect meticulous care and attention to detail in both the performance and recording of his survey. The draughtsmanship is of the highest standard, with particularly fine topography for Jersey, no doubt reflecting White's long residence there. The Hydrographer was certainly impressed and hailed 'a work of much labour joined to great scientific knowledge'. White had developed his technique since the survey of St Aubyn's Bay and used more colour on these sheets to depict his analysis of the drying areas around the Islands. He left in place the network of control stations which enabled him to tie in the off-lying islets and rocks and to lay down the sounding work around them. Little vignettes of *Fox* indicate positions where she was moored, and an observation of the tidal stream was made with a log-ship or free float. Both sheets have comprehensive keys to the symbology. They were accompanied by fine views – panoramas of the coasts high-lighting natural and man-made marks to guide the mariner past danger and into harbour. These views would be checked and modified throughout the coming decades.

As winter approached, White was directed to estimate when the survey of the whole archipelago would be complete. He had made full use of fair weather for field work and worked up and plotted the results 'during the bad weather'. He was well advanced with the survey of Alderney, Burhou, the Casquets and adjoining rocks and shoals. He had observed a chain of trigo-nometrical connections between the Islands and 'the French headlands as far to the southward as Cape Carteret' which he needed to extend to provide control towards the Îles Chausey and Plateau de Minquiers. He estimated that

---

19 TNA ADM 1/228 K91, letter dated 22 June 1813; Cap W283 dated 2 Nov. 1813; ADM 1/1230 A181, dated 30 Jan. 1814 and ADM 1/2715 Cap W204, dated 28 July 1814.
20 UKHO 842 on 5f.
21 UKHO 824 on 5f, with the accompanying Rough Remark Book at OD 542A.

this work would take another year if he were permitted to work through the winter and to have the loan of a boat from the squadron on station for investigation of the many shoals. This analysis was endorsed by Hurd who noted the extensive dangers and commended White's ability and local knowledge. The result, the Hydrographer judged, would finally enable the publication of a chart 'of that part of the French coast containing this group of islands [...] for the benefit of His Majesty's Ships employed on that Station [...] and advantage to the Naval Service'.[22]

A year passed, work was still outstanding, and in December 1814 White was compelled 'to offer to their Lordships my reasons for having failed'. It was, he noted, 'notwithstanding every exertion on my part, as well as on the part of the Seamen serving with me, whose cheerful dispositions under fatigue, and ready acquiescence on all occasions deserves my best thanks'. Quite apart from the logistical difficulties which constantly hampered him, the task was just vast:

> the space committed to my charge for investigation becomes considerably more complicated as I proceed eastward and southward and comprehends a greater number of real dangers than I was first aware of, or indeed was thought possible.

White now asked for an additional nine months, but, undoubtedly conscious of the retrenchment, which was underway, offered to continue on half pay, and suggested paying off the *Fox* and substituting a 'fitted 6 oared cutter' which would be more suitable for the examination of the shoals at low water. The matter was referred to Thomas Hurd who did not hesitate to support White, recalling how his own Bermuda survey had taken over twice as long as foreseen. The clinching argument reflected White's background of active service in the area. The results would benefit 'the service in general [...] and [...] the Cruisers in particular who may be hereafter destined to watch the motions of an enemy in this neighbourhood'. There was also a shrewd allusion to 'the favourable opportunity which the present pacific disposition on both sides holds out'.[23]

The new arrangements were put into effect in the following spring. Hurd's continued advocacy with the Board was assisted by the quality of the work which reached his office, now depicting Alderney and the adjacent sea area.[24] Once again it showed how the Casquets and other outlying hazards had been linked into the control scheme extended from stations on the main island.

---

[22] TNA ADM 1/2713 Cap W300, dated 15 Nov. 1813.
[23] TNA ADM 1/2715, Cap W365, dated 10 Dec. 1814.
[24] UKHO 843 on 43A.

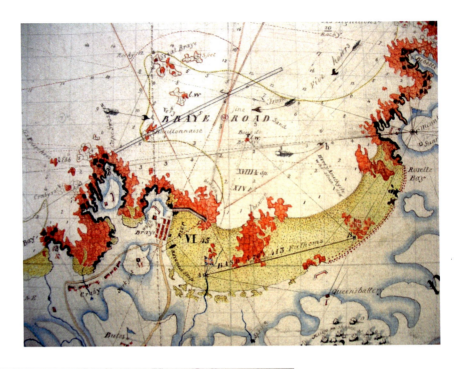

Figure 1 (above)   Example of White's control networks, here extending from a baseline on Braye Beach, Alderney, and his depiction of complex drying areas (Courtesy United Kingdom Hydrographic Office).

Figure 2 (left)   Detail from White's English Channel survey in *Shamroc*, showing 'Hurd's Pit' extending round Alderney and the Casquets (Courtesy United Kingdom Hydrographic Office).

Figure 3 Detail from White's 'Rough Sheet' of progress, showing a vignette of *Pigmy* marking a good anchorage used by the squadron watching the Breton ports (Courtesy United Kingdom Hydrographic Office).

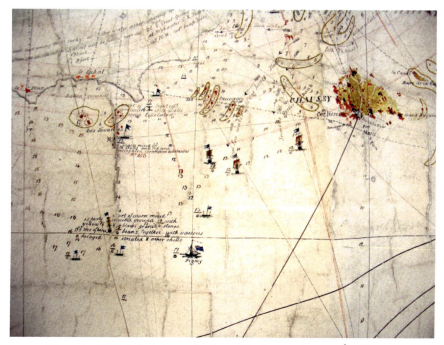

Figure 4 White's initial examination of the dangers between Île Chausey and the Plateau des Minquiers, including Les Sauvages where he would ground in *Lion* (Courtesy United Kingdom Hydrographic Office).

There a baseline had been measured on the strand in Braye Road. Extensive tidal and tidal stream information was shown throughout.

The task of depicting the complex area to the south and east of Jersey was more demanding. In September 1815 White submitted his 'Rough General Chart' comprising the sea area from Alderney round to the vicinity of St Malo.[25] This stunning work of draughtsmanship showed the detailed survey based on control extended trigonometrically from stations on the French coast. This had been carried to the complex area of the Minquiers. It was nonetheless work still in progress, and a 'Supplement' would arrive a year later, with corrections and additions.[26] These sheets, approximately five feet by four feet in extent, are clearly products 'during the bad weather'. Expansive annotations explained White's computations to achieve the Mercator projection, with complex symbology indicating his geodetic and astronomical work. All would be amplified in another Remark Book which was under preparation. To keep the patient Hydrographer on side White selected and reported extracts of his calculations, declaring 'I [...] earnestly hope they may find favour'.[27]

The comprehensiveness of this office work in no small part reflected the fact that, despite representations from the Hydrographer, the authorities in London and the Channel Islands were slow in putting the administration of White's naval party on a sound footing. He was left without any manpower at all as the season of 1816 ebbed away. By September a deeply frustrated and anxious man was writing to explain his circumstances. In July a crew had at last been selected in Portsmouth 'after much difficulty' but they were 'suddenly ordered to join the Algerine expedition, under the orders of Lord Exmouth'. Finally, in mid-August the Navy Board had given him permission to hire some men, enabling him to get 'occasionally afloat'.[28] On 25 October, in part anxious to 'clear his yard arm' if complaints should arise from the admiral on station, White wrote another letter which paints a vivid picture of the challenge of the survey. With the weather precluding work in the cutter on the investigation of the dangers 'between Chausey Island and Les Minquiers' which he was extremely anxious to pursue during the equinoctial spring tide, he had leapt at an offer of help from Mr John Betts the Commander of the *Lion* Revenue Cutter. He now reported:

> About one o'clock PM Chausey Island then bearing SE by E, and distant 5 miles, the *Lion* came suddenly from 10 to 3 fathoms, and eventually struck on

---

[25] UKHO 841 on 5k.

[26] UKHO 817 on 5k.

[27] UKHO Original Document (henceforth OD) 537, NMM ADM 359/36B, letter dated 4 Aug. 1816.

[28] NMM ADM 359/36B, correspondence dated 4 Apr. and 1 Sept. 1816.

the rocks denominated Les Sauvages, the actual existence of which 'though inserted in all the Charts now extant' are doubted by most of the nautical persons in this quarter, and most positively so by the pilot of the *Lion*, who with myself, had been anxiously looking out most part of the morning from the masthead of the cutter, and where in fact we both happened to be, when the accident took place, whilst Mr Betts the Commander was equally anxious with the helm and lead.

He was happy to report that the *Lion* had floated free with trifling damage 'already made good, and with very little expense to Government, probably less than three pounds sterling'. He hoped that no exception would be taken to his actions in consideration of 'the importance of the channel between Chausey and Les Minquiers (either with regard to advance and retreat in time of war, hitherto so extremely dangerous and doubtful)'.

Hurd would not miss the reiteration of White's clear appreciation of the military significance of his work, based firmly on his war experience:

> You may rely, Sir, on my most earnest endeavours to prosecute through every difficulty, this important service, that in the event of any future war, this part of our Channel navigation may be resorted to by the blockading frigates with confidence and security.[29]

On 26 November the Hydrographer addressed the Board, emphasising the difficulties of the survey and the 'masterly manner' in which it had been conducted, concluding: 'Captain White appears to be one of the most zealous and capable officers employed on Survey Service'. He had already assured White of his 'great anxiety to have the survey of so intricate a part of our Channel navigation on the copper' so that 'the abilities you have manifested in its execution' should be widely acknowledged'.[30] These 'rare talents' would be acknowledged by the Board when they inspected White's final product and they directed that they continue to be employed 'to the very best advantage of the public service'.[31]

HMS *Shamroc* and the English Channel survey

White was clearly the man to employ if Hurd achieved his objective of setting in hand a thorough re-survey of the English Channel in 'a small sloop of war furnished with necessary instruments and time-keepers'. The Admiralty Board had responded to a further minute from him in 1816 by requiring the

---

[29]   NMM ADM 359/36B, 25 Oct. 1816.
[30]   NMM ADM 359/36B letters dated 24 Aug. and 26 Nov. 1816.
[31]   UKHO Outgoing Letter Book (henceforth LB) 1, minute dated 26 May 1817, underlining as in original.

preparation of two vessels 'to have surveys carried on in the British Channel and North Sea'.[32] In 1817 White would commission the gun-brig *Shamroc* for Hurd's high-priority survey of the English and St George's Channels.[33] The Hydrographer's 'Hints or Memorandums' annexed to the instructions for White are of particular interest. Though he had provided similar memorandums for the masters employed as Admiralty Surveyors at home and overseas, this was the first issue for a survey vessel under the command of a suitably qualified 'Surveying Officer'. Hurd had to tread carefully in his role as head of specialisation, watching the reaction of the Board and, more particularly, that of the First Secretary, John Wilson Croker. The latter read Hurd's draft and annotated it: 'The variation of the compass to be particularly attended to in the different parts of the Channel'. Hurd, with knowledge of the acumen demonstrated in White's Channel Islands surveys, had kept such guidance to the minimum: 'With respect to the mode of executing the Duties here directed, you must be guided by your own judgment'.[34]

What Hurd's memorandums did provide was a clear definition of the strategic importance of the work committed to White. The objective was to enable 'better Navigation' by taking 'correct soundings [...] and correct description of the ground brought up by [the lead], taking due care to make the necessary calculations both of latitude and longitude for every position' and paying 'close attention to the different direction or sets of the currents and tides'. 'The particular object' of the survey was to confirm and delineate the Great and Little Sole Banks shown on old charts. If accurately charted, these would provide an aid to incoming vessels as they crossed onto the continental shelf seeking a safe landfall. Similarly:

> a small spot named Jones's bank with between 30 and 40 fathoms marked thereon [...] must be searched for and its position noted as being an excellent spot if fortunately sounded on in thick or foggy weather to mark a vessel's situation with regard to the dangers surrounding the Scilly Islands.

Hurd closed by noting the outstanding work on the dangers between the Channel Islands and the coast of France.

In the approaches to the Dover Strait at the eastern end of his area, White could use the same techniques as in his earlier work. This is evident in a surviving compilation sheet 'Beachy Head to South Foreland and Fécamp to Cap Blanc Nez'.[35] Liaison with the French authorities gave access to occupy

---

[32] TNA ADM 12/179, Cut 57.

[33] The spelling of the ship's name varies, but that adopted here was used invariably in White's records.

[34] TNA ADM 1/3460, minute dated 18 Feb. 1817.

[35] NMM G 218: 6/12 with the resultant fair sheet at UKHO E164 on 0b.

control stations, including that at Mont Lambert above Boulogne which had been used in the first connection of the two national geodetic networks. White extended his triangulation offshore by laying beacons on the banks, over which the sounding was intensified. The directions and rates of the tidal stream, observed at different states of the tide, are shown by curved arrows.

These techniques were being stretched to their limit as White worked off the British coasts at the extreme western end of the Channel. He laid down his work with reference to the marks and stations of the Trigonometrical Survey. Colonel Mudge and his assistants had established these on a day of perfect visibility in the summer of 1796, observing from their mainland triangulation to the lighthouses on the Scilly Islands. White drew up a diagram indicating the quality of the fix of his soundings by sketching in the rays from these shore stations.[36] When resurveying this area 170 years later, Commander Barritt used a similar diagram to assess the strength of fixes from electronic positioning aids set up on triangulation pillars ashore. White remarked on the impossibility of defining the edge of dangers such as Wolf Rock, but the depths which he plotted compare well with the modern chart. His effort to obtain the best results with the technology available was an inspiration for our endeavours in *Bulldog* in the 1980s when sounding in the deep water of the seaway between the Islands and the Cornish coast.

Further out of sight of land the challenge was much greater in White's day, with complete reliance on estimation of position between astronomical observations. White tackled the challenge with characteristic rigour. Every source of error is analysed with diagrams in his workbooks. He lists no less than 14 'contingent corrections' to courses and distances before entry in a traverse table to compute the track.[37] A sheet rendered to show 'Shamroc's rough Progress since 1st June 1818' reads like a strict report against the criteria laid down in the Hints and Memorandums, including the First Secretary's addition. Values for variation are shown in prominent lozenges! Track from off the Eddystone to the Little and Great Sole Banks and onwards to the shelf edge off Mizen Head is plotted with regular soundings. A set of symbols covers the means of laying down the track: latitude by the sun's meridian or lunar altitude, longitude by chronometer with the sun in altitude or in horizon. Little vignettes denote the brig's position at noon and ship's head for local attraction.[38] The completed work was rendered in a 'General Rough Chart', another imposing product some five feet square.[39] A vastly expanded reference table explained symbols for control, tidal information, soundings and natures of the bottom, with some additions denoting White's alert eye and indefatigable curiosity:

36 UKHO 826 on Oi*.
37 UKHO OD 537.
38 UKHO 815 on 15e.
39 UKHO D845 on 15e.

'an aurora appeared', 'Birds disappeared – stragglers excepted {species to be denoted}'. The sheet provides a dramatic picture of the extent of White's achievement, providing a pattern of sounding which had enabled him to define the features which Hurd had listed and to add others, such as Shamroc Knowl.

Acknowledging the 'particular object' which the Hydrographer had specified, separate plans were rendered showing 'the Sinuosities' of the Little Sole Bank and the Nymph Bank. A note on the latter records that 'upon and around this Bank there has been twenty-two Celestial Observations taken for Latitude and twenty by Chronometer for Longitude'.[40] Similar sheets were drawn up for new discoveries, 'named after and in honor of those Friends who first selected him for the important investigation and who have subsequently been pleased to patronize and support him so handsomely and so liberally thro' it'.[41] The First Lord could add Melville Knowl and Melville Pit to other surveyors' tributes around the globe. Another knoll was named after the senior naval commissioner, Admiral Sir George Cockburn, who had informed White of his promotion to Post Captain in December 1818, telling him that their Lordships 'wish you still to continue in the command of the Shamrock, to pursue the surveying duties on which you have already effected so much'.[42] The Hydrographer provided the label for a bank and for the most important discovery of all, 'Hurd's Dyke', a deep running almost from the meridian of Cap de la Hague round to the north of Alderney, giving a mariner who sounded in it the opportunity to sheer away from the danger of the Casquets. The approaches to important landfalls such as Ushant were depicted in other detailed sheets, to which soundings were added in the course of White's subsequent work.[43] So the first strategic imperative in the Hydrographer's remit was addressed. Information on soundings and natures of the seabed had been memorised and passed on since at least medieval times, and the wording is still discernible in today's Admiralty Pilot. In his published *Sailing Directions for the English Channel* White would note, however, the neglect of sounding in his day and lay down detailed guidance for the approaches to Scilly or Ushant.[44]

White spent the early part of the season in 1818 closer inshore, starting at Cape Clear and working northwards to establish correct latitudes and longitudes of the most prominent headlands on the western coast of Ireland. The Hydrographer had supported this proposal, noting the shipwrecks and loss

40 UKHO 813 and 810 on Oi*.

41 UKHO 816 on Ps*.

42 Copy enclosed with the Return of Service at TNA ADM 9/59, No. 4276.

43 UKHO 807a on Oi*.

44 White, Captain Martin RN, *Sailing Directions for the English Channel* (London, 1835), 1–13.

caused by the erroneous positions shown on published charts.[45] This task was complete by the end of 1819. Thereafter White completed ten surveys of Irish harbours from Valentia to Larne which were of interest to the Admiralty, in each case revealing significant errors in existing charts.[46]

Similar work in support of Royal Naval operations was conducted on the Channel coast of England. Accurate positions were observed at landfalls, and larger scale surveys were completed of anchorages and hazardous areas. The construction of the great breakwater in the strategic naval anchorage of Plymouth Sound was well advanced, with some modifications following a great gale in 1817. In 1821 White was directed to resolve discrepancies in existing surveys working from a firm triangulation scheme extended from the Ordnance Survey's stations. His thorough work filled in the soundings around the breakwater and extended through Asia Pass into the channels leading westwards to the naval dockyard in the Hamoaze and eastwards to the commercial harbours of Sutton and Cattewater.[47]

When the first catalogue of the holdings in the Hydrographical Office was completed in 1826, it listed 51 'original surveys of Captain M. White'. More than 20 others would subsequently be added including work in the Bristol Channel in 1825 and on the west coasts of Wales in 1827. There were new soundings in White's original survey area of the Channel Islands.[48] He had returned there throughout his survey when easterly winds made conditions unfavourable out in the fairway of the Channel.[49] These sounding sheets were destined to accrue fresh annotations in the years yet ahead.

The Hydrographer's regular tributes to White's 'zeal, perseverance and talents as a surveyor' were readily endorsed by the Board. Commending White's 'uncommon genius and talent' Hurd had emphasised that 'the remark books accompanying his charts are replete with useful and scientific observations and calculations, and strongly mark the preserving industry and great abilities with which this officer has followed up the service he has chosen to conduct'.[50] The 'Rough Remark Books' were to be preserved as prized Original Documents in the UKHO. White had arranged for the engraving and printing of at least one magnificent title page. Some were contained in beautifully illustrated covers; others were provided by the Admiralty with fine bindings.[51] The books provide invaluable descriptions of his survey methods and equipment.

[45] UKHO LB 1, letters dated 25 Nov. 1817 and 21 Mar. 1818.
[46] UKHO LB 1, report dated 31 Dec. 1819 and letter dated 17 Jan. 1820; TNA ADM 12/194, Cut 68.1, 29 Oct. 1819.
[47] UKHO B873/6 on Di.
[48] UKHO 818 on Ps.
[49] UKHO LB 1, letter dated 2 May 1817.
[50] UKHO LB1, letters dated 12 Feb. and 26 May 1817.
[51] UKHO OD 537, 537A, 541, and 542A.

In an early volume from the Channel Islands survey he illustrates a log-ship capable of measuring water flow down to 20 feet, 'here supposed to be the greatest quantity of water that any cruiser destined for these Islands will draw'. These observations were of the utmost importance in this quarter where the Coriolis effect and the configuration of coast and seabed result in a huge tidal range and concomitant powerful water flow.

Hurd was a constant champion of White's work, declaring that he had rejoiced in being able to publish charts of the Channel which demonstrated 'the difference between a real survey upon scientific principles, and an imaginary one, formed from loose materials occasionally picked up and badly put together.'[52] He would declare:

> It is unnecessary for me to express the particular satisfaction I feel when works such as yours come to my possession and most devoutly do I wish for the sake of the public service [...] that all my Naval correspondents were as well gifted as yourself or would consent to take a lesson from your highly valuable labours.

He allayed White's concern over the difficulties of estimating the time needed to conclude the English Channel survey, 'works of science and of such an extent of space subject to all the vicissitudes of winds and weather', and urged him to 'look forward to a continuance of your own and Shamrocs labors till the whole is completely finished and also to an extension of them on other parts of the coasts immediately after'.[53]

In his final months in harness, which were punctuated by illness and absence, Hurd sustained his support, indicating further work off the coasts of Brittany and Ireland.[54] White returned regularly to the complex area between Cap de la Hague and Cap Frehel, confirming in 1826 that he would need approval to land on the French coast to complete his work.[55] His letters reflect the ever-present challenges and hazards. Reporting the loss of a sextant 'off St. Maloe's, by the upsetting of the Boat' he added the terse note that by 'this calamity, seven of our companions have met a watery grave'.[56] One of them was his assistant, Mr Frost, whose loss he particularly lamented.

White appears to have retained the support of Thomas Hurd's successor, William Edward Parry, until shortly before he in turn handed over to Francis Beaufort in 1829. White reported from Jersey on additions and changes to the charts published in 1824 and 1827 from his earlier work.[57] Twelve new

---

[52] UKHO LB 1, letter dated 20 Nov. 1818.
[53] Ibid., letter dated 16 Oct. 1820
[54] Ibid., letters dated 27 Feb. and 15 Oct. 1822.
[55] UKHO Minute Book 1, ff 32–4, letters dated 22 Mar. and 10 Apr. 1826.
[56] Ibid., letters dated 27 Oct. and 24 Nov. 1828.
[57] British Admiralty Charts 60–3; UKHO LB 2, letters dated 23 Feb. and 5 Mar. 1829.

sheets would be rendered for the west coast of Normandy and the north coast of Brittany as far west as St Malo, with le Banc de la Schole and the area around Î. Chausey.[58] White's response to yet another call to estimate when work would be complete was that this depended 'how far I may go Westward of St Malo (for as far as the French Government are concerned, I could I believe go even to Brest, if required)'. He had detected errors in the existing French charts and noted that 'I was originally warned by the French maritime préfet' that these 'were not to be depended on'.[59]

Shamroc had been paid off, replaced by the smaller *Linnet*. She was commanded by two young protégés, Lieutenants Henry Mangles Denham and Edward Barnett, who had flourished whilst others had found the regime of Matthew White too much to bear.[60] White was aware of 'the French academicians who are working Northeastwards from Rochfort'. Eventually Barnett encountered the French survey party of M. Beautemps-Beaupré and on 2 July *Linnet* took White into the Rade de Solidor off St Servan, where an amicable meeting took place. White undertook to take two ingénieures hydrographes to Jersey to plan a geodetic connection with the mainland and to establish a tide gauge for their work.[61] The potential of this liaison was to be curtailed. There was pressure to economise, bring charting surveys to a satisfactory close, and pay off ships. There was also reluctance in Whitehall to cause any offence in France. Strict bounds were now placed on White's operations as he sought to improve control in areas where his survey depended on very early work in *Pigmy*.[62] He was directed to confine his efforts to the coast between Cap de la Hague and Cap du Rozel. Finally, he was informed that the survey was to be discontinued in the winter of 1830.[63]

The latter years and a summary of the legacy

White was far from ready to hand over the baton and rest on his laurels. He would lobby Beaufort for employment, in 1837 expressing 'a feeling of chagrin at being so long left upon the shelf'. He declared that he could match the efforts of 'the French Gentlemen [...] now occasionally at work among the Minquiers'.[64] His daughter Ellen wrote to the Hydrographer to seek acknowl-

---

[58] UKHO LB 2, letters dated 5 Feb. and 14 Nov. 1828 and 28 Mar. 1829.

[59] UKHO Surveyors' Letters 1c, dated 1 Mar. 1829.

[60] One such man was the talented Lieutenant William Mudge. TNA ADM 1/4917 Pro M11, TNA ADM 1/629, L150, letter dated 5 Jul. 1817, 1/1272, A226, letter dated 25 Mar 1818, and 1/1272, M96, letter dated 6 May 1818.

[61] Archives nationales de la France, Marine 3JJ 84, letter of July 1829. I am grateful to Isabelle Delumeau for this reference.

[62] UKHO Surveyors' Letters 1a, letter dated 7 June 1829.

[63] Ibid., letters dated 18 and 19 Sept. 1829.

[64] UKHO Surveyors' Letters 1a, dated 9 Jul. 1830.

edgement of his ongoing efforts. In response to the subsequent payment of a guinea a day he stated that:

> [...] ever since the termination of my late survey, as well in Jersey as during my sojourn in France, I have been constantly on the alert [...] occasional visits to various parts of the coasts in pursuit of Hydrographical matter, together with boat hire and certain douceurs to fishermen, have [...] not been effected without some sacrifice, private considerations however have never had weight with me when placed in competition with opportunities of benefitting the Service I belong to [...][65]

White appears to have been resident in Avranches during 1837–8 for the benefit of Ellen's health. He had asked for a short allocation of the cutter *Cracker* once she could be released at the end of the season from her fishery protection duties on the oyster grounds. He proposed to embark at Granville to revisit and check parts of the original survey.[66] He would soon report that 'I find the *Cracker*, her officer and crew [...] everything I can desire'. With their help he sent in a list of changes around the Minquiers and Chausey, some the effect of 'the continued disruption of the ground there during the last 15 or 16 years by the oyster dredges and its consequent deposition elsewhere'. Another list was accumulated in 1839.[67] He retained his warfare focus, reasserting, for example, the cautious guidance in his published sailing directions for RN cruisers seeking anchorage among the Chausey Islets.[68]

In the years which followed he would continue to submit tracings and reports of changes and new information from pilots and fishermen, even after he went onto the Retired List in 1846 at the age of 64.[69] These were years in which his letters would also express his frustration at the doubts which he felt were expressed over his survey and knowledge as new harbour works were taken in hand in the Channel Islands, including those for a watch on the expanding French naval station at Cherbourg. By contrast he continued to have very cordial relations with M. Beautemps-Beaupré, now the French Hydrographer.[70] In 1847 he reported achieving just six whole days afloat checking reported dangers when the station cutter *Sylvia* could be spared. In 1848 he was out in a boat tracing 'such alterations as the winds and waves have of late years effected in this exposed region' and checking for necessary

---

[65] UKHO Incoming Letters Prior to 1857 W, letter dated 5 May 1839.

[66] UKHO Surveyors' Letters 1a, dated 27 Jul. 1837 and 28 May and 13 June 1838.

[67] Ibid., letters dated 14 and 30 Sept. 1838 and 1c, dated 30 June 1839.

[68] UKHO Surveyors' Letters 1c dated 4 Aug. 1833, and 1a, letter dated 20 June 1837.

[69] UKHO 818 on Ps*, L1798 on Pr.

[70] Ibid., letters dated 1 and 12 Sept. 1845.

changes in his sailing directions as a result of the new piers at St Helier, St Catherine's and Braye in Alderney.[71]

Apart from his contributions to the Hydrographical Office's compilation charts of the English Channel, 11 charts were attributed to White in the catalogue of 1839. As his contemporary William Henry Smyth had predicted with perhaps rather more composure, their work would be steadily displaced as their successors came on the scene with steamships and more advanced equipment. By 1870, just five years after his death, White's name did not appear in the Catalogue of Admiralty Charts. He had left, however, a shining example of devotion to duty, superior skill, meticulous attention to detail and fine draughtsmanship. Above all else he retained an unswerving operational awareness of the strategic significance of his work. This last attribute remains the justification for the military survey specialisation envisaged by Thomas Hurd, which would see plenty of action in the centuries ahead.

[71] Ibid., letters dated 20 Oct. 1847 and 13 July 1848.

PART 4

ENGINEERING STRATEGIC CHANGE

6

Channel 'Harbours of Refuge' – Their Origins and Failures

WILLIAM ALLSOP

Reasons for 'harbours of refuge'

Throughout the early 1800s, Britain feared the 'Napoleonic threat' of invasion. The more explicit threat from France abated with the defeat of Bonaparte's armies at Waterloo in 1815 and his death in 1821 on St Helena. But latent fears of a resurgence of French naval power in the mid-1800s, emphasised by the construction of the large harbour at Cherbourg, fuelled proposals in Britain for 'harbours of refuge' in the English Channel, debated at length through the 1840s. The perception of this new threat drove harbour construction at Portland, Jersey (St Catherine's) and Alderney (Braye Bay), and later at Dover where work had already started. This paper will outline the history of these harbours/breakwaters, and the extent to which they failed or succeeded.

Harbours of refuge were notionally conceived to provide shelter from storms for commercial vessels, including mail packets, fishing and general trade. Use for naval purposes was sometimes less than explicit. Most of these harbours had difficult gestations, often with repeated shortages of money, particularly for Cherbourg. At the time of their design (~1840) most naval vessels were powered by sail. Harbours and trading practices would have adapted to the restrictions so imposed. For instance, it was very difficult for a sailing vessel to leave harbour in the face of an onshore wind. This limitation was understood in commercial operations. But even as these harbours were being developed, the propulsion (and form) of vessels changed, with greater use of steam power rather than sail, and iron (later steel) replacing wooden hulls.

A partly hidden sub-text of the 'harbours of refuge' debate was, however, the development of new harbours for the Royal Navy for deterrence, ie. defence. A further sub-text, less commonly discussed, was their potential use for offensive purposes. For the Channel Islands, this would essentially be to blockade or stage attacks on the major French port at Cherbourg.

Possible sites in Britain for 'harbours of refuge' were at Holyhead, Peterhead, Harwich, Dover, Seaford, Portland, Jersey (St Catherine's) and Alderney (Braye Bay). Both Jersey and Alderney are close to the coast of France, seen as the major military threat. So, whilst possible harbour developments here might be shrouded under the cloak of 'harbours of refuge', the truth is more certain that these harbours were simply military enterprises, and the Admiralty might be detected pulling strings behind the scenes. This paper will primarily focus on the two Channel Islands' harbours, but will also introduce those at Cherbourg, Portland and Dover, and comment on their fates into the twentieth century.

Cherbourg

Lack of a natural harbour on their Channel coast persuaded French military leaders to protect the bay at Cherbourg as a roadstead harbour (rade de Cherbourg). Three breakwaters were first mooted as early as 1665, but were only commenced in June 1784 by construction of the 4km-long central breakwater. The design by de Cessart used timber cones, abutting each other at the toe. Each cone was 46m in diameter at the seabed, 20m in diameter at the top and 20m high. The timber cones were then filled with stone over the lower part, and masonry-faced concrete on the upper part. Gaps between adjoining cones were blocked by chains, but wave action would still have passed around each cone.

De Cessart's concept did not survive early construction storms which severely damaged or destroyed many of the 18 cones placed. In 1789, the remaining cones were cut down to low water and incorporated into a rubble mound of about 1:3 on the seaward face, and 1:1 on the lee side. As at other sites, wave action eroded the seaward rubble slope down to about 1:10 over the upper part. In doing so, the reduced crest level became ineffective for carrying gun batteries protecting each end. Construction of the breakwater needed over 300 vessels to ferry stone from Becquet. Work on this design was terminated in 1788.[1]

In 1802, Napoleon 1 ordered work on the central breakwater to restart, reinforcing the central section to accommodate cannons. Large stones were then used to raise and protect the crest in 1802-03 for these gun batteries. This rock was, however, moved by storms, and it was decided in 1811 to take the foundations of the battery down to LW, and to construct it in masonry protected by a granite facing. Some 13,300 cubic metres of 'the largest stone procurable' was placed in 1811, but by 1813 the works were stopped before completion. That work recommenced some 11 years later. Works to raise the main breakwater crest above water restarted in 1830. Concrete blocks cast in

[1] J. M. F. Cachin, *Mémoire sur la digue de Cherbourg* (Paris, 1820).

place on the rubble mound formed a toe / foundation. The lower slope was protected by large stones down to 5m below LW at a slope of 1:5. The new superstructure suffered uneven settlement in the somewhat variable mound, so the final part was delayed '3-4 years to allow the mound to consolidate'. The central breakwater superstructure was completed in 1846 in the reign of Louis Philippe, and the pier-head forts in 1853 under Napoleon III.

When Queen Victoria and Prince Albert attended the grand opening of the new port in August 1858, at the invitation of Napoleon III, they rapidly appraised the potential threat of such a large military harbour, even though their host was keen to reassure Britain that the new naval base was not a threat. The Queen and Prince Albert took the new harbour so seriously that they instructed the Royal Yacht to sail, which cut their visit short and made them miss the ceremony to unveil a major statue of Napoleon I.

After 1846, the two side breakwaters of Digue de Querqueville and Digue de l'Est were completed by 1895, thus enclosing one of the largest harbour areas in the world. Naval use of the full harbour declined quickly, apart from specialised submarine construction, whilst it flourished as a commercial port with the growth of the transatlantic liners. The harbour has continued as a significant ferry port, it accommodates a fishing fleet and in recent years it has expanded work in marine renewables (both offshore wind and tidal stream turbines) with attendant reclamations within the harbour.

Portland

Portland Harbour is again a roadstead harbour like Cherbourg, formed in the shelter of Chesil Beach and the Isle of Portland. The harbour was created initially by two breakwaters: the short inner or southern breakwater connected to the island; and a detached breakwater to the north-east with a 120m-wide entrance. Construction of the breakwaters began in July 1849, when Prince Albert laid the foundation stone. They were designed by J. M. Rendel, with work supervised by J. T. Leather and John Coode as resident engineer. Both breakwaters were formed as rubble mounds with superstructures from low water. Portland stone was obtained from the island quarries by convict labour and run-out onto the breakwaters over timber staging extending over the gap between the inner and outer breakwaters.[2] Timber piles (spaced about 10m apart and surmounted by creosoted crossbeams about 5.5m above HW) were founded on iron screws set into the clay bed. Stone was dumped in ridges from the staging; 'the waves gradually levelled these ridges'. Large stones (3–7 tons) were included in the material dumped at an average of 500,000 tons per year from 1853 to 1860, reducing to 140,000 tons per year to 1866, giving a total of 5,800,000 tons. The outer (eastern) breakwater was then

---

[2]   L. F. Vernon-Harcourt, *Harbours and Docks: their Physical Features, History, Construction, Equipment, and Maintenance* (London, 1885).

completed by two pier-heads formed in masonry founded at 7.3m below LW. The harbour was declared complete by the Prince of Wales in 1872. But as part of additional defence works against torpedo attack, two further breakwaters were added between 1893 and 1906.[3]

Portland Harbour was used for many important naval activities, initially as the base for the Channel and later the Home Fleets, providing coaling and oiling depots. The harbour also became a base for the Admiralty's Underwater Weapons Establishment, and a factory and pier for torpedo testing. The harbour was active in both world wars, and the docks were used until closed in 1959. The main use of the Naval Base was in officer-training until Royal Navy operations at Portland ceased in 1995. The helicopter base closed in 1999. Portland Port was founded in 1996 as a private company to provide commercial and leisure uses, accommodating cruise ships and hosting sporting activities, including the 2012 Olympics.

Alderney

Alderney is just to the west of Cherbourg in an area of high velocity tidal streams, the Race of Alderney. The western coast of Alderney is exposed directly to Atlantic storms. As a possible base for a harbour of refuge, Alderney is well south of any English coastal traffic, and most transatlantic trade in the 1800s ran from either Bristol or Liverpool, far to the west of the Channel Islands. Almost no mercantile vessels would require a refuge harbour at Alderney, and even if they did, they would prefer to shelter on the less wave-exposed south-east side of the island, although there the tidal currents are even more severe.

The truth behind the selection of this site is suggested by its closeness to Cherbourg. The harbour blockade remained a major naval tactic, in which one fleet traps an enemy's fleet in its own harbour; a reason for Cherbourg and Dover each having two entrances. A convenient naval anchorage capable of holding an offensive force close to the enemy's main harbour would certainly be highly attractive to the Admiralty. But why site this harbour on the coast most exposed to waves? Again, the reason was military, to hide any British fleet from the telescopes of the French on the cliffs of the Cherbourg peninsula. In choosing to locate the harbour on the west side, Admiralty planners effectively sealed the ill fate of the harbour, and certainly of the breakwater.

The background to the selection of the Channel Islands' sites is discussed by L. F. Vernon-Harcourt (1873)[4] in the proceedings of the Institution of Civil Engineers (ICE) and in his book in 1885, reviewed at length by W. Davies

---

[3]   A. Smith, 'The Encyclopaedia of Portland History' (2019) <http://www.portlandhistory.co.uk/>.

[4]   L. F. Vernon-Harcourt, Paper no. 1347, 'Account of the Construction and

(1983).[5] In searching for Government grounds for the selection of these sites, Davies notes that reasons '... have not been easy to trace... [in] Admiralty papers on this delicate subject'.

In discussions on Vernon-Harcourt's paper (1873), Admiral Sir Edward Belcher explained that he had been summoned by the Government in August 1842 to examine (military) defences in the Channel Islands and advise on '... what guns should be added or withdrawn, and what harbours should be made ... .' He was asked to report as early as possible to allow estimates to be laid before Parliament. At Alderney, he found the tidal race across '... the mouth of the proposed harbour [probably Braye Bay] ... would render it utterly impossible for any disabled vessel to get in ... .' His advice to the Admiralty in September 1842 was that a harbour at Longy on the south-east side of the island would cost £1,500,000.

Even so, construction of the Alderney breakwater started in 1847, to a design by James Walker, second ICE President. The initial design included a mound to low water, surmounted by blockwork walls with rubble infill. Most of the stone for the mound and walls was obtained from the Mannez quarry on the opposite side of Alderney. But almost immediately, the weakness of Walker's design became apparent, with frequent breaches of the breakwater wall. Shortly into construction, the design was revised. The formation level was lowered to 3.5–4m below LW. The foundation stones, until then simply placed tightly, were laid using cement, and the wall batter was steepened. This construction continued to 823m by 1856. The design was then revised again, further lowering the wall foundation level. Construction of the outer section was nominally completed in 1864, giving a total length of 1,430m.

In 1852, five years after construction had started, following repeated breaches and cost increases, Sir Francis Baring summoned Sir Edward Belcher back to the Admiralty to tell him that ' ... the former Commission was still in force ... [he was] ordered to go to Alderney harbour and report upon it'. Further, ' ... you are not to entertain any of the opinions that you entertained before; you are to examine the place and tell us what has been done, and whether it is worthwhile to expend £600,000 more on the eastern arm.' James Walker was also instructed to go ' ... in order that he might be there in a gale'. It appears that both Walker and Belcher advised against an additional eastern arm, perhaps convinced that the concomitant concentration of tidal flows across the breakwater heads would scour their foundation mounds. Belcher concluded his contribution to the Vernon-Harcourt discussion in 1873 with the barbed comment: 'The present works were certainly a credit to British engineers and

---

Maintenance of the Harbour at Braye Bay, Alderney', *Proceedings of the Institution of Civil Engineers*, vol. XXXVII (1873–4), pp. 60–108.

5   W. Davies, *The Harbour that Failed* (Alderney, 1983).

showed what Englishmen could do when they were determined – whether right or wrong.'

At ICE in 1873, Vernon-Harcourt also noted that the idea of the eastern breakwater had not been abandoned until 1862. Whilst agreeing with Sir John Coode and Colonel Jervois that the eastern arm should be added ' … if the harbour was to be rendered perfect …' he felt that it was little use as a 'harbour of refuge' being away from the main shipping routes, and it was '… a bad harbour in easterly gales'. He disagreed with Sir Edward Belcher on the 'rapid scouring' fear ' … as the harbour area was not large and the rise of tide at Alderney was not peculiarly great', but he was probably not taking full account of current velocities along the breakwater.

After completion, the breakwater continued to be damaged, and on occasion the superstructure was breached completely. The Board of Trade appointed engineers to visit the breakwater and to report on measures to secure all or part of it. In 1870, Sir John Hawkshaw, eleventh ICE President, and Colonel Sir Andrew Clarke noted the instability of the mound and recommended changes, but the Government did not consider that the costs were merited, and none of their recommendations were implemented. By this time, no Government department wanted ownership of the Alderney breakwater problem.

In an attempt to strengthen the mound and protect the wall, Mannez stone was dumped onto the mound from rail tracks along the wall to maintain the foreshore level. About 300,000 tons were tipped between 1864 and September 1871. From 1873, repair and maintenance work covered the inner 871m only; the outer portion was abandoned, and the wall quickly collapsed. Partridge (2018)[6] reports 'destruction of the seaward end' by 1879 and the complete collapse and submergence by 1889, leaving a mound crest about 4m below LW. For the shortened section, work was still required to repair breaches in the superstructure, and approximately 20,000 tons of stone were dumped annually until that operation ceased in 1964. The shortened breakwater now protects the commercial quay used for the supply ship and oil tanker. The remaining mooring area is occupied by visiting yachts during the summer sailing season, which are a major source of tourist income.

Jersey

There are two issues that affect the utility of any 'harbour of refuge' on Jersey: whether Jersey is a useful location at all; and if so, where on Jersey might a harbour be useful? Again, the processes of decision-making in Parliament, the civil service, and the Admiralty have been obscured by the 'weeding' of

---

6   C. W. Partridge, 'Alderney Harbour Breakwater – summary of damage / repairs / maintenance', compiled for The Henry Euler Memorial Trust (Alderney, 2018), 3pp notes.

papers referred to by Davies (1983), so we must work hard to reconstruct the possible reasons.

The plan shown by Hold (2010)[7] and by Davies starts with two break-waters, both of which were begun in 1847: St Catherine's to the north; and Archirondel to the south. The St Catherine's breakwater exists to this day, and the outer end has recently been refurbished. The Archirondel breakwater was planned to be very much longer, protecting the harbour from southerly and south-easterly waves, and from the northerly running tidal currents. But in July 1849, Walker instructed the contractor, Jackson & Bean, to stop work, notionally to divert effort to the completion of the northern breakwater, but perhaps because the putative harbour started to silt up with the northern breakwater trapping sediment from the northerly drift. A mere stub of the Archirondel breakwater exists today, probably in a similar state to when it was abandoned.

It is pretty much impossible to disagree with Davies that siting a harbour of refuge on Jersey made no sense. This is an island of 12m tides, surrounded by inter-tidal rocks. It is close to (but separate from) France, to which it is nearly 'joined' by submerged rocks that run out east-south-east to near Coutances. Together with the substantial tidal flows between Jersey and France, these rocks significantly limit any commercial traffic along the east side of Jersey, most vessels from the United Kingdom passing to the west. In any event, very little traffic leaving the United Kingdom for further destinations will pass near Jersey, unless trading direct, in which case it has little use for a 'harbour of refuge' per se.

So, what about military use, even if not declared as such? Again, Davies rehearses the convoluted discussions at length. In 1831, Captain (later Sir) William Symonds favoured Bouley Bay on the north coast, although this had been countered by Admiral Martin White (Retired), a naturalised Jerseyman and former Admiralty hydrographer, who 'unmistakably showed up the defects' of that option.

During the early 1840s, the issue of a new harbour at Jersey was compli-cated by the involvement of Sir William Napier, Lieutenant-Governor of Guernsey, who appears to have been inveigled by Whitehall 'to prepare a military appraisal of the Channel Islands as a whole', for which 'he personally inspected Jersey, Guernsey, Alderney, Sark and Jethou'. Sir William was not impressed by the civilian administrations of either Jersey or Guernsey, and 'crossed swords with everybody who did not agree with his point of view, whether they be military or civil'. The British Government then set up a commission to revisit Sir William's work, including Admiral Belcher, Colonel Cardew and Lieutenant-Colonel Colquhoun, to be supported later by James

---

[7] S. Hold, 'Restoration of St. Catherine's Breakwater Roundhead, Jersey, Channel Islands', *Proceedings ICE Conference, Edinburgh, 2009* (London, 2010).

Walker and Captain Sheringham (surveyor), some of whom would be involved in the harbours commission of 1844. But by 1842, Government was minded to act. There were competing claims for Noirmont Point on the south-west coast of Jersey, or Bouley Bay towards the north-east corner, or none at all. For reasons that are still opaque, and not supported by any of the main protagonists, the Government opted to construct the harbour at St Catherine's on the north-east coast.

Davies notes that the Royal Commission on Harbours of Refuge of 1844, set up by the Treasury, did not mention the Channel Islands yet, in only three years, both 'the St Catherine's and Alderney projects had been proposed, authorised and commenced. No sound reason can be found for such a hasty decision, and this aspect must remain a mystery.' The 'haste' is illustrated by the act being dated 2 April 1844 and the report being submitted to their Lordships on 7 August 1844.

But even if this harbour could have been maintained, its utility would have been severely limited by the tidal conditions under which it could be accessed, when there would be sailing space (of appropriate depth and currents) between Jersey and France. The second issue was the threat of siltation, particularly of sand driven by waves and the northward running tidal flows, which was likely to enter the harbour under each flood, depositing over slack water. If that was not bad enough, the early cancellation of the Archirondel breakwater increased the probability of the nearshore current being trapped by the St Catherine's breakwater, probably significantly increasing rates of siltation.

Dover

The Royal Commission of 1840 favoured a deep-water harbour in Dover Bay to enclose 450 acres at LWOST (18.2 square kilometres) at a cost of £2,000,000. The 1844 Royal Commission reconsidered whether it was desirable to establish a harbour of refuge here, requiring any site to deliver, in order of precedence:

   a) Ease of access for vessels 'requiring shelter from stress of weather',
   b) For armed vessels in event of hostilities, both offensive and defensive,
   c) It should 'possess facilities for ensuring its defence' against attack.

So, whilst this harbour was in theory to be for the refuge of civilian vessels, the military purposes were clear from the start. This commission accepted the proposed site and general plan layout of the new outer harbour. A third commission of 1845 considered plans by eight engineers for a harbour of some 520 acres (21 square kilometres) out to seven fathoms (12.8m). The outer breakwater was to be aligned with the tidal currents to reduce siltation. The commissioners reported in 1846 in favour of Mr Rendel's design. In comment, Vernon-Harcourt (1885) noted damage to sloping solutions at Cherbourg and

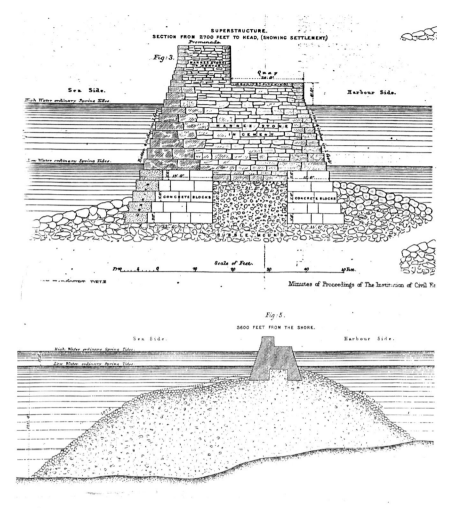

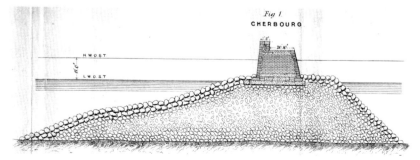

Figure 5 (a and b)   Alderney breakwater. The scale of the rubble mound required to create the harbour is obvious in this view, and can still be traced in the island's landscape to this day. Note the rise and fall of the tide. Vernon-Harcourt 1873.

Figure 6   Cherbourg breakwater. Artificial harbours have always been expensive, and although Cherbourg did not require such deep rubble foundations as Alderney, it was a far larger harbour – and equally costly. Vernon-Harcourt 1873.

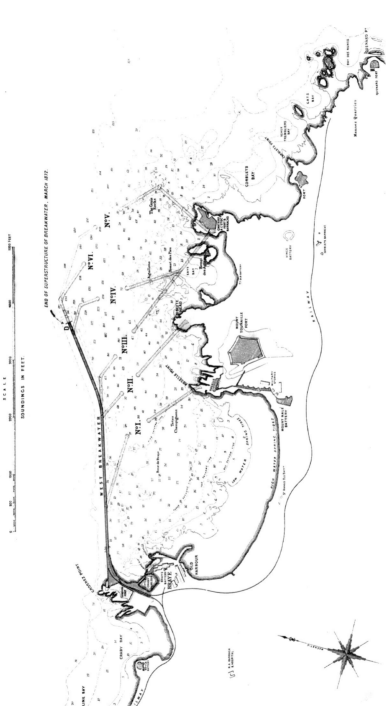

Figure 7 The evolution of the harbour was complicated by the exposed site, extreme weather and the vast quantity of rubble required as a foundation, a reality reflected in the railway line on this diagram. This prompted a variety of plans for the completion of the harbour, dated in the plan. The largest project stretched into deep water, and would have taken many years to complete. Vernon-Harcourt 1873.

Plymouth, and the lack of suitable stone at Dover. He also notes the shortage of experience in concrete. But given the chalk bottom, absence of local rock, 'and a moderate depth, the upright wall was the best system to adopt'.

The issue of siltation was again of significant concern, although this commission commented rather testily: '... if liability to silt were deemed an objection, it would be idle to attempt such works on any part of our coasts'. A contract was let in October 1847 for 244m of the Admiralty Pier. Subsequent contracts in 1854 and 1857 covered a further 305 metres, so that in 1871 the work was essentially completed to 640m from the shore.

Admiralty Pier was formed by 7–8 ton concrete blocks with outer stone facings. The main wall was 'surmounted by a high parapet, overhanging considerably to the seaward'. But on 1 January 1877, about 300m of this parapet at the outer end was swept away down to quay level. Wilson (1919)[8] ascribes the blame to the curved overhang, although the slender nature of the up-stand wall and absence of any tensile reinforcement must surely have contributed substantially. The damaged section was rebuilt with a significantly thicker (about 3.3m) vertical face, and 'proved perfectly satisfactory' up to 1919.

This single pier did not however give adequate shelter from easterlies, and a contract was let by Dover Harbour Board in 1892 to Sir John Jackson to construct the Prince of Wales Pier to some 503 metres, supervised by Coode, Son & Matthews. Then in late 1895, Coode were requested by the Admiralty to prepare drawings to facilitate expansion to the full Admiralty Harbour by:

a) Extension of Admiralty Pier by a further 610m.
b) A detached breakwater, the South Breakwater, of 1,284m.
c) The Eastern Arm of 1,012m.

This revised layout altered the length and overlap of the Admiralty Pier extension, and the position and width of the Eastern entrance, with the aims of improving accessibility to vessels and reducing siltation. The Coode design was approved by the Admiralty, and a contract let for construction to S. Pearson & Son in November 1897.

The Eastern Breakwater (termed the East Arm) projects south for 900m. The section was essentially like the Admiralty Pier extension, although the parapet wall was lower with the harbour coping set at +8.8m LWOST. Foundation blocks for the East Arm wall were laid direct on the chalk inshore, or the chalk marl / flint matrix further seaward, down to -16.2m LWOST. The East Arm was intended to provide berthing, so the harbour face was made vertical, timber fenders were provided and an L-shaped head provided some shelter from wave action along the inner face.

---

[8] M. F-G. Wilson, Paper no. 4274, 'Admiralty Harbour, Dover', *Proceedings of the Institution of Civil Engineers*, vol. CCIX (1919–20), pp. 31–112.

The South Breakwater (occasionally termed the Island Breakwater) runs 1,284m parallel to the shoreline. Placement of blocks for this wall started short of the eastern end, allowing a later adjustment of the width of the eastern entrance on the basis of wave penetration and flow experience during construction. A curved section connected the eastern end to the main run of wall using curved (radial) blocks to preserve block tightness. No parapet wall was used along the main section of the South Breakwater, simply being added at the ends to provide shelter to buildings close to the roundheads.

The new walls were formed by concrete blocks (one part cement to six parts sand / shingle). Blocks were 2.3m wide and 1.8m high, depth varying from 2.4–4m to accommodate the 12:1 batter and ensure adequate bonding. Facing blocks included a face of granite cast into the rest of the overall block. Granite was mainly supplied from a Pearson-owned quarry at Gunnislake in Cornwall, supplemented by a supply from Sweden, requiring special permission from the Admiralty. Pearson eschewed the use of Titan block-placing cranes that would run along the constructed works, in favour of temporary staging above and beyond the works, supporting Goliath and other steam-powered travelling cranes. The rail level for these cranes was generally above +8.2m HWOST. Ahead of block placing, the seabed was prepared by excavating 1.5m of surface material, most by a 'Hone grab'. The chalk or chalk / flint matrix was loosened where needed by a cast-iron breaker fitted with protruding chisels and dropped from the leading (60 ton) Goliath. The final 0.3m of excavation was removed by four men using picks and shovels within a large diving bell. These excavated a strip about 4.6m wide across the running face, sufficient to place two rows of blocks. The bell was passed over each strip once to give a coarse levelling, 'within a few inches', and then a second pass for final levelling.

Block-setting was supervised by two helmet-divers, blocks being placed hard against their neighbours. Significant effort was devoted to checking and regularising these courses to ensure an even base for the subsequent blocks. Bag joggles were placed by the divers, or from within the bell that had returned to deal with several blocks, and to regularise any unevenness in the completed surface. Helmet-diver working was limited to tidal velocities below one knot, restricting these operations to about four to five hours each tide, during which six blocks were placed per hour at best.

Further trimming or filling at the base of the 'Low-water course' compensated for any level errors in the lower layers. Blocks above were set by masons during the two to three hours of low water on spring tides. All the upper courses were set / bedded in 2:1 Portland cement mortar, and significant effort ensured that all lower joints were caulked by sacking/rope, pointed in neat, quick-setting cement, to avoid any loss of jointing/bedding mortar downwards.

Toe protection blocks were laid along the seaward face using essentially similar procedures, with a smaller diving bell operated from the small luffing-jib crane running along the completed surface of the wall. As these protection aprons were completed, so the parapet walls were added above. A capping layer of in-situ concrete with granite paving completed the deck, allowing for rails, gas / electric / telephone cables and water pipes.

Following the breakwater construction, minor contracts were let to expand rail and ferry facilities in the western harbour. On declaration of war in 1914, ferry and commercial activities were moved to Folkestone and Dover reverted to naval use. After the 1914–18 war, the harbour remained in the hands of the Admiralty, but the Commercial Harbour was managed by Dover Harbour Board (DHB), who had to deal with years of neglect and adaptations to the harbour that were not relevant to a passenger port. Ferry and commercial trade increased, and, in September 1923, the Admiralty Harbour was transferred by Act of Parliament to DHB, with the Admiralty retaining some rights. The most important was that the harbour was to revert to the Admiralty should the Defence of the Realm so require.

The generality of harbours of refuge

In considering the harbour of refuge options, it is worth noting that developments in steamships were in their infancy in 1830–40 (Barnes, 2014),[9] but that over the following years requirements for harbours, particularly naval harbours, were significantly altered by the changing forms of propulsion, the reduced mooring and swinging space required, and the ability to sail under adverse wind directions. This was potentially of significant benefit to the French ports of St Malo and Granville, as well as Cherbourg, where the new steamships could more easily depart under prevailing Westerly winds than would sailing vessels.

The often-heated discussions at ICE on 'harbours of refuge' may have been fuelled in some part by struggles for prominence, and the apparent proximity of a large pot of money. This might be illustrated in discussions at ICE in 1858 in a paper by Scott (1858).[10] G. P. Bidder (ICE Vice-President) discussed the generality of Government supervision of the 'harbours of refuge', primarily Holyhead, Portland, Dover and Alderney. He had found it necessary to examine 'the formidable and not very lively documents, the Parliamentary Blue Books … which confirmed his own previous observations … these great works were being executed without any efficient responsible supervision or control', asserting further that ' … the Government itself had been kept utterly in the

[9] J. Barnes, *Oceans of Power: 125 Years of Marine Engineering Milestones*, IMarEST (London, 2014).

[10] M. Scott, Paper no. 991, 'Description of a Breakwater at the Port of Blyth, and of Improvements in Breakwaters, applicable to Harbours of Refuge', *Proceedings of the Institution of Civil Engineers*, vol. XVIII (1858–9), pp. 72–161.

dark ... The time had now arrived when these matters should be brought before the bar of public opinion ... the Institution of Civil Engineers appeared to be the most fitting arena for the discussion of the question.' Bidder referred to several Reports of the Committee on Harbours of Refuge from 1845, noting that they could not agree on the preferred form of breakwater, '...chiefly arisen from the Committee not having arrived at a clear understanding of the terms used, and of the basis of the various arguments employed'. He continued, somewhat acidly: ' ... facts derived from the Blue Books ... appeared to contain everything except the specific information sought for'.

Considering Alderney, the wall section 'appeared to be of a disadvantageous form ... the effect of the waves upon this wall must be very prejudicial ... and greater than upon any other form which could be devised'. Bidder continued in an attack on James Walker (past-President of ICE, and designer of both breakwaters at Alderney and St Catherine's) who had signed the report of 1845, stating that the costs of a vertical wall or rubble mound 'would be nearly identical'. Yet the vertical pier at Dover was costing £415 per foot, whilst the rubble mounds at Portland were less than half of that. Of four works recommended, three had been commenced, and two 'had been intrusted [sic] to Mr James Walker, himself one of the Commissioners'. Bidder continued; ' ... it seemed that the Government authorised works ... without any idea being given of the cost of such works, or of the time that would be occupied in their construction, or even of the mode in which they were to be executed'.

Bidder then turned to the harbours at Alderney and Jersey, the former being 'nearly valueless' and that at St Catherine's offering 'scarcely shelter for a few fishing boats'. In conclusion, Bidder criticised (in fairly immoderate language) the shortage of independent members in the commissions, and the prevalence of 'foregone conclusions' and 'hocus pocus' in decision-making. He called for 'the attention of some independent Member of the House of Commons ... pertinaciously attacking and exposing the present objectionable system ... .'

Breakwater design and construction

The initial Walker designs for both Alderney and St Catherine's breakwaters were essentially the same, using a mound of quarried stone to low water, surmounted by blockwork walls with rubble infill. Most stone for the mound and walls was from the Mannez quarry on Alderney, or from Verclut on Jersey, although both required imported granite facings to reduce abrasion damage. Shortly into construction, the design at Alderney was revised. The mound was lowered to improve the stability of the foundation stones. Those, until then simply placed tightly, were now laid using cement mortar. The batter of the wall itself was steepened to give a greater 'pinching force' on the lower blocks. This continued to 823m until 1856, when the section design was further revised. Construction of the outer portion was completed in 1864, giving a total length of 1430m.

At both sites, the main construction was from staging (as later adopted by Pearson at Dover), using timber staging with some steam power to assist. At Alderney, an innovative rock chute was devised to get rock into the barges. Rock slid down the chute was slowed by a reversal of direction at part-height to avoid punching a hole through the bottom of the barge! Mound rock at St Catherine's was simply tipped from the staging, where the greater tidal range and lower wave exposure made placement of the wall blocks in the 'dry' far easier.

When these harbours were first considered (~1845), breakwater design was by trial and error with no calculation of loads or resistance. Designs advanced by experience. Two comments from the time give an indication of the problem. Scott Russell (1847)[11] remarked: 'Perhaps it may be considered rather hard by the young engineer, that he should be left to be guided entirely by circumstances, without the aid of any one general principle for his assistance.' In discussing his innovative wave dynamometer, Stevenson (1849, 1874)[12] [13] remarks: '… the engineer has always a difficulty in estimating the force of the waves with which he has to contend …. . The information … derived from local informants … is not satisfactory'. Those uncertainties were substantially compounded by very significant general misunderstandings on wave behaviour over submerged mounds, although not for want of trying many different descriptions. Here, the textbooks by Vernon-Harcourt (1885), and by Shield (1895),[14] might have been helpful had they been available in 1845–7. Even without formulae on near-structure wave transformations, it is still a little surprising to modern eyes that the designs were so similar when the exposure was so different; and perhaps also to more perceptive contemporaries (see comments by G. P. Bidder, above).

The site at St Catherine's, on the lee side of Jersey, is sheltered from major storm waves. Waves from the Atlantic are substantially reduced by refraction and diffraction along the north coast of Jersey, so that when reaching St Catherine's they are strongly oblique to the breakwater, and much reduced in height. The only direct attack on this breakwater is by waves from north and east which are strongly fetch-limited. The tidal range at Jersey at ~ 12m is one of the greatest in the world (a few sites reach ~14m), but the general tidal currents are not focussed here, except in local flows around the roundhead.

[11] J. Scott Russell, Paper no. 755, 'On the Practical Forms of Breakwaters, Sea Walls, and other Engineering Works, exposed to the action of Waves', *Proceedings of the Institution of Civil Engineers*, vol. VI. (1847), pp. 135–48.

[12] T. Stevenson, 'Account of Experiments upon the Force of the Waves of the Atlantic and German Oceans', (communicated by D. Stevenson) in *Transactions of the Royal Society of Edinburgh*, vol. XVI (Edinburgh,1845), pp. 22–33.

[13] T. Stevenson, *The Design and Construction of Harbours: a Treatise on Maritime Engineering* (Edinburgh, 1874), repr. (Cambridge, 2011)

[14] W. Shield, *Principles and Practice of Harbour Construction* (London, 1895).

So, this breakwater is very lightly attacked, as evidenced by the significant lack of damage or demand for repair until very recently.

Wave conditions at Alderney are very different. The tidal range is less at 5.2m, but currents may exceed 7–8 knots (3.6–4.1m/second) in the Race of Alderney. Modelling of waves and currents discussed by Allsop et al. (1991)[15] show that waves are refracted by these currents in somewhat surprising fashion. Tidal currents are often greatest at mid-tide, with slack water at high and low tide levels. At Alderney the contrary is true with tidal velocities being greatest around high and low water. Those high currents reduce wave heights at the breakwater at high and low water, but no wave-current refraction applies at mid-tide so wave attack is greatest. Modelling in 1989 (see Allsop et al. 1991) gave a 1:50 year condition of Hs=11m offshore reducing to Hs=8.0–8.5m at the breakwater. [Note: At simplest, the significant wave height, Hs, is taken as the average of the top one third of wave heights, $H1/3$. It fits well with the assessment of seasoned mariners by discounting the very largest waves, but biasing the assessment towards the larger wave heights.] Combining direct wave attack at mid-tide, and the effect of shoaling over the submerged mound, causes waves to break impulsively over the mound onto the breakwater wall.

The debate on wave behaviour was discussed by Shield (1899), who reminds his reader of '… one or two leading points … generally accepted as the theory of waves', discussing the change from circular wave orbits to ellipses as waves move into shallow water. He notes that waves 'break on entering water of a depth which but little exceeds their height …' (implying that the effects of steep bed slopes and, perhaps, wave period on wave-breaking limits were little appreciated). The following comment: '… swell waves however … are often transformed into waves of a dangerous character', whilst being somewhat oblique, does illustrate a growing appreciation of these effects. Shield then uses work by Airey (1845)[16] to derive relative particle displacements for different depths below the water surface, concluding that, for all depths in which it is practical to construct breakwaters, storm waves will (mostly) have transformed to 'waves of translation'. In discussing wave action at a vertical quay with an approaching bed slope of 1:10, Shield noted that as the tide recedes, waves are 'quickly transformed into angry waves of translation by being tripped up by the foreshore …' He then draws the similarity with Alderney, noting that the returning wave often causes damage to the foundation, and that high parapets 'greatly intensify this action … and are objectionable'. He notes that rubble may be washed away at the outer end of a breakwater down to depths >12m. At Alderney, with a bed depth of -14m LW at 300m from the root, the

---

[15] N. W. H. Allsop, M. G. Briggs, T. Denziloe and A. E. Skinner, '18. Alderney breakwater: the quest for a final solution', in ICE, *Coastal structures and breakwaters, 1991* (London, 1992).

[16] G. B. Airey, 'On Tides and Waves', in *Encyclopaedia Metropolitana*, vol. V (London, 1845), pp. 241–396.

mound at -1m LW was not stable even at a slope of 1:6.5, the foundation being withdrawn leading to breaching.

But not only did the lack of clear understanding of wave forces severely hamper the design, key technologies that would greatly assist construction at the end of the century were yet to be developed. Ordinary Portland Cement (OPC) had been patented by Aspedin in 1823 but was not available in commercial quantities until 1840–50. Perceptively, Pearson ensured the supply needed for Dover by buying the cement works, and then selling it off afterwards at a profit.

Cement mortar (initially Medina, later OPC) and helmet divers were, however, both included in the design revisions. In discussions with Vernon-Harcourt (1873), John Jackson (the contractors' agent, 1857–66), described using helmet divers to excavate holes to receive support piles. Six divers operated at any one time, four on the sea side, and two on the harbour side, working in four-hour shifts, three shifts per day. Jackson discussed the operation of delivering blocks to the divers, and then to the masons once the blockwork emerged above LW.

How did they fail?

Alderney

Even early during construction, the Alderney breakwater was damaged on multiple occasions, with the wall sometimes being breached completely. That led to changes of section and incorporating cement mortar in placing foundation blocks. Even so, damage continued, although Vernon-Harcourt (1873) claims that most had been at points where the mound crossed/inter-cepted rock outcrops and that other instances of damage were relatively minor. A storm in January 1865, however, forced two breaches (widths 15m and 40m), both completely through the superstructure. Another breach occurred in January 1866, a smaller one in February 1867 and another 18m wide in January 1868. There were further breaches in December 1868, and fresh ones in February and March 1869. However, the Government did not consider that the costs of the works proposed by Hawkshaw and Clarke following their inspection in May 1870 were merited and, consequently, no significant recommendations were implemented.

The wall toe had been partially protected by stone dumped to maintain the foreshore level. About 300,000 tons were tipped between 1864 and September 1871, after which the de facto decision was made to abandon the outer length. From 1873, repair and maintenance work covered only the inner length of 870m. The outer portion was abandoned to the sea and the wall quickly collapsed, leaving a mound crest about -4m LW. For the shortened section, approximately 20,000 tons of stone were dumped annually, and further work was still required to repair breaches in the superstructure. Dumping of foreshore rock ceased in 1964.

Waves at Alderney are frequently severe. Depths off the breakwater generally exceed 15–20m. Atlantic storms reach the breakwater with little reduction, with the 1:50 year storm condition of Hs=11m offshore corresponding to Hs=8.0–8.5m at the breakwater. The severity of wave impact on the wall is then increased by waves shoaling over the mound, causing waves to break impulsively against the wall. Storms at Alderney usually persist for many hours, so that the breakwater is exposed to the full range of possible wave and water level combinations, particularly those which allow waves to break directly against it.

Responsibility for the maintenance of Alderney breakwater was transferred to the States of Guernsey in 1987. Maintenance costs up to 1990 were estimated at around £500,000 per annum, excluding direct costs of storm damage. That damage takes two main forms. Direct wave impact on the wall shakes the breakwater, and cracks mortar joints. The impact pressures force water into the joints, and into voids behind. Loose rock from the mound is thrown against the wall, abrading the wall by a depth greater than 1m. Over time, the typical size of rubble on the mound has reduced, and the process has generated considerable quantities of gravel and sand on Little Crabby and Platte Saline beaches to the westward.

Up to 1990, a team of eight men repointed the face of the wall above mid-tide level, filled cracks and replaced damaged masonry each summer. A team of six civil engineering divers carried out repair work at the toe, working both below and above water. During 1989/90, storms battered the breakwater for six weeks. At its peak on 25/26 January 1990, the storm had a return period of about 1:25 years, with offshore conditions of Hs=10–10.5m. During the next six days, the storm subsided slowly, then rose again to $Hs > 7$m. On 11/12 February, storm conditions again exceeded $Hs = 9$m. This continuous pounding cracked the masonry facing, and a large cavity was formed in the wall. Finally, it was breached by an explosive failure clearly audible in and around Braye Bay. Other sections of the structure also suffered damage. An emergency procedure had previously been formulated, and permanent repair work was underway within ten days. The cost of repair work occasioned by these storms was estimated in 1990 at £1.1 million. Studies by Coode & Partners and HR Wallingford explored various potential solutions, see Allsop et al. (1991). Later work on alternative approaches to protecting this breakwater have been described by Jensen (2017).[17]

---

[17] O. Jensen and A. Bisgaard, 'Alderney Breakwater, a developed rehabilitation solution', in K. Burgess (ed.), *Coasts, Marine Structures and Breakwaters, 2017: Realising the Potential* (London, 2018).

Jersey

At St Catherine's, the failure of the harbour was simply one of utility, compounded by the lack of depth, the inherent failings of the location and the lack of interest of the States of Jersey and the Admiralty. The breakwater itself has suffered very little damage, most being confined to the outer end, described by Hold (2009). The rapid siltation of the harbour area was accelerated by constructing the breakwaters in the wrong sequence, capturing the sediment-laden northerly current by St Catherine's breakwater, rather than deflecting it by extending the Archirondel breakwater. No records exist of the changes of depth, but they must have been sufficient to cause doubts about the wisdom of continuing within the first two years of construction.

Cherbourg, Portland and Dover

Each of these (initially) military harbours has continued in use, although only Cherbourg retains a naval function. The breakwaters at Cherbourg require an annual supply of large rock. Portland, facing essentially away from any significant wave action, has required relatively little remediation. Dover harbour is probably one of the most successful harbours anywhere, substantially due to the large volumes of cross-Channel ferry traffic. There have been many changes to the internal harbour structures, but the main breakwaters have required little repair work given their 110+ year age!

PART 5

ALDERNEY AND THE CHANNEL ISLANDS – NAVAL STRATEGY FROM 1815 TO 1905

7

The Channel Islands in French Naval Strategy from 1815 to 1906

JEAN DE PRÉNEUF

Within French naval strategy between 1815 and 1906, the Channel Islands were part of France's global rivalry with London. Several elements of this strategy and the interactions between them merit consideration. France is an amphibious nation. Both continental and maritime, it has faced numerous land- and sea-based threats, from both within Europe and overseas. The country is surrounded by sea on three sides and also has to deal with the lock that is Gibraltar. The unifications of both Italy and Germany, followed by the signing of the Triple Alliance, increased the complexity of this geostrategic challenge. France's strategy involved prioritising and identifying links among the threats posed by Germany, Britain and Italy. It was only Italy's neutrality and then the Entente Cordiale that would change matters in the early twentieth century.

This complexity could be seen in the English Channel when it came to selecting a main naval base within it. While siting the base at Dunkirk would have made it possible to block the Hochseeflotte (hereafter HSF)'s entry into the Channel from the north, as well as posing a threat to London, the port was isolated and exposed. At the western end, Brest was well protected, but it was far not only from France's industrial base but also from the British centre of gravity and the Dover Strait. Meanwhile, Cherbourg, right in the middle of the Channel, was isolated from Paris until the mid-nineteenth century and vulnerable to the Royal Navy and the HSF. This vulnerability was increased by the development of Portland and Alderney. The narrowness of the central section of the Channel meant that fluidity was limited: British bases were close, navigation difficult and the legal framework restrictive. The configuration of the waters and the coastline favoured denial of access and raids on commerce or bases. This combination of limiting factors was reinforced by the technological revolutions that came along after 1850. The debate, which mainly concerned coastal protection and commerce raiding, was arbitrated by civil society because naval policy partly escaped experts' control owing to statements made in parliament and the press.[1] Many actors therefore contributed to the development of naval strategy.

This article focuses on the French navy's central authorities. Their archives, in particular the papers of the Admiralty Council (Conseil d'Amirauté), which became the High Council of the Navy (Conseil supérieur de la Marine, hereafter CSM) in 1889, are kept at the Defence Historical Service (Service historique de la Défense, hereafter SHD). I draw upon these archival sources, supplementing them with the courses offered at the French War Academy (École supérieure de guerre), established in 1896 and placed on a permanent footing in 1898 as the French Higher Naval Academy (École supérieure de Marine, hereafter ESM). I also make use of the correspondence received from forces stationed in the Channel,[2] and writings published by civilian and military experts. The historiographical output on this topic is uneven: little has been written about the first half of the nineteenth century, and the same goes for the Second Empire,[3] with Michèle Battesti's thesis serving as one of the few sources on the subject. On the other hand, the 1871–1914 period has been considered a great deal,[4] including recently.[5]

This corpus allows two periods to be identified. First, between 1815 and 1871, French strategy in the Channel served a foreign policy that aimed for neutrality in London with a view to amending the order set by the Congress of Vienna. Then, from 1871 to 1906, we see the predominance of a stance that is both anti-British and anti-German, and which was influenced to varying

---

[1]   Sébastien Nofficial, *'Le Parlement et la marine de guerre en France (1871–1914)'* (Unpublished Hist. Thesis, University of South Brittany, 2015).

[2]   Éric Barré, 'L'organisation défensive de Cherbourg et de la presqu'île du Cotentin de la fin du XIXe au début du XXe siècle', *Revue de la Manche*, 150–1 (1996).

[3]   Michèle Battesti, *La marine de Napoléon III. Une politique navale* (Vincennes, 1996), 2 vols. On the local dimension, see Guy de Saint-Denis, 'La station navale de Granville sous la deuxième République', *Revue de la Manche*, 183 (2004) and Sébastien Chatelain, 'La place de Cherbourg dans la guerre franco-allemande de 1870–1871. Etude du rôle stratégique d'une place forte maritime' (Unpublished MA thesis, EPHE, 2007).

[4]   Martin Motte and Jean de Préneuf, 'L'écriture de l'histoire navale française à l'époque contemporaine: un modèle national?', *Revue historique des armées*, 257 (2009), 27–43.

[5]   Emmanuel Boulard, 'La défense des côtes. Une histoire interarmées (1815–1973)' (Unpublished Hist. Thesis, Sorbonne University, 2013); Jean de Préneuf, 'Entre Londres, Rome et Berlin. Les marins français et la figure mouvante de l'ennemi 1871–1914' in J. Ülbert (ed.) *Ennemi juré, ennemi naturel, ennemi héréditaire. Construction et instrumentalisation de la figure de l'ennemi. La France et ses adversaires (XVIe–XXe siècles)* (Hamburg, 2011), pp. 289–302; Frédéric Saffroy, *Le bouclier de Neptune. La politique de défense des bases françaises en Méditerranée (1912–1931)* (Rennes, 2015).

degrees by France's naval strategy at the time, known as the Jeune École [The Young School].

1815–70: a strategy aimed at deterring the British superpower

Up until the mid-nineteenth century, Paris wanted to amend the order arising from the Congress of Vienna and sought London's support or neutrality in this endeavour. Its aim was to place France at the heart of continental affairs and to obtain room for manoeuvre overseas. This is why the first two *ententes cordiales* were agreed between the two states in the 1830s and 1850s. A country that distrusted Caesarism and lagged behind Great Britain in terms of industry, France's priority was defending French territory, protecting trade and having a capacity for projection, even if there was no clear and immediate threat.

At sea, this involved adopting a stance of deterrence vis-à-vis the Royal Navy. When the Bourbon Restoration period began, the French navy had to make do with the fleet inherited from the First Empire, and it envisaged engaging in commerce raiding. It wanted to raise a select, modernised battle corps that operated on a war footing and was capable, in the event of crisis, of deterring a pre-emptive British attack or engaging in a conflict with a lesser navy. In the event of a global conflict with the British, the idea was to undertake commerce raiding and try to rally the continental powers around France's squadrons.[6] In 1857, the minister of the navy, Admiral Ferdinand Hamelin, believed that the navy would have to 'undoubtedly remain in second place' and, therefore, have 'a very effective, very threatening elite fleet' that was capable of unleashing 'terrible reprisals' on the shores of an aggressor in order to 'inspire a certain respect from her'. Britain was the target here, despite not being explicitly named.[7] To compensate for a structural inferiority, this strategy was based on innovation from the late 1840s. *Napoléon*, the first propeller-driven warship, and then the *Gloire*, the first ironclad steam frigate, were emblematic of this. However, Paris's initiatives aroused naval scares in Great Britain, such as those during the Oriental Crisis of 1840 and after Queen Victoria's visit to Cherbourg in 1863.

Down to 1870, the central part of the Channel was important in France's naval strategy. Protecting the coast was a priority, but funding for it was not forthcoming, resulting in coastal batteries being hastily built in times of crisis. On the other hand, costly investments were undertaken throughout the first half of the nineteenth century to make Cherbourg the main operating base in the Channel. Its development, begun under Louis XIV, was resumed

---

[6] P. Masson, *Histoire de la marine française*, vol. 2 (Paris, 1992), pp. 17–24, 48–61.

[7] Ferdinand Hamelin, *Rapport de son excellence M. le ministre de la Marine à l'Empereur sur la transformation de la flotte* (Paris, 1857), pp. 6–7.

from the First Empire. The artificial harbour was completed in 1813, and four slipways entered service in the same year and were then covered in 1820. The Bourbon Restoration saw the excavation of a second wet dock, which became operational in 1829. In 1838, the July Monarchy devised a plan for fortifications to protect an 850,000 m² dockyard, with a vote for a special budgetary allocation to complete them passed in 1841. The navy became a priority after an investigation into its state was launched in 1849 by the Second Republic. Strategic vision and budgetary spending therefore transcended changes in regime, even if efforts were sporadic and only resumed in times of crisis.

The Second Empire pursued the same policy, but the constancy of the effort, the priority given to Cherbourg, and the will to deploy part of the battle corps there represented a clear shift. In 1852, the decision was made to connect Cherbourg to the rail network, and until 1857 the completion of the port accounted for 40% of total spending on the French navy's port infrastructure. The completion of the Napoléon III basin in 1858 enshrined this initial effort. It included four dry docks, seven slipways and impressive hydraulic installations. The increased investment was also a response to the development that Portland and Alderney had been undergoing since the 1840s. France's momentum led to a British reaction: Alderney's port was enlarged, and its main powerful forts were built between 1856 and 1859.[8]

Between 1857 and 1870, Cherbourg had a real 'industrial quarter' of its own.[9] The port was given the explicit mission of becoming the French navy's second base, behind Toulon but ahead of Brest. Receiving a quarter of total infrastructure spending between 1853 and 1870, the Normandy port was the top priority between 1857 and 1869. Ultimately, the navy required it to have ten dry docks, compared to six in Brest, in order to support a first-rate force. In 1858 and 1859, keels were laid for one of the ironclad frigates that made up the backbone of the battle corps. The French navy's deterrent strategy was based on its ability to strike at the heart of the Royal Navy before it had finished mobilising. In 1863, an 'Ironclad Squadron' bringing together the most modern units was created. Major manoeuvres were organised in the western part of the Channel from Cherbourg, while in the 1840s, the battle corps was structured around the 'Squadron of Evolutions' stationed in Toulon. At this time, the Ironclad Squadron operated at sea for thirty-six consecutive days.[10]

The fact remained that Cherbourg was more a base in the making than one operating at its full potential. Most shipbuilding was done in Toulon and,

8   Trevor Davenport and Colin Partridge, *The Fortifications of Alderney* (Alderney, 1993), pp. 16–25.

9   Marlène Née, 'Arsenal et activités associées : les industries militaires à Cherbourg 1900–1939' (Unpublished Hist. Thesis, University of Caen, 2008).

10   Battesti, *La marine de Napoléon III*, pp. 174, 540, 564–72.

in this respect, Cherbourg was the second last of the five port-dockyards.[11] Meanwhile, the publicity surrounding the new offensive capabilities in the Channel weakened the era's *entente cordiale* and restarted an arms race that France could only lose to the British superpower. By the end of the Second Empire, the French navy had clearly been left behind, and Cherbourg still appeared vulnerable to the modernised bases facing it. As a result, from 1865, there began a rebalancing of investments and of deployment of forces that favoured Brest and, further afield, Toulon.

The war of 1870–1 revealed both the vulnerability and usefulness of Cherbourg, though the enemy was Prussian on this occasion. Although there was no fear of a major attack from the sea, the base's vulnerability to a ground assault became clear, especially once the Prussians crossed the Seine. Forced to improvise a defensive redoubt, the maritime prefect criticised the weakness of its close fortifications and lack of a defence in-depth system that included the capacity to flood the Cotentin Peninsula. On the other hand, mastery of the sea having been obtained by France during the conflict, Cherbourg supported operations in the North Sea and in the Baltic, despite its remoteness limiting how useful it could be. At a time when France's railways were overburdened or in Prussian hands, Cherbourg played a decisive role as a rear base from which to provide seaborne support to an isolated Army of the North, which was pinning down enemy forces far from Paris.[12] For the first time, Cherbourg, which was designed with Great Britain in mind, was used against Germany. Afterwards, from 1871 to the signing of the 1904 Entente Cordiale, a stance that was both anti-German and anti-British formed the core of France's strategy in the Channel.

1871–1905: British and German threats and the Jeune École

Following its defeat in the Franco-Prussian War and the end of the Paris Commune, France was in a weak state, and it faced the threat of intervention from Bismarck's Reich. A cautious policy vis-à-vis London and Berlin was adopted, and the priorities were to ensure political stability was maintained and to secure the departure of the occupying troops. In the short term, the most likely enemy was, unsurprisingly, Berlin, which had limited naval capabilities. Priority was therefore given to the army and to the north-east borders.

The French navy's proposed strategy in response to Germany was a continuation of what had prevailed during the Second Empire – that is, blocking its ports and raising the threat of a landing to pin down troops far from France. Cherbourg would play an important role in this arrangement. The strategy for countering Britain, which was deemed only a hypothetical threat, would now

[11] Battesti, *La marine de Napoléon III*, pp. 594–9.
[12] Chatelain, 'La place de Cherbourg dans la guerre franco-allemande'.

be limited to protecting the coast, defending interests in the Mediterranean and having the capacity – a deterrent one, it was hoped – to attack shipping in a way that did not contravene the Treaty of Paris of 1856. France's naval leadership took the view that this strategy had to be based on an ironclad fleet that required a partial update, fast and poorly protected cruisers that were being built and, finally, coastguard vessels and monitors.[13]

Although the overall strategy was endorsed by politicians, parliament only partially followed the recommendations made by the general staff, because the Republicans, who held a majority from 1876 and downplayed the threat at sea, sought to demonstrate their pre-eminence. As a result, parliament postponed completion of the 1872 programme to 1885. The navy was reduced to using the assets inherited from the Second Empire, whether these were already afloat or under construction. Just one modern ironclad was launched in 1876.[14] Amidst budgetary restrictions, priority was given to wooden cruisers that had multiple propulsion forms and little iron cladding or protection and which could carry out commerce raiding and overseas interventions. Laying the keel of six expensive coastguard vessels and monitors in the 1870s shows the importance accorded both to defending the coasts against London and bombarding the German coast.[15] In the Channel, the assets available were very modest. The navy relied primarily on Brest and, to a lesser extent, on Cherbourg. Investment in the latter was scaled back, particularly because the British stopped expanding Alderney's port in 1872. The Channel and North Sea Division only had an aviso and a cutter to monitor fisheries.[16]

However, from the late 1870s, the strategic stance was updated because the threat of a conflict with Berlin was now combined with rising tensions with Rome and the return of overseas tensions with London. Although everyone agreed on the perspective of a war with Italy, debate over how to prioritise and manage potential adversaries was fierce. This debate attracted much attention from politicians and the public. It was influenced by the analysis of the leading proponent of the Jeune École, Théophile Aube, whose followers remained a minority in the high command until 1914. The Jeune École advocated a more aggressive attitude towards both Great Britain and Italy. Aube also backed the

13 Conseil des travaux, *Procès-verbal de la séance du 18 octobre 1871*, SHD-MV BB8 1168 and Conseil d'Amirauté, *Procès-verbal de la séance du 28 février 1873*, SHD-MV BB8 1171, cited in Guy Pedroncini, *La défense sous la Troisième République*, vol. 2 (Vincennes, 1986), pp. 60–1, 356–69.

14 Theodore Ropp, *The Development of a Modern Navy. French Naval Policy, 1871–1904* (Annapolis, 1987, orig. 1937), pp. 26–42.

15 Robert Gardiner (ed.), *Conway's All the World's Fighting Ships. 1860–1905* (London, 1979), pp. 299–300.

16 *Inspection générale de la station de la Manche et de la mer du Nord*, 1878, SHD-MV 1001–4.

use of technological innovations to deter the Royal Navy. However, within this approach he did not prioritise fleet-on-fleet warfare. Instead, he called for a 'weak to strong' strategy in response to Britain, under which fleet-on-fleet combat would only be attempted around Toulon and on the basis of temporary local superiority. The main strategy that he proposed to deter London and to make the British seek a compromise peace in the event of conflict was commerce raiding. He took the view that, in order to prevent conflict, it was necessary to raise the threat of widespread terrorising warfare that was directed at civilian targets and waged through attacks on undefended coasts and the destruction of merchant ships − that is, through targeting populations and ships' crews. This 'industrial war' or 'all-out war' would be a release from the restrictive legislation that favoured British interests based on the control of trade flows. The stance was intended to act as a deterrent to a liberal nation whose government had to take civil society into account.[17] Aube ultimately saw unrestricted commerce raiding as part of a more aggressive coastal defence on the basis that 'only the threatening front created by maritime skirmishers will be able, by pushing the blockading squadron away from shore, to ensure that our ironclads can leave'. This would in turn allow commerce raiding to take place.[18]

Reflecting the majority opinion within the naval elites, Admiral Bourgois, president of the Commission for Submarine Defences from 1872 to 1879, accepted the use of commerce raiding. But he challenged the legitimacy and effectiveness of the Jeune École's interpretation of it, variously for technical and ethical reasons and, above all, for political and strategic ones: in his view, failure to respect the law would cause neutrals to side with Great Britain. Above all, more so than Rome or London, the main enemy could only be Germany, as it would be able to reach Paris.[19] Ultimately, until 1914, the Jeune École's approach was followed not at all or only partially by the majority of naval figures and members of parliament alike. Despite the torpedo boat, armoured cruiser and submarine crazes, a balanced approach was adopted. Until 1914, warfare instructions prohibited the bombarding of undefended cities and unrestricted war on commerce.[20] After the Triple Alliance was signed in 1882, the French naval leadership ceased to rule out the prospect of a war in

---

[17] Martin Motte, *Une éducation géostratégique. La pensée navale française de la Jeune Ecole à 1914* (Paris, 2004), pp. 167–75; Arne Røksund, *The Jeune Ecole: The Strategy of the Weak* (Leiden, 2007), pp. 7–23.

[18] Théophile Aube, *La guerre maritime et les ports militaires de la France* (Paris-Nancy, 1882), p. 73.

[19] Motte, *Une éducation géostratégique*, pp. 218–23; Røksund, *The Jeune Ecole*, pp. 24–38.

[20] *Facsimile des instructions de guerre*, SHD MV BB4 2437 and 2680b (1895–1908), 2681 and SS Ed 38 (1908–14).

two theatres. The threat of the Triple Alliance continued to be prioritised over that of the British, except during the Fashoda Incident. To counter the alliance, the battle corps continued to be made up of ironclads. The Jeune École's influence was nevertheless felt, especially during the ministries of Aube in 1886–7 and of Pelletan in 1902–05, with, on the one hand, the construction of flotillas to protect the coast and, on the other hand, the establishment of a force for attacking shipping.

Specifically, Aube required priority to be given to the Mediterranean[21] because 'it is first of all necessary to envisage joint action by Germany and Italy against us'.[22] He convinced the Admiralty Council to bring together in Toulon the first-class ironclads and the best vessels from the flotillas. The idea was to gain control of the sea there through a decisive battle fought against the Italian navy at the start of a war, then to bombard the transalpine coastline and, in the event of a conflict with London, to attack the route to India. For Aube, whom the naval general staff followed on this point, fleet-on-fleet combat in the Channel would be hopeless. In the absence of control over this sea, the aim would be to prevent a close-range blockade. This would involve stationing flotillas of torpedo boats all along the coast. These would be responsible for mobile defence, alongside the coastguard vessels already in service in military ports, where it was also necessary to strengthen the fixed defences. In this narrow sea with heavy traffic, these flotillas could also operate against British merchants. Because Cherbourg was a poorly defended 'trove of bombs and shells' that was exposed to bombardment by a fleet, to attacks by torpedo boats sent from Alderney, or even to a raid, the main units had to be based in Brest. However, during Aube's ministry, this strategy's lack of credibility was revealed during manoeuvres organised in the Mediterranean in 1886, around Toulon and Corsica. Torpedo boats failed to halt passage through a strait, destroy a fleet at anchor or prevent an attack on a base.[23] This did not bode well for what could happen around Cherbourg, which, unlike Toulon, could not be located closer to the Royal Navy's centre of gravity and its advanced support point in Alderney.

Coastal defence was another blind spot. Most fortifications were being made obsolete by advances in artillery technology. A commission meeting in January 1887 recommended the immediate modernisation of batteries and the abandonment of the idea of a fortified line to focus on military ports. While the ministry of war controlled reform, the law of 27 May 1889 decommissioned a thousand structures, many of which had been built in the 1840s. A decree dated 13 May 1890 specified the division of responsibilities between

---

21 EMGM/1, 3 March 1887, SHD MV BB4 1452.

22 Note from VA Jaurès to the minister, 1887, SHD-MV BB4 1452.

23 VA Bourgois, *Les torpilleurs, la guerre navale et la défense des côtes* (Paris, 1888), pp. 273–8, analysed in Motte, *Une éducation géostratégique*, pp. 217–18.

the ministry of the navy and the ministry of war, but it only heightened the confusion. Maritime prefects commanded the defence of the coasts only in wartime and under the authority of the minister of war (and these provisions did not apply, for example, in Dunkirk).[24] These coastal-defence shortcomings jeopardised the credibility of the strategy, which had in part been readjusted in line with Aube's ideas.

From 1890, as a result of the Triple Alliance's persistent hostility and the lack of credibility of Russia, France's ally, Paris continued to prioritise the combination of German and Italian threats while targeting London to a greater degree, Britain's objective having been the 'two-power standard' since 1889. France's naval policy consequently evolved towards a multi-directional stance that was made official by the programme of 1890. It lasted until around 1905–06 – even, perhaps, until as late as 1908. The French navy anticipated a conflict against each of the other powers, and the possibility of a confrontation with the Royal Navy alone was reassessed. At the same time, the naval general staff readied itself for the scenario of a coalition between Great Britain and the Triple Alliance.

This strategy was inevitably flexible in nature. By 1895, the overall plan had been established. Major operations off the coast of Brittany, whether against the Triple Alliance or the Royal Navy, were anticipated. From 1889, the First Ironclad Division was stationed in Brest; it was renamed 'Northern Squadron' in 1892 and became commanded by a vice admiral rather than by a rear admiral, as it previously had been. A lack of dry docks in Toulon was the primary reason why a substantial force continued to be stationed in Brest; the Mediterranean Squadron otherwise remained a priority. The plan in the event of a war against the Triple Alliance was for the fleet concentrated in Toulon to fight an initial battle of attrition against the Italian navy before the latter could combine with the Austrian fleet. Only afterwards would they move to an offensive stance against the HSF in the Channel and North Sea.[25] At the outset, the seven ironclads (only one of which was recently built) and the four coastguard vessels of the Northern Squadron would have to be confined to 'defending and protecting our coasts' for the time that it took for the Mediterranean Squadron to reach Brest, or even Cherbourg. The two squadrons, brought together in a 'naval armed force', would then wage a second battle of attrition off the coast of Brittany. Enabling forces from the south to reach Brest before the HSF's arrival was therefore essential. The commander-in-chief of the Northern Squadron took the view in 1891 that Cherbourg was the best support point for slowing down the HSF's descent towards the Atlantic; Dunkirk was considered too exposed and Brest too far away.[26]

[24] Saffroy, *Le bouclier de Neptune*, pp. 40–5.
[25] CSM, *Procès-verbal de la séance du 2 décembre 1894*, SHD-MV BB8 2424-2.
[26] Letter from VA Gervais to the minister, 19 December 1891, and correspondence

While the Northern Squadron's commanders focused on the German threat, the CSM was equally preparing for a conflict against Great Britain. As was the case during the Aube ministry, the naval leadership believed that waging a fleet-on-fleet war in the Channel would be suicidal, especially since war plans emphasised Cherbourg's vulnerability to Alderney, which was turned into a torpedo base in 1891.[27] This analysis led to a continued preference for Brest as an operating base over Cherbourg. In this context, Lieutenant Degouy unsuccessfully pleaded with the ESM for the battle corps to be concentrated in Brest, pointing out that deploying part of it in Cherbourg would be perceived as a provocation by London.[28] The failure to complete the building of dry docks at Cherbourg that would have been capable of accommodating the recently built armoured cruisers, some of which were longer than the old ironclads, also favoured their being based in Brest. Against the Royal Navy in the Channel, the French navy had to settle for providing close-quarter self-defence of bases and waging a campaign of commerce raiding. The CSM issued a reminder that these operations needed to be conducted in accordance with international law.[29] This restriction was rejected by supporters of the Jeune École such as Degouy; they were still a minority, though they were well represented at the ESM. In Degouy's view, from the start of a conflict, the fastest cruisers based in Brest should attack Britain's slower coastal shipping trade. They would also have the mission of launching attacks against the coast, which would be aimed at civilian and military ports alike. The objective of these rapid attacks was to disrupt the enemy's mobilisation and to hit their morale.[30]

The ships responsible for carrying out these operations and assisting the ironclads had partly been updated. Henceforth, rather than using coastal-defence torpedo boats that were not well suited to the high seas, commerce raiding would be conducted using 'armoured cruisers' that were well armed and protected as well as fast; and capable of surprising squadrons with their speed and then escaping as quickly as they had attacked. The most influential backer of them was Rear Admiral Fournier. His book, published in 1896 and completed before his appointment to the command of the new ESM, attracted significant attention.[31] Emblematic of this strategy was the *Dupuy de Lôme*,

received from the commander-in-chief of the Northern Squadron, in particular SHD-MV BB4 2437.

27 Confidential memorandum from the naval general staff envisaging measures to be taken in the event of war with Britain, 2 April 1898, SHD-MV BB⁴ 2681.

28 LV Degouy, *Marines étrangères. Marines anglaise, allemande et italienne*, vol. 2 (Paris, 1897–8), p. 291 et seq., SHD-MV 1 CC 211.

29 EMGM/3, *Opérations de guerre. Guerre maritime contre l'Angleterre*, décembre 1892, SHD MV BB4 2437, cited in Røksund, *The Jeune Ecole*, p. 109.

30 LV Degouy, *Marines étrangères*, vol. 2, p. 291 et seq., SHD-MV 1 CC 211.

31 CA F. E. Fournier, *La flotte nécessaire. Ses avantages stratégiques, tactiques*

a solidly armed and fast vessel with a long range, which entered service in 1895 and was stationed in Brest. Several increasingly imposing and expensive ships inspired by it were ordered, and until 1898 the navy was determined to line up no fewer than twenty-five 'protected cruisers'. With their light artillery, their weakly armoured bridge and their lack of an armoured belt, these vessels were intended for overseas operations. But their value was limited: they were slower than liners and vulnerable to the Royal Navy.[32]

Whereas the development of cruisers did not improve the French navy's credibility vis-à-vis British commerce on the high seas, the beginnings of submarine weaponry were promising. This was particularly the case when it came to deterring a close-range blockade or to attacking bases. During the 1898 manoeuvres, the *Gustave Zédé* successfully launched torpedoes against the ironclad *Magenta* while the latter was moored by Toulon. Above all, during the 1901 manoeuvres, having admittedly been towed to the scene from Toulon, it managed to launch an inert torpedo at the flagship *Charles Martel*, which led the fleet that played the role of a British squadron blockading Ajaccio.[33] According to Maxime Laubeuf, the linking of the submarine with the mobile-defence torpedo boat was the solution to finally making the ban on the close-range blockade credibly enforceable. In his view, submarine weaponry also had to make it possible to attack the Royal Navy in its ports.[34] The *Narval*, a submersible torpedo boat launched in October 1899, designed by Laubeuf and built in the Cotentin Peninsula, had a longer range, both when submerged and on the surface, than its predecessor. The vessel ought to 'arrive, having left Cherbourg or Brest at nightfall, at the English ports before daylight, go underwater and torpedo the ships entering the harbours'.[35] When it was tested in May 1900, the *Narval* demonstrated its offensive capabilities: departing from Cherbourg, it reached Brest having travelled, partially submerged, along the Brittany coast for forty-eight hours, surfacing in harbour at Brest without having been spotted.[36] Edouard Lockroy, the minister of the navy who encouraged its construction, immediately ordered similar units to be built, but parliament limited how many would be commissioned. The submarine's contribution to French strategy remained limited.

At the same time, criticisms of France's coastal defence were increasing: Should a continuous mobile defence be maintained, or should the focus be on naval bases? Should the deployment of specialised flotillas combining torpedo

---

et économiques (Paris-Nancy, 1896).

[32] Ropp, *The Development of a Modern Navy*, pp. 284–90 and 294–7.

[33] T. Ropp, *The Development of a Modern Navy*, p. 351.

[34] Armor (pseudonym of Maxime Laubeuf), *Les sous-marins et la guerre contre l'Angleterre* (Paris, 1899), pp. 12–17.

[35] Laubeuf, quoted by H. Le Masson, *Propos maritimes* (Paris, 1970), p. 97.

[36] Reported by Røksund in *The Jeune Ecole*, pp. 192–3.

boats and coastal submarines continue, or should operations be confined to a static defence coupled with offshore actions by squadrons? How could a choice be made between torpedo boats, submarines and coastguard vessels? And should all coastal defence be entrusted to the navy?

Like almost all the sailors and elected officials from the coast, Lieutenant Albert Grasset, assigned in 1894 to the naval general staff to define coastal-defence doctrine, argued in vain for the navy to have sole control over this domain. He believed that

> operating bases must be few in number so as to be better defended. Indeed, they must be able to repel the enemy's attacks by their own means and without cooperation from vessels, which must have full freedom of action and be sure that these positions will always be able to support them when they return to the coast.[37]

On this point, however, he was almost alone. Supporters of an almost continuous defensive cordon found powerful intermediaries among the coast's elected officials, who dominated the Naval Commission. Coastal populations were reassured by the proximity of these small units. Moreover, because the Cotentin Peninsula's landings seemed conducive to naval guerrilla warfare, hydrographic missions were launched, a route book was drafted and pilots were trained. In early 1898, the navy amassed 180 numbered torpedo boats that were deployed from Dunkirk to Tunis. But their military value remained questionable, as did that of the four coastguard vessels on duty within the Northern Squadron. The squadron's commander-in-chief complained about their inability to operate in rough seas, which amounted to a crippling handicap in the Channel. One of the most critical members of parliament was Charles Cabart-Daneville, a deputy and then a senator from Manche, an influential member of the Extra-Parliamentary Commission for the Navy in 1894 and the author in 1895 of a work entitled *La défense de nos côtes* [Defence of Our Coasts].[38] Cabart-Daneville was close with Vice Admiral Jules Cavelier de Cuverville, who had been Cherbourg's maritime prefect and was now naval chief of staff, as well as with Edouard Lockroy, the minister of the navy during the Fashoda Incident, and he denounced the coastal defence system's unfitness by using the examples of the Cotentin Peninsula (viewed from Great Britain) and Corsica (viewed from Italy). Although he thought that Cherbourg was fairly well defended against an attack from the sea, he believed it remained very vulnerable to a ground assault launched following a raid on the western coast of the Cotentin Peninsula.[39]

---

[37] LV Albert Grasset, *La défense des côtes* (Paris-Nancy, 1899), p. 601.
[38] Charles Cabart-Danneville, *La défense de nos côtes* (Paris, 1895).
[39] Saffroy, *Le bouclier de Neptune*, pp. 46–50.

On the eve of the Fashoda Incident and at the end of a decade of controversy, the 1897 operational plan (completed in April 1898, as it could not be submitted to the CSM before the crisis) was a continuation of the stance sketched out in 1890. It envisaged that the Northern Squadron's ironclads would converge on Brest to play the role of a 'fleet in being' to pin down as many British forces as possible far from Toulon. Only the armoured cruisers *Dupuy de Lôme* and *Pothuau*, accompanied by the cruiser *Friant*, would leave Brest to 'create disturbances among commercial arrivals near the British coasts, taking care to avoid fighting a superior force', while flying divisions would engage in commerce raiding in the Atlantic and the flotillas would push back the close-range blockade.[40]

This stance was unrealistic, and Fashoda put an end to it. In the summer of 1898, the French navy did not have a credible operational plan, and it remained a 'fleet of samples' that was inferior to the Royal Navy in quality and quantity.[41] And so the minister noted in late 1899 that 'if we are proposing to hunt British commerce with armoured cruisers, we will see that the English have enough to chase our own cruisers and destroy them before ours have taken or destroyed Great Britain's merchant ships'.[42] Moreover, at the start of the Fashoda Incident, the navy was not ready. Between 40% and 50% of the ironclads and cruisers and 60% of the torpedo boats were unavailable, and the ironclads of the Northern Squadron were fully equipped for only eight months of the year. The situation was critical in Brest and, especially, in Cherbourg. Its stocks of ammunition and coal were insufficient, with coaling taking more than eight days, while its forts were not ready to repel a surprise attack. In Brest, a quarter of the guns could not be armed owing to a lack of personnel. Emergency measures were taken, including the deployment of artillerymen from the French army in October.[43] Lockroy had a law passed on bases and support points so that the main ports, including Cherbourg, could be equipped with modern dry docks and thus accommodate ironclad squadrons. Lastly, he submitted a bill on coastal defences, but it was not voted on prior to his departure. The text provided for new torpedo-boat stations equipped with rapid-fire cannons, which would act as flank guards for the main bases. So that they could operate in a coordinated manner, the torpedo boats were then subdivided into offensive and defensive flotillas that were linked by telegraphs

[40] Renée Masson, 'La marine française lors de la crise de Fachoda (1898–1899)' (Unpublished PhD dissertation, Sorbonne University, 1955), pp. 54–6.

[41] For a detailed analysis of the French fleet's weaknesses, see Masson, 'La marine française', p. 34.

[42] Jean-Louis de Lanessan, *Rapport sur la flotte française*, November 1899, SHD-MV BB4 2437.

[43] Masson, 'La marine française', pp. 72, 87–90, 94–6.

and semaphores to the squadrons. The deep-sea torpedo boats with a larger tonnage would operate in direct contact with the squadrons.[44]

Owing to the scale of the crisis that the Fashoda Incident entailed, in January 1899 the admirals were consulted on the strategy to be followed. A war against the Triple Alliance or Great Britain was to be considered, 'these two possibilities needing to be contemplated without the possibility of ordering them urgently'. Only three admirals wanted to make the Atlantic the main theatre in order to counter both the Royal Navy and the HSF. Ten of the CSM's fourteen members thought that 'the scenario of a possible agreement between Italy and England suggested to the admirals even more forcefully the need not to give up playing the important role in the Mediterranean that our situation requires of us'. A consensus was reached to maintain the defensive stance in the Channel and to provide de facto validation of the rationale behind the division of forces decided in October, only for Lockroy, concerned with strengthening the squadrons' homogeneity, to approve the transfer of a recent ironclad and four coastguard vessels from the Northern Squadron to the Mediterranean Squadron. Once again, a lack of infrastructure in Toulon was primarily what prevented the transfer of the six second-line ironclads still stationed in Brest.[45]

Only the compromise negotiated by France's ministry of foreign affairs allowed an end to the Fashoda Incident. At no point did the French navy appear to be capable of deterring the Royal Navy, let alone of winning a protracted global war. In the words of Théophile Delcassé, the architect of the rapprochement with London, 'France does not have the navy of its diplomacy' and vice versa. He also pointed out the mismatch between naval strategy and both financial and industrial resources.[46]

Paris's uncertainty over the attitude to adopt towards London continued for several years. In 1899 and 1900, deterring a preventive attack remained the most pressing issue. The operational plan, which still foresaw the Mediterranean Squadron's moving north to Brest, was once again deemed unrealistic by Vice Admiral Alfred Gervais, who would be admiral of the fleet in the event of war. This anglophile was responsible for devising the major manoeuvres of 1900, which centred on a conflict with the Royal Navy. Due to Gibraltar acting as a lock, he envisaged conducting separate operations in the Mediterranean and the Atlantic. Because the former was considered a priority, he wanted to keep the bulk of the first-rate vessels in Toulon.[47] In *La défense navale*

---

[44] Ropp, *The Development of a Modern Navy*, pp. 341–3.

[45] CSM, *Résumé de ses avis et décisions prises par le ministre séance du 11 janvier 1899*, SHD-MV BB8 2424–5.

[46] Daniel Moucheboeuf, 'L'œuvre navale de Delcassé de 1907 à 1913: Élément d'une politique de puissance' (Unpublished MA thesis, Sciences Po, 2001), p. 44.

[47] VA Alfred Gervais to the minister, 'Manœuvres navales de 1900', January 1900, SHD-MV BB4 2437.

[Naval Defence], a work that had a major impact, Lockroy acknowledged the structural imbalance of forces as well as divergences between London's and Paris's interests. He therefore did not rule out a rapprochement with Berlin and imagined an alliance of the continental navies that would bring France, Germany and Russia together against Britain.[48] This stance found backers within the navy – for example, Vice Admiral Bienaimé, the navy's chief of staff between May 1900 and February 1902, as well as certain instructors at the ESM[49] – but remained a minority position. Lanessan, a supporter of the Entente Cordiale and Lockroy's successor, disapproved of it. At its meeting of 31 May 1901, the CSM definitively rejected the idea of concentrating the bulk of the fleet in Brest in order to be able to confront the Royal Navy and the HSF, a proposal that had previously been put forward by the first section of the naval general staff, which was under Bienaimé's orders, in May 1900.[50] The strategy implemented by Lanessan aimed to give credibility to the ministry of foreign affair's policy of seeking to convince London that following the logic of confrontation that had prevailed since Fashoda was risky, and also that Great Britain had an interest in finding a modus vivendi with France. This approach required a fleet rebalanced around an updated and homogeneous battle corps. Lanessan ensured that the six *PATRIE* battleships provided for under the 1900 naval programme, voted for under Lockroy, were built. In May 1902, keels were laid for thirteen *AIGRETTE*-type 'submersible torpedo boats' that were based on the *Narval*. These units were intended to operate with squadrons or to attack enemy bases. In July 1902, a simulated attack carried out by four units from Cherbourg seemed to prove him right: without having been spotted, they surfaced in Brest's harbour, four hundred metres from the coastal-defence ironclad *Fulminant*.[51]

When it came to the central Channel, however, doubts persisted about France's ability to prevent an attack. Lockroy believed that Alderney made a 'vigorous unannounced offensive' against Cherbourg possible.[52] The front page of *Le Petit Parisien* described these islands in the spring of 1899 as 'the British vanguard against France'.[53] The Channel Islands became part of public debate because many voters made a living from fishing and supporting the mobile-defence forces. The position of the Franco-British maritime boundaries

[48] Edouard Lockroy, *La défense navale* (Paris-Nancy, 1899), pp. 54–5.

[49] Motte, *Une éducation géostrategique*, pp. 202–3.

[50] CV Henri Saulces de Freycinet, *Étude sur la concentration des forces maritimes, 11 mai 1900*, SHD-MV BB4 2427. Cited in John R. Walser, 'France's Search for a Battlefleet. French Naval Policy, 1898–1914' (Unpublished PhD thesis, University of North Carolina, 1976), p. 166 and J.-L. de Lanessan, *Notre défense maritime* (Paris, 1914), p. 153.

[51] Motte, *Une éducation géostrategique*, p. 481.

[52] Lockroy, *La défense navale*, p. 28.

[53] *Le Petit Parisien*, 30 April 1899.

around the Islands also took on a military dimension. In 1903, Camille Pelletan, the minister of the navy from June 1902 to May 1905, complained, for example, about 'the occupation of the Minquiers, English ownership of which, if I am not mistaken, has never been recognised, [which] would be a most serious threat to our shores'.[54] Alderney's proximity was therefore taken into account in the plan to revise the Northern Squadron's war plans in 1902. This was one of the reasons why the naval general staff favoured Brest.[55]

The last flames of an anti-British stance could be seen burning until around 1905 or 1906.[56] Pelletan, the architect of a return to the ideas of the Jeune École that was as parodical as it was ineffective, was obsessed with defending the coast. He decreed an end to large-scale manoeuvres, halted the construction of the *PATRIE* and *AIGRETTE* vessels, and encouraged the building of small units configured to continuous coastal defence.[57] The decree on these measures, issued on 18 September 1904, stipulated that the ministry of war would continue to share responsibility for coastal defence.[58] Notwithstanding a few flare-ups after 1905, an anti-British stance became a fringe position. To call the Royal Navy the 'hereditary enemy' in the course of service − as in 1906 did Captain Darrieus, a Mahanian officer in charge of strategy and tactics at the ANS − was extremely rare.[59] In December 1905, the most influential heir of the Jeune École, Vice Admiral Fournier, who was designated admiral of the fleet in the event of war, proposed a programme that aimed more at deterring London than at confronting it. The CSM rejected his idea of a navy whose core of offensive capabilities would consist of a force of deep-sea submarines.[60] Having to envisage operations against Germany, Fournier questioned the credibility of the war plans, especially in relation to the Channel. Proving that he was not obsessed with a conflict with London, he advised against the concentration of first-rate forces in Brest, because doing so would leave none in the Mediterranean to counter Italy, and there would be a risk of being blockaded at Brest once the HSF travelled southwards at the outbreak of a conflict. For Fournier, Cherbourg remained a secondary base whose flotillas could slow down the HSF. But the most likely scenario was that the decisive fight would be fought in the Bay of Biscay against the Germans, who would have bypassed the British Isles. He therefore argued

---

[54] Letter to the minister of foreign affairs, 28 May 1903, MAE 161 CPCOM 5.

[55] *Instructions secrètes A4, du ministre au vice-amiral commandant en chef l'Escadre du Nord*, n.d. [1902], SHD-MV BB⁴ 2681.

[56] Préneuf, 'Entre Londres, Rome et Berlin', pp. 298–300.

[57] Røksund, *The Jeune Ecole*, pp. 216–17.

[58] Saffroy, *Le bouclier de Neptune*, pp. 54–6.

[59] CV Gabriel Darrieux, *Stratégie et tactique. La doctrine*, 1906, SHD-MV, 1 CC 197.

[60] CSM, minutes of the sessions held in December 1905, SHD-MV BB4 2437.

for a second option that was adopted by the naval general staff. It consisted in concentrating the first-rate forces at Toulon, including the cruisers from Brest, and in keeping only coastguard vessels in the westerly port, with the coastguard vessels in Toulon added to those in Brest.[61] From mid-1906, a turn was taken towards adopting a Mahanian strategy based on a partnership with London. The navy would combine in the Mediterranean against the Italian fleet and would entrust the Royal Navy with deterring the HSF. Henceforth, rivalry with London in the Channel was limited to the distribution of responsibilities vis-à-vis the HSF.

Conclusion

Before 1906, the Channel Islands had a bearing on France's naval strategy in the Channel owing to the challenge that they represented for Cherbourg. Before Germany emerged as a threat, when only the anticipation of a conflict with London was at stake, the development of infrastructure on the Islands did not prevent impressive development of the Cherbourg base. It was the linchpin of a deterrence strategy that was based on linking a 'stone navy' with a fleet at the cutting edge of technological developments. Although the proximity of modernised British bases ultimately led the French navy to choose Brest as the main base in the Channel, Cherbourg, 'this pistol pointed at the City', continued by its mere presence to play the role of what one could describe as a 'base in being', in the same way as one speaks of a 'fleet in being'. Between 1871 and 1906, Cherbourg's status also depended on the link that was made between the threats from Britain and Germany, a matter that was a real squaring of the circle for the French navy. Brest was clearly prioritised, and Cherbourg played an auxiliary role to protect the coast, take the lead in anti-British commerce raiding and slow down the HSF's journey southwards. Fashoda sealed the failure of this strategy, before the Entente Cordiale partially changed the situation. The place of the Channel Islands in French naval strategy is therefore an excellent barometer of French foreign policy, which from 1815 sought, in part via the deterrent effect provided by the French navy, to obtain a margin of independence in the face of the British superpower, and even obtain support from it.

---

[61] VA E. Fournier, *Mesures préparatoires à prendre d'urgence dans la flotte française en prévision d'une brusque agression de l'Allemagne, Rapport au ministre,* 18 January 1906, SHD-MV BB4 2437.

8

Commanding the Channel: the Channel Islands in British Grand Strategy, 1814–1914

ANDREW LAMBERT

Beginning in the late 1780s the strategic geography of the English Channel and Western Approaches would be fundamentally altered by the construction of large artificial harbours, extending existing ports into deep water and enhancing their security against wind and tide. While Cherbourg, Plymouth and Holyhead pre-dated steam shipping, later works at Dover, Portland and Alderney and French harbour upgrades at St Malo, Granville, Dunkirk and Calais, were influenced by the prospect that future wars in the Channel would be fought by steam ships. Steam navigation posed a particular challenge for the Channel Islands, which lacked the local capital to acquire and operate steamers, and the floating harbours needed to operate them efficiently. While some islanders tried to persuade the British Government to build such harbours, the new technology significantly reduced the Islands' offensive strategic potential. After 1830 local naval operations would be shaped by steam, not small sailing vessels. Island privateering was no longer a significant asset, but the Islands remained critical to commanding the Channel. Their security became a national priority and required new harbours.

The Channel resumed its central place in British grand strategy after the 1814–15 Treaties of Paris and Vienna, where British diplomacy helped shape a European system to resist French expansion in Europe, while the Waterloo campaign demonstrated how the Castlereagh/Wellington diplomatic and strategic 'System' worked. With France constrained by the 1815 borders the only significant strategic threat it could pose to Britain would be against merchant shipping, especially at the focal point in the Channel and Western Approaches. As all French regimes between 1815 and 1870 attempted to secure domestic support by overturning the Vienna Settlement, these attempts frequently reduced Anglo-French relations to diplomatic crises and arms racing. It would be against the background of heightened tension that Britain developed a series of new naval stations to support steam warfare in the Channel, specifically to counter the emerging naval base at Cherbourg.

The Channel Islands remained a critical element in this response. In late 1830 former Prime Minister Wellington became anxious about their security, fearing a 'Revolutionary' French government would use war to maintain domestic credibility, encouraged by a francophile Whig administration that deliberately weakened links with Austria, Prussia and Russia, which had hitherto restrained France, and secured Britain's vital interests in Europe, keeping Belgium and the River Scheldt outside France.[1] When Anglo-French relations improved in the mid-1830s strategic anxieties shifted to the challenge of Imperial Russia.[2]

Concern for the security of the Channel Islands emerged in the 1820s, achieving national prominence as part of the wider strategic priority of securing command of the Channel, from the Thames Estuary to the Scillies, when Anglo-French relations deteriorated in the late 1830s. The Channel became the focus for a complex of naval, navigational, engineering, technological and economic issues that reshaped British strategy for industrial warfare. In 1828 Captain John Ross RN called for 'Harbours of Refuge' on the coasts of Kent and Sussex as bases for steam warships to defend Britain's floating trade from enemy vessels.[3] The limited endurance of contemporary steamships necessitated one or more secure floating harbours between Sheerness and Portsmouth.[4] The initial focus was on Dover, the packet station and fortress commanding the narrows. After a decade of inaction, Dover MP Edward Rice called for an inquiry into the harbours on the south-eastern coast in May 1839, linking security with the needs of rapidly expanding cross-Channel steam communications. Although Whig Chancellor of the Exchequer Sir Thomas Spring-Rice recognised the need he implied the matter might be addressed by 'private and local efforts'. Admiral Sir Edward Codrington, Liberal MP for Devonport, shifted the debate to national security, amending the motion to ensure any harbour project would consider the needs of war, because: 'if war arose, it was in the narrow seas more especially, ... because, ... steamers

[1]   Lambert, A. D. 'The Wellington system and national strategy, 1814–1852'. Unpub conference paper. Wellington Congress Southampton University, April 2019. Muir *Wellington Waterloo and the Fortunes of Peace 1814–1852*. London, Yale 2015 pp. 404–5.

[2]   Partridge, M. S. *Military Planning for the Defence of the United Kingdom 1814–1870*. London, Greenwood Press 1989 pp. 18–19.

[3]   Ross, Captain John. *A Treatise on Navigation by Steam, comprising a history of the steam engine, and an essay towards a system of the naval tactics peculiar to steam navigation as applicable to commerce and maritime warfare, including a comparison of its advantages as related to other systems in the circumstances of Speed, Safety and Economy, but more particularly in that of National Defence*. London, Longman 1828 pp. xviii–xix.

[4]   Hasenson, A. *The History of Dover Harbour*. London, ASPE 1980 pp. 80–1.

could run over very rapidly'.[5] In July the Admiralty appointed a six-man committee to examine the options for a floating harbour on the south-east coast of England, led by Rear Admiral Sir James Alexander Gordon.[6] It included a hydrographer, officers of the Royal Engineers and Royal Artillery, an Elder Brother of Trinity House and two Civil Engineers, including James Walker, the leading authority on harbours. Tasked to consider the strategic issues and advise on harbour construction the Committee reported in May 1840. While 'a perfect harbour of refuge is capable of receiving any class of vessels, under all circumstances of wind and tide', there were no such harbours between the Nore and Selesy Bill. The Committee recommended new harbours at Dover, Beachy Head, Margate and Foreness, at the alarming cost of £2 million, providing shelter from the weather and 'stations for armed steam vessels'.[7] Dover was the critical location, requiring a large artificial harbour. Francis Baring, the new Chancellor of the Exchequer, requested an estimate for building such a harbour in three years.[8] While Lt Colonel Thompson RE and Captain Francis Beaufort, Hydrographer of the Navy, reported favourably on the design nothing was done.

Edward Rice revived the issue in March 1841, shortly after Britain and France went to the brink of war over Syria.[9] He cited Codrington's clinching argument, 'in the narrow sea of the British Channel, in consequence of the application of steam navigation, this country was most assailable', and remarks by new French Prime Minister Francois Guizot, that strong defences were the best method of preserving peace, before observing that France had recently voted £5.6 million for harbour work over ten years. With the Cherbourg breakwater approaching completion, and other French harbour works in hand, 'better harbours on the south-eastern coast were not only necessary for our public navy but for our commercial marine'. Pointedly reminding the House that the 1840 Commission estimate for new and improved harbours was approximately £2 million Baring advised rejecting the motion. While agreeing there was no need to review the report Tory leader Sir Robert Peel skilfully blamed the Government for inaction and blocked the motion.

Within weeks the Whig ministry had fallen. Peel's intervention ensured his new Government was not saddled with a potentially costly enquiry. The Channel faded into the background while Peel exploited another brief Anglo-French entente to balance the budget. Although there was no budget for new

5   Commons Debate 2.5.1839 *Hansard* vol. 47 cc734–7.
6   O'Byrne, W. R. *A Naval Biographical Dictionary.* London, John Murray 1849 pp. 409–10.
7   PP 1840 (365) XXVIII pp. 1–18.
8   Hasenson. pp. 99–100.
9   *Hansard* HofC Debate Harbours on the South East Coast 18.3.1841 vol. 57 cc337–48.

defences or harbours the military authorities were processing the lessons of the Syrian Crisis and the rapid growth of steam navigation, prompting the Government to act in the late spring of 1842. General Sir George Murray, Master General of the Ordnance, checked the local fortifications and discussed the issue with the Home Secretary, former First Lord of the Admiralty (1830–4), Sir James Graham.[10] With existing forts being inadequate against a serious attack by steam warships, Murray began practical, economic improvements.[11] His first thought was for the security of Alderney, which would depend on steam communications with the mainland. It needed a fort to protect the harbour if the rest of the island was overrun.[12] Graham was anxious to avoid a vote in Parliament.[13]

In early July Codrington, now Commander-in-Chief at Portsmouth, used a private letter to the Admiralty to highlight the weakness of coastal artillery in the Islands, and cited local experts; hydrographer Martin White, Jersey militia Colonel John le Couteur and Commander Robilliard of the Jersey-based fishery protection vessel HMS *Seaflower*.[14] Codrington put the Channel Islands back on the Admiralty agenda; Lord Haddington, First Lord of the Admiralty, forwarded the letter to Murray and Peel, who was 'quite alive to its great importance'.[15]

To counter the speed and mobility of steamers coastal batteries needed traversing platforms and powerful artillery. Jersey had two 8-inch shell guns and a few 32-pounders, which could stop war steamers, but Guernsey relied on inadequate old 24-pounders.[16] When the Cabinet met to discuss 'the defences of the Channel Islands', on 23 July, Chancellor Henry Goulburn was anxious

---

[10] George Murray to Sir Frederick Mulcaster IGF 30.5.1842: WO/9/16–17. Sir James Graham to Murray 8.6.1842: WO 80/4/24.

[11] Murray to Graham 1.6.1842: WO 80/4/11 The inconsistency in dating needs to be addressed.

[12] Murray to Mulcaster Draft 3.6.1842 & Mulcaster to Murray 6.6.1842: WO 80/4/1 & 7–8. Murray to Graham 4.6.1842 Private: WO 80/4/16–7. see Partridge 1989 pp. 96–7 for the 1830s.

[13] Graham to Murray 6.6.1842: WO 80/4/14–5.

[14] Bourchier, Lady. *Memoir of the Life of Admiral Sir Edward Codrington: with selections from his public and private correspondence.* London, Longman 1873 2 vols, 2. p. 516. There is ample evidence of Codrington's interest in the Channel Islands in his papers, e.g. COD 20/4 One Jersey Papers; Codrington to Sidney Herbert 11.7.1842 No.116 with enclosures and plan on chart; Colonel le Couteur to Codrington 25.6.1842; Captain Martin White to Codrington 25.6.1842.

[15] Haddington to Murray 15.7.1842: WO 80/4/48–9. Peel, who had visited Jersey and St Malo in 1836, had some understanding of the location; Gash, N. *Sir Robert Peel: the life of Sir Robert Peel after 1830.* London, Longman 1972 p. 150.

[16] Drummond to Murray 23.7.1842: WO 80/4/42.

to avoid 'universal alarm at home and great jealousy in France'.[17] Island garrisons stood at 378 infantry, 81 Artillerymen and 2,175 militia spread across four islands; Alderney depended on 126 militiamen.[18] Murray observed that steam navigation negated the old advantages of tide and rocks that had enabled the defenders to predict the timing and direction of attacks in the age of sail. Future attacks would be more powerful, and more likely to succeed: 'having a naval force always at hand' to provide early warning and support the defences was a matter of 'peculiar importance for the security of the Channel Islands'. As there were no suitable floating harbours; 'it is only by the construction of a Breakwater that an adequate degree of security can be obtained for War Steamers employed upon the above service'. To counter the Chancellor's economic anxieties, Murray reminded his Cabinet colleagues of their collective responsibility for the Islands, while a new harbour would improve trade, a point stressed by Colonel le Couteur.[19] Le Couteur also warned that the Chausey Islands, twenty-two miles south of Jersey, would be the rendezvous for a steam invasion from St Malo and Granville.[20]

Although Murray linked naval and military force his primary focus remained insular defence, ignoring such key naval concerns as trade defence. The Islands were finally placed at the centre of national policy by the appointment of Major General Sir William Napier as Lieutenant Governor of Guernsey. Both Wellington, soon to become Commander-in-Chief, and Home Secretary Graham directed Napier's attention to local defences. Napier was already familiar with the Islands, having visited Guernsey in 1827–8, when his friend and precursor Sir John Colborne had urged the need for a harbour at Alderney.[21] Within twenty-four hours of landing Napier had condemned the coastal batteries, praised the militia and cast doubt on the commitment of their landowning officers. Advised the Government would appoint a commission to recommend improved defences Napier pre-empted their conclusions, providing Wellington and Graham with a masterpiece of joint service strategic analysis.[22]

[17] Goulburn to Murray 22.7.1842: P&C WO 80/4/34–5.

[18] Militia Return by General William Napier Lt Gov. 14.6.1842: WO 890/4/90. Return of Troops 6.6.1842; WO 80/4/93. Barrack Accommodation – Channel Islands 1.7.1842: WO 80/4/46–7.

[19] Defence of the Channel Islands 25.7.1842: WO 80/4/36–40 draft. Fair copy /56–60.

[20] Le Couteur to Murray 26.6.1842: Jersey: WO 80/4/52–5; Stevens, J. *Victorian Voices: An Introduction to the Papers of Sir John le Couteur.* St Helier 1969.

[21] Bruce II. p. 77. Home Office to Colborne: HO 99/6 3/9/26. Moore-Smith, G. C. 'Letters from Colonel William Napier to Sir John Colborne, chiefly in Connexion with His "History of the War in the Peninsula" ', *English Historical Review* vol.18 no.72 Oct. 1903 pp. 725–53, at p. 747.

[22] Bruce, H. A. *Life of General Sir William Napier* London, Murray 1864 vol. II p. 84. Napier had recently edited his cousin Commodore Charles Napier's *The War*

Napier discussed the defence of the Islands 'as a group by the naval power of England', prioritising 'their means of offence'; their defence as military positions was a secondary issue, while the defence of individual islands was a tertiary concern. Their strategic role was to support 'the maintenance of English supremacy in the Channel'; their defence was only important in the context of Britain's 'general control of the Channel'. Steam squadrons based in the Islands would control St Malo, Granville and St Servan, the ports linking Cherbourg and Brest, which would be blockaded by the main fleets. Naval forces at Alderney would ensure French warships could not leave Cherbourg without being observed and reported to the Channel Fleet. Not only did Napier prioritise the defence of floating trade over local security, but he advised recovering the Chauseys, returned to France in 1815 to support the blockade of St Malo. He anticipated the French would fortify the islands. In his view naval command of the Channel would secure the Islands, protect the mainland and defend floating trade, but it depended on steamship harbours in the Islands. While it would be ideal to station 'heavy steamers and ships of the line ... at Alderney, Jersey, Guernsey and the Chaussy's ... Alderney alone would nearly attain those objects if it became a great naval station'. Critically Alderney was small enough to be militarily defensible, ideally placed to watch Cherbourg and close to the mainland.[23]

Having elevated local anxieties into a matter of national strategy Napier's report shaped that of the Joint Commission.[24] The Commissioners were hydrographer Captain Edward Belcher RN, Lt Colonel Colquhoun of the Royal Engineers and Colonel Cardew of the Royal Artillery.[25] 'Summoned to the Admiralty on secret service' on 4 August Belcher received verbal orders from First Naval Lord Admiral Sir George Cockburn, who considered Guernsey the most important location for a new harbour, then Jersey and only lastly Alderney. He wanted harbours 'calculated to accommodate ships of the line, and not mere fishing-boats'. Belcher found the eight-knot Alderney race made it impossible for a disabled vessel to get into Braye harbour, while the foul anchoring ground made it: 'no place for a ship of war'. He advised excavating a massive harbour at Longy, inside the Isle of Raz. 'The great object was "to be able to watch the French coast, to keep an eye upon Cap de la Hague, and

---

in Syria, London, John Parker 1841, which examined the latest steam-powered coastal warfare.

23 Napier to Graham July 1842: HO 45/1345.

24 Bruce *Napier II* pp. 97–8.

25 Graham to Murray 30.7.1842: WO 80/4/62; Murray Memorandum 1.8.1842: WO 80/9/18–21; Murray Draft to Mulcaster and Dundas 1.8.1843: WO 80/4/64; Winfield, R. *British Warships in the Age of Sail. Vol IV.* Barnsley, Seaforth 2014 pp. 281–2. Belcher had just returned to London from an Asian survey mission.

be ready to send out ships to sea as soon as a vessel was seen coming out of that place [Cherbourg]".'[26]

Cockburn wanted to circulate the Commission report to the Cabinet and, if Murray agreed, despatch James Walker to inspect sites and estimate costs.[27] Haddington sent the papers to Prime Minister Peel in February 1843.[28] There the matter rested for fifty-three weeks, until Murray prompted Haddington to remind Peel.[29] As a result nothing had been decided, let alone done, when the Tahiti and Moroccan crises broke in the summer of 1844. The Islands remained vulnerable.[30]

In the interval Lymington MP W. A. Mackinnon had called for a Committee to investigate the harbours between the Thames and Portsmouth, 'a subject of very great importance to the trade of the empire, and to the security of navigation', in peace and war.[31] Napier's cousin Captain Charles Napier RN MP emphasised the security issues, while Major Beresford called for Harwich, his constituency, to replace Foulness as the Harbour of Refuge for the Thames Estuary. The Liberal MP for Durham North, Mr Lambton, observed: 'these national harbours of refuge would be important as great national defences in time of war. The French were not idle on this subject.' Peel agreed: new harbours in the Channel should provide: 'defence in time of war, as well as of refuge for trading-vessels in bad weather', 'their location to be settled by the Admiralty', not the House of Commons. He opposed Mackinnon's motion, and it was withdrawn.

Peel finally acted in February 1844, blocking a Commons proposal to build at Dover by appointing a Harbour of Refuge Commission.[32] As he explained to Wellington his concerns were strategic.

> Seeing the naval preparations of France in the vicinity to the Channel and the probable results in any future war of steam navigation, it appears to me that regardless of the state of our finances we should immediately and seriously apply ourselves to the question of a great harbour of Refuge and Defence in the Channel.[33]

[26] Belcher comments on L. F. V. Harcourt's paper to the Institution of Civil Engineers on 25.11.1873: 'Account of the Construction and Maintenance of the Harbour at Braye, Alderney': *Minutes of the Proceedings of the Institution of Civil Engineers* vol. 37, iss. 1874 pp. 60–83 at pp. 96–8. Belcher's reliability when discussing his own actions is open to question.

[27] Haddington to Murray 17.1.1843: WO 80/4/72.

[28] Haddington to Peel 16.2.1843 Add 40525 f20.

[29] Haddington to Murray 26.1.1844: WO 80/4/70–1.

[30] Ordnance Mounted 30.6.1844: Guns by calibre 30.6.1844: WO 80/4/19–20. Officer of the Jersey Militia to Graham 5.9.1844: WO 80/4/30–1.

[31] *Hansard* Commons Debate 27.4.1843: vol. 68 cc.1002–1010.

[32] *Hansard* Commons Debate 29.2.1844: vol. 73 cc. 395–406.

[33] Peel to Wellington and Haddington 6.3.1844 copy: Peel Ms BL Add. 40,460 ff.61–4, 98.

Peel may have been advised by Cockburn, the dominant figure at the Admiralty, a relative by marriage and a trusted confidant.[34] Cockburn had a critical role in developing Government policy on Harbours of Refuge, the Channel Islands and trade defence in the Channel. He selected four naval officers for the Commission, Admiral Sir Thomas Byam Martin, hydrographer Captain John Washington, Captain James Dundas and Sir William Symonds. Dundas, a Whig MP, could secure cross-party support, while the 'whiggish' Symonds was 'the best qualified' on local issues.[35] He hoped to avoid partisan disputes in the House, which might excite unwelcome interest in France.[36]

Byam Martin, Dundas, Symonds and Washington were appointed to a ten-man Commission.[37] On 2 April 1844 Peel directed it to settle where to build the harbour recommended by the 1843 Select Committee on Shipwrecks. Chairman Byam Martin was an experienced policy maker, Lieutenant General Sir Howard Douglas had expertise in artillery and engineering, and both were Conservatives; Captain Dundas MP was a former Whig Naval Lord of the Admiralty. Hydrographer John Washington represented the Navy's scientific elite, working with Lt Colonel Colquhoun and Lt Colonel Anderson, scientific soldiers from the Royal Engineers and Royal Artillery, on harbour locations, structures and defences. The appointment of Sir John Pelly, a Master of Trinity House, reflected his powerful City of London connections, including a Directorship of the Bank of England, while Captain Peter Fisher RN was closely connected to Wellington.[38] The final nominee, James Walker, was the President of the Institution of Civil Engineers, an expert on harbour construction and a potential project engineer.

Evidently Peel understood the issues, probably from discussions with Cockburn: he wanted to know if a harbour was necessary, if it could be afforded and if so which location would best serve the needs of peace and war. It must be accessible at all times, 'a station for vessels of war in the event

---

[34] Peel secured Cockburn a seat in the House of Commons after forming the Ministry: Gash *Peel 2* pp. 279, 520–1; Cockburn's brother William, the Dean of York, had married Peel's sister. Heathcote, T. A. *British Admirals of the Fleet: 1734–1995.* Barnsley, Pen & Sword 2012 pp. 49–50; Gash, *Peel 2.* pp. 172, 279.

[35] Haddington to Peel 6.3.1844: Add. 40,457 f.100–1. Symonds had lived on Jersey for several years.

[36] Peel to Wellington 24.3.1844: Add. 40,460 Peel had been admitted as an Honorary Member of the ICE in May 1842 Add. 40,508 at Walker's request.

[37] Haddington to Peel 27.3.1844: Add. 40,457 f.102 & Symonds to Peel 29.3.1844: Add 40,451 f.441.

[38] Fisher died on 28.8.1844, while serving as Superintendent of Sheerness Dockyard. He was also Captain of Sandown Castle, a post in Wellington's gift, and Magistrate for the Cinque Ports and the County of Kent. Haddington to Peel 27.11.1841: Add.40,456 f.34. He was appointed to Sheerness 'to please the Duke': Haddington to Peel 30.3.1844: Add. 40,457 f.113.

of hostilities, both for the purposes of offence and defence'. Finally, it had to be fortified. The Commissioners could suggest more than one harbour.[39]

Within weeks the Moroccan crisis had made Graham, the responsible Minister, 'a little anxious' about many more exposed points.[40] His main concern was an attack by French steamers, armed with shell-firing guns. The Chancellor belatedly accepted the need to improve defences, but remained anxious to avoid expense, especially asking the House of Commons for additional funds.[41] In September Graham urged Murray to improve the Islands' batteries and re-arm the militia, although he hoped 'the "Entente Cordiale" is not at an end'.[42]

The defence of the Channel Islands and Harbours of Refuge project began to coalesce in early December 1844, when Peel asked Murray for the report on Harbour Defences, which he shared with Cockburn and Wellington.[43] Then Murray asked for the Admiralty's final decision on the location of Alderney harbour, an issue raised eleven months earlier.[44] Peel belatedly accepted James Walker's report recommending Braye, a decision that may be traced to Cockburn. Murray adjusted the shore defences accordingly.[45] The Admiralty emphasised that the defence of the Crown's insular possessions, near and far, was an Army responsibility, while the Cabinet set the level of naval force on each station, primarily on the advice of the Foreign Secretary.[46] The Navy had no wish to be tied to any location.

The defence of the dockyards became a priority in the summer of 1844, the Admiralty urging a committee of senior officers from the Navy, Engineers and Artillery to examine those of the Medway and Pembroke, the Navy's largest building facility.[47] Cockburn advised Murray to consult the Navy's leading gunnery expert, Captain Thomas Hastings of HMS *Excellent*, who joined George Hoste RE and George Mercer RA on a Committee to consider defence against steam-powered naval attacks and raids.[48] The Committee visited Sheerness, Pembroke, Plymouth and finally Portsmouth and reported

---

[39] PP 1845 (611) XVI Harbour of Refuge Commission Report 1845 p. 3.

[40] Graham to Murray 25.5.1843 and 8.10.1843: WO 80/4/160–1, 150.

[41] Goulburn to Murray 17.7.1844: WO 80/13 confidential.

[42] Graham to Murray 5.9.1844 Private: WO 80/4/32–3.

[43] Haddington to Murray 3.12.1844: WO 80/4/95 and Haddington to Murray 10.12.1844; WO 80/4/115.

[44] Murray to Haddington 18.12.1844 Confidential: WO 80/4/26–7.

[45] Haddington to Murray 20.12.1844; and 1.1.1845 and Murray to Mulcaster draft 3.1.1845: WO 80/4/28–9, 74 and /24–5. The key to the plans box of Walker's Report is in Murray's archive, having been returned by Mulcaster: WO 80/4/82.

[46] Admiralty Minute on Colonial Office to Admiralty 4.7.1845: ADM 1/5555.

[47] Admiralty to MGO 24.8.1844: WO 80/9 ff 66–7.

[48] Cockburn to Murray Confidential 6.9.1844: WO 80/9 f.113.

on 10 October 1844.[49] Hastings recommended that old 74-gun battleships and 46-gun frigates fitted with screw propulsion should be stationed at these ports to reinforce the fixed defences. His initiative reflected recent propeller trials and discussions with Codrington at Portsmouth in 1842.[50] With reduced masts, no poop deck and reduced water and stores these ships could steam at seven knots, while the engines were safely below the waterline. With a small crew trained to their guns these ships would protect vital bases, and then 'proceed to any part of the coast which might be menaced with a descent'. Two propeller battleships and six frigates would secure Spithead, the Isle of Wight and Southampton, supported by fast steam vessels and cross-channel packets, to provide advanced warning.[51]

Armed with guns of the heaviest calibre these battleships 'would be equal to five of the largest steamers', with a similar draught of water. They would destroy hostile paddle-steamers, in combination with shore batteries.[52] Once the Solent, Spithead and the Isle of Wight were secure Britain would command the Channel. Hastings proposed using the 5–6,000 Coastguard men to man these ships for local service.[53] He also explained an enduring principle of maritime strategy:

> no invasion of this Country on a large scale, by an Army with a battering train will ever be attempted, until the invading power has obtained by a succession of naval combats and victories undisputed superiority at sea, and further that the Commerce and Coast of this Kingdom may be fully protected against sudden and predatory expeditions.

But defence was merely the strategic base line:

[49] Cockburn to Murray 26.8.1844 Private: WO 80/9 ff.70–1. Bound file 'Coast Defences' 10.10.1844: ADM 1/5543. This file was updated for at least two years. Report on Defences of Home Ports. 1844: ADM 13/185 Secret and Confidential Board Room Journals.

[50] Codrington to Sidney Herbert 11.7.1842 NMM. COD 20/4 One Jersey Papers No.1116. Codrington was an early advocate of the screw propeller as an auxiliary in battleships and frigates. He may have discussed the subject with Hastings, under his command at HMS *Excellent.*

[51] O'Brien, F. T. *Early Solent Steamers: A History of Local Steam Navigation.* Newton Abbott, David & Charles 1973 pp. 93–139 for local cross channel services including the Channel Islands.

[52] Thomas Hastings to Haddington 4.11.1844: Adm 1/5543.

[53] Captain Sir William Bowles RN to Haddington 31.3.1845: encl. Hastings to Bowles 2.4.1845: Bowles, W. *Naval Administration.* London, Ridgeway 1854 pp. 218–20.

> PS It is hardly necessary to observe, tho' the question has been considered as a system of defence, that it may at all times be converted into a system of offence, when it is considered expedient to do so.[54]

Although initially serving vital defensive functions the steam battleships were a 'moveable and powerful means of aggression' that would release troops from fixed defences for the field army.

> the ships I have spoken of might also be moved for the purposes of aggression to any part of the Channel, and they might also serve for the defence of the Channel Islands if they were attacked, as 10 hours would carry them 80 miles ... no cowering idea of defence only entered into our consideration, but that we felt when proposing what would be a powerful means of defence, if well carried out, that we were also placing at the disposal of the Admiralty means of attack of the most valuable and overwhelming character...

Furthermore:

> ... their steam power might also prove most valuable in taking up positions against batteries. I trust I have said enough to shew the plan I have advocated is not only one of defence, but one which may be made powerfully aggressive.[55]

Hastings' offensive imperative provided the core of a strategy to destroy hostile naval bases by bombardment – beginning with Cherbourg. In autumn 1845 the Admiralty detached John Washington to inspect French naval bases and commercial harbours at St Malo, St Servan, Granville, Cherbourg, le Havre and Dieppe, to inform the Harbours of Refuge Commission. St Malo's new floating basin had failed, at Granville there were plans for a basin and forts while smaller works were in progress at Le Havre and Dunkirk. At Cherbourg 5,000 men were employed, while the defences were advancing rapidly:

> Cherbourg will thus be impregnable by sea... But although impregnable I am far from thinking it indestructible. Either a fleet lying in the roadstead, or a number of ships fitting out in the basin, or the dockyard itself might be destroyed by steamers armed as bomb vessels, supposing they can throw shells with tolerable precision at a distance of 2 miles or 4000 yards, and the late experiments, I believe, prove this to be quite practicable. Now a steamer by bringing the dockyard to bear SSW by the compass might place herself so as to be within 2 miles of it, and still at a distance of one mile, 200 yards from the nearest battery on the breakwater. The length of this

---

[54] Hastings to Haddington 1.2.1845: Adm 1/5543.
[55] Hastings to W. A. B. Hamilton 5.7.1845: Adm 1/5543.

structure, which is known, would form a ready base to measure an angle for taking up an exact position.[56]

John Ross had created an improved sextant specifically for the last task in the 1820s, while Thomas Hastings tested the steamer HMS *Scourge* as a bomb vessel in early 1846. Clearly hydrographers and gunnery experts were working together. Washington's report shaped British thinking about naval bombardment for the next decade. He played a critical role in the development of war plans to attack Russia and wrote the war orders for the main British fleet.[57] Those orders were addressed to Vice Admiral Sir Charles Napier, another man to visit Cherbourg in the mid-1840s, and plan its destruction from the sea.[58]

Meanwhile the Harbour of Refuge Commission travelled round the coast, starting in the Thames, taking evidence at potential sites from local politicians, pilots, fishermen, packet skippers, Masters of Ordnance transports and coastguard and revenue officers. Byam Martin, Dundas and Douglas, who believed the Navy needed operational bases for steam warships, and staging posts for coastal convoys, led the interviews.[59] Once the senior men had shaped the agenda the remaining members provided supplementary questions, on technical points. John Washington and the junior soldiers dutifully followed their seniors.

The report was dominated by the defence of floating trade.

> Without any except tidal harbours along the whole coast between Portsmouth and the Thames, and none accessible to large steamers, there is now, when steam points to such great changes in maritime affairs, an imperative necessity for supplying, by artificial means, the want of harbours throughout the narrow part of the Channel.

These harbours would facilitate 'powerful naval protection' for the country and its commerce, questions of 'life, property and national security ... of vast importance'.[60] The Commissioners concluded three harbours were needed: Dover, at the Channel narrows, Portland to the west, and Harwich, which occupied a superb strategic position to control the Thames Estuary,

---

[56] Washington to Admiralty 3.12.1845 details of works at Cherbourg. Washington to Admiralty 24.12.1845; Berkeley MS Gloucester Record Office. [I assume the letters were extracted by Berkeley after the Whigs returned to office].

[57] Lambert, A. D. *The Crimean War; British Grand Strategy against Russia 1853–1856.* Aldershot, Ashgate 2011.

[58] Napier to Peel 5.6 and 18.9.1845: Add 40568 ff.295–7 Add 40574 f.135. Dear, I. *The Royal Yacht Squadron 1815–1985.* London, Hutchinson 1985 pp. 43, 49.

[59] For an example see: HofR 1845 p. 91.

[60] HofR 1845 p. 13.

support North Sea and Baltic shipping in storms and sustain operations on the German, Dutch and Belgian coasts. Harwich was cheap, the harbour only needed dredging and a breakwater to end damaging erosion. It was: 'the proper place for a squadron of steamers ... as well as for a Harbour of Refuge for merchant ships, while the neighbouring anchorage of Hollesley Bay is favourably suited for ships of the line'.[61] It was also, 'of very great importance to the trade of the country'.[62] Harwich obviated the need for an expensive harbour at Foreness.

The decision for Dover was categorical. While Ramsgate's new steamship harbour offered useful refuge for merchant shipping, it was too far east of the narrows. Dover's wet harbour, small dry dock and storehouses could support naval operations, while adding a Harbour of Refuge would give it 'the efficiency as naval station which is necessary in order to provide for the security of this part of the coast, and the protection of trade'.[63] It appears the naval men expected to take over the port in wartime.

The Commission also recommended Portland, at the western end of the Channel Narrows, stressing its close proximity to the Channel Islands and, by inference, Cherbourg. The secure inner harbour at Weymouth, cheap local stone, good holding ground and ample fresh water (crucial for early steamers), prompted Byam Martin and Dundas to conclude that a 'Harbour of Refuge' squadron at Portland would cover the shipping and the coast between Portsmouth, Dartmouth and Plymouth; completing 'the chain of communication and co-operation between Dover and Falmouth, a distance of 300 miles'. These harbours, separated by only sixty miles, would support a steam convoy system along the Channel coast. Portland was a similar distance from Alderney and Cherbourg.[64] The Army officers agreed Dover and Portland could be defended by fixed works, to be built once the harbours were complete.[65] In conclusion, the Commissioners expressed.

> in the strongest terms, their unanimous opinion and entire conviction that measures are indispensably necessary to give the south east frontier of the kingdom means and facilities, which it does not now possess, for powerful naval protection.[66]

This defensive tone was for public consumption. In a confidential covering letter Byam Martin emphasised the ultimate purpose of the new harbours was

---

61 HoR 1845 p. 6. Battlefleets often used the Bay for North Sea and Baltic operations.

62 HoR 1845 p. 10.

63 HofR 1845 p. 9.

64 HofR 1845 p. 10.

65 HofR 1845 p. 12.

66 HofR 1845 p. 15.

to augment the steam force, placing 'the government in a posture to commence vigorous measures of assault in the first burst of war'.[67]

The carefully crafted report persuaded the pacifist/francophile Foreign Secretary Lord Aberdeen to support the project: 'although these works may be highly useful during war, their immediate and manifest object is the protection of the commerce of the country in time of peace'.[68] When estimates were presented to Parliament in June 1845 work at Dover had been reduced to a single pier, while harbours at Alderney, Jersey and Guernsey joined the list, at a cost of £2 million. Combining these harbours into a single motion emphasised their strategic character.

In July 1845 James Walker produced a strategic analysis emphasising: 'the immense importance of having stations for armed vessels, particularly armed steam vessels, in the Channel Islands'. Cherbourg and St Malo were France's only low water, or wet harbours between Ushant and Ostend in Belgium, a distance of 360 miles. He advised building the three Channel Island harbours, because, as Sir Francis Beaufort had told him, 'whoever has the Channel Islands has the lock and key of the British Channel'. Walker recognised that the Hydrographer had become a pivotal figure in British strategic planning, his officers providing the navigational expertise needed for sustained operations in the Channel. The Islands would be a serious threat in French hands. 'Looking therefore at all the circumstances, I doubt if Dover, or any other place be so important as the Channel Islands in case of a war with France.' He expected the French would attack at the outbreak of war. The best defence would be locally based squadrons, and it was 'sound policy' to act now. Wellington had told him as much eight years earlier. Boulogne and Calais, which faced Dover, were only open for six hours in every twelve, and therefore 'vastly inferior to Cherbourg and even to St. Malo'. Building new harbours at Jersey, Guernsey and Alderney would cost £1 million, using local stone. Jersey was belatedly spending £200,000 on the harbour at St Helier, 'making the dock gates wide enough for the largest steamers', where Walker was the project engineer.[69] It is probable Cockburn shaped the report, hoping an 'expert' opinion would unlock the political decision-making process. Walker's anxiety to secure the million pound contract was obvious, but he was not a strategist.

The decision to build harbours on all three Channel Islands was heavily criticised by William Napier: 'Alderney is of far greater importance than either Guernsey or Jersey' but it required suitable fixed defences. Alderney was critical to the security of floating trade in the Channel. If it were lost:

> French steamers and privateers will see an English vessel two or three hours before she can be seen distinctly from Portland: they will pounce upon

---

[67] Byam Martin to Admiralty: ADM 1/5553.

[68] Aberdeen to Peel 31.12.1844: Add. 40454 f.368.

[69] Walker to Cockburn 1.7.1845: WO 30/116.

her. ...What Mercantile losses! what an immense expense! what dangerous
chances are thus opened! what a number of ships of war must be employed!
what difficulty of blockade!

Yet a single steamer based at Alderney could blockade Cherbourg. The harbour
at Jersey was ill-placed, while the proposal for Guernsey was too expensive
and ignored a better option that the States would help fund.[70]

By 1845 the defence of the Channel Islands had become inextricably
intertwined with wider concerns about national security and the protection
of commerce. To be secure the Islands needed at least one advanced naval
station, linked to Harbours of Refuge on the English coast, that would operate
the steam squadrons that protected commercial shipping in wartime. At the
same time the Islands and the Royal dockyards must be protected against
steam-powered raids.

These issues became urgent in 1844–5 as Anglo-French tensions were
exacerbated by French aggression in Tahiti and Morocco. While Lord
Aberdeen doubted the French had any intention of going to war, Wellington
took the opposite view, using alarmist rhetoric to press for enhanced defences.
Peel balanced these divergent approaches, competing economic demands
and alarmist rhetoric in the House of Commons by opposition spokesmen
Captain Charles Napier and Lord Palmerston. That he did so against the
background of another Irish crisis, while the Conservative party split over
agricultural protection, further complicated the process, and encouraged his
use of defensive terminology.

Although he had most of the information by late December 1844, Peel
allowed any decision to stand over.[71] The key players met, belatedly, in Downing
Street on 7 August 1845 and agreed to spend £50,000 addressing obvious
weaknesses at Sheerness, the Thames batteries, Portsmouth and Plymouth,
but ignored the exposed dockyard at Pembroke, where Cockburn concluded
that Hastings' steam battleships 'would be quite sufficient for the defence of
the mouth of the Haven'.[72] Haddington concurred: he planned eight blockship
conversions, as soon as the engines could be contracted. 'Two of the large
ships and two frigates are at present destined for the Medway – & we hope and
believe that with the land defences – we shall then be sufficiently fortified'.[73]

Although Peel's ministry decided to build six harbours in the Channel,
domestic problems, reduced Anglo-French tension and the re-emergence of
a strategic challenge in the New World ensured little had been accomplished

[70] Napier to Graham November 1845: Bruce *Napier II* pp. 125–8.

[71] Peel to Wellington 26.12.1844: Parker III pp. 197–8.

[72] Murray to Cockburn 19.8.1845; Cockburn to Murray 19.8.1845; Tait to Murray
4.9.1845: WO 80/9 ff.5–7, 26.

[73] Haddington to Murray 5.9.1845: WO 80/9 8–11.

before it fell from office in June 1846. Cockburn had authorised James Walker to buy land for quarries and construction work in Alderney and Jersey, while Lord Ellenborough, Haddington's successor, placed the harbours on the 'to do' list left for Lord Auckland, the Whig First Lord.[74]

Shortly after taking office Auckland advised Prime Minister Lord John Russell that the new harbour at Dover was 'indispensable to the defence of our coasts in time of war', adopting James Walker's 1845 enclosed harbour design, but only building the western pier, to prevent shingle deposition, rather than an enclosed war station. Auckland recognised the Channel Islands would be 'among the first objects of attack' in war:

> In our hands they would be a check upon all privateering, and even upon other more serious enterprises. In the hands of an enemy, they would give facilities for the most injurious attacks upon our trade.[75]

Privateers, the primary threat to British commerce for the past two centuries, shaped strategy into the 1850s, including decisions about Channel Island harbours. French and American privateer activity had been especially acute in the Channel between 1793 and 1815, with Channel Island-based privateers providing a critical element of the defensive effort. This threat made it imperative to ensure all French harbours were observed, and to provide the Islands with floating harbours to operate steam warships. Satisfied that France could not challenge British sea control, or stage an invasion, the Admiralty focussed on trade defence, anxious to avoid the criticism that erupted whenever the City or Parliament thought it was not doing enough. Anxiety about privateers endured through the Crimean War, prompting Lord Palmerston to secure their abolition in the 1856 Declaration of Paris, being convinced privateers were the only effective strategy that America, France and Russia could use to challenge British naval dominance. He ensured that if they resorted to privateers Britain would be free to apply a harsh economic blockade.

Britain built a large force of steam cruisers between 1830 and 1854, primarily to counter privateers. It needed a large force of sloops for the critical linked missions of trade protection and economic blockade. Screw propeller sloops and brigs, designed to cruise under sail, with powerful engines, full broadsides and heavy pivot guns transformed Britain's ability to defend floating trade. Once the prototype, HMS *Rattler*, had proved the concept, in April 1845 a major building programme produced enough ships to blockade Russia in 1854–5.

On taking office Auckland recognised Alderney was 'a much more important naval position' than the other islands, delaying work at Guernsey to provide

---

[74] Ellenborough Memo for successor 6.7.1846: PRO 30/12/34/12.
[75] Auckland to Lord John Russell, Admiralty 3.7.1846: PRO 30/22/5B f.59–63.

savings for Chancellor of the Exchequer Sir Charles Wood.[76] A year later he asked James Walker and Wellington to revisit the issue. Walker suggested the 'easy' harbour Jersey should have priority, ignoring the strategic issues. Wellington took a more tactical position, one that may have reflected William Napier's report. The new harbours were:

> not for the mere defence of the islands, that object could be obtained by constructing Harbours at a moderate expense. But … to augment the maritime means of defence of the country: to give to the Gov't facilities for a greater development of its naval force, by a great naval station in the seas surrounding these islands and to manoeuvre there its fleet to westward between those of the enemy at Cherbourg and those at St. Malo, Brest, Rochfort etc.[77]

Everything pointed to Alderney, where work started in January 1847, Walker's self-serving advice ensured work started at Jersey, but Guernsey, the most expensive harbour, was quietly dropped. Auckland was anxious to complete Alderney 'without appearing too aggressive'.[78] Speed was of the essence, which may explain the poor choices.

In 1848 Sir Charles Wood advised Prime Minister Russell against a new Militia Bill on strategic grounds:

> The invasion of England with a great army calculated for conquest, I firmly believe to be utterly impracticable as long as we maintain decided superiority at sea….. It is in the Channel and not on this side of it that the attempt at a descent must be defeated.

As a former Admiralty Civil Lord Wood stressed the offensive role of the mainland 'Harbours of Refuge'.[79] Three years later he justified harbours at Alderney and Jersey by referring to commercial losses inflicted by French privateers in the last war.[80]

Not only did Auckland visit the Channel Islands, and consult the Duke, but he reinforced the intimate connection between the Islands, Dover, Portland

---

[76] Auckland Memo. 3.7.1846: PRO 30/22/5B ff.59–64. Auckland to Wood & reply 3.10.1846: Hickleton MS cited Partridge p. 24.

[77] Auckland to Wellington 17.9.1847: Wellington to Auckland 19.9.1847: Wn MS Southampton University WP 2/155/67–73. Walker 24.9.1847 copy Melville MS SRO at GD 51/1/320. The copy dates to Captain Richard Dundas's inspection of the islands in 1853.

[78] Auckland to Earl Grey 2.10.1847, 28.2.1848: 3rd Earl Grey MS Durham Univ. Lib.

[79] Charles Wood Memorandum 5.1.1848 sent to Russell: *LCLJR* vol. 1. pp. 258–61 at p. 260.

[80] Davies, W. *The Harbour that Failed.* Alderney, Ampersand Press 1983 p. 25.

and screw propeller warships. Harbours would enable screw sloops to prevent French steamers leaving harbour for raids, invasions or destroying commerce. He remained sceptical about St Catherine's, but deferred to the Duke and Walker. Lord Anglesey, Master General of the Ordnance, and an experienced yachtsman with local knowledge, condemned the location of the Jersey harbour. He only agreed to continue because the threat was so obvious.[81]

Anxious for clarity Auckland consulted younger officers with experience of steam warfare. In 1847 Prince Albert asked him how many troops existing French steamers could carry. Captain Lord John Hay, a junior Naval Lord, reported that the entire French steam marine, about a hundred small vessels, could not lift 30,000 men with the necessary guns and horses. Ten to twenty war steamers would check or destroy any such attempt. Although Hay's report exploded the invasion scare, the Admiralty did not rest content with a purely defensive programme.[82]

A year later Auckland consulted Captain Charles Hotham on a potential Anglo-French conflict.[83] Hotham had no doubt Britain would prevail. He believed the French Navy would be divided into ten 'corsair' squadrons to attack British trade. Three would be based at Cherbourg, operating in the Channel, off the Thames Estuary and in the North Sea. To control them Britain should blockade Cherbourg with a mixed force of sailing battleships and steamers and pursue any ships that put to sea. He anticipated annihilating the French fleet within a year.[84] 'Harbours of Refuge' would secure merchant shipping, while steam would ensure more effective blockades, especially if the steamers could refuel quickly. Fourth Naval Lord Captain Alexander Milne would report on mechanised coaling facilities for Portsmouth, Portland and Plymouth in late 1851.[85] By August 1849 Dover pier had solved the shingle problem, and improved conditions in the anchorage.[86]

Throughout the defence debates of the 1840s British ministers attempted to avoid offending or alarming France, their public utterances creating the impression British measures were purely defensive. However, Auckland

[81] Anglesey to Wellington 10.10.1847: WP 2/155/93. Dear, I. *The Royal Yacht Squadron 1815–1985.* London, Paul 1985 pp. 17–62.

[82] Hay to Auckland 16.1.1848: PRO 30/22/7A (Lord John Russell MS).

[83] Captain Charles Hotham 'Remarks as to the result of a probable war with France' 12.1.1849: ADM 13/185 ff.54–80. see also Hotham to Auckland 24.11.1848: Hotham MSS DDHO/10/11 Secret and Confidential Letter Book, Captain Charles Eden RN (Auckland's cousin and secretary) to Hotham 25.4.1849: Hotham MS DDHO 10/2/29b.

[84] Charles Hotham 'Remarks as to the Result of a probable war with France' 12.1.1849: ADM13/185 ff.54–80.

[85] Evans, D. *Building the Steam Navy: Dockyards, Technology and the Creation of the Victorian Battlefleet, 1830–1906.* London, Conway 2004 Ch.14.

[86] Hasenson pp. 121–3.

and others recognised that Alderney harbour was the key to controlling the Channel, and projecting power against French ports – they wished to hide the appearance of being 'aggressive', the underlying reality.

After Auckland's sudden death in late 1848 the Admiralty proved less effective at co-ordinating the many strands of policy required to create a Navy capable of seizing the initiative in a future war. By 1851 Russell's economically challenged Government faced mounting costs at Dover, Portland and two harbours in the Islands. With over £2 million still outstanding defence planners had to accept reality. Both Sir Henry Hardinge, Master General of the Ordnance, and Sir John Burgoyne, Inspector-General of Fortifications, stressed Alderney's greater strategic value. The screw sloops' improved cruising capabilities enabled Britain to dispense with two of the harbours Sir George Cockburn thought necessary to operate paddle-steamers and sailing battleships.

The decision to concentrate on Alderney also reflected the wider reality that the British response to France's naval challenge, symbolised by Cherbourg and paddle-steamers, had been effective. Admiralty insiders were confident there was no threat, although they continued to talk one up in public, to secure funds for ongoing projects. In early 1852 outgoing First Naval Lord Admiral Sir James Dundas reflected on the latest alarm. His bullish analysis linked hydrographic expertise, intelligence, careful analysis of French shipping, the steam reserve and naval recruitment.

> Invasion – we were never in less danger. France has enough on her hands at home – if not her power by steamers is very small, and most of her large boats are employed between Toulon – Algiers and Italy. Another thing is – all the Harbours in the Channel (except Cherbourg) are dry harbours – and we know to a moment, at what time their vessels can come out – there we should be to meet them, and I am happy to say – both our men of war reserve steamers, and our merchant steamers are increased to that degree, we could seal up every port in France in 10 days. I never hold an enemy too cheap, but I state that is fact.[87]

In 1853 Palmerston wrapped up the Aberdeen Cabinet's Defence Committee discussions of Channel Island harbours with a decision to stop work at Jersey and complete Alderney, echoing William Napier's decade-old assessment.

> Alderney with such a harbour and such defensive works will become a most important post for watching the French ports, for intercepting communications between Brest and Cherbourg, for commanding, in co-operation with the Squadron at Portland, the navigation of the Channel, and for checking

---

[87] Dundas to Henry Drummond nd. early 1852: C4 f.1 Drummond of Allbury MS Alnwick Castle.

the swarms of steam privateers that could otherwise sally forth from the French Channel Ports, and prey upon our trading vessels.[88]

The ministry also invested in Charles Lancaster's long-range rifled cannon, specifically to bombard dockyards.[89] They would fulfil that role in 1854 and 1855.

The Jersey harbour had failed *and* it had been rendered unnecessary. With screw sloops, steam gunboats and rifled cannon Alderney, Dover and Portland were the keys to the Channel.[90] As Anglo-French relations oscillated between alliance, arms races and war scares, work on the harbours and forts continued into the late 1860s as Louis Napoleon III sought a progressive Anglo-French entente to shape a post-Vienna Settlement Europe and enhance French power, by challenging British sea control. Britain rejected his policy and re-established naval dominance with a series of arms races, while Alderney enabled the Royal Navy to observe Cherbourg, and cut the connection with Brest.[91] After 1871 French naval policy shifted to radical forms of commerce warfare using torpedo boats, cruisers and submarines rather than privateers.[92] Yet the strategic logic of the Channel was unaffected.

For Britain, which had no desire to go to war with France, Braye harbour repaid the cost of construction as a critical element in a strategic posture that deterred war. Overt British preparations reminded France that it could not win at sea and would suffer massive economic damage in war. Sinking millions into a harbour at Alderney produced no obvious economic benefit, nor did it save the lives of any distressed mariners[93]; instead, it provided a potent demonstration of Britain's determination to retain command of the Channel, countering the strategic and symbolic challenge posed by Cherbourg, and enabled British warships to hold station to the west of Normandy. It would have been a major asset in any war: that it was never tested does not mean it was unnecessary.

Alderney was central to a highly offensive strategy. As the Crimean War approached ministers and service chiefs planned the destruction of Russian naval bases, using the naval bombardment and amphibious operations initially planned against France. The war also undermines the assumption that a French war would have been fought on defensive lines. The Royal Navy would have

---

[88] Palmerston Memo Carlton Gardens 9.4.1853: ND/D 8/1–3.
[89] Graham to Aberdeen 26.1.1853: Aberdeen MS BL Add. 43,191 f.16.
[90] Partridge p. 22.
[91] Treasury Minute 1.7.1859 Somerset MSS Devon Record Office 59/1.
[92] Hamilton C. I. *Anglo-French Naval Rivalry 1840–1870.* Oxford, Clarendon 1993 pp. 316–19; Ropp, T. ed. Roberts, S. S. *The Development of a Modern Navy, 1871–1904.* Annapolis, 1989 Annapolis, Naval Insitute Press Ch.8.
[93] Partridge p. 23.

moved to secure battlefleet command of the Channel, blockaded French naval bases, and convoyed merchant shipping with steam cruisers, before assembling specialist coast attack forces to destroy French naval bases and privateer ports. The harbour at Alderney was pivotal to that programme in 1847 *and* in the Fashoda Crisis of 1898.

The reputation of the new harbour suffered when the French naval challenge temporarily lapsed in the 1870s, making it appear a costly folly, but the commerce raiding threat re-emerged in the 1880s and Alderney remained ideally placed. The harbour transformed Alderney into an advanced strategic base, ideally located to observe and address threats to merchant shipping from the west coast of Normandy and the north coast of Brittany and prevent the French from moving battlefleets or invasion shipping into the Channel. The only serious question that the harbour ever raised was one of cost.

In October 1901 the Admiralty advised the War Office that France would 'attempt to seize the Channel Islands' at the outbreak of war, inviting the Army to set the level of military force necessary to hold out for 2–3 days. The soldiers settled on 3,000, mostly on Alderney, the strategic naval facility. In April 1904 a joint Naval and Military Committee advised the Cabinet to send an additional infantry battalion to Alderney, raising the garrison to 1,300 infantry, 110 artillerymen and 85 engineers and submarine miners. The extra battalion would be moved from Ireland, and it would train on the mainland in the summer.[94] In November 1904 the new Committee of Imperial Defence agreed that the loss of the Islands would 'deprive our destroyers of advanced anchorages, which would facilitate their operations on the French coast in the vicinity of Cherbourg', leading to 'disruption of trade'.[95] While the strategic base at Alderney remained secure the other islands were not vital.

Conclusion

Existing studies of British coast defences, on the mainland and offshore islands, assume their purpose was to prevent the occupation of territory.[96] This inference is incorrect. At the strategic level no combination of troops and forts in the United Kingdom could prevent the loss of sea control, economic disaster and ultimate defeat, a reality that French strategists understood. Britain did not fortify the country, which would have been a grotesque waste of resources, only the naval dockyards, key ports and the Thames. These bases and harbours were essential to securing command of the sea, without which Britain was vulnerable to loss of food supplies and trade, leading to mass

---

[94] Defence of Alderney 1904: CAB 38/4/33.

[95] Naval Aspects of Channel Islands Defence 11.1904: CAB 38/6.

[96] Partridge pp. 20, 38; Strachan, H. *From Waterloo to Balaklava: Tactics, Technology and the British Army 1815–1854*. Cambridge UP 1985 pp. 6–7, 15.

unrest, political turmoil and the withdrawal of the City of London's support for the Government. Public discussion of invasion was invariably driven by service agendas. Richard Cobden claimed that 'nine tenths of all the clamour for more defences ... had a professional origin'. In 1909 Lord Esher observed: 'an invasion scare is the mill of the Gods which grinds you out a Navy of Dreadnoughts and keeps the British people war-like in spirit'.[97]

There was no danger of invasion at any stage in the nineteenth century, because no sane French or German general would risk embarking an army for Britain before securing command of the sea. A raid on the Royal dockyards was possible, necessitating defensive upgrades there and at the new Harbours of Refuges for 'distressed merchant shipping' on the south and east coasts. No one mentioned that the 'distress' the new harbours were built to protect would come from the guns of French cruisers, rather than the tumult of wind and ocean. The British state was not worried about 'defending' the Channel Islands, because such anxieties were a local matter: it looked to exploit a prime strategic location that would cripple French coastwise shipping, lock up major harbours and observe Cherbourg. The security of floating trade in the Channel was the foundation of British strategy, not the capstone. The Channel Island harbours, along with the mainland 'Harbours of Refuge', were strategic bases for naval steamers to link local defences with naval reinforcements, blockade French ports and escort merchant shipping. As an ensemble they would support the destruction of Cherbourg. This offensive strategy, refined during the Crimean War, would influence British naval thinking down to 1915. The naval offensive was one element in a time-honoured strategy that exploited command of the sea to break the enemy's resistance through economic warfare.

---

[97] Cobden to John Bright 10.1.1861: Add. 43,651 f.213. Partridge p. 13. Esher to Fisher 1.10.1907: cited in Morgan-Owen, D. *The Fear of Invasion: Strategy, Politics, and British War Planning, 1880–1914.* Oxford University Press, 2017 p. 2.

PART 6

CIVIL SOCIETIES AND ANGLO-FRENCH NAVAL RIVALRY – THE 19TH CENTURY TO WWI

9

Hydrographic and Nautical Knowledge in French Coastal-Defence Strategy: the Case of the Channel Islands Area

ISABELLE DELUMEAU

The waters around the Channel Islands and the Gulf of Saint-Malo are known to be dangerous. Treacherous rocks that scatter the sea and strong tides produce rapid currents.

The weather is frequently difficult, and fogs are not unusual. The need for accurate charts drawn at an appropriate scale and precise nautical instructions appears then to be quite obvious. The French hydrographic service, known during the major part of the nineteenth century as the Dépôt des cartes et plans de la Marine before changing in 1886 to the Service hydrographique,[1] made efforts to provide seamen with a collection of documents of great quality.

It is interesting to explore further the sequence of the different surveys and to replace them in their political and economic context whenever possible. It creates a rather contradictory image. The maritime activities whose prosperity was the final aim of these efforts were languishing during the nineteenth century. The harbours of the western coasts of Cotentin Peninsula and northern Brittany were lagging behind, unable to make the necessary investments in order to attract freight. Saint-Malo missed out on industrial development and never regained its former grandeur from the previous century. The port collapsed and did not even rank among the first twenty in France.[2] Granville, despite some improvements and the construction of two wet docks in 1856 and 1873, never emerged and remained a fishing port. Few coasters exploited the sea routes between Cherbourg and the harbours of Brittany. Moreover, the trade that was mostly made up of agricultural

---

[1] 'Notice sur le service hydrographique de la Marine', *Annales hydrographiques*, (Paris, 1914), p. 44.

[2] Bruno Marnot, *Les grands ports de commerce français et la mondialisation au XIXe siècle* (Paris, 2011), p. 150.

products was in the hands of British shipowners and businessmen. They enjoyed preferential terms and prospered on the commercial relationships between France and the Channel Islands.

There were few shipowners in this area, and they concentrated mostly on high-sea fishing on the Grand Banks and in Iceland. This activity was more rewarding and attracted the major part of the available capital and able seamen. The port of Granville held 50 fishing boats, Saint-Malo nearly 70 and Saint-Brieuc 60 in 1866. The activity employed at that time almost 7,500 people. Coastal fishing was by comparison fruitless. Every year the statistics bulletin[3] described the fishing practices as a routine and regretted that fishermen lacked a spirit of enterprise. With limited access to capital, they could only have small day boats and dredgers. Oyster fishing was a seasonal activity,

At first sight it seems that the Navy lost adequate investment and that the documents the Dépôt published did not find their audience. We must admit it to some extent. No economic impetus explains the two years' exceptional survey that the engineers performed in 1888 and 1889 in the Minquiers Islands. The major reason that justified all the efforts the Navy made to chart the Gulf of Saint-Malo was political. Two issues must be considered. First, hydrography not only played an important role in the matter of sovereignty at sea but also on land. Second, when France implemented her new strategy of coastal defence from 1880, the Navy needed new documents which the Dépôt hastened to draw. The task had been demanding and absorbed an appreciable part of the resources of the service.

The first modern charts of the Gulf of Saint-Malo and the coasts from Cherbourg to Saint-Brieuc had been published after the important survey conducted by Beautemps-Beaupré. In 1816, he proposed that a systematic survey was financed, aiming at finally giving to navigation the most precise image of the coasts of France. He had proved some years before, as the hydrographic engineer of the team of Joseph Antoine Bruny d'Entrecasteaux on board *La Recherche* and in the Scheldt River, that his method was revolutionary and that he would complete his mission successfully.[4]

Beautemps-Beaupré started the survey in Brest in 1816 and in the following years his team explored the coast of southern Brittany before sailing down to the Spanish border. In 1829, it had been decided to survey the northern part of the French coast. The starting point of the new mission was Saint-Malo. The

---

    3   *Statistique des pêches maritimes*, Imprimerie administrative de Paul Dupont (Paris, yearly publication since 1866).

    4   The reader will find useful information on the outstanding works of Beautemps-Beaupré in Olivier Chapuis, *A la mer comme au ciel: Beautemps-Beaupré & la naissance de l'hydrographie moderne, 1700–1850 : l'émergence de la précision en navigation et dans la cartographie marine* (Paris, 1999), especially in chapters 5 and 6 of the first part and chapter 2 of the second part.

reason for this choice lay in political matters. Indeed, the British government intended to improve the charts of the Channel Islands and officially sought from the French authorities the right to land and fix some stations on the shore.[5] The minister reacted immediately, considering the British initiative as a major threat to the honour of the Navy. France let Great Britain give to posterity the first modern charts of this part of her territory. In great haste the mission was sent to Saint-Malo and Beautemps-Beaupré got down to work.

The French government decided to authorise the British surveyor, Captain Martin White, to land on the coast of France and as a way of balancing the relationship asked the same favour for her engineers. Beautemps-Beaupré made the most of the situation and obtained new and better equipped ships to conduct his survey. The first encounter between Beautemps-Beaupré and Martin White occurred when they were approaching Hébiens Island. They agreed to share information on the position of submerged rocks and especially the dangerous 'Basse trouvée' that the French team recognised. White himself offered to ship Thomas Daussy to Jersey in order to complete the geodetic framework he oversaw and to display and use his tidal gauge.[6] Daussy managed to connect the points of the French geodetic framework that had been made by the cartographers of the Ministry of War to three points in Guernsey, Sark and Alderney.[7]

Due to the goodwill and civility of the two teams, this sensitive survey was a success. As Beautemps-Beaupré explained, Captain White and himself were both motivated by the interest of the navigation of all nations.[8] It took three more years to cover the coast from the island of Bréhat to the Raz Blanchard. In 1835 and 1836 the Dépôt published a collection of sixteen charts. They had been printed on a large scale and featured many details. The quality of the engravings was very high. The Dépôt made special efforts to draw the charts of the Ecrehous, the Minquiers and Chausey Islands[9] since the engineers considered that they belonged to France.

5   Charles-Dominique-Maurice Rollet de l'Isle, 'Étude historique sur les ingénieurs hydrographes et le Service hydrographique de la marine, 1814–1914' *Annales hydrographiques* (1951), p. 170 and Chapuis, *A la mer comme au ciel*, p. 417.

6   'Lettre de Beautemps-Beaupré au Directeur du Dépôt des cartes de la Marine', 4 July 1829, Archives Nationales, fonds Marine, 3JJ 84.

7   It is interesting to note that the observations made by Daussy in 1829 had been the only ones until the great triangulation made during World War II by the German Army in 1942 and 1943, see : Cyril Ernest Everard, 'The Isles of Scilly and the Channel Islands: "bench-mark" hydrographic and geodetic surveys, 1689–1980' (unpublished DPhil thesis, University of London, 2004), vol. 1, pp. 254–5.

8   'Lettre de Beautemps-Beaupré au Directeur du Dépôt des cartes de la Marine', 4 July 1829, Archives Nationales, fonds Marine, 3JJ 84.

9   Beautemps-Beaupré drew Chausey Island on two sheets : *Iles Chausey* and

The Dépôt des cartes found it necessary to write new nautical instructions. The task had been given to Alexandre Pierre Givry and from 1842 to 1851 the service published *Le Pilote français* in three volumes, which described the coasts and the routes from the Belgian border to Bréhat Island.[10] This publication had been the last before the revision of the collection of charts that was begun here in 1863. The lack of more precise nautical instruction was obvious, but engineers were overwhelmed by more pressing tasks and had to rely on some Navy officers. Charles Thomassin was one of them, who accepted to write in three volumes the *Pilote de la Manche*, published from 1871 to 1875.[11] Then regularly, the Dépôt asked an experienced officer for upgrades. In 1880 Edgar de Courthille, with the help of a pilot, took over from him.[12]

Nevertheless, the chiefs of the naval station of Granville, who were assigned to monitor fishing fleets and defend the French fisheries to prevent infractions committed by Jersey fishermen, contributed to developing the hydrographic knowledge of the area.[13] From time to time, they gave the Dépôt information about some submerged rocks. Their contribution was limited, however.

In January 1862 the *Commission des phares et balises*[14] decided to install a light vessel to mark the dangerous islands of the Minquiers. This decision had been triggered by the loss of the *Marie*, a brick that was sailing back to Granville after her fishing expedition on the Grand Banks of Newfoundland. In the fog she hit a rock around the Minquiers on 30 November 1861. The master mistook the shoals he had in sight for the first rocks of the Saint-Malo channels. The crew tried to escape from the grounded boat; some of them reached Chausey but fifty-one died.[15] The next year another brick, *Les Trois Frères*, sank with all its crew of seven seamen.[16] The government was pressed by the Deputy of the Manche department to officially ask his British counterpart to build a lighthouse on the main island.[17] Then, for fear that

---

Sound de Chausey. These charts had been compiled by the Hydrographic Office and published under the number 63.

[10] Pierre Givry, *Pilote français, Instructions nautiques...*, (3 vols, Paris, 1842–51).

[11] Charles Athanase Thomassin, *Pilote de la Manche, côtes nord de la France, par M. Thomassin,...* (3 vols, Paris, 1875, 1871).

[12] Edgar de Courthille and F. Hédouin, *Pilote de la Manche. Côtes nord de France, par E. de Courthille,... avec le concours de F. Hédouin,...* (2 vols, Paris, 1880).

[13] The reader will find some interesting information about the naval station of Granville in : Guy de Saint-Denis 'La station navale de Granville sous la deuxième République', *Revue de la Manche* (2004).

[14] The *commission des phares et balises* is a committee that organises the network of lighthouses and beacons.

[15] Robert Sinsoilliez, *Histoire des Minquiers et des Écréhou* (Saint-Malo, 1995), pp. 127–31.

[16] Ibid., p. 132.

[17] 'Rapports et délibérations du Conseil général de la Manche' (Saint-Lô, 1863), p. 117.

inaction should be taken by the British as a renunciation of sovereignty, the French authorities decided to react. Anatole Bouquet de la Grey, an engineer of the Dépôt, took part in the commission and sailed to the Minquiers to take some soundings.[18] On that occasion he experimented with a new method by plotting numerous soundings with only a few landmarks. As far as we can judge from the account of Bouquet de la Grey himself this method is probably the one referred to as 'inscribed angles', which had been commonly used for navigation.

This first mission had not been very conclusive and during the summer of 1865 Xavier Estignard, an engineer of the Dépôt des cartes, was sent to survey the southern part of the Minquiers. It seems that the mission had been decided in a great hurry and was poorly equipped.[19] Estignard had to wait for almost a month for neap tides, and the ship he intended to use had needed repairs. Very few days remained for the survey. On 6 August, he was at last able to sail to the Minquiers with the *Hoque* and the *Faon*. The second boat was equipped with a dredger they had hastily borrowed from oyster fishers. Estignard had in mind to determine precisely the nature of the bottom of the sea in order to find a suitable mooring place. He was confident that he could rely on the conclusion drawn previously by Bouquet de la Grye but he soon became disillusioned and concluded that his method of plotting soundings was not accurate enough. Instead of the sandy bottom he expected to find he encountered granite.

On top of the difficulties, Estignard even wondered if it was feasible to moor a light vessel around the Minquiers. He sailed to Jersey and asked the harbour master of St Helier for advice. The general opinion among Jersey seamen was that mooring a light vessel would have been very useful for them because they were frequenting this area very often, but he doubted that it was a profitable investment for the French government since national fishermen were scarce.

Nevertheless, Estignard recommended that they wait for the November storms to take a final decision. Eventually, in December 1865, the light vessel was successfully moored.[20] The event went rather unnoticed. Local newspapers gave barely any account of it. The *Vigie de Cherbourg* simply informed mariners 'that a new light vessel [would] enter in service on 23

---

[18] Anatole Bouquet de La Grye, *Notice sur les travaux scientifiques de M. Bouquet de La Grye* (Paris, 1879), p. 10.

[19] Xavier Estignard related his mission in a report he sent to the Minister on 29 September 1865, Service historique de la Défense à Vincennes, archives de la Marine (noted thereafter SHDMV), BB3 750.

[20] The reader will find interesting information about the life of the light-vessel *Les Minquiers* in : Guy de Saint Denis, 'Le bateau-feu Les Minquiers (1865–1891)' *Revue de la Manche* (1999).

December'.[21] It was only some years later that the light vessel served the French claims for sovereignty over the Minquiers.

In 1864 the Dépôt des cartes undertook the general revision of the charts of the French coasts. The collection appeared outdated and ill-adapted for steam navigation. Yet the director had some difficulties in convincing the minister of the necessity of the enterprise. Estignard was assigned to the survey of the northern coasts of France from Brest to the Belgian border. With his team on board the *Phoque*, a rather uncomfortable ageing ship, he spent the summer of 1868 along the coast between Granville and Barfleur. He also took some soundings in the Gulf of Saint-Malo. With his colleague Felix Vidalin, Estignard drew a new map of the Rance River and corrected eight charts in the collection. The same year the British Hydrographic Office[22] in turn undertook a new survey of the Minquiers Islands, but with greater accuracy. The mission had been given to staff Commander John Richards[23] who spent the summer of 1868 between the north of the plateau and the southern part of Jersey, searching for submerged dangers. He relied mostly on the crew of the ship assigned to monitor the fishing fleet.[24]

Xavier Estignard, somewhat hypocritically, explained to the minister that such efforts were in vain because the area was so dangerous that no one dared to sail there anyway. Yet Estignard demanded that a team should be commissioned to take some soundings around Ecrehos Island and Raz Blanchard, at least to save the honour of France and take up the challenge.[25] The Dépôt never missed an opportunity to exploit Anglo-French rivalry in order to draw the minister's attention. Afterwards, many corrections were made on existing charts, but it is difficult to determine precisely their importance and who did them. After the revision conducted by Estignard, twelve maps were concerned. It is very likely that data had been gathered under the supervision of the officer who settled the training programme of the *Pilotes de la flotte*. This new corps was created in 1862 due to the tenacity of Alfred Moulac, who had been

21 *Vigie de Cherbourg*, 7 December 1865.

22 The Admiralty appointed nearly permanently a small team to the survey of the Channel Islands.

23 John Richards spent many years surveying the Channel Islands. In June 1859 he was appointed assistant surveyor under the commander, Frederick William Sidney. He finally replaced him in 1861 and spent the end of his career charting the Channel Islands and the west coast of England. Sidney and Richards drew and corrected five charts of the Channel Islands and the Gulf of Saint-Malo between 1858 and 1872, see: Dawson, *Memoirs of hydrography, including brief biographies of the principal officers who have served in H.M. Naval Surveying Service between the years 1750 and 1885* (Eastbourne, 1883), pp. 119–21.

24 *Proceedings of the Royal Geographical Society* (1869), p. 275.

25 'Lettre d'Estignard à l'amiral directeur du Dépôt des cartes', 16 April 1869, SHDMV, BB3 789.

the chief of the station at Granville between 1852 and 1856. He understood the necessity of training some able seamen to navigate in difficult areas. He persuaded the minister to formalise his initiative and create a training school. The method was rather simple. On a seaworthy ship (the) young volunteers learnt landmarks and safe routes in order to develop an impressive spatial knowledge. At the end of their training, those accomplished pilots had learnt by memory more than 7,000 landmarks[26] and were able to follow a route without a map. This knowledge had been formalised in the *Livres de Pilotage*; of course, but they were unpublished and even kept secret. The first version had been written by Lieutenant Charles Kerros and published in 1869.[27]

During their *tournées de pilotage*, they had many opportunities to analyse the charts and search for errors.[28] Their action, although discreet, enabled the Dépôt des cartes to increase the hydrographic data related to the coast of France. In the 'Channel Islands' file that contained the archives of the data gathered on the subject, we can find an example of the contribution of a pilot. On the *Faon*, in April 1879, he made a report to update information on the beacons and fires around Guernsey, Sark and Jersey. As a map user, he gave precious information to the engineers of the Dépôt and made, for example, some recommendations for modifying the beacons near Chausey. Finally, he made topographic stations where he suspected some errors on the chart. Thanks to the quality of his work, the chart of Chausey (n°829) was corrected.[29]

Nevertheless, behind what appears to be a fruitful cooperation lay some dissension. Chiefs of the pilots' school and experienced pilots themselves kept notifying the Dépôt of some 'dangerous rocks' that were not inscribed on maps. Engineers who had to address these critics constantly explained that their concerns were baseless. During their *tournée de pilotage* crews were looking for new routes that small steam ships would be able to take; thus they carefully explored the limits of the safe channels already sounded by engineers and ventured among shoals that had not been previously recognised. In the bay of Saint-Malo, indeed a very rocky place, they certainly found uncharted rocks and – to their great amazement – even drying rocks. In 1877 criticism rose to a high level as the Dépôt was asked to publish several notices to mariners. A bit irritated, Estignard felt the necessity to explain formally the Dépôt's methods. Beautemps-Beaupré in his time and his successors after him chose

---

[26] This figure is given by André Marquis in 'Histoire de l'école de pilotage de la flotte 1862–1924' Service historique de la Défense à Brest, 5W.

[27] Charles-Marie Kerros, *Manuel du pilote-côtier, par Ch. Kerros,...* (Paris, 1869).

[28] 'La Bible de l'école de pilotage à lire par tous les officiers, Histoire de l'école de pilotage de la flotte par le capitaine de frégate André Marquis', Service historique de la Défense à Brest, 5W.

[29] 'Rapport du pilote du *Faon*', 22 April 1879.

to concentrate on sounding channels in order to chart routes for mariners. They delineated with small dots the area where they could tack and informed sailors that some zones between reefs would remain uncharted because they were considered inaccessible. Estignard conceded that some local and trained pilots would take the risk to venture into small channels. But he reminded them that maps were not designed for them because their practical knowledge was far more accurate than the charts.

Estignard strove to destroy the idea that white parts on charts meant safe waters and hence that rocks found there were 'dangerous'.[30] Nevertheless, he had to give up and corrected the maps anytime an officer or a pilot from the school noticed some new rocks, even in inaccessible areas. The changing political situation also drove the Dépôt to change its methods. First, a sovereignty conflict emerged between France and Great Britain and each state made a plan to chart contested areas to give credit to its claim. Second, as relationships deteriorated between them during the last decade of the century, the Gulf of Saint-Malo was being considered as an active maritime border. This new situation brought the Navy to build a new defensive strategy.

The sovereignty issues arose at the beginning of the 1880s. Jersey fishermen tried to prevent their French colleagues from exploiting the waters near the rocks of the Ecrehos and soon they requested the State of Jersey to ask the Privy Council to claim sovereignty over the islets. In March 1884 the French government backed down and the minister of the Navy warned fishermen that they would sail around the Ecrehos at their own risk and that the Navy would take no action to support them.[31] It was only when the rumour arose that the British were building a battery on the main island that many journalists spoke up to defend national pride.[32] The question emerged again in 1886 and then all newspapers published on the subject. The main issue was concerning strategic matters and some journalists dared to compare the Deroute Channel with the Strait of Gibraltar.[33]

In 1888, the quarrel reached an even higher level when France planned to draw better charts of the Minquiers and the Gulf of Saint-Malo. The mission was settled in April 1888 and the minister cautiously forbade the surveying team 'to do anything' in the British waters around the Channel Islands.[34] During the first days of May, the *Chimère*,[35] under the supervision of the engineer

---

[30] 'Lettre au ministre', 12 January 1877, Archives Nationales, fonds marine, IJJ 122.

[31] Robert Sinsoilliez, *Histoire des Minquiers et des Écréhou*, p. 224.

[32] Some newspapers such as *Le Gaulois* or *L'Avranchin* and *La Vigie de Cherbourg* that were local titles gave information about the battery in December 1884.

[33] 'La question des Ecrehous', *Le Gaulois*, 10 December 1884.

[34] 'Lettre du ministre à l'ingénieur en chef', 20 April 1888, SHDMV, BB2 667.

[35] The *Chimère* was the first ship the French Navy designed specifically for hydrographic survey.

Ferdinand Isidore Hanusse, headed for the Minquiers. The programme was ambitious. This area had been charted by Beautemps-Beaupré in 1831 but he purposely limited his survey to the outlines of the plateau and the main channel. It is worth mentioning that during his time on board a sailing ship, because of strong tide currents, it would have been difficult to obtain better accuracy. The survey of 1888 had been a great effort, for the financial situation of the service was difficult. At the same time another team was struggling to finish charting the coasts of Corsica, an even more pressing task.[36]

The major part of the survey took place in the islands themselves but Hanusse devoted time to improving the accuracy of the chain of big triangles that would frame his future work. He used as a base the line between Granville and Cancale.[37] While on the Minquiers Islands, the team made the most of difficult weather and managed to land in order to take some geodetic measurements. The Jersey fishermen who had settled in during summer showed no sign of hostility and even welcomed the crew and the two persons hired by the hydrographic service as tide observers. Hanusse emphasised that the mission had been run normally without anything that could have been taken as a provocation.[38] Nevertheless, some journalists in a Guernsey newspaper spread the rumour that the French flag had been flown on the main island and a dispute arose. Soon many articles appeared, claiming to defend French rights even though the majority of writers recognised the poor strategic value of these small rocks.[39]

Hanusse gave a detailed account of his mission. For the first time a French team had been able to land and perform a triangulation, even if it was modest. It took five days for the workers hired by the service to construct a signal of eight metres high on the main island, and five more on the biggest rocks. Two tide gauges had been constructed and the tide observers were accommodated in one of the tiny houses on the island at a very cheap price. The weather had been exceptionally awful; strong winds alternated with thick fog and interrupted the work. When it was too dangerous to stay at anchor, the ships had to sail back to Saint-Malo or Granville, which delayed the mission even more. In addition, during daytime, the tides allowed the team to perform soundings for only three to four hours. Between 7 May and the latest day of July, the team had completed only thirty days of work. Maurice Rollet de l'Isle who

---

[36] 'Lettre du ministre au directeur du Dépôt des cartes', 7 April 1888, SHDV, BB2 667.

[37] Charles-Maurice Rollet de l'Isle, 'Étude historique sur les ingénieurs hydrographes et le Service hydrographique de la marine, 1814–1914', *Annales hydrographiques*, p. 190.

[38] 'Rapport de la mission hydrographique du plateau des Minquiers', 7 June 1888, 'Dossier Minquiers' Archives du service hydrographique de la Marine à Brest.

[39] *Le Petit Parisien*, published three articles on the subject on 1, 3 and 6 June 1888.

was in charge of the topographic part of the survey was able to achieve little more than half of the task.[40]

Nevertheless, a dispute arose when a Guernsey newspaper described the French survey as an attempt to take the island. Soon the French journalists replied in defence of what they considered as the right of their country and all of them took the light vessel as proof of sovereignty. The public, generally unaware of the reality of the sea, thus had a good idea of what it could be like. In 1866 Victor Hugo published *Les Travailleurs de la mer*, in which he contributed to emphasising the dangers of the seas around the Channel Islands. The efforts that France had made to light the Minquiers were worth any title of property.[41] As a response to France in August 1888, the government of Great Britain sent a mission of inspection to the Minquiers.

Then France asked for an explanation and for the first time claimed sovereignty over the islets, which led to an exchange of diplomatic notes. On 21 November 1888 the Foreign Office officially denied all the arguments the ambassador of France had put forward in August. The note said that neither a hydrographic survey nor the light vessel France had moored could be taken as proof of sovereignty.[42] Somewhat discountenanced, the French minister of foreign affairs asked his colleague the minister of the Navy for advice, who in turn tasked the hydrographic service with researching archives for any more solid proof. Indeed, so far the French authorities had never questioned their rights on the Minquiers. In February 1889, the chief engineer Anatole Bouquet de la Grye gave a response. [43] He found nothing to assert any claim of sovereignty over the plateau and concluded that the rights of France and Great Britain were both weak.

The service faced a dilemma. Due to the bad weather, only limited data had been gathered to draw a new map. Unless a new survey was planned, all the effort would have been lost. Under these circumstances, and despite the risk of a political issue, the minister gave the hydrographic service the mission to achieve the task.[44] The *Chimère* headed again to the Minquiers during the

---

[40] 'Lettre de l'ingénieur Hanusse à l'ingénieur en chef du service hydrographique', 28 July 1888, 'Dossier Minquiers', Archives du Service hydrographique et océanographique de la Marine conservées à Brest.

[41] Among many examples, an article of *Le Matin*, on 31 May 1888, expressly linked the lighthouse and the question of sovereignty.

[42] The dispute between France and Great Britain had been settled by a decision of the International Court of Justice in 17 November 1953. The Minquiers and Ecrehos islands had been awarded to Jersey.

[43] 'Note confidentielle sur les Minquiers', 10 February 1889, 'Dossier Minquiers', Archives du Service hydrographique et océanographique de la Marine conservées à Brest.

[44] 'Lettre du ministre à l'ingénieur en chef du service hydrographique', 12 February 1889, SHDMV, BB2 676.

first days of summer. Due to better conditions the survey was easier, and the team, led once more by Hanusse, concentrated on soundings and improved some topographic details. When the inhabitants got notice of the *Chimère*'s arrival, they hoisted the Union Jack, but despite some tensions the survey ran normally without any event that could have triggered a diplomatic incident. The team deplored the death of two sailors who were making soundings in a dinghy that had drifted away.[45]

The chart that was drawn after these surveys was published in 1891 and titled 'Plateau des Minquiers – entrée de la Déroute' and took the number 4599. At a rather large scale (one nautical mile to 45 millimetres) it shows a high density of soundings, but some had been copied from the British chart.[46] It is difficult to know if the document had been of some use to French seamen. We can reasonably have doubts. The Minquiers were indeed very dangerous and anyone without an experienced pilot might have hesitated to risk his ship. The map was of some use to sail on the Deroute Channel, which was also dangerous but frequented by coasters. However, the charts numbered 826 and 827 also featured this area with enough accuracy and were certainly more useful since the balance between the price and the extent of the charted area was better. It was the last survey that the French hydrographic service performed until 1923 but in 1895 it published a useful collection of charts of the currents of the Channel drawn by Captain Alfred Houette after a long and meticulous study. The cartographic documents were accompanied by a manual that explained how to use them.[47]

The survey of the Minquiers had been decided when France took a strategic turn and acknowledged that the best defence against a hostile fleet would lie in the deployment of torpedo boats.[48] It was generally acknowledged that coastal fortifications were weak and outdated because France had to concentrate its efforts on the eastern borders. This new strategy is known as *défense mobile.* In these schemes the probable enemy was Great Britain, but the theory could have been applied to any other nation that would have landed on the coasts of France. Many officers advocated this strategic concept and spread a coherent doctrine among the public. The most famous of them is surely Admiral Hyacinthe Aube, the leading figure of a group known as

---

[45] Charles-Maurice Rollet de l'Isle, 'Étude historique sur les ingénieurs hydrographes et le Service hydrographique de la marine 1814–1914', p. 189.

[46] The French hydrographic chart used is probably the number 62, in three sheets that shows at a large scale the island of Jersey and the surrounding islets, first published in 1867 and corrected in 1884 and 1897.

[47] Alfred Houette, *Les Courants de la Manche, par M. Houette,...* (Paris, 1894).

[48] Among copious publications it is worth mentioning the book of Admiral Léon Bourgois that had a significant impact on public opinion: Siméon Bourgois, *Les torpilleurs, la guerre navale et la défense des côtes / par le vice-amiral Bourgois* (Paris, 1888).

Jeune École.[49] The general public, primarily the populations of Normandy and Brittany who were directly concerned by the possibility of an invasion or at least hostile manoeuvres, became gradually more anxious. The conseil général de la Manche[50] reflected this fear, as it asked the government to strengthen the naval forces in Cherbourg.[51]

The Channel Islands were perceived as an outpost from which the British Navy or any other enemy such as the German Navy could launch an attack. In this context it is interesting to focus on the publication of what we would call today a political fiction novel titled *La prise de Cherbourg*,[52] published in 1889. The book can be compared to *The Battle of Dorking*,[53] published in 1871, which depicts the landing of a likely German enemy.[54] This atmosphere surely increased the feelings of vulnerability among coastal populations.

Such feelings were deeply rooted in the dramatic past of the Anglo-French wars and resurfaced from time to time. The construction of the port of Braye in Alderney that started in 1847, even disguised under the benign name of 'port of refuge', gave good reasons to the French public opinion to feel insecure.

Secondly, the Gulf of Saint-Malo since the second decade of the nineteenth century had witnessed a long conflict between French and Jersey oyster fishers. This activity thrived up to the middle of the century as urban markets developed a new appetite for oysters, which Jersey fishermen hastened to meet.[55] They built a fleet of fast and seaworthy boats which were much better than the small, undecked ones of their French counterparts[56] and in general gained a certain prosperity.

Rapidly, harsh competition arose between French and Jersey fishermen, worsened by the depletion of oyster beds. Soon some incidents occurred at sea. The difficulties rose to a crescendo in 1828 and again during the months of March and April 1834, when gunfire had been exchanged between some

---

[49] The reader will find an exhaustive analysis of the question in Martin Motte, *Une éducation géostratégique: la pensée navale française de la jeune école à 1914* (Paris, 2004).

[50] A *conseil général* is the elected assembly of a *département*.

[51] Bourgois, *Les torpilleurs, la guerre navale et la défense des côtes*, p. 192.

[52] *La Prise de Cherbourg* (30 avril 1889). The author remains unknown.

[53] George Tomkyns Chesney, *The Battle of Dorking* (1871).

[54] Patrick M. Kirkwood, 'The Impact of Fiction on Public Debate in Late Victorian Britain: The Battle of Dorking and the "Lost Career" of Sir George Tomkyns Chesney', *The Graduate History Review* (vol. 4, n°1, 2012).

[55] The reader will find some important information about the efforts made by the State of Jersey to regulate oyster fishing in Alan G Jamieson, *A People of the sea: the maritime history of the Channel Islands* (London, 1986), p. 434.

[56] This difference is often noticed by the chiefs of the naval station in their reports to the minister. In 1861, Palasne de Champeaux paid particular attention to the working conditions of the seamen he had to monitor, SHDMV, BB4 797.

British fishing boats and the warship committed to the protection of the French fisheries. In 1837 both the French and British governments agreed to find a reasonable settlement. It took almost three years for arduous negotiations to lead to the Convention of August 1839, which resolved the problem.[57] Both states took strong measures to enforce the treaty and orders were given to the commanding officers of facing naval stations in Jersey and Granville to patrol the sea and control ships as much as they could.[58] They had a twofold function. First, they had the mission to repress any illegal access by foreign fishermen and second they also monitored the local fishing fleet. Despite the joint efforts of the French and British navies, local maritime societies cultivated mutual distrust if not pure hatred. It is also likely that they didn't differentiate between the mission of the *station navale* of Granville and that of the new torpedo boats settled in Cherbourg, especially when in 1892 the *Sainte Barbe*, an *aviso-torpilleur*,[59] was assigned to monitor fisheries.

This new strategic turn had some specific aspects in the Gulf of Saint-Malo. The entire area became even more of 'a maritime border' close to the neighbour's land. The small torpedo boats of *défense mobile* with only 54cm of draught were somehow very well adapted to the configuration of the coasts with many islands and rocks. Their main mission was patrolling in narrow and shallow waters. In the mind of its designers, the success of the strategy relied on the capacity of the torpedo boats to sail out of their ports, lurk behind shoals and harass the enemy's ships. It was necessary to exploit every route and to survey new ones. There lies the main reason why the hydrographic service had been ordered to draw more accurate maps of the Gulf of Saint-Malo.[60] The minister grounded his decision on the expertise of the chief of the school of the *Pilotes de la flotte*. Since 1882, each pilot was provided with a complete set of charts of French coastal waters and in 1890 the hydrographic service created a new collection, especially for the service of the torpedo-boat flotillas.[61]

Each route was given a number that figured on these special and secret charts. Only a few have been preserved. These charts were expensive to print

[57] Alan G. Jamieson, *A People of the Sea*, pp. 436–43.

[58] The activity of the naval station in Jersey had been studied by Victor Coysh in 'Admiral Lefebvre and HSM *Dasher*', Société Guernesiaise, *Transactions of La Société Guernesiaise* (1966), p. 60.

[59] An *Aviso-torpilleur* is a rapid patrol boat. The *Sainte Barbe* was 59m long, displaced 395 tons and made 19 knots.

[60] 'Note sur le programme proposé sur les côtes nord de la Bretagne et sur le plateau des Minquiers', February 1889, Archives du Service hydrographique et océanographique de la Marine conservées à Brest.

[61] 'Lettre du ministre au Service hydrographique', 1 April 1890, SHDV, BB2 686.

because they displayed several colours and needed four lithographic stones.[62] Three hundred of them had been issued by the service, but they became quickly obsolete as the Navy failed to update and correct them.

Soon, pilots received ordinary maps which they were ordered to complete themselves. On the chart of Alderney and the Casquets,[63] for example, we can see numerous routes that weave among rocks. Some are very close to the one printed by the hydrographic service but diverged to some extent in order to avoid submerged rocks. Some routes were totally specific to the torpedo boats and, as far as we can see, were rather dangerous. Indeed, they dared to sail in the middle of the Casquets islets.

As bigger torpedo boats were being constructed at the beginning of the twentieth century, it appeared necessary to revise some routes that were too dangerous. Nevertheless, the pilots argued that in time of war, difficult passages of the Deroute Channel could be used by a torpedo boat as a shelter that protected her from the enemy warships that were too big to sail there. According to the commanding officer of the torpedo-boat flotilla, the passage could also be used to shelter an entire squadron of small destroyers in case Cherbourg Harbour should be blockaded.[64] In 1909, when he wrote this note, it was very unlikely that the British would attack Cherbourg and thus the French Navy still clung to this idea more from habit than for good reasons.

The method of navigation that the *Pilotes de la flotte* developed is puzzling and had been criticised in its time. They learnt their environment through the landmarks and the routes they delimited, with a view to navigating without a map and, in a way, it was the chart itself they assimilated. But the officers were not convinced of the validity of these practices and were very doubtful whether the pilots would have been able to safely alter their course if it had been necessary. They drew the conclusion that this method led them to navigate as if they were in a tunnel and once they wandered out of the routes they admitted that they felt disorientated. The advantages of such a practice were few compared to the normal use of a good chart.[65]

During the nineteenth century the French hydrographic service made efforts to draw up a coherent collection of charts of the coasts of France. It led to

---

[62] 'Note interne du Service hydrographique', 4 July 1894, Archives nationales, fonds Marine, 3JJ 133.

[63] This chart had been published in 1902 by the French hydrographic service after a British map published in 1863.

[64] 'Rapport au sujet de l'extension et de la révision des zones de pilotage', 8 May 1909, SHDMV, BB4 2333.

[65] The most complete and interesting criticism of the methods developed by *l'école des pilotes de la flotte* had been made by Pierre Célérier as late as 1950. His report allows us to understand how the French Navy addressed the complex question of spatial cognition that was and still is a major problem. The document is held by the Service historique de la Défense à Brest (5W).

the publication of the *Pilote français*, published first from 1823 and revised between 1864 and 1870. The surveys performed in the Gulf of Saint-Malo and up to Cherbourg occupied a special place. French coasts had been unsurprisingly surveyed meticulously, but the charts were afterwards corrected very frequently at a pace that changed with the configuration of the seabed or that navigation networks cannot explain. It was the consequence of the new strategy the Navy implemented here to defend the maritime borders against a British enemy. New data were steadily gathered by the *Pilotes de la flotte* and commandants of torpedo boats that sailed back and forth around the Channel Islands and in the Gulf of Saint-Malo, which was considered a major strategic area. The two years survey of the Minquiers Islands in 1888 and 1889 is ultimately one of the first and best examples of the ambiguous links that hydrography and sovereignty may share. These two missions stand as an exception in the history of the hydrography of the French coasts.

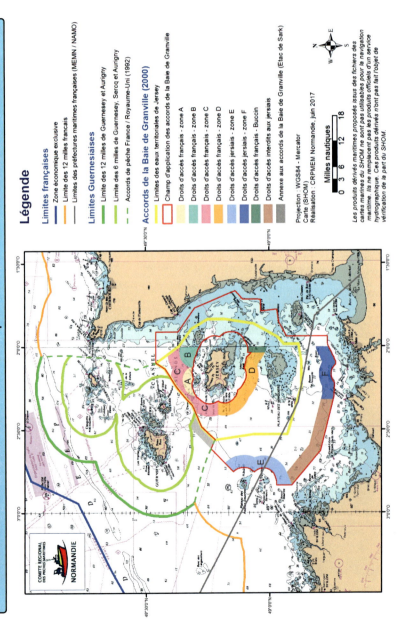

Plate 1 The sea as territory. The close proximity of the Anglo-Norman Islands to France has created a wide range of territorial and juridical complications, notably for fishing. In 2004 the Treaty of Granville, of July 4th 2000 became law, setting the fishery boundaries between Jersey, Guernsey and France, but these do not coincide with the international boundaries. Comité régional des pêcheurs maritime de Basse-Normandié, 2016.

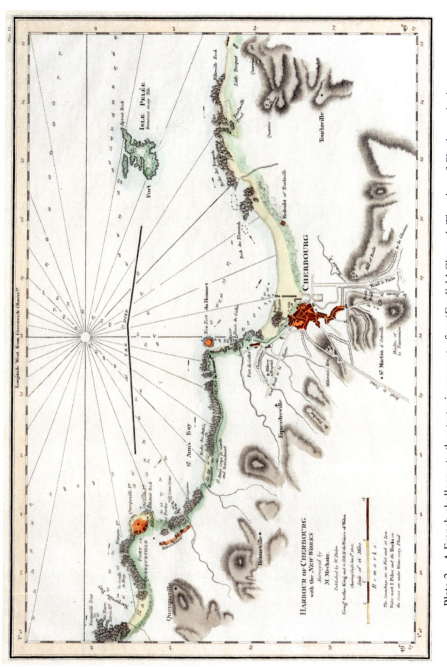

Plate 2   A French challenge to the strategic concept of an 'English' Channel. The plan of Cherbourg harbour in 1805, published by W. Faden, Geographer to the King and to H.R.H. the Prince of Wales. Joseph Cachin was the project engineer at Cherbourg. Courtesy of The Trustees of The Henry Euler Memorial Trust.

Plate 3   Cherbourg today. Google Maps.

THE FOUNDING OF A HARBOUR OF REFUGE AT ALDERNEY.

Plate 4   The start of work on the harbour at Alderney was an event of national significance in Britain, suitably captured by the Illustrated London News in February 1847 for a mainland audience anxious about a potential invasion. It was also the beginning of dramatic changes in the life of the island. © Illustrated London News Ltd / Mary Evans Picture Library.

Plate 5   With the French coast so close Captain William Jervois' concept of a fortified island surrounding the new harbour, in this updated version dated May 1st 1854, stressed the critical connection between insular security and marine capabilities. The forts and fortified barracks could accommodate wartime garrisons. TNA MR1-1299(2) permission granted.

Plate 6 By 1852 the harbour works had made considerable progress, with the first major section of the 1,300 feet of breakwater completed, along with the supporting defences at Fort Grosnez alongside the inner harbour. The inner harbour was critical for supply ships and, in the event of war, refuelling naval paddle steamers deployed off Cherbourg. Lithograph by George S. Reynolds, dedicated to supervising engineer James Walker G.S.Reynolds 1854 / Courtesy of the Mignot Memorial Hospital.

Plate 7 The 1858 Admiralty Chart of the Harbour combined the work completed, the projected eastern breakwater and the ongoing western breakwater. TNA WO 1/5754 permission granted.

Plate 8   Fort Touraille, and the Roselle Battery, were the final pieces of the defensive plan, completed in 1859. The fort combined substantial barrack accommodation, headquarters, a parade square, landward defensive works and heavy gun batteries covering the entrance to the new harbour. The fort also acted as a central redoubt for the entire defensive system of the island. It was renamed Fort Albert in 1861, a fitting memorial for a man who had visited the harbour and the forts on three separate occasions. TNA WO 78/2761(4) permission granted.

Plate 9   After the fall of the Second Empire in 1870 France no longer posed a significant threat at sea, leaving Alderney harbour without an obvious role, widely criticised as a waste of money. Two decades later that judgement was reversed, as France once again posed a strategic threat, primarily to shipping in the Channel. This prompted the Royal Navy to return to Alderney in 1890, to test blockading local harbours, with Alderney acting as an 'enemy' torpedo boat station during the annual strategic exercises. Cherbourg, still only 25 miles away, contained the armoured cruisers and torpedo boats that France would use in wartime to attack British merchant shipping. The exercises proved the utility of the harbour as a base for torpedo boats, destroyers and small cruisers, which were accompanied by the essential colliers and storeships. Priaulx Library, Guernsey.

10

Alderney: The Impact of National Defence

COLIN PARTRIDGE

The coastal landscape of Alderney is dominated by the relics of its former strategic maritime prominence – a prominence based on British naval planning of the mid-Victorian period which would transform the island over a critically brief interval of thirty years in the mid-nineteenth century. However, it would be misleading to suggest that this was the first and last occasion on which the Channel Islands archipelago would find itself in the front line of international conflict.

Islands in the front line

The idea that the Channel Islands – as we now call them – would provide an advanced station for English and British warships and a base from which to observe and intercept enemy shipping, may be truly said to have originated as far back as the thirteenth century after King John's loss of Normandy,[1] but more recently – during the War of American Independence – the British government would support modest plans to improve the coast defences of the islands, and build major works at Fort Regent in Jersey and Fort George in Guernsey.[2] At this time, and following French commitment to develop the port of Cherbourg,[3] more serious attention would be given to the provision of improved harbour facilities in the three principal islands in order to secure military support and naval protection in time of war. The threat from France was real and ever-present: for instance, an attack by a French squadron on Elizabeth Castle and a foiled *coup de main* in St Ouen's Bay, Jersey, in 1779; the attempt by three French privateers to seize Alderney in 1780,[4] and the

---

[1] N. A. M. Rodger, *The Safeguard of the Sea* (London,1997), pp. 50–1, 59.

[2] C. W. Partridge, unpub. MS, *Harbours of Refuge in the Channel Islands 1775–1904* (Alderney, 2012).

[3] Y. Murie, *Le digue qui a fait Cherbourg* (Cherbourg-Octeville, 2006), pp. 30–1.

[4] A. G. Jamieson, *A People of the Sea* (London, 1986), p. 222; TNA, WO 33/65.

defeat of Baron de Rullecourt's forces at the Battle of Jersey after a successful landing in 1781.[5]

Fears of imminent attacks on the Channel Islands during the French Revolutionary and Napoleonic Wars were given renewed impetus after Napoleon's visit to Cherbourg in April 1803, relaunching Vauban's project of over a century earlier to create *un port militaire*, and appointing Joseph Cachin as *Directeur des travaux maritimes*.[6] Writing to Lord Pelham, Lieutenant-Governor General Sir John Doyle urged: 'Your Lordship knows we are the advanced posts and that the fate of these islands would have an influence upon publick opinion.'[7] Any lingering doubts as to Napoleon's aggressive intentions towards the islands were dispelled in the later publication of his correspondence with Marshal Berthier,[8] and his order to le comte Decrés to concentrate a naval force and 8,000 troops at Cherbourg for that purpose.[9]

Meanwhile, Brigadier-General J. R.Mackenzie in command of the troops in Alderney, writing to his sister in Inverness shortly after his arrival in August 1806, laments: 'From this sterile place I can give you nothing entertaining – There is but little society, but the place is healthy.'[10] Notwithstanding General Doyle's repeated calls for maintenance and improvement of the island's coast defences, Alderney was now defended with a total of 93 guns in 19 open batteries, and an island militia force of 384 men of all ranks under detailed orders for mustering on the approach of enemy vessels and taking up defensive positions around the coast, night and day.[11] The island possessed its own hired local vessel to act as a scout, while the gun-brig *Assault* patrolled the adjacent French coast from Dielette to La Hague, just seven miles distant and within clear sight from the island on a fine day, reporting on enemy shipping and troop movements.[12]

Any prospect of forming a deep-water harbour in Alderney before 1815 was linked only with unsuccessful attempts to construct a place of arms into which a garrison force might retire but, in the aftermath of inevitable post-war retrenchment, the dismantling of coast batteries and withdrawal of garrison forces, Alderney had fallen progressively into a period of depression. After appealing unsuccessfully to the Home Office for an extension of the existing

---

5 R. Mayne, *The Battle of Jersey* (Chichester, 1981), pp. 51ff.

6 Murie, *Le digue*, p. 60.

7 TNA, WO 1/772, f. 589, Doyle to Pelham, 28 July 1803.

8 HC Deb. cit. vol. 167, cols 814–17, Napoleon to Berthier, 2 June 1805.

9 R. Glover, *Britain at Bay: Defence against Bonaparte, 1803–14* (London, 1973), pp. 182–3.

10 BL, Add Ms 39197, f. 208, Mackenzie Paper, vol. XI.

11 BL, Add Ms 39199, f. 116, ibid., vol.XIII.

12 TNA, HO 99/2, Home Office to Brigadier-General MacKenzie, 26 August 1806.

small pier at Braye, not only to stimulate trade but to provide a naval facility,[13] the hereditary governor, John Le Mesurier, informed the Home Office in 1821 of the 'recent and total loss of trade', with upwards of 200 islanders having emigrated to France, America and the neighbouring islands, those remaining only being employed in cultivating their respective portions of land and common handicrafts.[14] With the earlier demise of privateering and the suppression of smuggling in 1808, the sea could no longer sustain them.

John Le Mesurier would eventually surrender his patent in 1825 for an annuity of £700, property reverting to the Crown on terms which, though unfavourable with regard to rents, would prove most advantageous for the future defence of the nation.[15] At the same time, the Lieutenant-Governor of Guernsey's civil authority became coextensive with his military command of Alderney.[16] The effect on Alderney was immediate and far-reaching after a period of almost two and a half centuries of relative independence as a Crown *fief*. By 1830, there was such widespread distress in the northern island that it was determined to accept the Lieutenant-Governor's earlier recommendation that the common land should be partitioned and distributed among the poorer section of the population, which numbered just 1,045 in 1831.[17]

At this *partage*, the British Crown took the further step of reserving to itself areas of land with appropriate access, suitable for works of defence which would, in time, be transferred to the Admiralty and Ordnance. Reservations marked out in 1832 by General Cardew and placed under the control of the Office of Woods, included the '100 Feet' along the shoreline between Clonque Rock and Mannez Garenne established by an earlier Order in Council of 4 August 1830, together with land around existing barracks, magazines and other older government works.[18] This was an opportune moment, with political disarray over the creation of Belgium as a separate state, when Lord Aberdeen – who as Foreign Secretary in Peel's later administration would completely reverse his opinion – argued in the House of Commons: 'If France was not England's natural enemy, she was certainly her natural rival. It might be true that, in order to preserve peace, it was necessary to prepare for war, but it was hard to interpret France's conduct in this light. In a great state, such preparations usually meant aggression.'[19]

[13] TNA, HO 98/42, J. Le Mesurier to Home Office, 29 February 1816.
[14] TNA, HO 98/43, J.Le Mesurier to Home Office, 3 January 1821.
[15] *Fifth Annual Report of the Commissioners of Her Majesty's Woods, etc. 1826*, XIV, p. 10.
[16] Guernsey Greffe, LG-14, Lieutenant-Governor's letter-book, 31 December 1824.
[17] TNA, HO 98/53, Major-General Sir J. Colborne to Alexander Milne, 26 October 1826.
[18] Guernsey Greffe, *Plans des Communes de l'Ile d'Aurigny 1831*.
[19] M. E. Chamberlain, *Lord Aberdeen: a political biography* (London, 1983), pp.

Public awareness of French interest in the Channel Islands, prompted by
the French hydrographic service's survey of the waters around Jersey and
Guernsey under the direction of M Beautemps-Beaupré, was a further spur to
latent concerns which would be echoed later by the Duke of Wellington.[20] In
his report to Lord Melbourne on the defenceless state of the island in 1832, the
Lieutenant-Governor of Guernsey, Major General John Ross, stressed: 'It is
only necessary that Alderney should possess a floating harbour, accessible at
all times of tide and respectably protected, to render it a port of observation
on the harbour of Cherbourgh [*sic*] of infinite consideration.' A pencilled
margin note − 'a naval question' − portended the Treasury's prompt refusal
of this premature application.[21] This was not the first occasion on which
appeals had been made to the government for naval anchorages in the Channel
Islands, notably by Captain (later Rear Admiral) William Symonds in recognition of the harbour building at Cherbourg,[22] while Major General John
Ross persisted in approaching Lord John Russell in 1836, after noting the
large sums voted recently by the French government for improvement to
the harbours at Granville and St Malo, stating: 'I have long since invited the
attention of His Majesty's Government to the expediency of providing, at all
events for steamers, a protected Anchorage at Alderney ... A secure Harbour
or Anchorage at all times of the tide in this Island must, I should imagine,
be highly conducive to the Interests of His Majesty's service in the event of
War, and more particularly of a french War.'[23]

The government responds to the threat

The eventual catalyst for action would be the Treaty of London of 15 July
1840 − the quadripartite settlement of the Levant crisis − from which France
was excluded, leading to a tense confrontation with Britain, which was resolved
by Palmerston's bold diplomacy in the wake of the bombardment of Acre.
Large sums voted in the French chambers for the re-fortification of Paris and
the completion of the works at Cherbourg, mingled with strident support in
the French press, again drew attention to the exposure of the Channel Islands.
This led directly to the first commission of 1842 to investigate the development of naval anchorages in the three principal islands 'where a squadron
of steam-vessels may be collected and protected' under the euphemistic title
of harbours of refuge, this in a thinly veiled attempt to avoid causing offence
to France. A second commission would determine the final location for the

---

270−2, n. 17.
   20 *Colburn's United Service Magazine*, September 1829, p. 373.
   21 TNA, WO 44/75, Treasury minute, 27 September 1832.
   22 Jamieson, *A People*, pp. 228−9.
   23 TNA, HO 98/58, Major-General J. Ross to Lord John Russell, 30 May 1836.

harbours in Alderney, Jersey and Guernsey, though the latter would not be proceeded with.[24] At the local level, these proposals would be championed in Jersey by Sir John Le Couteur, ADC to Queen Victoria, and in Guernsey by the Lieutenant-Governor, Sir William Napier, while at national level the Duke of Wellington and Lord Palmerston would prove active and persistent proponents of the Channel Islands' harbours in successive administrations, and of the Alderney project in particular. Concerned at the delay in the provision of defensive works for the new harbour, the Duke of Wellington would assert in a letter to the prime minister before the end of 1847: 'But we must get forward with these works! and above all we must immediately take care of Alderney!'[25]

In order to appreciate the impact that these harbour works, and their defences would have on Alderney between 1847 and 1872, it is important to understand who was responsible for ordering the works in the first instance, and how these orders were put into effect. The Admiralty took the initiative in promoting the first Channel Islands' joint naval and military commission in the summer of 1842, with the cooperation of the Ordnance Department, subsequently appointing the civil engineer, James Walker, second president of the Institute of Civil Engineers, who would accompany the second commission in 1844 and eventually design and superintend the harbour projects in the Channel Islands.[26] The prime minister, Sir Robert Peel, fully upheld the initiative privately, but wished publicly to play down the strategic importance of the new harbours for warlike purposes in Jersey, and Alderney just seven miles from the French coast.[27] Significantly, the votes raised in parliament for harbours of refuge would be taken under the civil estimates and not under the naval budget. The harbour works at St Catherine's on the east coast of Jersey would commence on the same date as those in Alderney under the same contractor but would be abandoned prematurely in 1853 due to the silting up of the anchorage.[28]

The knowledge in all three islands that major projects of national defence were being contemplated did not escape the attention of the local press. Speculation was rife in Guernsey that the government was intent on placing the Channel Islands in the forefront of British naval strategy, and every visit

[24] M. S. Partridge, *Military Planning for the Defense of the United Kingdom, 1814–1870* (Connecticut, 1989), pp. 34–8.

[25] TNA, PRO 30/22 6F, f. 43, Duke of Wellington to Lord John Russell, 6 September 1847.

[26] PP, 1847–8, vol. XVIII, *Minutes of Evidence: Miscellaneous Expenditure*, Sir Charles Wood, 8 May 1848.

[27] BL, Add Ms 40444, f.234, Sir Robert Peel to Henry Goulburn, 9 September 1844.

[28] The full story of St Catherine's Breakwater is told in W. Davies, *The Harbour that Failed* (Alderney, 1983).

of Admiralty board members and their representatives was faithfully recorded in the local press, accompanied by lively editorial assessment.[29] With a population barely on a par with that of 1831, Alderney was descended upon by the full weight of government initiative with the commencement of the harbour works at Braye on the north side of the island in January 1847. At the laying of the harbour foundation stone, portrayed in *The Illustrated London News*, who among the large crowd which had assembled to witness the ceremony and join in the festivities, including excursionists from Guernsey, could have foreseen the transformation of the island which would ensue?[30] The following year, Europe was riven by revolution and King Louis Philippe fled the country, as France became a republic under the hand of Louis Bonaparte, the nephew of Napoleon I.

The appointed contractor, Jackson & Bean, from Eltham Park in Kent, had worked on railways and canals, but had no previous experience of marine works. With what would be recognised as a beacon of Victorian enterprise and engineering resourcefulness, they set about mastering the elements and developing the necessary infrastructure for such an enormous undertaking. First, it was essential that they should provide their own shipping facility, the steamer *Princess Royal*, which would open twice-weekly communications with Guernsey, together with a safe haven for unloading cargoes and sheltering the craft employed in the breakwater works by building the inner harbour in Little Crabby Bay in 1849. Second, it would be necessary to construct a railway linking the principal Admiralty quarry at Mannez, some two and a half miles to the east, where stone for the breakwater would be obtained. Third, they would need to accommodate the large labour force that must be brought to the island, at first by taking up empty dwellings and disused former barracks and, later, by building terraces of workers' cottages.[31]

The land required for a project of such magnitude – the fortification of the island would follow three years later – entailed the acquisition of large tracts of ground in private ownership, as well as the transfer of Crown land to the respective service departments.[32] It was later admitted that the works now being carried on in Alderney could not have been undertaken unless the property had been acquired previously by the Crown. These acquisitions, commencing with James Walker's instructions from the Admiralty in September 1845 and those of the Treasury subsequently, had amounted to £9,022 17s 8d by February 1849, rising to some £13,800 8s 3d four years later, inclusive of legal fees – well in excess of £1m at today's prices. The Crown

---

[29] *The Star*, Guernsey, 20/24 August 1842; 11 July 1844.

[30] *The Illustrated London News*, 20 February 1847, p. 128.

[31] These details and those which follow are taken from PP. 1850, vol. LIII, *Harbours of Refuge and Breakwaters*.

[32] TNA, WO 44/514, 51 T. 205, James Walker to Sir Charles Trevelyan, April 1851.

land was transferred to the respective service departments on a valuation agreed with the Treasury of £25 per acre (roughly equivalent to £2,000 current). The private land purchases in Alderney were facilitated by Judge Gaudion and the Procureur, T. N. Barbenson, who acted as law agent, considerable problems being experienced due to the unreasonable demands of some landowners and the great number of very small lots in the divided common land.[33] The passage of an 'Expropriation Act' by the States of Alderney thereafter, based on the similar law currently in force in Guernsey and subject to prior authorisation by the Lieutenant-Governor, went some way to simplifying and speeding up this process in many of the transactions in the following decades. In 1852, James Walker would be instructed to purchase the whole of the shoreline of Braye Bay, in anticipation of the need to provide the wharfage, quays, docks, slips and stores for a naval station which would never materialise. Land which remained in Crown ownership or which had already been transferred to the service departments would be let until needed for harbour or defence works.

The harbour at Braye Bay

The plan first presented to the House of Commons in 1850 shows the extent of these purchases to date for quarrying (51 acres), the mineral railway (13½ acres), and the projected works of defence (116½ acres) required by the Ordnance, which were now becoming a matter of some urgency as the harbour works progressed. At this point, the harbour plan comprised a modest area of 67 acres, three fathoms and above in depth with two breakwaters, the larger being to the west of 2,550ft (777m) from Grosnez Point with that to the east of 1,027ft (313m) from Roselle Point. Already, £97,806 9s had been expended on the Alderney harbour works before the end of 1849 out of the initial estimate of £610,000. In order to gain an impression of the transformation imposed on Alderney in the space of just six years, the monochrome lithograph from *The Illustrated London News* may be starkly contrasted with the vibrant colour print by G. S. Reynolds after the painting by the accomplished Guernsey artist, Paul Naftel, showing the harbour of refuge and fortifications in 1852. The unspoilt coastal scene has become what may be inferred in the title and from the content of Thomas Jackson's later biography – *Industry Illustrated* – a hive of industrial activity.[34]

The first intention to open a quarry near the western breakwater revealed stone of an inferior quality and led to the purchase of land for more extensive quarries at Mannez at the east end of the island, requiring the construction of

[33] PP, 1854, vol. LX, *Statement of Lands purchased in the Island of Alderney*, pp. 5–7.

[34] The London Borough of Bexley Public Library, The Memoirs of Thomas Jackson, *Industry Illustrated* (1884).

the railway which was begun on 15 March and opened on 7 July 1847, including several substantial rock cuttings and road crossings. A steam locomotive and wagons had carried some 90,000 tons of stone to the breakwater before the end of the year, where 320 workmen were already engaged. A year later, the rubble stone base upon which the breakwater superstructure was to be built extended out some 450ft (137m) from the shore, and a start had been made on the outer sea wall and inner harbour wall, with the foundations for a slipway at its base. The total quantity of stone deposited that year was 198,000 tons and the workforce employed had increased to a daily average of 487 men as the project gathered momentum.[35]

The industrious scene at the harbour in 1852 demonstrates not only the progress made in the harbour works – the extended breakwater superstructure, the travelling gantries and timber staging, the chute for loading the barges towed by a steam tug for depositing stone for the base of the breakwater, the blacksmith's shop, the lime kilns, the fabrication of large concrete blocks for the breakwater foundations – but also the commencement of the intensive programme of fortifications with the commissioning of Fort Grosnez at the base of the western breakwater. The scene was again graphically encapsulated in the portrait by G. S. Reynolds of Walker's partner, Alfred Burges, which now hangs in Alderney.

Anxious to complete the eventual chain of eighteen forts and batteries that would be built over the next eight years, the design and supervision of the remaining works would be placed under the direction of Captain William F. D. Jervois RE from June 1852, with the oversight of the Inspector-General of Fortifications, Sir John Fox Burgoyne.[36] In an unprecedented move, the Board of Ordnance had passed the work of constructing the defences to Jackson & Bean without competitive tender, since the breakwater contractor already monopolised the transport and labour infrastructure of the remote island.[37] Later that year, considering Alderney to be 'by far the most important Station, as containing a Naval Establishment', Burgoyne wrote in a confidential memorandum after visiting Alderney: 'The position of the French for the attack of these Islands, is very imposing; they have on one flank, the great Port and Naval Arsenal of Cherbourg, within 25 miles of Alderney; and on the other the excellent Harbours of Granville & St. Malo, with the fine roadstead of the Chaussée [sic] Islands, as an advanced rallying Point, with a large amount of substantial, decked fishing and coasting vessels along their shore, manned by Crews well acquainted with the peculiarities of that

35 PP, 1850, vol. LIII, *Harbours of Refuge and Breakwaters.*

36 C. W. Partridge and T. G. Davenport, *The Harbour and Fortifications of Alderney* (Alderney,1993), pp. 44–7.

37 TNA, WO 55/815, f. 253, Sir J. F. Burgoyne, Minute to Board of Ordnance, 14 October 1852.

Navigation.'[38] In this widely supported belief, shared among leading British naval and military figures, the defensive works in Alderney would be pressed forward with some degree of urgency and completed within the decade.

From as early as the summer of 1852, plans for the first royal visit to Alderney had been eagerly anticipated by the population, only to be thwarted at the last minute by bad weather after elaborate preparations had been made.[39] There was a particular purpose behind such a visit: Prince Albert had taken a close interest in national defence, and his immaculately kept files survive to chart the pursuit of his enquiries, ostensibly on behalf of the monarch. By September of that year, following the death of the Duke of Wellington and the establishment of the Second Empire in France under Louis Bonaparte's reincarnation as Napoleon III, the Ordnance was pressing the Treasury for increased expenditure on the national defences, supported by Sir John Burgoyne's detailed assessment of priorities, in which he stated: 'Of all the works of defence required for the British Empire at home and abroad, I consider those for Alderney as first in importance.'[40] The Queen herself, claiming to be 'no alarmist', addressed her concerns on the subject to the Earl of Derby.[41] At the same time, the earlier mixed naval and military commission was reconvened and returned to Alderney in early 1852, now recommending the adoption of James Walker's plan for the first of several proposed increases in the size of the harbour to accommodate the larger warships then under construction. In the eight months that it took the Admiralty to come to a decision, several hundred workmen were unemployed.

Islanders would have to wait until the 1854 Channel cruise of the royal yacht, *Victoria and Albert*, for the first visit of the Queen and her consort. Her Majesty first set foot on the island on 9 August 1854, marked by the renaming of the principal thoroughfare Grosnez-street, accompanied by great festivities in which the contractor's agent Thomas Dixon, and Captain William Jervois RE, played a prominent role in conducting the royal party around the harbour and fortifications at very short notice.[42] These momentous events in Alderney's history were again recorded in the paintings of Paul Naftel, while Victoria found time to record her own impressions in her diary and to paint and sketch scenes from her first visit to the island, which are preserved in the

---

[38] TNA, WO 55/816, Sir J. F. Burgoyne, *Memorandum, On the Defences of the Channel Islands*, 20 September 1852.

[39] *The Star*, Guernsey, 14 August 1852.

[40] RA, E44, f. 11, *Notes on the Above Items*, by Sir J. F. Burgoyne, in G. Butler to Treasury, 23 September 1852.

[41] A. C. Benson and Viscount Esher, *The Letters of Queen Victoria* (London, 1908), vol. II, pp. 396–7.

[42] The Royal Visit is fully described in *Industry Illustrated*, pp. 68–75, and *The Star*, Guernsey, 10 August 1854.

Royal Archives.[43] Prince Albert's interest in the works had grown from his earlier conviction that 'Alderney will be most important as a Naval Station when the Harbour now in progress is completed; & no risk must be run of its loss – It will probably require, therefore a garrison of not less than 2,000 men, all Regular Troops.'[44] From his first examination of the works, Prince Albert would take advantage of successive royal visits to Alderney, twice in 1857 and again in 1859, to chart their progress.

The transformation of the island

From the very beginning of the harbour works, the sudden influx of workmen from outside the island led to problems beyond the control of the local authorities. A riot occurred in November 1847 when a party of labourers forcefully released two of their number from jail, leading the Lieutenant-Governor, with Home Office approval, to send a detachment of the 47th Regiment from Guernsey to restore order.[45] From this date, Alderney once again became a garrison island with many of the principal British line regiments occupying the newly constructed barracks, without a break, until shortly before the Second World War. Unemployed labourers and quarrymen from Guernsey, navvies from Ireland and stonemasons from Cornwall, were all drawn to the island by relatively higher wages and the prospect of several years of continuing employment. Previously unoccupied houses were taken over, and Jackson & Bean began building new dwellings in terraces close to the harbour works in an area to become known as New Town. Older barracks surviving from the Napoleonic Wars were temporarily occupied with the agreement of the Ordnance Department, and new remote settlements sprang up in the neighbourhood of the quarry at Mannez and Longis Bay.[46] A growing number of French quarrymen and labourers added to earlier settlers from that country since 1815, and totalling around seventy within two years of the commencement of the works, were reluctantly accepted as residents by Judge Gaudion so long as they obtained work, noting in a report to the Lieutenant-Governor that several kept shops and owned smallholdings.[47]

The anticipated pressure on the island authorities was manifested further in the requirement to introduce criminal jurisdiction to Alderney in March 1850.

---

[43] RA, VR 1851–4, ff. 62–7 *Sketches from Nature*; Album no. K 56, ff. 77–9, 8/9 August 1854.

[44] RA, E44, f. 23, Memorandum by Prince Albert, *Distribution of Troops in Great Britain*, 10 November 1852.

[45] Island Archives, Guernsey, LG 18–01, pp. 13–14, Colonel Ward to Judge John Gaudion, 15 December 1847.

[46] Reports on the growth of Alderney which follow are to be found in successive editions of *The Comet*, Guernsey.

[47] Island Archives, LG 18–01, pp. 92–4ff, Judge J. Gaudion to Major-General J. Bell, 17 January 1849.

Prior to this date, offenders were tried in Guernsey and would continue to be so dealt with for serious crimes of assault and murder, of which there were several cases over the following decades. Opening at the Michaelmas Chief Pleas, henceforth all petty misdemeanours and other criminal charges would be dealt with in the newly erected Court house, with its attendant Greffier's house, jail and Jailer's house. Legislation would also be passed giving the Court powers to order offenders to give security for good behaviour over a specified period of time, failure to do so leading to removal from the island. The Court was also granted powers to solemnise matrimony between the growing number of dissenters and other Christian denominations who were being drawn to the island. This trend would be reflected in the later applications to build places of worship for these groups. Intermarriage between islanders and newcomers, including military personnel in the garrison, would see an increase in the birth rate that in turn added to a steady increase in the population to 3,333 in 1851, comprising 1,083 English and Welsh, 324 Irish, 99 Scottish, 156 French and 1,271 natives of Alderney and the Channel Islands. The total would rise to 4,933 in the census of 1861 – almost five times that of twenty years earlier.[48]

Another consequence of the rapid increase in the population over these two decades was the growth of the town of St Anne, again recorded in the Jersey and Guernsey newspapers. The contractor's steam vessels, the *Princess Royal* succeeded by *Queen of the Isles*, were put to good use in the summer months running well supported excursions to Alderney and, occasionally, beyond to attend the Cherbourg *fêtes*. Afterwards, the great progress with the Alderney harbour works and fortifications was reported in detail, as well as that of the town where the *Douzaine* attempted to apply rudimentary planning controls regarding the layout and paving of new roads. The building of new houses in extensions to High Street and Victoria Street (formerly Grosnez-street) was apparent, the latter supplanting the former with a growing number of new shops and the assembly rooms, together with schools for the children, a hospital, a library for the Mechanics Institution and lodges for the Oddfellows and Masonic Order. Perhaps the most significant landmark was the new church of St Anne, designed by the prolific English Gothic revival architect Sir George Gilbert Scott, and built with a generous gift from the Reverend John Le Mesurier, son of the last hereditary governor, who attended its consecration by the Bishop of Winchester in 1850. The nearby Wesleyan Chapel was built a year later with stone donated by Jackson & Bean.

As Alderney flourished, watched closely by its neighbours, there remained a number of continuing social problems. The short-lived introduction of the 'truck system' into the breakwater contractor's scheme of remuneration caused hardship amongst some elements of the workforce, drew criticism from the authorities and was soon abandoned. Drinking to excess was a perennial

---

[48] *Census of England and Wales 1861*, HMSO (1862), Table X.

scourge, with the issue of twenty-two liquor licences in January 1849, rising to as many as forty-six in January 1861.[49] At the latter date, these drinking establishments had doubled in number, ranging through the town of St Anne (21), New Town (5), Braye (8) and beyond, even in the area of Longis Bay (8). Objections were raised by the military to the proximity of a beer and cider shop close to Corblets Barracks and by the contractor for the government works at Braye and the quarries at Mannez, where it was considered that 'the granting of such a licence would be a serious injury to the cause of Order in the neighbourhood.'[50] Earlier, in September 1849, an outbreak of cholera giving rise to the death of eleven victims and said to have originated from France, was fortunately contained by the imposition of strict medical control and the timely provision of an isolation hospital on the Butes. All the while, there was the repeated danger of serious or fatal accidents on the harbour works, on the railway and in the quarries.

Accidents on the breakwater itself were a regular occurrence. In 1849, a Mr Findlater, the head mason, vanished without a trace and later the same year a foreman, William Ross, was washed off the advancing superstructure and drowned. The year 1853 was particularly bad when in June, following two earlier fatalities, thirteen men were seriously injured when the breakwater staging collapsed due to the overloading of stone wagons, one dying later from his injuries. The following month, four workmen were washed off the staging in heavy seas, three of whom were drowned. Fatalities on the railway included workmen falling between moving wagons, as well as small children being run over accidentally. Injuries in the government quarries figured prominently in the grisly statistics noted with regret by Walker and Burges in their quarterly reports to the Admiralty.[51] Most of these occurred due to falling rock or flying splinters, with a number of deaths caused by premature detonation of explosives or mishandling of the newly discovered gun cotton charges, first used in Alderney in August 1847 in the presence of the First Lord of the Admiralty, Lord Auckland, and Colonel Irvine, the Admiralty Director of Works.[52] In 1868, William Browning, who had been employed on the harbour works for many years, accidentally fell from the breakwater with his horse. The horse was found a few days later off the French coast; tragically, William Browning's body would not be recovered from the sea until several months later.

---

[49] Island Archives, LG 21-03, p. 407, Judge Thomas Clucas to Major-General M. Slade, 28 January 1861.

[50] Island Archives, LG 18-01, p. 111, W. Parkes to J. N. Barbenson, Queen's Procureur, 12 February 1849.

[51] PP, 1850, LIII, *et seq, Abstracts of Engineers' Quarterly Reports of Progress*, for the years commencing 1847.

[52] *The Comet*, Guernsey, 23 August 1847.

Questions and answers

While British ministers, naval and military men would continue to justify the great works of national defence publicly, there were doubters emerging at a very early date who questioned the enormous expenditure as the harbour plans were progressively enlarged. In the debate in the House of Commons on miscellaneous expenditure in June 1851, Joseph Hume succeeded in forcing a temporary suspension of the vote in the committee of supply on harbours of refuge, questioning the purpose of the works in the Channel Islands after having visited them earlier in 1849. He was vigorously supported by Richard Cobden who alleged that if the government now progressed their plans to fortify Alderney by transferring their 'engineering panic' to the Channel Islands, 'it would certainly be regarded as a work of aggression by the French'.[53] But the publication of the notes on the *Enquête parlementaire sur la situation et l'organisation des services de la marine militaire* in Paris just six months later, left the British government in no doubt as to the requirement for the harbour works at Braye. In submitting a confidential, detailed assessment of the French report to Prince Albert in 1853, the First Lord of the Admiralty, Sir James Graham, after earlier expressing his own reservations as to the expenditure, stated: 'I have now visited the great works at Dover, Portland and the Channel Islands, and I am quite satisfied, that none of them must be abandoned, but all pushed forward without exception steadily but with energy.'[54] Unsurprisingly the works in the Channel Islands had attracted the attention of France from the outset. Alluding to the Hobbesian precept arising from endemic suspicion and insecurity (so ably expounded by Azar Gat),[55] a defended base is held to reduce mutual deterrence by offering the potential for offensive action. As early as January 1848, a French war steamer anchored in the Alderney roads, four men going ashore to make observations particularly in the quarries, before steaming around the island for the purpose of surveying the coast. In subsequently granting Lieutenant Colonel William Le Mesurier additional powers as Town Major in Alderney, the Lieutenant-Governor ordered: 'You will further consider yourself fully authorized to take cognizance of all Foreigners – more particularly Military Men and Engineers, who may visit the Island, – if it appears to be their object to acquire knowledge of the works and defences; and to prevent if possible, the attainment of that object by their making Plans, Surveys, etc. ...'[56] Similar instructions would follow for keeping a proper surveillance over the islet of Burhou. Nevertheless, Félix-J-B. Reibell, charged

---

[53] HC Deb. vol. 117, cols. 816–19, 16 June 1861.
[54] RA, E45, f. 52, Sir James Graham to Prince Albert, 23 September 1853.
[55] A. Gat, *War in Human Civilisation* (Oxford, 2006), pp. 97–100.
[56] Island Archives, LG 18-01, p. 79, Major-General J. Bell to Lt. Colonel W. Le Mesurier, 6 November 1848.

with the inspection of *Travaux hydrauliques* in the *Premier arrondisement* at the port of Cherbourg, submitted his third report on Alderney after his inspection with fellow engineers in 1855, leaving his superiors in no doubt as to the purpose of '*des travaux importants pour un port de refuge et de concentration de forces navales et pour la défense militaire de l'Ile.*'[57]

Direct postal communications with Alderney were never realised at this time due to the absence of regular sailings from England, all mail having to be sent via Guernsey where the South-Western Railway Company's mail packets arrived every Tuesday, Thursday and Saturday morning from Southampton, returning on Monday, Wednesday and Friday morning. The mails closed each day at 9:00am, so that if the masters of ships plying between Alderney and Guernsey failed to deliver or collect the Alderney bags before that hour, the island could be deprived of mail for several days on end.[58] By the same token, Alderney was excluded from the benefits of the penny-postage system. The laying of the electric telegraph between Portland and Alderney for military objectives in 1858, inaugurated with a message sent by the Queen from Balmoral, would prove to be another unreliable link in the years immediately following when suffering intermittent breaks and long periods of silence while repairs were undertaken. With the prompt approval of the States of Alderney, the cable would be laid across the island and extended to Guernsey and thence to Jersey, before a final link to France was eventually established.[59]

Throughout the period of Anglo-French alliance in the war with Russia (1854–6), the harbour works in Alderney were pursued with unremitting vigour and would receive further impetus with the completion of the Cherbourg dockyard and arsenal, coupled with the opening of the railway from Paris in August 1858 by Napoleon III. The celebrations, with the attendance of Queen Victoria and Prince Albert, were widely reported in the British press, raising serious concerns about the facility now available for the assembly of a potential invasion force which could threaten Britain's principal naval bases. The following year, when France demonstrated the apparent ease of transporting by sea and landing a force of 12,000 men in Italy in the war against Austria, the rumour that the French emperor had issued orders for the immediate fortification of the Chausey Islands acted as an additional spur. The fortification programme in Alderney was speedily concluded in 1859 with the completion by Major Jervois of the Arsenal and Store Establishment, and the

---

[57] SHD-Cherbourg, Cabinet du ministres, *3ème Rapport de M. Reibell, etc. relatif aux travaux du Gouvernement Anglais à l'Ile d'Aurigny, près du Casquets*, 8 July 1855.

[58] Priaulx Library, Guernsey, *Guernsey Almanack 1850*, published by H. Brouard.

[59] Island Archives, LG 21-03, p. 255ff, Lt. Colonel W. Le Mesurier to W. Brock, Government Secretary, 27 July 1858.

adjoining principal work at Fort Touraille, to be known as Fort Albert when named for the Prince Consort who died in 1861.[60]

The Admiralty sheds responsibility

The subsequent inauguration of a royal commission to enquire into the defences of the United Kingdom, which gave rise to yet another 'invasion scare' at home, did not distract a growing number of critics in parliament from protesting at the ever-increasing annual expenditure in Alderney with what was claimed to be little apparent benefit.[61] In 1862, McClean and Stileman took over the engineering supervision of the western breakwater on the death of James Walker, who had been wrestling with contractual disputes between Jackson & Bean and the government over claims arising from delays and the cost of repairs from storm damage, and the Admiralty's decision not to proceed with an eastern breakwater a year later.[62] In 1864, the western breakwater had reached its extremity of 4,698ft (1,432m) from the shore in a depth of 130ft (39.6m) at low tide. The Admiralty, having lost the initiative, divested the responsibility for the 'harbour of refuge' to the Board of Trade with the Alderney Harbour Transfer Act of 1865.

During the second half of the 1860s, after expenditure on the harbour works alone had exceeded one million pounds sterling, although the average labour force had declined from a peak of just over one thousand men in 1856 to less than 300 ten years later, several violent storms of unprecedented severity caused repeated damage to the exposed outer section of the breakwater. In 1870, after several internal reports and recommendations for the repair and maintenance of the breakwater had been received, the Board of Trade commissioned an independent assessment by John Hawkshaw, engineer for the Holyhead harbour works, and Lieutenant Colonel Andrew Clarke, the Admiralty Director of Works. The Treasury responded with an assurance that HM Government had determined to maintain the breakwater until estimates were obtained for the necessary repairs, and to retain Mr Hawkshaw as super-intending engineer.[63] These plans were defeated in June 1871 by an amendment moved by Mr G. Bentinck, MP for West Norfolk, in the committee of supply on the civil service estimates, when the vote for Alderney was omitted from

[60] Partridge and Davenport, *The Fortifications*, pp. 61–9.

[61] HC Deb. vol. 164, cols 320–6, 4 July 1861; vol. 166, cols. 1849–60, 16 May 1862.

[62] TNA, ADM 1/5860, Admiralty Minute (following visit to Alderney), 11 September 1863.

[63] TNA, MT 10/140, Board of Trade to Treasury, 9 May 1870; Treasury to Board of Trade, 15 July 1870.

the sum for harbours of refuge on a pledge that no further money should be expended on it.[64]

The prospect of winding up the harbour works had already attracted the concern of the island authorities with critical observations made on a visit early the previous year by the Secretary to the Board of Trade, Mr George Shaw-Lefevre. Now, with the unanimous assent of the board members, instructions were issued for the immediate discontinuance of the works, notice to be given to the remaining labour force, and estimates to be prepared for closure of the facilities and settlement of all outstanding claims.[65] As the population of Alderney now declined rapidly to 2,718 in the 1871 census, parliament voted the necessary funds for closing down the works which finally stopped on 30 September.[66] While the Post Office and War Office became concerned at the prospective discontinuation of the contractor's steamship service to Guernsey, Alfred Bean gave an assurance that this would be maintained for the time being, though now running at a loss.

The future of Alderney harbour would now be determined by a Select Committee of the House of Lords under the chairmanship of the Duke of Somerset, the former First Lord of the Admiralty from June 1859 to 1866. While the committee sat during April 1872 and heard evidence from all the principal engineers who had reported on the harbour works, as well as prominent representatives from the Admiralty, the War Office and the Board of Trade, a remonstrance of the Court of the Island of Alderney on behalf of the inhabitants had been drawn up. Protesting at the decision of the Board of Trade to cease maintenance of the breakwater and of the alleged lack of knowledge of members of parliament, 'who by their influence tend to mislead others', this was referred to in the submissions before the committee by Thomas Barbenson, the Queen's Procureur and Colonel commanding the Royal Alderney Artillery Militia.[67] The effect of abandoning the works on the population and the island economy was forcefully expressed, together with the inevitable impact on trade with Guernsey, England and Cherbourg – all to no avail.

The final decision was based on military and naval factors alone – coinciding crucially with the defeat of France in the Franco-Prussian War. The harbour works would be abandoned, and the fortifications maintained to provide a token defence. In July 1873, prime minister William Gladstone informed the Queen that 'The Cabinet considered the state of Alderney Harbour, on which

[64] HC Deb. vol. 207, cols. 679–83, 27 June 1871.

[65] TNA, MT 10/112, Minute H.3060, Board of Trade to John Hawkshaw, 30 June 1871.

[66] Alderney Society Museum, Breakwater Diary, 30 September 1871.

[67] PP, 1872, IX, *Report from the Select Committee of the House of Lords on the Harbour and Fortifications of Alderney.*

there has been so vast an outlay with very small results.' Their decision was to keep up the maintenance of the breakwater at an annual expense of £4,000 rather than see the works destroyed. He would later add: 'That harbour affords a sad example of what is now generally admitted to have been more than a waste of a million and a half of public money, under the sanction and instigation of the highest professional authorities.'[68] – perhaps forgetting that as a member of Peel's cabinet from May 1843 he had been party to the creation of the Alderney project. By 1875, it was determined that the outer section of the breakwater would no longer be maintained, the Treasury having agreed with the Board of Trade's representations for it to be returned to the superintendence of the Admiralty by way of a second transfer act. In future all votes for repairs to the inner section of the breakwater only would be taken under the navy estimates under the strict control of the director of works.[69]

The Admiralty re-establishes its interest

Major storm damage to the outer section of the breakwater in 1879 led to its progressive collapse and the decision to build a new head at the point we see today at 2,800ft (853m) from the shore. If the Admiralty had been somewhat reluctant initially to take back responsibility for the harbour at Alderney, they were soon able to justify their commitment to the defence of British seaborne trade, faced with the advocates of the newly introduced torpedo boat by the French *Jeune École*. Amongst the British fleet's subsidiary objectives in the naval manoeuvres of 1890 would be to ascertain what form the tactics should assume, taking account of torpedo boats operating from a distant base against a reserve fleet and the Channel ports. For this purpose, 'enemy' torpedo boats stationed in Alderney would demonstrate all too clearly the danger of this new threat, notably in their attack on 'A' fleet in Plymouth Sound.[70] This event drew the attention of the War Office to maintaining appropriate defences for the harbour at Alderney.

In the wake of the Fashoda crisis of 1898 which had prompted tactical British and French counter-naval movements, and following a review carried out by a joint naval and military committee, a new battery of two 6-in BL guns would be mounted in Fort Albert, which continued to accommodate British garrison forces, with a 12-pdr QF battery and searchlights at Roselle Point to command the examination anchorage, both manned by the Royal Alderney

[68] RA, A 46/31, William Gladstone to Queen Victoria, 10 July 1873.

[69] PP, 1902, XLV, *Navy Estimates 1875–1876: Memoranda explanatory of Vote 11, (E) Alderney Breakwater.*

[70] PP, 189–1891, LI, *The Partial Mobilisation of the Fleet and the Manoeuvres of 1890.*

Artillery Militia.[71] Ironically, these works coincided with the publication of *The Last Great Naval War* – a fictional account of a war between Great Britain and France, written by Sir George Sydenham Clarke under the pseudonym of 'A. Nelson Seaforth', in which Alderney is not only successfully attacked and occupied by the French on the outbreak of hostilities, but is ceded to France under the terms of the imaginary peace settlement![72]

The first use of Alderney by the navy had brought renewed prominence to the island and a welcome boost to the economy, albeit short-lived. Licences issued for continued quarrying activity, the use of the railway and the development of the stone trade were accompanied by the construction of a massive stone-crushing plant at Braye, and the successful application by the States of Alderney for government assistance with the construction of a new commercial quay in 1895 after several years of bitter dispute between rival island factions. The establishment of the Alderney Steam Packet Company, after the withdrawal of the contractor's vessels in the mid-1870s, had assured the retention of an all-year-round, twice-weekly mail service between Guernsey and Alderney, and once a week with Cherbourg. The navy would use Alderney again as a defended base in its fleet manoeuvres of 1901, with a squadron attached to 'B' fleet operating from the Channel Islands; these manoeuvres were memorable chiefly for the total loss of the navy's fastest torpedo boat destroyer, HMS *Viper*, on the Renonquet reef to the north-west of the island, and the sinking of torpedo boat No.81 in the harbour, holed after striking the submerged section of the outer breakwater at low water.[73] Alderney would play only a minor role in the British naval manoeuvres of 1906.

A garrison island

Throughout this period, and beyond the First World War, Alderney remained a garrison island with the civilian population in 1901 standing at 2,062 – very much akin to today's figure – though with seventy-eight houses now unoccupied. A further 402 military personnel and their families were housed principally in Fort Albert, Fort Château à l'Étoc and the married quarters at Whitegates and Simon's Place.[74] As always, the military calendar impacted on island life with twice yearly inspections by the Lieutenant-Governor and visits by other senior officers, weekly church parades and festivities celebrating

[71] TNA, CAB 18/22, Joint Naval and Military on Defence: Report XXXVI, 24 April 1902.

[72] A. Nelson Seaforth (pseud. Sir G. Sydenham Clarke), *The Last Great Naval War* (repr. Forgotten Books, 2015).

[73] PP, 1902, LXI, *Report of Naval Manoeuvres, 1901*. Return to an Order of the House of Commons, 17 January 1902.

[74] *Census of England and Wales 1901*, Alderney, HMSO (1903).

the monarch's birthday, regular musket and rifle practice on the range at Longis Common, gunnery practice by the militia with regular drill at the Arsenal in Ollivier Street (now a car park) and the inevitable sporting and social events in which islanders were traditionally involved. In the event of war with France – a scenario still under consideration by the Committee of Imperial Defence despite the growing naval menace of imperial Germany – and while the retention of regular battalions in the Channel Islands could not be justified on strategic grounds, the maintenance of Alderney as a torpedo boat station by the Admiralty was considered, *ipso facto*, as conferring some measure of protection on the other islands. In 1905, the political aspects of so doing, one year after the formal e*ntente cordiale* had been agreed between Britain and France, were viewed as a question for the cabinet alone.[75] Having benefited from its brief interaction with advances in British technology and naval supremacy and experienced the impact of rapid growth in its social and commercial infrastructure, Alderney was once again left to make its own way in the world.

---

[75] TNA, CAB 38/8 (20), Committee of Imperial Defence: Minutes of 65th Meeting, 8 March 1905.

PART 7

TRADE WAR – THE PROTECTION OF CHANNEL ISLANDS SHIPPING IN THE GREAT WAR

11

The Channel Islands in French Naval Strategy During the First World War

THOMAS VAISSET

Thirty kilometres off the Cotentin Peninsula, the Channel Islands are the closest British territory to the French coast. Because of this, and as also indicated by their compound French name – Les Îles Anglo-Normandes – they are an integral part of the history of the Channel as a 'mer pour deux royaumes' – a 'sea shared by two kingdoms' – the term coined by Renaud Morieux to describe this stretch of sea, now a border between France and Great Britain.[1] For André Lespagnol, they 'have been heavily involved for centuries in the everyday life of this part of the French Atlantic seaboard'.[2] They have also long been a source of concern for the French navy. Island strongholds, they represent a threat to Cherbourg, the town whose dockyards were nevertheless chosen for the construction of a fleet intended to rival that of the Royal Navy.

But in the early years of the twentieth century, the Channel Islands' geostrategic worth decreased significantly. For the British, worried by German sea power, the islands were losing their importance in favour of bases in the North Sea.[3] For the French, the Entente Cordiale seemed to remove the danger of an attack from Britain. So, for both countries the Channel was a sea at peace in 1914. Should conflict break out and an alliance be formed between the two countries, it would even be a central part of their shared military strategy.

---

[1] Renaud Morieux, *Une mer pour deux royaumes La Manche, frontière franco-anglaise (XVIIe–XVIIIe siècles)* (Rennes, 2008). Translator's note: Our translation. Unless otherwise stated, all translations of cited foreign language material in this article are our own.

[2] André Lespagnol, 'Les îles anglo-normandes et la France de l'Ouest: une relation particulière', in Frédéric Chauvaud and Jacques Péret (eds), *Terres marines. Études en hommage à Dominique Guillemet* (Rennes, 2005), pp. 85–90.

[3] Alan G. Jamieson (ed.), *A People of the Sea. The Maritime History of the Channel Islands* (London and New York, 1986), p. 243.

Events proved them right, as the Channel quickly became both a hunting ground for German submarines and a lifeline for the Franco-British war effort. A closer look at the French navy, and at the Channel Islands during the First World War, can shed new light on relations between the two navies, specifically in respect of the protection of sea routes.

Since the in-depth studies of the 1920s, little research has been carried out into the role of the French navy during the First World War, particularly in the Channel, which has long been considered a secondary theatre of operations. That early work was very much of its time: mostly designed and undertaken by military institutions, navy-centred, nationalist in outlook, mostly in written form, and largely positivist and utilitarian in style. However, the centenary of the First World War has sparked renewed interest.[4] This paper draws primarily on diplomatic records and collections held in the archives of France's Defence Historical Service (Service historique de la Défense, hereafter SHD), where research has been carried out into the papers of the general staff of the French navy, the Directorate General of Submarine Warfare and the naval forces that saw service in the Channel. Most importantly, I have been able to make use of the archives of the Normandy Patrol Division (Division des Patrouilles de Normandie), which are still in the process of being catalogued.[5]

Entente Cordiale and maritime security in the Channel on the eve of war: Franco-British dominance in the Channel

For both the Royal Navy and the French navy, the Entente Cordiale fundamentally recast the situation in the Channel. Under the leadership of the ever-dependable Rear-, later Vice Admiral Charles Aubert, Chief of Staff of the French navy from November 1905 to August 1909, and again from November 1911 to January 1913, who enjoyed steadfast support from statesman Théophile Delcassé, *la rue Royale*[6] became one of the key elements in the transformation of the Entente from the colonial compromise of 1904 into the de facto compact against the Triple Alliance that it became by the outbreak of the First World War.

With pressure from Delcassé, the navy became a driving force in moves that led to the exchange of letters of November 1912, by which the French and British governments undertook to consult with each other over acts of

---

   4   Jean de Préneuf, Thomas Vaisset, and Philippe Vial eds, 'La Marine nationale et la Première Guerre mondiale: une histoire à redécouvrir', *Revue d'histoire maritime*, 20 (2015) 14–191.
   5   My sincere thanks go to Cyril Canet, head of the central archives of the French navy at the Service historique de la Défense for his help with these resources.
   6   This metonym is used to refer to the headquarters of the French Ministry of the Navy, located on rue Royale, Paris.

aggression by third countries and to strengthen contacts between the general staffs in order to facilitate military preparations for addressing such eventualities.[7] This Franco-British agreement was in fact pre-empted and made easier – if not officially sanctioned – by naval reorganisations carried out on both sides in response to developments in the Triple Alliance. Starting in 1906, the concentration of French naval power at Toulon crossed a decisive threshold in October 1911 with the creation of the First Battle Fleet (Première Armée Navale). This significant development was followed in the spring of 1912, at the instigation of Winston Churchill, by the British decision to recall most of the British Mediterranean Fleet to the North Sea. All that was then left was the French 3rd Battle Squadron at Brest, consisting of six ageing battleships, and the 2nd Light Squadron at Cherbourg. With the redeployment of the 3rd Armoured Squadron to the battle fleet in the Mediterranean, announced just a few days before the famous exchange of letters, the French navy played a key part in sealing the *rapprochement* begun in 1904.[8] The decision rested on a calculation about Britain's willingness to engage militarily in the case of conflict. It was tantamount to entrusting the bulk of the defence of the Western seaboard to the Royal Navy, with the French navy, having decided to prioritise its commitments in the Mediterranean, contributing only limited support.

The de facto partnership between London and Paris placed control of the Channel at the centre of the two countries' overall strategy against Germany. In the case of an unprovoked attack on France or a violation of Belgian neutrality, they would need to be able to transport a British Expeditionary Force to continental Europe. Despite a continuing lack of clarity regarding any guarantee of London's commitment to military action, the two countries envisaged moving six divisions of infantry and a brigade of cavalry plus all their materiel, amounting to 162,000 men including non-combatant troops. In order to guarantee the safety of this transport, baptised 'transport W' by the French military, its route would have to be as far as possible from German

[7]   Service historique de la Défense, French navy archives held at Vincennes (hereafter, SHD-MV), SS Es 11, a brief history of the Franco-British conventions and understandings concerning maritime operations in the case of war involving the two countries against Germany (undated). The venerable old book by Samuel Williamson, *The Politics of Grand Strategy, Britain and France Prepare for War 1904–1914* (Cambridge, MA, 1969), remains the most complete source on the role played by the French navy in the development of the strategic partnership between the two countries. For the role of Delcassé, see Daniel Moucheboeuf, *L'œuvre navale de Delcassé de 1907 à 1913. Élément d'une politique de puissance* (Thesis for a Postgraduate Diploma at l'Institut d'Études Politiques de Paris, under the supervision of Serge Berstein, 2001).

[8]   John R. Walser, *France's Search for a Battlefleet. French Naval Policy 1898–1914* (PhD thesis in history, University of North Carolina, 1976), pp. 236–72.

bases, but close enough to enable effective onward resupply to the operational area of the Expeditionary Force. For these reasons, Le Havre and Rouen were designated as disembarkation points for the troops and materiel in preference to similar ports further north, or to Cherbourg.[9]

In practice, the strategy of the Entente partners was founded on the ability of their navies to turn the Channel into a kind of Franco-British 'lake'. The prime guarantor of this was the presence of British squadrons arrayed against the German fleet in the North Sea. The second was based on tight control over the Channel approaches, both at the Dover Strait and further to the west, in the strait between the Cotentin Peninsula and the British coast. While the need to protect the former appears self-evident, sources indicate the importance also accorded to the latter by the French naval authorities. In the light of manoeuvres carried out by the Japanese navy in the war of 1904–05, *la rue Royale* feared this passage might be penetrated by enemy ships approaching from the west, having first sailed north around Scotland. The French general staff even believed such an attack might be carried out in the first hours of the war by detachments of Germany's Hochseeflotte (High Seas Fleet), setting out immediately prior to the outbreak of hostilities.[10]

In January and February 1913, discussions between the two countries' general staffs led to the signing of three agreements which, in anticipation of a formalised alliance, specified the kinds of practical cooperation to be undertaken in the various theatres involved. In the Mediterranean, tasks were split between the Royal Navy, which would prevent the Austro-Hungarian navy from leaving the Adriatic, and the French navy, which would take on the Italian navy. Operations in the Dover Strait were entrusted to the British Admiralty, the French navy contributing only a few submarines and torpedo boats in supporting roles.[11] Further west, in the Channel itself, the situation was different in that Paris and London took shared responsibility. Document F07, dated 10 February 1913, charged France with the defence of a stretch of the Channel from the Cotentin Peninsula to the British coast. It also specified that a French admiral was to be in command of this deployment. The document then continued at length to give details of the means and manner of the actions to be carried out. In order to prevent the entry of enemy shipping into the Channel, two lines of small submarines were to be set out. The first line was between Cap de la Hague and Portland; the second reached from Barfleur across to Saint Catherine's Point. The larger submarines were to be split into two groups off the coast of the Cotentin Peninsula, the first to the north of

---

[9]   SHD-MV, 1 CC 316, 'Le transport en France du Corps expéditionnaire britannique. Août–septembre 1914', Lt. de Toulouse Lautrec, École de Guerre navale, 1935–6.

[10]   Letter from the general staff of the French navy to the Admiralty, September 1912, cited in ibid.

[11]   SHD-MV, SS Es 10, classified document no. F06, 23 January 1913.

Cap de la Hague, and the second to the north of Barfleur. Anti-torpedo vessels would cover the submarines' flank, although in order to avoid any misunderstandings, they would not be authorised to cross a line running from Guernsey to Start Point. The other surface shipping would be tasked with intercepting any German attempt to force passage into the Channel by patrolling either side of a line between Lizard Point and the north coast of Finistère. These ships were backed up by reserve units whose job would be to attack any enemy ship that managed to break through.[12] On the eve of the war, French forces in the central part of the Channel were reinforced and regrouped into the 2nd Light Squadron, which in the summer of 1914 consisted of six armoured cruisers, three flotillas of submarines, and three flotillas of torpedo boats, now mostly equipped with vessels designed since 1905–06. But should London decide not to enter the war, they would have the suicidal mission of opposing any move south by the Hochseeflotte.[13]

This meticulous organisation was the result of a compromise reached between the French and British general staffs. Each side took care to limit the possibility of 'friendly fire' incidents; at the same time, each admiralty attempted to assert its primacy in what had long been an area of disputed sovereignty, while the two governments tried to demonstrate to their respective parliaments that they retained complete freedom of action. The proposals originally put forward by the French navy had placed more emphasis on the Channel Islands because their surface forces were actively patrolling the waters between Guernsey and Start Point, but this met with a muted response from the British Admiralty.[14] Be that as it may, these arrangements, with their bi-national means and cross-Channel area of operations, did also raise questions about the approach and access to the ports of one country by the warships of the other. These matters were only settled in April 1914 with the signature of a new convention that made explicit mention of Jersey, Guernsey and Alderney. The text of the document defined procedures for landing and the use of navigation lights and flagging. It made a particular point of prohibiting entry at night into British ports by small French vessels such as torpedo boats, anti-torpedo boats and submarines sailing on the surface.[15] Communications between the Channel Islands and the Cotentin Peninsula also had to be organised, making use of the cables that connected both Guernsey to Dartmouth, and Jersey to Cherbourg.[16]

The incorporation of the British into French naval strategy, the sharing of forces and the organisation of coastal defence that it entailed all came in

---

[12] SHD-MV, SS Es 10, classified document no. F07, 10 February 1913.

[13] SHD-MV, SS Ed 62, French navy telegram no. 2701, Paris, 3 August 1914.

[14] SHD-MV, SS Es 10, classified document no. F04, 10 January 1913.

[15] SHD-MV, SS Es 10, classified document no. F021, 3 April 1914.

[16] SHD-MV, SS Xa 1, letter no. 10-C from the naval attaché in London to the French Minister of the Navy, 16 December 1913.

for a great deal of vehement criticism between 1910 and 1920, most notably from areas along the French Atlantic and Channel coasts. Public opinion, along with several elected representatives, judged it imprudent to entrust the protection of the northern theatre to the goodwill of a partner that had shown little evidence to suggest a willingness to engage militarily on the French side should conflict erupt. One of the most acerbic voices raised belonged to the former Minister of the Navy, Jean-Marie de Lanessan. While reminding his audience that he had been one of the most fervent advocates of the Entente Cordiale, he was of the opinion that Paris was being culpably naive, not just with regard to the firmness of British commitment to action, but also in its belief in the capacity of the Royal Navy to honour the undertakings with which it was now tasked, highlighting moreover the weakness of the available French forces faced with their mission of preventing German incursion into the Channel and of defending the coast.[17] His concerns were echoed in the writings of numerous naval experts, such as Vice Admiral Bienaimé, former Chief of the General Staff, and senior naval officer Henri Rollin, who judged that it remained possible for the Germans to land behind Cherbourg, cut off the port and subsequently mount attacks against the French rear with an expeditionary force shipped in on liners from Hamburg.[18]

The Channel in 1914

At the outbreak of hostilities, the whole of the French navy in the Atlantic theatre turned to see what the British would do. During the night of 2 August 1914, having yet to receive any assurance that the Royal Navy would prevent the entry of the Hochseeflotte into the Channel, the French general staff gave orders to Rear Admiral Rouyer, commander of the 2nd Light Squadron, to put to sea immediately and to repel the German fleet alone.[19] While awaiting his arrival, the torpedo boats and submarines based at Dunkirk set sail and established a derisory barrier in the Pas-de-Calais. It was not until 3:30am on 4 August, when official notification was received of Britain's entry into the war, that Rouyer was authorised to switch to the arrangements set out in the 1913 accords. His forces then joined in surveillance operations in the western section of the Channel, the protection of Dunkirk and the support, under the

[17] Speech made by Jean-Marie de Lanessan to the Chamber of *députés* on 30 July 1913 (*Journal officiel de la République française. Débats parlementaires. Chambre des députés: compte rendu in-extenso*, 30 July 1913, p. 3163).

[18] Henri Rollin, *Marine de guerre et défense nationale* (Paris, 1912).

[19] SHD-MV, SS Ed 62, telegram no. 2701, from the French navy, Paris, 3 August 1914, at 1:40am.

auspices of the Dover Patrol, of combat operations against German troops in Belgium.[20]

On 9 August, in the central section of the Channel, and two days behind the plan made prior to the war, 'transport W' went into operation. For the first time since 1815, a British army was crossing the Channel to be deployed in Western Europe.[21] Two features characterise the theatre in which the vessels charged with this mission had to operate: the weakness of extended lines of communication, and the relative proximity of enemy bases. They were never less than forty miles from a friendly coast. This worked in their favour, since the tonnage needed to sustain the rotation of trips between the two coasts was not particularly great. It also reduced the vulnerability of the transport ships and decreased the requirement for military resources to guarantee their protection. Viewed from the other side, this situation was very demanding for any fleet that should decide to attack cross-Channel traffic. The narrowness of the strait offered little choice over where to strike, which militated against a surprise attack.[22] This combination of factors had direct implications for the organisation of the transport. Once loaded, vessels would set sail day or night and cross the Channel alone.[23] On 17 August, the transfer of front-line troops for the British Expeditionary Force was completed without loss. On 14 August, for example, forty-four ships made the crossing, and three days later a total load of 171,000 tonnes had been transferred.[24]

Developments in the land war, however, following on from the Battle of the Frontiers, threatened all plans for operations in the Channel. The extent of the defeat suffered by Franco-British forces was such that consideration was given to using armoured cruisers to protect the troops' left flank. To free up these ships, they were removed from patrolling at the western end of the Channel and gathered at Cherbourg.[25] The withdrawal from the front at Mons–Charleroi, which began on 23 August, placed at risk the French ports chosen as transit points for British soldiers and supplies. The following day, the Royal Navy sounded out their French colleagues to find out the French

---

[20] Auguste Thomazi (Capt.), *La guerre navale dans la Zone des armées du Nord* (Paris, 1925), pp. 33–77.

[21] James A. Williamson, *The English Channel. A History* (London, 1961), p. 355.

[22] SHD-MV, 1 CC 316, 'Le transport en France du Corps expéditionnaire britannique. Août–septembre 1914', Lt de Toulouse Lautrec, École de Guerre navale, 1935–6.

[23] SHD-MV, 1 CC 314, 'Communications en Manche et mer du Nord', Lt Pothuau, École de Guerre navale, 1929.

[24] SHD-MV, 1 CC 316, 'Le transport en France du Corps expéditionnaire britannique. Août–septembre 1914', Lt de Toulouse Lautrec, École de Guerre navale, 1935–6.

[25] SHD-MV, 1 CC 314, 'Organisation du commandement en Manche et Océan', Lt Cdr Nove-Josserand, École de Guerre navale, 1921.

government's position on a possible evacuation from the North Sea ports and Le Havre.[26] At the end of the month, the German advance forced the Admiralty's decision to transfer their main base on the continent from Le Havre to Saint-Nazaire.[27] The move was short-lived. With the German threat removed following victory on the Marne, Le Havre returned to the role it had been given at the outbreak of hostilities.[28] Between 9 August and 21 September, three-quarters of the 210,000 British soldiers landed in France had been landed there. A report to the French Ministry of the Navy in the autumn gives an idea of its importance:

> This port has become the base of operations for the British Army, and a hub for moving supplies up to the defensive works protecting Paris, as well as for the shipment of coal; it is a dockyard for the repair of auxiliary cruisers, and a port of call for hospital ships, and at the same time as addressing the military demands placed on it by the present situation, it must also, as far as was possible, play its part in the import of coal.[29]

Thus, by the end of 1914, the Channel had been turned into a Franco-British 'lake', in which the Allies enjoyed complete mastery of the seas. But this situation was increasingly challenged by the arrival of the U-boats, the appearance of which marked a turning point. The expansion of submarine forces shook the very foundations of Mahanian naval strategy. It undermined the primacy of the capital ship at the heart of a fleet and cast doubt on the likelihood of large-scale confrontation on the surface. It provoked a thorough-going review of the existing parameters of commerce raiding and opened up new lines of development for it at the expense of the set-piece battle between surface fleets.[30] The first attacks occurred in the North Sea, where on 22 September U-9 successfully carried out a torpedo attack, sinking three warships. Towards the end of October, the threat moved into the Channel. On 20 October, a British steamer, the *Glitra*, was first captured and later sunk by a submarine. More significantly, on 26 October, the *Amiral Ganteaume*, a cargo ship requisitioned from commercial shippers Chargeurs Réunis, was

---

[26]   SHD-MV, SS Xa 1, telegram no. 258, from the naval attaché in London to the French navy, Paris, 24 August 1914.

[27]   SHD-MV, SS Xa 1, telegram no. 291, from the naval attaché in London to the French navy, Paris, 31 August 1914.

[28]   Albert Chatelle, *La base du Havre et la guerre sous-marine secrète en Manche (1914–1918)* (Paris, 1949), pp. 55–7.

[29]   SHD-MV, SS Te 12, letter from the Commander of the Navy at Le Havre to the Minister for the Navy, 21 November 1914.

[30]   Jean Meyer, 'La guerre de course de l'Ancien Régime au XXᵉ siècle: essai sur la guerre industrielle', *Histoire, économie & société*, 16:1 (1997), 7–43.

torpedoed off Boulogne.[31] Of the 2,000 refugees on board, forty lost their lives.[32] The attack on this ship provoked a furore in the press and among the wider public, but had little political impact.[33] At sea, it prompted the implementation of the first countermeasures.

Adaptation to the submarine threat

The first thought of the Allied navies was to block off the Dover Strait in order to prevent German submarines from entering the Channel. Minefields were laid in the strait and torpedo boats were sent out on active search patrols.[34] To clear their way, severe restrictions were placed on fishing. While a six-mile coastal limit remained open to fishing boats between the Île de Batz and Carteret, no activity was permitted anywhere east of Cap de la Hague.[35] A review was carried out of the disposition of forces adopted at the outbreak of hostilities, some aspects of which appeared particularly vulnerable to submarine attack, in particular the line of cruisers.[36] At the end of October, the Admiralty proposed a division of the area under surveillance into two parts, each independent of the other. One of these would be the responsibility of British ships commanded by Rear Admiral Wemyss, while the cruisers of the French 2nd Light Squadron would take charge of the other.[37] This division of responsibilities between the Royal Navy and the French navy did not affect the Channel Islands, which remained under the protection of French forces.

These first measures proved, however, to be insufficient, as was clearly illustrated by the destruction of the steamer *Malachite* by U-21 off Le Havre on 23 November.[38] Two vulnerabilities were identified. The first was the

[31] SHD-MV, SS Eb 128, note from the 2nd bureau of the General Staff to the head of the cabinet, 14 December 1914.

[32] Jean de Préneuf, 'L'évacuation par voie maritime des réfugiés belges des ports du Nord et du Pas-de-Calais: octobre 1914–février 1915', *Revue du Nord*, 404–5 (2014), 102–3.

[33] Thomas Vaisset and Jean de Préneuf, 'Le Parlement, la Marine et la création de la direction de la guerre sous-marine, 1914–1917', *Revue d'histoire maritime*, 20 (2015), 67–89.

[34] Adolphe Laurens, *Introduction à l'étude de la guerre sous-marine* (Paris, 1921), pp. 15–16.

[35] Adolphe Laurens, *La guerre sous-marine. La protection de la navigation commerciale*, vol. 1, work produced by the Service historique de la Marine, place and date of publication unknown, p. 3.

[36] SHD-MV, SS Xa 2, message no. 764, from the naval attaché in London to the French Minister of the Navy, 24 October 1914.

[37] SHD-MV, SS Es 11, memorandum, 23 October 1914.

[38] SHD-MV, 1 CC 314, 'Communications en Manche et mer du Nord', Lt Pothuau, École de Guerre navale, 1929.

cross-Channel shipping route. To protect this, at the end of December 1914 specific ships deemed to be carrying precious cargo began to be escorted on the crossing.[39] This measure was only applied systematically to troop ships. Vessels were to sail at night with all lights extinguished, 'accompanied' by destroyers between their points of departure and Le Havre.[40] The second danger was congestion in the ports, which was forcing some incoming ships to wait outside the port, in open water. Such a concentration of stationary transport vessels made a tempting target for the U-boats, as demonstrated by the triple torpedoing off Le Havre on 1 February 1915 of the steamers *Tokumaru*, *Oriole* and *Ikaria*.[41] More significantly still, a few days later, Germany launched its first unrestricted submarine campaign, declaring the Channel to be a 'war zone' and threatening to sink any commercial ships found there.[42] The U-boats thus became the main concern of the French and British naval authorities in the Channel. Ships were sent to try to discover where enemy submarines were being resupplied from. As an archipelago of small islands, the Channel Islands now became a potential target, and several French units were despatched to explore the surrounding waters.[43]

In the Bay of the Seine river, the reaction of the Entente partners was primarily defensive. Control of anchorages was tightened, and permission was given for ships destined for Le Havre and Rouen to moor overnight in the outer harbour at Cherbourg, an option previously denied.[44] But these measures were not enough given the increasing amount of traffic. The volume of ships through Le Havre, for example, doubled between February and May 1915.[45] In June there were sixty vessels bound for Rouen choking up the approaches in the Rade de la Carosse at the mouth of the Seine – targets easy for a U-boat to destroy. This was a threat to the nation's supply lines, a matter of strategic importance. Proof of the increased importance of Le Havre was provided by the appointment there, in March 1915, of a Rear Admiral as 'Commander of the Navy'.[46] To deal with the increasing tonnage being unloaded in the ports

---

[39] SHD-MV, SS La 22, confidential letter no.16-S, from the Captain of the *Lavenir* to Vice Admiral Commander-in-Chief of the 2nd Squadron, 15 December 1914.

[40] SHD-MV, SS La 22, note from the head of the Patrol Division to Rear Admiral Chief of Staff of 2nd Light Squadron, 2 April 1915.

[41] SHD-MV, 1 CC 314, 'Communications en Manche et mer du Nord', Lt Pothuau, work of the École de Guerre navale, 1929.

[42] Paul G. Halpern, *A Naval History of World War I* (London, 1995), pp. 291–4.

[43] Archives du ministère des Affaires étrangères (hereafter, MAE), 1 CPCOM 1052, letter from the French Consul to Jersey, 30 January 1915.

[44] SHD-MV, SS Eb 27, confidential correspondence from the Minister of the Navy to Rear Admiral Governor of Le Havre, 16 February 1915.

[45] SHD-MV, SS Eb 27, chart 'Trafic mensuel du port du Havre (base anglaise)', undated.

[46] Emmanuel Boulard, *La défense des côtes: une histoire interarmées (1815–1973)* (PhD thesis supervised by Olivier Forcade, Université Paris-Sorbonne, 2013), pp. 476–8.

of Normandy, only a global approach taking in the whole of the Channel would be sufficient to avoid them becoming blocked up. The management of shipping traffic was henceforward viewed as a transnational undertaking and adapted accordingly. In the summer of 1915, for example, it was decided to require ships with a draft in excess of five metres bound for Rouen to put in and stop at Spithead or Cherbourg to obtain authorisation before continuing their journey to the Rade de la Carosse.[47] This system, although designed to ensure the safety of commercial shipping, was harshly criticised by the captains of the steamers forced to make those detours, whether they sailed under a neutral or an Allied flag. Complaints flooded in about the detours and the hold-ups caused by the compulsory stops imposed for military reasons.[48] They illustrate the difficulties of cooperation between military and merchant navies that arose during this first global conflict, and added to the persistent disagreements between *la rue Royale* and the Comité central des armateurs de France (Central Committee of French Shipowners) over the anti-submarine war in general and the defensive arming of merchant vessels in particular.[49] Faced with these dual obligations, consideration was even given to the possibility of unloading merchant ships in the outer harbour, and perhaps even in the military dock itself.[50] Studies carried out at the site estimated that it was possible to unload five ships simultaneously, including three of the larger ones: one would be in the harbour and the other two in the military dock, while two medium-sized vessels would be being unloaded in the commercial port. In any case, the plan suffered from a serious handicap − the existence of a bottleneck caused by a lack of infrastructure in the port itself: the Cherbourg depot was not able to move supplies quickly on into the rest of the country and the town did not have enough hard-standing areas or warehouses to handle the stocks involved.[51] The threat to supplies was considered sufficiently serious for the Ministry of War to take on the cost of the works to be undertaken to build a new road to serve Cherbourg's Charles X basin.[52]

Be that as it may, the German strategy soon reached its limits. There were an increasing number of incidents involving neutral countries, in particular the United States after the sinking of the *Lusitania*. From the autumn onwards, the

---

[47] SHD-MV, SS Eb 27, directives from the Ministry of the Navy, 25 June 1915.

[48] SHD-MV, SS Tgl, order no. 25 from Rear Admiral Commander of the Cherbourg Coast, 5 August 1915.

[49] Christian Borde, 'Le Comité central des armateurs de France face aux enjeux de la guerre maritime', *Revue d'histoire maritime*, 20 (2015), 91–102.

[50] SHD-MV, SS Eb 28, note from the Director of Inspections, 15 April 1916.

[51] SHD-MV, SS Eb 28, letter no. 51 from Rear-Admiral Didelot, major-general and commander in charge of the docks, to the Maritime Prefect of Cherbourg, 30 April 1916.

[52] SHD-MV, SS Eb 28, letter no. 27791 from the Minister of War to the Minister of the Navy, 22 July 1916.

Admiralstab, the general staff of the German navy, felt forced to abandon its approach and returned to more restrictive rules of engagement, more closely in line with international law. Nevertheless, the submarines were redeployed to the Mediterranean, which was not included in their February proclamation.[53] The U-boat threat in the Channel was only temporarily put off course. It returned with renewed force in early 1917.

French supply lines in the crosshairs

For war-stricken Europe, 1917 was the 'impossible year'[54], and for the French, a 'year of anguish'.[55] The entry into the war of the United States completely changed the balance between the alliances, as did the revolutions in Russia and the armistice signed there, which was to lead, by March 1918, to the separate peace treaty of Brest-Litovsk. At sea, 1917 was a crucial year. The German reverses at Verdun and on the Somme convinced the *Admiralstab* of the futility of large-scale land offensives. The German navy's high command was at the same time persuaded that a submarine war of attrition could swing the war in their favour. The German admirals estimated that they could strangle the Entente countries in six months by sinking 600,000 tonnes a month, forcing them to capitulate before the United States could intervene to stop it. In February 1917, after numerous delays, and lengthy debates in the Reichstag, Germany declared an all-out submarine war.[56] No merchant ship, even neutral ones, would be spared from attack by torpedo without warning. The risk of rupture in the Allies' lines of communication was very real. The two Entente navies immediately saw the extent of the threat, particularly given the serious impact they had already experienced in terms of coal supplies since the end of 1916.[57] With just Le Havre and Rouen between them handling a third of all French coal imports, the Channel became the front line.[58]

The causes of the crisis were numerous. Organising transport itself became a source of considerable difficulties. The British mining areas authorised to

---

[53] Paul G. Halpern, *The Mediterranean Naval Situation 1908–1914* (Cambridge, MA, 1971), pp. 148–70 and 190–205.

[54] Jean-Jacques Becker, *1917 en Europe. L'année impossible* (Brussels, 1997).

[55] Jean-Baptiste Duroselle, *La Grande Guerre des Français, 1914–1918. L'incompréhensible* (Paris, 2002), pp. 187–312.

[56] The debates were particularly well attended in the *Reichstag*. See Torsten Oppelland, 'Les débats sur la guerre sous-marine et la neutralité américaine au *Reichstag* 1914–1917', *Parlement[s]*, 10:2 (2008), 92–103.

[57] Pierre Chancerel, *Le marché du charbon en France pendant la Première guerre mondiale (1914–1921)* (PhD thesis supervised by Michel Lescure, Université Paris Ouest, 2012), pp. 88–107.

[58] Calculated according to SHD-MV, SS Ea 42, comparative table of British coal imports (all types), first six months of 1915 and 1916.

export coal were among the furthest from the French coastline, further compli-
cating deliveries already slowed down by congestion in the ports at which they
loaded and unloaded. Furthermore, the tonnage hitherto provided by neutral
ships, essential to the movement of coal, ceased to be available.[59] They had
been a target of choice for the U-boats, which destroyed a monthly average
of 100,000 tonnes of neutral shipping in the last quarter of 1916. Losses were
sufficiently great to dissuade Norwegian vessels, which carried the greater part
of France's supplies, from putting to sea whenever U-boats were reported in
the Channel or the North Sea. What is more, the Admiralty's anti-submarine
measures also further contributed to the crisis of resupply. As soon as an
area was believed to be under threat, traffic was suspended, intermittently
creating de facto blockades.[60] For example, sailing was interrupted on 30–40
per cent of days in November and December 1916.[61] This situation led to a
fall of nearly 25 per cent in the tonnage of supplies unloaded in France in
the second half of 1916.[62]

The impact of the crisis on provisioning was such that the French navy's
general staff proposed that a system of convoys be established to escort coal
ships bound for France.[63] But the idea of focusing on the targets in need
of protection – the ships – rather than on control of the sea ran counter to
prevailing Mahanian naval strategy. The British did not just lack the ships
necessary for escort duties, they also feared that moving to such a system
would deprive coal ships sailing under neutral flags of the legal protection
normally accorded to them.[64] To try to persuade the British, the French sent
Commander Pierre Vandier to London, a man then basking in the success
of the convoy system used to transport the Serbian army in 1916, which he
helped to set up while serving as Admiral de Gueydon's chief of staff. His
message was simple:

[59] SHD-MV, SS Ea 42, letter from Commander Vandier to the Minister of the
Navy, 19 January 1917.

[60] SHD-MV, SS Ea 42, letter from Commander Vandier to the Minister of the
Navy, 19 January 1917.

[61] SHD-MV, SS Ea 42, confidential note to the Minister of Public Works, 5 January
1917.

[62] Letter from the Under-secretary of State for Transport to the Minister of the
Navy, on the subject of coal convoys, 17 March 1917, quoted in SHD-MV 1 CC 309,
'Protection de la navigation dans la Manche et dans l'Océan depuis le début de la
guerre 1914–1918 jusqu'à la création de la D.G.G.S.M. (18–19 juin 1917)', École de
Guerre navale, 1922.

[63] SHD-MV, SS Ea 42, note on the protection of coal ships and the formation of
convoys, undated [December 1916].

[64] SHD-MV, 1 CC 314, 'Communications en Manche et mer du Nord', Lt Pothuau,
École de Guerre navale, 1929.

For us this is a matter of life and death; we cannot live, and we cannot fight without coal. Today we are suffering from a partial blockade. Tomorrow, that blockade will be total. You yourselves will be forced to form convoys and escort them if you wish to maintain trade. Twice in the past, our corsairs have forced you to do this. You will be forced to do it again. This plan for French coal that I am asking you to implement will be a chance for you to prepare.

In France, in any case, our decision has been made; we will cease to protect the sea and concentrate our efforts on protecting the ships. In order to facilitate this task, we are regrouping these ships into convoys to allow us to reinforce their protection. The escorts for these convoys will form one of the bases of our anti-submarine strategy.[65]

Vandier managed to reach an agreement thanks to semantic sleight-of-hand: the two countries would not use the term 'convoys', but 'controlled sailing'; thus, the 'French coal trade', too, was born. The British came around because of the importance of coal imports to the French war effort. Even so, the Admiralty had no intention of 'organising in the true sense a system of convoys, but merely to take steps so that ships can be more or less together in areas where patrols [were] weakest. Those patrols [would then be] organised in such a way as to be in the vicinity, ready for any eventuality'.[66]

The so-called 'French coal trade' began to operate on 6 February 1917 but was not reserved exclusively for coal ships. Crossings were made via four routes: two each at the eastern and western ends of the Channel. Route A ran from Falmouth/Penzance to Brest, and route D from Ramsgate harbour to Boulogne, while two further routes crossed in the central section: route B from Portland to Cherbourg, and route C from Portsmouth to Le Havre. While the latter was used by ships bound for ports from Fécamp to Caen, route B was taken both by the coal ships heading to ports from Cherbourg to Morlaix, and those vessels sailing at less than eight knots and aiming for Brest and the Bay of Biscay, with the fork in the route located not far from Jersey. These two routes were among the most important in the French coal trade. Between them, in June 1917, for example, they carried 20 per cent of overall traffic.[67] The Channel Islands found themselves in close proximity to a communication route of vital importance to the Entente powers. Sailing in the waters around the islands proved to be very challenging, and the early

---

[65] SHD-MV, SS Ea 42, letter from Commander Vandier to the Minister of the Navy, 3 January 1917.

[66] SHD-MV, SS Pn 10 (3), translation of Circular no. 06321, British Admiralty, 21 May 1917, concerning controlled sailing. Translator's note: Back-translated from the French translation of this circular.

[67] Data calculated according to SHD-MV, SS GR 53.

attempts made by the convoys met with limited success. The Maritime Prefect of Cherbourg noted that it was virtually impossible to cross the Alderney Race when the wind and tide were not favourable.[68]

From the spring of 1917, in order to keep the coal trade safe, great efforts were made to improve patrol forces. The 1st Patrol Division of the Atlantic and the Channel (1ère Division des patrouilles de l'Océan et de la Manche), rapidly christened the Normandy Patrol Division (Division des Patrouilles de Normandie), was based at Cherbourg. Its operational area stretched from Antifer to Île-de-Bréhat. It had two squadrons, the first stationed at Cherbourg, and the second in Le Havre. Each of these had thirteen patrol vessels and two sloops or gunboats.[69] A remarkable document held by the SHD gives an insight into the way in which these ships were expected to carry out their missions: the 'Patrol Commander's Guide', written by a joint commission set up at the end of 1917 on the initiative of the Chief of the Normandy Patrol Division.[70] The text, which is divided into five chapters, is intended as a guide for the commanders of these small units. Among the instructions they were given was the following: do not hesitate 'to sacrifice the lives of the crew to the last man' to bring about the destruction of the enemy. That aim was to override all other considerations, except in the case of a convoy escort. In those circumstances, the sole aim of the commander was to 'lead it safely to its destination'.[71]

Another conspicuous new feature of these patrols was that they were henceforth to include the third dimension: air power.[72] Air units were attached to the Normandy Patrol Division in December 1917. While all aircraft were progressively incorporated into anti-submarine warfare, each carried out missions specific to its technical capabilities. Airships and tethered balloons afforded immediate protection to the convoys, while seaplanes were used to carry out offensive patrols in an attempt to locate enemy submarines.[73] Close to several coal trade routes and to several Channel crossing routes, the position of the Channel Islands was a great asset. The operational potential of Guernsey, situated halfway between the lighthouses at Casquets and Roches-Douvres, was immediately identified. The new aviation programme adopted by the French navy on 21 February included plans to establish a permanent

---

[68] SHD-MV, SS Pn 7, note from the Vice-Admiral Maritime Prefect to the Officer-in-Command, Cherbourg coast, 15 February 1917.

[69] Adolphe Laurens, *La guerre sous-marine*, p. 526.

[70] SHD-MV, 1 CC 311, 'La Division des Patrouilles de Normandie de sa création (avril 1917) à la l'armistice (novembre 1918)', Lt. Huré, École de Guerre navale, 1924.

[71] SHD-MV, SS Pn 10 (3), *Guide du Commandant de Patrouilleur*, undated [1917].

[72] Adolphe Laurens, *La guerre sous-marine*, p. 528.

[73] MV, SS Vb 1, general instructions from Commander Copi, commander of the Normandy air patrols, 22 May 1918.

armed base on the island.[74] At the end of March 1917, a French officer was sent to investigate the possible infrastructure requirements. The governor and the local authorities declared their enthusiasm for the idea. No charge would be made for land purchase, a slipway, or warehousing.[75] From June onwards, this first military base became a significant centre for seaplanes.[76] It was situated at Saint Peter Port, and was initially home to twelve aircraft, increasing to sixteen in the autumn of 1917. It was garrisoned by approximately 120 sailors of all ranks. The air station monographs produced by the Ministry of the Navy show that the Guernsey base was one of the most important in the region, second only to that of Cherbourg.[77] It was active across a vast sector of the theatre. Every day, one seaplane section had to patrol a route between Sark and Roches-Douvres, while another took responsibility for convoys sailing south from Sark towards Brest, accompanying them for as long as possible.[78]

The anti-submarine war in the Channel provides a good opportunity to observe the parallel between warfare and hunting, which has been highlighted in the case of land warfare, for example, in Christian Ingrao's work on the 'Black Hunters' of the German Dirlewanger Brigade.[79] The structure of military organisation in the Channel offers an early example of this. From 1 December 1917, the Normandy Patrol Division saw the arrival of a 'hunter squadron'. The counter-torpedo boats that formed part of it were equipped with Walser hydrophones, a device that depends on the ability of its operator to detect sounds so that his ship can 'seek out, follow [...] and attack submarines'.[80] Sea conditions in the Channel and the North Sea make demands on the crews' senses of smell and hearing, which are precisely those needed in hunting. The often difficult sea conditions in these waters support the analogy, and apply not only to those sailing on the surface, but also to the officers in charge of the hunt for submarines, whose daily duties are similar to those of a hunter tracking his prey. Thus, we find the commander of the Guernsey

---

[74] SHD-MV, SS Ga 154, letter from the Minister of the Navy to Vice Admiral Maritime Prefect of Cherbourg, 21 February 1917.

[75] SHD-MV, SS Ga 154, report of Lt Douillard to officer-in-command of the airbase, 1 April 1917.

[76] SHD-MV, SS Ga 154, ministerial directive no. 431, 13 June 1917.

[77] SHD-MV, SS Ga 154, monograph on the maritime airbase at Guernsey, prepared by Sub Lt Flandrin, 28 September 1918.

[78] SHD-MV, SS Pn 1, letter no. 183, from Commander Faivre to the commander of the Normandy Patrol Division, 16 October 1917.

[79] Christian Ingrao, *Les chasseurs noirs. La brigade Dirlewanger* (Paris, 2006). See also Stéphane Audoin-Rouzeau, *Combattre* (Paris, 2008).

[80] Letter no. 2346 from Commander, Normandy Patrol Division to the Maritime Prefect, 21 September 1918, quoted in SHD-MV, 1 CC 311, 'La Division des Patrouilles de Normandie de sa création (avril 1917) à l'armistice (novembre 1918)', Lt. Huré, École de Guerre navale, 1924.

airbase, Captain Lecour Grandmaison, complaining of not finding any enemy in the 'rich hunting grounds' patrolled by the aircraft under his command.[81]

Conclusion

During the First World War, the Channel Islands were never the lynchpin of French naval strategy. They did, however, allow the French fleet to meet its obligations in the Channel. While often considered a secondary theatre, events there undoubtedly played a role in the outcome of the war at sea. The ability of the Entente countries to control the sea lanes despite the U-boat threat enabled them, at the height of the storm, to prevent the collapse of the Western Front.

The Channel was also one of several places that saw military experimentation. Two examples of this stand out in particular: the convoy system introduced with the 'French coal trade', and the use of naval aviation, which was born shortly before the First World War, but earned its spurs in that conflict. The Channel Islands were part of both stories. They are located next to some of the busiest coal ship convoy routes, and were home to a seaplane base on the front line of the anti-submarine war. The signing of the Entente initiated a change in the way the French navy perceived the Channel Islands, a transformation brought to full fruition by the experience of the First World War.

[81] SHD-MV, SS Pn 2, note no. 1136 from the Commander, Normandy Patrol Division to the Vice Admiral, 17 January 1918.

12

Royal Navy Trade Defence in the English Channel During the First World War

ALEXANDER HOWLETT

Introduction

The primary role of the Royal Navy in the First World War was to protect seaborne commerce and communications, and there was no greater challenge to the flow of oceanic trade than Germany's unrestricted submarine campaign of 1917–18. Since the wars with Louis XIV the protection of trade had been critical to England's national survival, with the Western Approaches and English Channel the decisive maritime theatres. William III crossed the English Channel at the beginning of the War of the League of Augsburg, and the privations of Spanish, Dutch and French commerce raiders during the War of Spanish Succession were so significant that the newly created United Kingdom was forced to introduce compulsory convoys in 1707. The defence of trade was no less significant for the conduct of distant colonial campaigns during the Seven Years War, and the protection of merchant shipping neces-sitated a strict convoy policy during the American Revolutionary War.[1] The Act of 1798 once again granted the Admiralty the power to enforce the convoy system on oceanic merchants,[2] and indeed it was control of these vast supply lines, and the mobilization of capital and credit this enabled, that contributed so profoundly to victory against Napoleon's Empire.[3]

The legal basis for the protection of oceanic trade, and the rules of engagement for maritime warfare, became codified during what Stephen

---

[1] Andrew Lambert, 'The Royal Navy and the Defence of Empire, 1856–1918', in *Imperial Defence: The Old World Order 1856–1956*, ed. Greg Kennedy, Cass Military Studies (London: Routledge, 2008), 111–32, p. 112; N. A. M. Rodger, *The Command of the Ocean* (New York: W. W. Norton, 2006), pp. 359, 367.

[2] John Terraine, *Business in Great Waters: The U-Boat Wars, 1916–1945*, Kindle ebook (Barnsley: Pen & Sword Military, 2009), part 1, chapter 3, loc. 1223.

[3] Roger Knight, *Britain Against Napoleon: The Organization of Victory, 1793–1815* (London: Penguin, 2014), pp. 390–414.

Cobb described as the new 'liberal age of free trade' that emerged in the decades following the Congress of Vienna.[4] Privateering was abolished by the 1856 Declaration of Paris and the rights of neutrals during a naval blockade reinforced by the 1907 Hague Conference and the 1909 Declaration of London.[5] Warships engaged in trade interdiction were expected to follow prize law, necessitating basic consideration for the crews of captured ships and assuring the safety of passengers.[6] By 1914 the Royal Navy's conceptualization of trade defence had transitioned from the traditional 18th century combination of convoy escort and close blockade to a geographically globalized *laissez-faire* model that provided for the security of oceanic communications and trade routes through command of the sea.[7]

The outbreak of the First World War put Britain's global strategy to the test. The Royal Navy, working with the *Entente* navies of France and Russia, quickly swept Germany's merchant shipping from the seas and began intercepting neutrals bound for North Sea ports, so as to confiscate goods destined for Germany.[8] A proposal to restrict Germany's imports was hammered out by the Restriction of Enemy Supplies Committee, supplemented in November by the Foreign Office's Contraband Committee, and an elaborate diplomatic treaty framework was negotiated between Whitehall, Paris and the European neutrals, to financially and economically isolate the Central Powers.[9]

After Germany's offensives on the Marne and at Ypres failed to generate a decisive outcome on land, Britain and the Allies tightened their economic blockade. Early in November the Admiralty, in an effort to force neutral shipping through the Dover Strait where it could be more easily inspected

---

[4] Stephen Cobb, *Preparing for Blockade, 1885–1914: Naval Contingency for Economic Warfare* (Farnham: Ashgate, 2013), p. 62.

[5] Ibid., pp. 62–76. Eric Osborne, *Britain's Economic Blockade of Germany, 1914–1919* (London: Frank Cass Publishers, 2004), p. 26 et seq.

[6] Steve Dunn, *Bayly's War: The Battle for the Western Approaches in the First World War* (Annapolis: Naval Institute Press, 2018), p. 30.

[7] R. M. Bellairs, 'Historical Survey of Trade Defence since 1914', *Royal United Services Institution Journal*, vol. 99, no. 595 (1954): 359–77, p. 363. See also, Andrew Lambert, 'The Royal Navy and the Defence of Empire, 1856–1918', in *Imperial Defence: The Old World Order 1856–1956*, ed. Greg Kennedy (London: Routledge, 2008), 111–32, pp. 112, 124–6.

[8] This procedure involved both a liberal application of the controversial 'continuous voyage' justification for seizure and the expansion of the contraband list to include essentially anything imported by the Central Powers, a serious aggravation of neutral interests including that of the United States. Arthur Marder, *From The Dreadnought to Scapa Flow* [hereafter *FDSF*] II, 5 vols (Barnsley: Seaforth Publishing, 2013–14), pp. 372–7. See also, Osborne, *Britain's Economic Blockade*, pp. 59–63.

[9] A. C. Bell, *A History of The Blockade of Germany and of the Countries Associated with Her in the Great War*, reprint (Uckfield: Naval & Military Press, 1961), p. 61 et seq.; Osborne, *Britain's Economic Blockade*, pp. 64–72, 75–7.

and controlled, declared the entire North Sea a military area.[10] In retaliation, Admiral Hugo von Pohl, Chief of Germany's *Admiralstab*, threatened to unleash the U-boats by January 1915.[11] Initial opposition to Admiral von Pohl's plan was overcome when he was promoted to command of the High Sea Fleet as Friedrich von Ingenohl's replacement following the Battle of the Dogger Bank. On 4 February 1915 the U-boats were indeed loosed against Britain's merchant shipping in the 'War Zone' established around the British Isles.[12] This was a dangerous gamble, likely to add neutral powers to the growing list of nations fighting against the Central Powers.[13]

During the following years of maritime conflict Germany's submarines dealt a heavy blow to British and indeed global merchant shipping. There was a marked reluctance at the Admiralty to admit that the pre-war conceptualization of trade defence based on independent sailings was no longer viable. As Nicholas Black observed, the Admiralty's Naval War Staff attitude towards the regulation of oceanic trade constituted a 'mental block' that had 'clearly formed in the age before the advent of the submarine'.[14] Archibald Hurd, the official historian of Britain's merchant navy, stated that 'there was no conception that any Power, in however desperate straits, would not merely ignore the recognised principles of international law as they applied to naval warfare, but would disregard customs of the sea which for centuries had been considered a binding code of honour by seamen of all nations'.[15] The U-boats, sinking targets on sight and undetectable beneath the waves, posed a serious threat to Britain's vital system of seaborne communications and demonstrated, as Paul Kennedy phrased it, that the Admiralty's pre-war defence schemes were 'quite out-of-date'.[16]

Ultimately the Admiralty Naval Staff began to implement schemes for oceanic, and later coastal, convoys that gradually, between April 1917 and June

---

[10] Osborne, *Britain's Economic Blockade*, p. 74.

[11] Lawrence Sondhaus, *German Submarine Warfare in World War I: The Onset of Total War at Sea* (New York: Rowman & Littlefield, 2017), pp. 15–6, 28.

[12] Ibid., pp. 30–1; John C. G. Rohl, *Wilhelm II: Into the Abyss of War and Exile, 1900–1941*, trans. Sheila de Bellaigue and Roy Bridge, Kindle ebook, III, 3 vols (New York: Cambridge University Press, 2014), p. 1151.

[13] Steve R. Dunn, *Blockade: Cruiser Warfare and the Starvation of Germany in World War One*, Kindle ebook (Barnsley: Seaforth Publishing, 2016), pp. 117–19; V. H. Danckwerts, '1807–1917: A Comparison', *Naval Review Journal* 8, no. 1 (1919): 14–30, p. 23; See also, Osborne, *Economic Blockade of Germany*, pp. 128–32.

[14] Nicholas Black, 'The Admiralty War Staff and Its Influence on the Conduct of the Naval War between 1914 and 1918' (PhD thesis, London, University College London, 2005), pp. 72–3.

[15] Archibald Hurd, *The Merchant Navy*, III, 3 vols, reprint (Uckfield: Naval & Military Press, 1921–9), pp. 365–72.

[16] Paul M. Kennedy, *The Rise and Fall of British Naval Mastery* (New York: Humanity Books, 1976), p. 253.

1918, became comprehensive. It was this extensive convoy system, constituting the near total regulation of trade in the Atlantic, Western Approaches, English Channel, North Sea and Mediterranean, that finally staunched the Allies' shipping losses. By the summer of 1918 new construction in British and Allied shipyards began outpacing sinkings and the crisis was at last surmounted.

The submarine war in the Channel was fought across three key districts: Dover, the bottleneck controlling access to the North Sea; Portsmouth, where supplies for the British armies and the critical coal trade crossed into France; and Plymouth, the base for operations in the vital Atlantic approaches, upon which Britain's capacity to continue the war relied. Analysis of shipping losses in the areas of responsibility for these three Channel districts reveals interesting details that have hitherto been subsumed by the broader conflict. The Royal Navy's Channel Senior Naval Officers (SNOs), in cooperation with their French counterparts, developed three distinct approaches to sea control and the protection of trade, reflecting geographical and operational variances across the theatre. It was ultimately this complex aggregate of methods and materials that demonstrated, as Andrew Lambert has phrased it, that 'there was no easy answer' to the submarine crisis.[17]

The statistical struggle

At the macroeconomic scale the events of the submarine crisis are well known: unrestricted submarine warfare, on the basis of calculations supplied by Germany's Chief of the Naval Staff, Admiral von Holtzendorf, at a sustained monthly sinking rate of 600,000 tons, would force Britain to a negotiated peace before the end of 1917. Towards this goal, the U-boats' operational tempo accelerated in February 1917, with 520,000 tons of merchant shipping sunk that month.[18] The loss rate increased in the spring, with the U-boats achieving their greatest monthly total in April, when British losses neared 600,000 tons and total world losses surpassed 860,000 tons.[19] The result of this action, as had been expected by the German supreme command,[20] was that the United States declared war against Germany on 6 April, a grave development for the future of Germany's war effort and a boon to Allied trade defence efforts which could now be systematically coordinated across the Atlantic.

[17] Marcus Faulkner and Andrew Lambert, *The Great War At Sea, A Naval Atlas, 1914–1919* (Barnsley: Seaforth Publishing, 2015), pp. 35–7.

[18] Andreas Michelsen, *Submarine Warfare, 1914–1918* (Miami: Trident Publishing, 2017), pp. 37–8; Reinhard Scheer, *Germany's High Sea Fleet in the World War*, Kindle ebook (Shilka Publishing, 2013), pp. 301–8.

[19] Kennedy, 'The War at Sea', p. 339.

[20] Erich Ludendorff, *Ludendorff's Own Story, August 1914–November 1918*, Forgotten Books reprint, II, 2 vols (London: Hutchinson, 1919), pp. 415–8; Rohl, *Wilhelm II: Into the Abyss*, III, p. 1154.

Although the submarine crisis came to a head in April, in the Channel itself the peak destruction of tonnage had been reached in March, when 178,167 tons of British, Allied and neutral shipping was sunk or damaged. This included neutral ships such as the 5,225-ton American oil tanker *Illinois*, scuttled by *UC21* north of Alderney on 18 March, one of a string of indiscriminate sinkings of American merchantmen that contributed to President Woodrow Wilson's decision to intervene.[21] After March the total tonnage sunk in the Channel districts declined, reaching a local nadir in August when not much more than 85,000 tons were sunk or damaged. This local trough coincided with the introduction of outbound, and later inbound, Atlantic convoys which forced the U-boats to refocus on coastal waters and the Mediterranean.

As we have seen, in March 1917 the coastal U-boats based in Flanders reached their greatest effectiveness, destroying the largest quantity of Channel shipping in a single month. Following the American declaration of war on 6 April the Channel became less significant as both the High Sea Fleet and Flanders U-boats concentrated on the crowded shipping lanes in the Atlantic and Western Approaches. The rolling introduction of inbound and outbound convoys had by September dramatically reduced the effectiveness of the High Sea Fleet's long-range U-boats as their targets became organized and defended, although this meant renewed importance for the Flanders boats which increased their mining and coastal operations against the convoy dispersal points along the Welsh and Irish coasts at Milford Haven and Queenstown, and in the Channel.[22] In the Mediterranean the introduction of convoy methods in October likewise reduced the value of that theatre compared to the increasing value of the Channel.[23] In December 1917, 172,196 tons were sunk or damaged in the Channel, a performance that was nearly repeated in January 1918 when 140,621 tons were sunk or damaged, at which point the Channel in fact became the most significant theatre in terms of *ship* sinkings, although at this time still only representative of 47% of the total *tonnage* sunk, with the Mediterranean accounting for 50%.

This German success early in 1918 was short-lived, however, as operational and at sea U-boat numbers had in fact reached their wartime peak between October and December 1917, declining steadily thereafter.[24] After January 1918 U-boat operations in the Channel became significantly more

---

[21] Sondhaus, *German Submarine Warfare*, pp. 114–15.

[22] Dunn, *Bayly's War*, pp. 184–5; Sondhaus, *German Submarine Warfare*, pp. 145–8; McCartney, 'The Archaeology of First World War U-Boat Losses in the English Channel', p. 199.

[23] Marder, FDSF, IV, p. 261.

[24] R. H. Gibson and Maurice Prendergast, *The German Submarine War, 1914–1918*, Reprint (London: Naval & Military Press, 1931), p. 205. See also Marder, *FDSF*, V, p. 81; Michelsen, *Submarine Warfare*, pp. 196–8.

difficult as a result of increased mine quality and mass production combined with patrol reforms implemented by Vice Admiral Roger Keyes in the Dover district. Within a few months it was clear that the Allies had successfully contained the situation in the Channel, and the audacious raids at Zeebrugge in April and Ostend in May highlighted the difficulty the Flanders boats were experiencing concurrent with the introduction of coastal convoys. This final regulation of coastal trade was the missing element in the convoy equation, and indeed it was at this time that the U-boats first attempted to concentrate for prepared attacks against the convoys themselves. This development, as John Terraine phrased it, cast 'ominous shadows towards the distant future', – the deadly convoy battles of the Second World War.[25] In May 1918, however, this effort was premature, in fact exposing the attacking U-boats to the British Direction-Finding (D/F) system that was capable of locating U-boats by their Wireless-Telegraphy (W/T) transmissions.[26] The U-boats instead abandoned the Western Approaches altogether and extended their cruises to the limits of their endurance for attacks against shipping near the American and Canadian coasts.[27]

The High Sea Fleet U-boats were having more success in the Mediterranean, sinking 65 ships or 173,172 tons in May 1918. The Channel meanwhile yielded only 94,698 tons that month, representing a meagre 24 ships. Furthermore, the situation for the Flanders boats was becoming increasingly difficult. Between mid-June and the end of August Brigadier-General Charles Lambe's Royal Air Force (RAF) bombers, based at Dover and Dunkirk, dropped 135 tons of bombs on the Belgian U-boat bases.[28] Although in August shipping losses in the Channel increased somewhat to 77,844 tons (22 ships sunk, six damaged), the effectiveness of the coastal U-boats was clearly declining. In September, 58,141 tons were sunk or damaged in the Channel, enough at this late stage of the war to account for 34% of the total tonnage destroyed, but this was the final effort by the Flanders U-boats as their bases were evacuated between 17 and 19 October and then overrun during the Hundred Days offensive.[29] The Allies promptly demanded the cessation of the submarine campaign as a condition

[25] Terraine, *Business in Great Waters*, part 1, chapter 6, loc. 2413; Newbolt, *Naval Operations*, V, pp. 278–81.

[26] Sondhaus, *German Submarine Warfare*, p. 145; Dwight Messimer, *Find and Destroy: Antisubmarine Warfare in World War I* (Annapolis: Naval Institute Press, 2001), p. 177; Patrick Beesly, *Room 40: British Naval Intelligence 1914–1918* (London: Hamish Hamilton, 1982), pp. 254–6.

[27] Newbolt, *Naval Operations*, V, pp. 283–4.

[28] Abbatiello, *Anti-Submarine Warfare in World War I: British Naval Aviation and the Defeat of the U-Boats* (New York: Routledge, 2006), p. 76.

[29] Gibson and Prendergast, *German Submarine War*, p. 324.

for armistice negotiations,[30] and on 20 October Admiral Scheer ordered the recall of the U-boats still at sea, formally abandoning the campaign.[31]

Between February and December 1917 the percentage of sinkings in the Channel at first decreased, as the submarines focused their efforts outside of the Channel, but then increased dramatically when the introduction of Atlantic convoys restricted the U-boats' activities in that ocean.[32] The total of 958,619 tons of British shipping sunk and damaged in the Channel between February and December 1917 is approximately equivalent to the combined total losses, in all theatres, of Norway (659,949), Greece (236,070) and Sweden (65,978) that year.[33] In terms of the total submarine campaign between 1917 and 1918, Norway at 167,689 tons lost the most tonnage in the Channel districts after the British Empire, followed by France, with 146,838 tons sunk and damaged. France and Norway combined account for 56.5% of the total 556,890 Allied and neutral, i.e. non-British Empire, tonnage sunk and damaged in the Channel area during the study period.

As total losses continued to fall during 1918, the importance of the Channel again shifted. In February the Channel percentage of Home Waters losses decreased to 29.4% (71,388 tons out of the 185,555 British and 57,597 foreign tons sunk), but then climbed to 80,499 tons in April, representing 42.5% of the Home Waters figure. This brief upswing in sinkings was not sustained, however, as the introduction of coastal convoys thereafter dramatically improved merchant protection and by July only 18,559 tons or 9.4% of the Home Waters tonnage was sunk in the Channel (out of 133,355 British and 64,734 foreign tons).[34] The U-boats redoubled their efforts, sinking 51,677 tons or 23% of the Home Waters total in August, and another 45,363 tons or 29.3% in September but, as we shall see, this final effort was at much greater risk of detection and counterattack.[35]

These statistics demonstrate that the Channel was a central battleground in the submarine campaign, at times *the* significant region of the conflict. The importance of the Channel for the submarine campaign, however, is best illustrated by comparing the corresponding figures for another crucial district: the Mediterranean. Between February and December 1917, in that theatre, at least 651 British, Allied and neutral steamers and sailing vessels were sunk (and another 35 damaged), representing 1.43 million tons, or close

[30] Scheer, *Germany's High Sea Fleet*, p. 427.

[31] Marder, *FDSF*, V, p. 170.

[32] Julian Corbett and Henry Newbolt, *Naval Operations*, 5 vols, reprint (Uckfield: Naval & Military Press, 1920–31). See, Newbolt, *Naval Operations*, vol. V, Appendix E.

[33] Salter, *Allied Shipping Control*, p. 358.

[34] Marder, *FDSF*, V, p. 85.

[35] Gibson and Prendergast, *German Submarine War*, pp. 328–9.

to a quarter of the total world tonnage destroyed in 1917. This regional figure for the Mediterranean is in fact closely comparable to the 1.42 million tons of all nations sunk and damaged in the Channel districts during those same months.[36] The corresponding figures for 1918, between January and September, are 800,084 tons for the Channel districts and 1,032,000 for the Mediterranean. Although the total rate of successful merchant sinkings declined in the spring of 1918 as new A/S counter-measures and coastal convoys dramatically reduced losses, the Channel actually increased in importance as targets in other theatres became scarce.

The statistics indicate the Channel's significance as an operational theatre when compared to the macroeconomic scale of the entire U-boat campaign, but to fully appreciate the situation in the Channel itself, it is necessary to increase the resolution beyond the theatre level and examine where shipping losses were occurring at the district level. In fact, between the Royal Navy's three major Channel districts, most merchant losses nearly always occurred in the Plymouth district, as the ports in that sector were, after all, Britain's primary assembly point for the Atlantic and world shipping routes. The Western Approaches traffic that funnelled into the Plymouth district made this sector the scene of the most furious U-boat activity, and the location where the largest tonnages of shipping were sunk. Interestingly the Plymouth command, despite its importance for the submarine war, has been almost entirely ignored in the historiography with very little written about A/S measures or trade defence in this district.

The second most important district, Portsmouth, varied in significance. Portsmouth was one of the first districts to implement cross-Channel convoys but was also a fertile source of mine warfare and U-boat concentration once convoys had been implemented in the Atlantic. Although less significant than Plymouth in terms of Britain's global maritime trade, Portsmouth was decisively significant in terms of cross-Channel supply – vital for fuelling the French economy and feeding the British Expeditionary Force (BEF).

The Dover district, although undeniably tertiary in terms of merchant sinkings, controlled the Channel's North Sea entrance and was a fortified military region in its own right. Dover was effectively the aero-naval front line, where the Royal Navy fought a combined surface, submarine and air battle over the contested Dover Strait in defence of the variably effective Channel barrage. Dover, despite the mere handful of merchant losses, has for this reason been the subject of the most thorough historiographical study.

---

[36] Newbolt, *Naval Operations*, V, Appendix C I, pp. 410–12.

Dover: the bottleneck

Dover's role in the war is inseparable from its principal commander, Vice Admiral Reginald Bacon, SNO Dover between April 1915 and January 1918.[37] While Bacon was responsible for a number of wartime innovations, his development and maintenance of the Dover barrage remains controversial.[38] Recent scholarship has emphasized the complex nature of the Dover defences, and specialized studies of the Royal Naval Air Service (RNAS) have clarified the essential role of Wing Captain Charles Lambe, whose Dover and Dunkirk based squadrons were responsible for conducting extensive coastal patrols and U-boat base bombing operations.[39]

From the outset of the war Dover was a critical naval district, an area of responsibility that included not only the Channel narrows at the Dover Strait but also operations along the French and Belgian coasts. Rear Admiral Horace Hood, who assumed command of the Dover district in October 1914, began the effort to secure the Strait against German naval assets. Hood was responsible for introducing the outlier indicator net system that by mid-February 1915 constituted some 17 miles of nets overseen by 30 drifters.[40] Construction of the heavy Folkestone to Cape Gris-Nez barrage line also began under Hood's tenure, with French and British destroyers patrolling the coasts.[41] These measures were, however, only marginally effective as losses in the Channel continued at the rate of two to three merchant ships per week.[42]

Rear Admiral Hood's aggressive temperament made him better suited to the Battle Cruiser Fleet (BCF) where, after briefly commanding the Eleventh Cruiser Squadron, he was transferred on 24 May. Hood's replacement at Dover, and the central protagonist in the Patrol's history, was Vice Admiral Bacon: a career technocrat and underwater warfare specialist who had been brought out of retirement and appointed on 12 April as C-in-C Dover.[43]

---

[37] Reginald Bacon, *The Dover Patrol, 1915–1917*, 2 vols (New York: George H. Doran, 1919).

[38] Cecil Aspinall-Oglander, *Roger Keyes* (London: Hogarth Press, 1951), pp. 222–54; Steve Dunn, *Securing The Narrow Sea: The Dover Patrol, 1914–1918* (Barnsley: Seaforth Publishing, 2017), pp. 180–95.

[39] John J. Abbatiello, 'British Naval Aviation and the Anti-Submarine Campaign, 1917–1918' (PhD thesis, King's College London, 2004); Abbatiello, *Anti-Submarine Warfare in World War I*; James Goldrick, *After Jutland: The Naval War in North European Waters, June 1916–November 1918*, Kindle ebook (Barnsley: Seaforth Publishing, 2018).

[40] Corbett, *Naval Operations*, II, p. 271; Newbolt, *Naval Operations*, IV, p. 331.

[41] Fayle, *Seaborne Trade*, II, pp. 21–5.

[42] Ibid., p. 26.

[43] Messimer, *Find and Destroy*, p. 40. See also, Marder, *FDSF*, II, p. 353fn; R. G. Studd, '"The Dover Patrol 1915–1917" By Admiral Sir Reginald Bacon', *Naval Review*

Bacon's appreciation of the Dover Patrol's mission was the following: 1) defend shipping at the Downs anchorage, 2) prevent the transit of raiders through the Straits, 3) provide an A/S patrol, and 4) sink U-boats.[44] Upon taking command he reviewed the efforts to block the Channel and determined that Hood's efforts so far had been impractical. Bacon refocused efforts on a barrage line between the Goodwin Sands and the French coast.[45] The Folkestone–Cape Gris-Nez passage obstructions were replaced by an eastern drifter line that by June was comprised of 132 drifters.[46] The nets were fitted with explosive mines and smoke emitters meant to detonate on contact, hopefully either revealing or destroying enemy submarines.[47] In practice the nets proved temperamental affairs, and in fact the Channel remained generally traversable until the deep minefields were introduced in January 1918.[48] Bacon's critics point to this failure to secure the Dover Strait as a black mark, and indeed, Bacon did not consider the submarine a decisive weapon, a position he maintained even after the war, writing in 1919 that 'the stiletto of the submarine, [was] a weapon too weak, too short in reach to inflict really vital blows at our sea-borne trade' and with hindsight recommended instead a German strategy based on armed merchant cruisers.[49]

Some A/S successes were nevertheless obtained by Bacon's methods, such as when *U32* was temporarily caught in a drifter net on 6 April 1915, and more spectacularly when *U8* was destroyed or scuttled after becoming tangled in an indicator net and then subjected to explosive sweep and destroyer gunfire on 4 March.[50] On 10 April, as a result of these upsets, the High Sea Fleet command ordered that its submarines were not to attempt the Channel crossing and should instead use the northern route between Scotland and Norway, orders that technically remained in force until December 1916, although the daring High Sea Fleet U-boats, under Kommodore Andreas Michelsen, and the Flanders U-boats, under Korvettenkapitan Karl Bartenbach, continued, nevertheless, to sail down the Channel and in fact no further U-boats were

---

Journal 8, no. 3 (1920): 423–4, p. 424; Arthur Marder, ed., *Portrait of an Admiral, The Life And Papers Of Herbert Richmond* (Cambridge, MA: Harvard University Press, 1952), p. 260.

[44] Studd, '"The Dover Patrol 1915–1917" By Admiral Sir Reginald Bacon', p. 428.

[45] Reginald Bacon, *The Dover Patrol, 1915–1917*, II, 2 vols (New York: George H. Doran, 1919), p. 393.

[46] Michelsen, *Submarine Warfare*, p. 93; Messimer, *Find and Destroy*, p. 40.

[47] Bacon, *Dover Patrol*, II, 1919, p. 394; Messimer, *Find and Destroy*, pp. 41–2.

[48] Messimer, *Find and Destroy*, p. 43; Marder, *FDSF*, II, p. 353.

[49] Studd, '"The Dover Patrol 1915–1917" By Admiral Sir Reginald Bacon', p. 426; Bacon, *The Dover Patrol*, I, pp. 47–9.

[50] Dunn, *Securing The Narrow Sea*, pp. 31–2. See also, Messimer, *Find and Destroy*, pp. 51–2 and Dwight Messimer, *Verschollen: World War I U-Boat Losses* (Annapolis: Naval Institute Press, 2002), pp. 21–4.

caught in the barrage for the remainder of 1915 or indeed during 1916.[51] The Dover barrage remained a veritable sieve during the first six months of 1917, with U-boats successfully transiting the Strait 190 times between December 1916 and June 1917.[52]

Efforts to improve the Dover barrage were made as the unrestricted submarine crisis worsened during the spring of 1917. The year began with the Allies successfully reverse-engineering the effective German mine (Type H, or 'horned' mine),[53] and although by October only 1,500 had been manufactured, mass production thereafter accounted for 12,450 mines between October and December, with 10,389 laid in the Dover Strait and Heligoland Bight.[54] The new mines allowed for the Folkestone to Cape Gris-Nez barrage to be replaced and strengthened, such that by December 1917 a 'mine wall' ten rows thick, containing 4,000 mines and covered by powerful surface illumination, had been installed.[55]

The improvements to the Channel defences were partly the result of the November 1917 Channel Barrage Committee, of which the chairman was Rear Admiral Roger Keyes, formerly the Director of the Plans Division of the Naval Staff.[56] The Committee's report was circulated on 29 November, and Bacon promised reform; both he and Keyes had endorsed the deep minefields, to be deployed between Gris-Nez and the Varne,[57] but it was clear that he objected to the Admiralty dictating his deployments.[58] At an Admiralty meeting on 18 December Bacon was pressured into implementing an illuminated flare patrol along the Folkestone–Gris-Nez deep line, the success of which was dramatically demonstrated the following day when *UB56* dived into the barrage and was destroyed.[59] On New Year's Day 1918 the energetic Keyes replaced Bacon as C-in-C Dover.[60]

---

[51] Marder, *FDSF*, II, p. 352; Messimer, *Find and Destroy*, p. 45; Sondhaus, *German Submarine Warfare*, p. 78.

[52] The annoyance of the barrage line prompted retaliation and, in June and July 1915, newly commissioned short range UC-type minelaying boats began placing minefields near the Dover harbour and off the Thames estuary. Dunn, *Securing The Narrow Sea*, pp. 87–8, 130.

[53] Jellicoe to Beatty, 2 April 1917, #39 in A. Temple Patterson, ed., *The Jellicoe Papers, 1916–1935*, II, 2 vols (London: Spottiswoode, Ballantyne, 1968), pp. 154–5.

[54] Michelsen, *Submarine Warfare*, p. 94; John Jellicoe, *The Submarine Peril* (London: Cassell, 1934), p. 13.

[55] Michelsen, *Submarine Warfare*, p. 94.

[56] Newbolt, *Naval Operations*, V, pp. 178–9.

[57] Ibid., p. 180.

[58] Ibid., pp. 182–3.

[59] Dunn, *Securing The Narrow Sea*, p. 158; Newbolt, *Naval Operations*, V, p. 183. See also, Messimer, *Verschollen*, p. 177.

[60] Dunn, *Securing The Narrow Sea*, p. 157.

The deep mine wall soon proved effective: six U-boats were suspected to have been destroyed by barrage mines between September and the end of the year,[61] another four boats were mined in the Channel between 19 December 1917 and 8 February 1918, and *UB35* was depth-charged by HMS *Leven* on 26 January. A total of 12 enemy submarines were destroyed between November 1917 and May 1918.[62] Maritime archaeology and underwater survey have recently verified that of the 35 U-boats destroyed in the English Channel and approaches, 16 were in fact sunk by mines.[63] After the war Bacon claimed he had been a motive force behind the new barrage. However, Lieutenant-Commander R. G. Studd, a lieutenant aboard the Dover Patrol monitor *General Wolfe* from September 1915 until the end of the war,[64] in a critical review of Bacon's book for the *Naval Review*, demonstrated that Bacon's conceptualization of the barrage differed entirely from the measures adopted after his dismissal.[65]

Even after the installation of the deep mine wall, U-boat commanders willing to accept the risks could still penetrate through the Straits. During January 1918 eight cruiser-type boats and 15 UB and UC-types utilized the Channel crossing.[66] In view of the increased risk of destruction, however, Commodore Michelsen, responsible for the High Sea Fleet's U-boats, could no longer advocate the use of the Channel route, instead mandating the northern route around Scotland (location of the Northern Barrage),[67] effectively adding five days of transit to the U-boats' cruise.[68]

The situation for the Flanders boats was worse in another way as by June 1918 RAF Brigadier-General Charles Lambe's No. 5 Group (Dover and Dunkirk, the latter soon replaced by the US Navy's Northern Bombing Group) was dropping 60 tons of bombs on the Flanders U-boat bases at Bruges and Zeebrugge every two weeks.[69] Peak sinkings in the Dover district occurred under Keyes' tenure during the period March–May 1918, before the introduction of coastal convoys, when one or two U-boats operating in the confined eastern Channel waters managed to destroy or damage 63,700 tons of shipping

---

[61] Marder, *FDSF*, IV, p. 226.

[62] D. W. Waters and Frederick Barley, *The Defeat of the Enemy Attack on Shipping, 1939–1945*, ed. Eric Grove (Aldershot: Ashgate, 1997), p. 13.

[63] McCartney, 'The Archaeology of First World War U-Boat Losses', p. 191.

[64] Service record of Ronald Granville Studd, TNA ADM 196/144/500.

[65] Studd, '"The Dover Patrol 1915–1917" By Admiral Sir Reginald Bacon', p. 440.

[66] Newbolt, *Naval Operations*, V, p. 209.

[67] Marder, *FDSF*, V, pp. 66–75.

[68] Ibid., pp. 41–2.

[69] Abbatiello, *Anti-Submarine Warfare*, p. 75; Geoffrey Rossano and Thomas Wildenberg, *Striking the Hornets' Nest* (Annapolis: Naval Institute Press, 2015), p. 181 et seq.

in the Dover district. Between 28 and 30 April *UB57*, commanded by the reckless Oberleutnant zur See Johannes Lohs,[70] sank five ships collectively worth 14,000 tons. In May *UB57* and *UC71* sank or damaged another five ships, totalling 21,700 tons, representing a quarter of all losses in the Channel districts that month. Although Lohs continued to harass Dover district shipping over the following months, he and his crew were killed when they drove into a mine off the coast of Zeebrugge while attempting to return to base on 14 August.[71] Likewise, *UB109*, patrolling in the Plymouth district, was destroyed in the Dover district when it drove into a mine while attempting to pass through the Folkestone minefields on the 29th.[72] These examples demonstrated the grave danger associated with U-boat operations in the Dover district late in the war.

Both Bacon and Keyes had attempted to counter the U-boats with their own forms of offensives, Bacon through bombardment of the U-boat bases with monitors, and Keyes through deep minefields and aggressive aerial bombing and blockship operations such as the Zeebrugge and Ostend raids. If Bacon's response to the U-boat threat during 1917 had been hesitant, the concern over aerial and surface threats was real. Technical improvements in mine warfare, and methodological reforms introduced by the Naval Staff, decisively closed the Strait by the summer of 1918.[73]

Portsmouth: the lifeline

The Portsmouth district was the main departure point for the cross-Channel trade that kept the BEF supplied and the French economy functioning while its coalfields were under enemy occupation. Since 1912 Portsmouth had been under the command of Admiral Sir Hedworth Meux, who oversaw a constant stream of transports departing England for the continent as the BEF ballooned in size and the Western Front swallowed up men and munitions.[74] Admiral Meux's forces were concentrated at Southampton, base of the Portsmouth Extended Defence area, and by January 1915 had been built up to include 14 destroyers (6 old, 8 *Beagle* class), 11 minesweepers, 17 TBs, 17 armed trawlers and 83 net drifters.[75]

Admiralty policy for Portsmouth, resulting from the initial German 'War Zone' declaration of February 1915, was that troopships should cross

---

[70] Gibson and Prendergast, *German Submarine War*, p. 318.

[71] Messimer, *Verschollen*, p. 178; Tomas Termote, *Krieg Unter Wasser: Unterseebootflotille Flandern, 1915–1918*, Kindle ebook (Hamburg: E. S. Mittler & Sohn, 2015), UB-Boote, loc. 5328–82.

[72] Messimer, *Verschollen*, p. 220.

[73] Letter from Jellicoe to Sims, 6 October 1919, #125 in Temple Patterson, *Jellicoe Papers*, II, pp. 395–6.

[74] Corbett, *Naval Operations*, I, pp. 73–5.

[75] Corbett, *Naval Operations*, II, pp. 133–4.

the Channel to Le Havre only when escorted, preferably at night, unless the transports were fast enough to steam independently, although even this allowance was soon modified to require an escort.[76] The C-in-C Portsmouth was thus in command of one of the first organized escort systems implemented by the Royal Navy outside of the Grand Fleet. In February 1916 Admiral Meux departed for Westminster,[77] and was succeeded at Portsmouth by Admiral Sir Stanley Colville, formerly the C-in-C Orkneys.[78]

During Colville's tenure the Portsmouth command's trade protection role expanded in February 1917 to incorporate the newly established cross-Channel coal trade.[79] This was a highly successful example of grass-roots convoy organization that, along with the Scandinavian ore trade (organized and convoyed by the C-in-C Orkneys and C-in-C Rosyth), and the Dutch beef trade (convoyed and organized by Commodore Tyrwhitt of the Harwich Force late in 1916), is often cited as one of the key examples of cross-Channel cooperation that convinced the Admiralty of the viability of Atlantic convoys in 1917.[80] The French coal trade was divided into four protected routes across which 37,927 coal transport voyages were convoyed with the loss of only 53 ships.[81]

Route A, between Penzance and Brest, over which there were 10,204 sailings with only 39 losses, was controlled by the SNO Falmouth, after April 1917 Rear Admiral John Luard, and the Prefet Maritime Brest, from March to November Vice Admiral Pierre Ange Marie Le Bris and then Vice Admiral Frederic Paul Moreau.[82] Route B, between Portland and Cherbourg, with 7,355 sailings and three losses, was controlled by the SNO Portland, Rear Admiral Richard Harbord until November, and then Rear Admiral Vivian Bernard, and the Prefet Maritime Cherbourg, Vice Admiral Antoine-Auguste

[76] Ibid., pp. 273–4.

[77] After winning the unopposed by-election for MP Portsmouth where he replaced Admiral Charles Beresford who had been elevated to the peerage. V. W. Baddeley and Roger T. Stearn, 'Meux [Formerly Lambton], Sir Hedworth (1856–1929)', in *The Oxford Dictionary of National Biography* (Oxford University Press, 2008); John Bullen, 'Colville, Sir Stanley Cecil James (1861–1939)', in *The Oxford Dictionary of National Biography* (Oxford University Press, 2004).

[78] *The Naval Who's Who, 1917* (Polstead: J. B. Hayward, 1981), pp. 40, 106.

[79] Marder, *FDSF*, IV, pp. 138–9.

[80] Waters and Barley, *Defeat of the Enemy Attack on Shipping*, pp. 7, 40. See also, John Jellicoe, *The Crisis of the Naval War* (London: Cassell, 1920), p. 48.

[81] Marder, *FDSF*, IV, p. 139.

[82] <https://actu.fr/bretagne/brest_29019/histoire-frederic-paul-moreau-1858-1929-prefet-maritime-brest_8600000.html>; <http://ecole.nav.traditions.free.fr/officiers_lebris_pierre.htm> accessed 7 June 2020. See also, Auguste Thomazi, *La Marine Francaise Pendant La Grande Guerre (1914–1918)*, I, 5 vols. (Paris: Payot, 1925). Service record of John Scott Luard, TNA ADM 196/42/350.

Tracou until November and then Vice Admiral Louis Jaures.[83] Route C, between St Helens or Weymouth and Havre, was controlled by the C-in-C Portsmouth, Admiral Colville, and the French SNO at Havre, since February Port Admiral and Major General Charles Baron Didelot, who was assisted by a number of Royal Navy transport officers as arranged at the end of 1915.[84] This Portsmouth district route, with 14,754 sailings and 12 losses, included traffic between Southampton and Havre which was the main line of supply for the BEF that, significantly, had been escorted by both Royal Navy and Marine Nationale destroyers since 1914.[85] Route D, with 6,757 sailings and zero losses, between Southend or Dover and Boulogne (SNO Captain William Benwell), plus Calais, was controlled by the VA Dover Patrol, Vice Admiral Bacon until his replacement by Vice Admiral Keyes at the beginning of 1918.[86] The French naval forces at Dunkirk were initially under the command of Rear Admiral de Marliave, until he was replaced in May 1916 by Vice Admiral Pierre Ronarc'h, who commanded at Dunkirk and worked closely with Bacon.[87]

The statistics summarized above demonstrate how highly successful this prototypical convoy system was, organized between the Royal Navy and Marine Nationale SNOs, and by Captain Reginald G. H. Henderson, a member of the Anti-Submarine Division (ASD) of the Royal Navy's Staff, an influential proponent of Atlantic convoys and Third Sea Lord from 1934 until his death in 1939.[88] The cross-Channel convoys were provided with trawler escort from the Auxiliary Patrol: zones XIV (Falmouth and Plymouth), XIII (Portland), XII (Isle of Wight) and XI (Dover) representing the key Channel trawler bases. Each trawler base included several trawler groups, each group composed of six trawlers and a yacht, at least one vessel of which was equipped with

[83] Jean Moulin, 'France: La Marine Nationale', in *To Crown the Waves: The Great Navies of the First World War*, ed. Vincent P. O'Hara, W. David Dickson and Richard Worth (Annapolis: Naval Institute Press, 2013), chapter 2; <https://www.naval-history.net/xGW-FrenchNavyWW1Admirals.htm> accessed 7 June 2020, service record of Richard Morden Harbord-Hamond, TNA ADM 196/42/332 and service record of Vivian Henry Gerald Bernard, TNA ADM 196/43/15.

[84] <http://dreadnoughtproject.org/tfs/index.php/Le_Havre> accessed 7 June 2020; Bacon, *Dover Patrol*, II, 1919, p. 443.

[85] Anthony Clayton, *Three Republics One Navy: A Naval History of France, 1870–1999*, Kindle ebook (Solihull, West Midlands: Helion, 2014)., chapter 5, loc. 1084.

[86] Newbolt, *Naval Operations*, V, Appendix B III. Jellicoe, *Crisis of the Naval War*, pp. 94–5, Service record of William Francis Benwell, TNA ADM 196/43/214.

[87] Bacon, *Dover Patrol*, II, 1919, pp. 443–5.

[88] Jellicoe, *Crisis of the Naval War*, p. 95; Fayle, *Seaborne Trade*, III, p. 100. See also, Nicholas Black, *The British Naval Staff In The First World War* (Rochester: Boydell & Brewer, 2011), pp. 182–4.

W/T – and supplemented with an airship and aircraft escort during the day.[89] Furthermore the Channel convoys were supported by hydrophone-equipped flotillas, of which there were four motor launch patrols (six vessels each) established for submarine hunting at Dartmouth, Portland, Portsmouth and Newhaven.[90] An additional group of six British trawlers, four minesweepers and 26 net drifters operated out of Trouville to cover the approach to Le Havre.[91] In October 1917 the first shore-based Channel hydrophone station was opened at Cuckmere Haven near Eastbourne, followed in 1918 by stations outside Plymouth at Rame Head (January), on the Isle of Wight at Freshwater (March), at Lulworth (May) and at Margate (August).[92]

The Admiralty, in cooperation with the French, was steadily exerting control over all Channel trade. Fishing vessels, initially easy targets (675 British fishing craft totalling 71,765 tons were sunk in all theatres during the war),[93] were also organized into groups. Each group comprised a dozen vessels, several of which were armed, and at least one equipped with W/T, the same scheme used for merchant convoys.[94] The militarization of the merchant seafarers and fishermen required expanded training facilities. Commander E. L. B. Lockyer, working under Captain Webb of the Trade Division, proposed wartime standards that would prepare the merchant crews for convoy duty, including lighting discipline and submarine observation training.[95] In February 1917, based on the success of the volunteer 'submarine menace course' available at Chatham and Cardiff, HMS *Excellent* at Portsmouth was selected to train officers and masters. The course was expanded to include Devonport and, on 14 May 1918, made mandatory for 'masters and chief officers of British merchant ships of 1,600 tons gross and above'. At Portsmouth 207 masters and 1,267 officers took the volunteer course, while 396 masters and 477 officers attended the compulsory course. The figures for Devonport were 455 masters and 548 officers. All told this training scheme graduated 4,620 masters and 5,606 officers during the war, one of the lesser-known achievements of the Royal Navy's trade defence system.[96]

---

[89] Faulkner and Lambert, *The Great War At Sea, A Naval Atlas, 1914–1919*, pp. 119–20.

[90] Hurd, *The Merchant Navy*, III, chapter 2, et seq.

[91] Hurd, *The Merchant Navy*, II, p. 288.

[92] Willem Hackmann, *Seek & Strike: Sonar, Anti-Submarine Warfare and the Royal Navy, 1914–54* (London: Her Majesty's Stationery Office, 1984), pp. 65–6.

[93] Hurd, *The Merchant Navy*, III, Appendix C.

[94] Richard Webb, 'Trade Defence in War,' *Royal United Services Institution Journal* 70, no. 477 (1925): 31–55, p. 34; Black, *British Naval Staff*, p. 186.

[95] Jellicoe, *Crisis of the Naval War*, p. 81.

[96] Hurd, *The Merchant Navy*, 1929, III, chapter 5, pp. 135–63.

Furthermore, the district was well supported from the air: Portsmouth's RNAS contingent was under the command of the Channel Group CO, Wing Commander A. W. Bigsworth, who had formerly been a pioneering Squadron Commander stationed at Dunkirk.[97] Bigsworth was supported by the former Director of Air Services (DAS), Rear Admiral Charles L. Vaughan-Lee, who had been appointed the Admiral Superintendent of the Portsmouth Dockyard in January 1917.[98]

Bigsworth's forces were significantly expanded as 1917 progressed, with new stations opened at Portland and Bembridge, followed by bases at Newhaven (11 May) and Cherbourg (26 July), and the Polegate airship station was transferred from Wing Captain Charles Lambe at Dover to Bigsworth's command (23 July). Lastly, a kite-balloon station, crucial for providing day and night reconnaissance over convoys, was opened at Tipnor on 28 September.[99] Commander Jean de Laborde, who at the beginning of the war had been in charge of the centre d'aviation maritime (CAM) Dunkirk and was now chief of the French Naval Aviation Service, attended a conference at the Admiralty on 11 May in which British and French air patrol zones were arranged and common W/T signals organized.[100]

The French aviation patrol system was divided into three districts, the first responsible for the North Sea and Dunkirk region, the second for the English Channel and Atlantic approaches, and the third for the Mediterranean. The first district was divided into two zones, with 32 seaplanes at Dunkirk and Saint-Pol commanded by Lt de vaisseau Lofevre, and 22 seaplanes at Boulogne and Dieppe commanded by Lt de vaisseau Serre. The Atlantic and Channel district was composed of three divisions, representing Normandy, Brittany and Gascony, of which the first was responsible for the Channel and the second and third for the Atlantic approaches. The Normandy division included Le Havre, commanded by Lt de vaisseau Flamanc with 16 flying boats, Cherbourg, with 24 aircraft, and Capitaine Lafay at Lion-sur-Mer with 12.[101]

The Channel Islands area with its numerous shoals and reefs was a hazardous area for a submarine to operate in, but nevertheless U-boats did attack targets there. On 26 February 1917 *UC17* captured and then sank the

---

[97] Alexander L. N. Howlett, 'The Royal Naval Air Service and the Evolution of Naval Aviation in Britain, 1914–1918' (PhD thesis, King's College London, 2019), pp. 124, 194; David Hobbs, *The Royal Navy's Air Service in the Great War* (Barnsley: Seaforth Publishing, 2017), p. 116.

[98] Portsmouth General Orders, 7 January 1917, TNA ADM 179/78.

[99] Jones, *WIA*, IV, p. 48.

[100] Newbolt, *Naval Operations*, V, pp. 35–6.

[101] Terry Treadwell, *The First Naval Air War* (Stroud: The History Press, 2010), p. 113.

716-ton French bark *Le Lamentin* 30 miles west of Guernsey, while simultaneously *UC65* stopped and then scuttled the 134-ton Dutch sailing ship *Alberdina* north of Alderney. *UC65* returned to the Channel Islands late in April and sank two more sailing ships of 79 and 146 tons north of Alderney on the 26th. *UC66* sank the 335-ton French bark *La Manche* north-east of Guernsey on 1 May, and *UC70* sank the 268-ton steamer *Dromore* south of Guernsey on 18 May. *UC36* sank two sailing vessels, one of 120 and one of 182 tons, north of Guernsey on 20 May, and on 6 June *UB18* sank the 170-ton Dutch schooner *Cornelia* west of Jersey. On 19 June the 164-ton brigantine *Mary Ann* and then the 96-ton ketch *Kate And Annie* were both sunk by *UC17* north-west of Guernsey. The 317-ton steamer *Solway Prince* was sunk north of Alderney by *UB40* on 27 June, and the 91-ton schooner *Industry* was sunk by *UC42* north-west of Guernsey on 5 September, which was also the location where, on 4 December, *UB35* sank the 343-ton Swedish steamer *Helge*. Nine days later the 114-ton British schooner *Little Gem* was sunk by *U87* amongst the Casquets off Alderney, a trend of sinkings near the Channel Islands that continued when *U90* sank the 78-ton schooner *Charles* 16 miles from the Casquets on 24 January 1918.[102]

As these examples suggest, the development of a flying boat base on Guernsey was essential to cover this gap in the Channel patrol scheme. A French seaplane base was indeed established at Castle Cornet, Guernsey, after the location was scouted by Lt de vaisseau Pierre Le Cour-Grandmaison during the summer of 1917. In August a team of Royal Engineers began construction of the base and by September there were 12 flying boats on station.[103] The proof that U-boats were slipping through the Channel Islands gap was demonstrated repeatedly during 1918, as CAM Guernsey flying boats attacked and damaged transiting U-boats on 31 January, 23 April, 6 and 31 May.[104]

Combined with the RNAS bases in Wing Captain Gerrard's South West Group (see below), and the other French flying boat bases in the Channel,

---

[102] <https://uboat.net/wwi/ships_hit/3534.html>, <https://uboat.net/wwi/ships_hit/6759.html>, <https://uboat.net/wwi/ships_hit/930.html>, <https://uboat.net/wwi/ships_hit/116.html>, <https://www.wrecksite.eu/wreck.aspx?155057>, <https://www.wrecksite.eu/wreck.aspx?2640>, <https://uboat.net/wwi/ships_hit/1447.html>, <https://uboat.net/wwi/ships_hit/7326.html>, <https://uboat.net/wwi/ships_hit/3267.html>, <https://uboat.net/wwi/ships_hit/5643.html>, <https://uboat.net/wwi/ships_hit/7318.html>, <https://www.wrecksite.eu/wreck.aspx?2627>, <https://uboat.net/wwi/ships_hit/2793.html>, <https://uboat.net/wwi/ships_hit/3637.html>, <https://www.wrecksite.eu/wreck.aspx?2616>, accessed 7 June 2020.

[103] <http://ecole.nav.traditions.free.fr/officiers_lecour.htm>, accessed 7 June 2020. Terry Treadwell, *The First Naval Air War* (Stroud: The History Press, 2010). See also, Raoul Lempriere, *History of The Channel Islands* (London: Robert Hale, 1974), p. 211.

[104] Treadwell, *The First Naval Air War*, p. 114. English Channel, German Submarines, May 1918, TNA ADM 137/1479.

this overlapping and coordinated seaplane and airship patrol system provided a daytime patrol and escort capability that severely restricted the U-boats' freedom of operation. During 1917 the Channel Group flew 1,540 patrols, in addition to 406 Sea Scout and Coastal-type airship sorties.[105] This air coverage provided the Portsmouth zone with an unprecedented degree of protection and between March and May 1917 there were only nine ships lost sailing with convoys, all at night when there was no air coverage, out of the 4,000 ships convoyed. Between May and August the figure was 8,825 vessels convoyed with only fourteen losses.[106] Even independent merchant ships began to join the convoys, de facto recognition of the success of the protected sailings.[107]

Despite this comprehensive scheme of sea and air escorts, losses of vessels travelling outside the convoy system in the Portsmouth district remained at a rate averaging 28% of all Channel losses during the 1917–18 crisis. Although the absolute tonnage lost in the Portsmouth district fell after the spring of 1918 when coastal convoys were implemented, the overall *percentage* of losses in the district remained high as losses elsewhere tapered off. Once again this included the work of Johannes Lohs and his *UB57* crew, who sank the 5,306-ton British steamer *Shirala* on 2 July 1918 and damaged two more steamers worth a collective 8,971 tons over the next four days. *UB103* (one 731-ton steamer sunk) and *UB88* (damaged a 6,045-ton steamer) were also active around Portsmouth that month. On 9 August *UB57* sank the *Glenlee* for another 4,915 tons, while Oberleutnant zur See Walter Warzecha in *UC71* damaged two steamers worth a combined 12,826 tons, and the less lucky Hans Kukenthal in *UC49* sank the 7,713-ton *Warilda* on 3 August. As these cases indicate, the Flanders U-boats could still inflict a few notable wounds, although at great risk to their safety: less than a fortnight after these attacks both Lohs and Kukenthal had been killed.

Plymouth: the linchpin

The Plymouth command gradually increased in significance as the U-boats were forced to extend their area of operations into the Atlantic and away from the coasts. The Plymouth district, commanded from the HQ at Devonport, was part of a broader group of districts known as the South West Approaches that included the base at Falmouth on the Cornwall peninsula, Vice Admiral Lewis Bayly's Ireland command at Queenstown which was supplemented in the summer and autumn of 1917 by USN forces organized energetically by

---

[105] Wing Commander A. W. Bigsworth, RNAS Portsmouth Group, General Report of Work Carried Out During Year 1917, 2 December 1917, TNA AIR 1/659/17/122/609.

[106] Waters and Barley, *Defeat of the Enemy Attack on Shipping*, p. 7; Jellicoe, *Crisis of the Naval War*, p. 96.

[107] Black, *British Naval Staff*, p. 177.

Admiral William Sims, including flying boats under the command of Captain Hutch Cone,[108] and lastly the Bristol Channel approach that funnelled shipping into Milford Haven. The C-in-C Plymouth was responsible for the largest area of operations in the Channel districts and, unlike Dover or Portsmouth, his command involved protecting traffic from North and South America, Africa and the Mediterranean.

The established system of trade defence at this time was based on 'approach routes', originally organized in July 1916.[109] This system provided for four approach 'cones' which were swept by patrol ships to keep the routes clear of enemy raiders.[110] The randomness of the system might usefully confuse surface raiders but was ultimately to prove disastrous as it funnelled shipping into dangerously crowded and exposed lanes. A great number of destroyers and patrol craft were needed to sweep the approach areas, and it was unlikely that patrol ships alone would encounter U-boats not wanting to be found. As Henry Jones phrased it, the approach-lane system had the effect of 'concentrating great numbers of [merchant] ships along the patrol routes off the south coast of Ireland and in the Bristol Channel' where they were easy prey for waiting submarines.[111]

The Plymouth district was initially under the command of Admiral George Le C. Egerton, although he was superseded in 1916 by Vice Admiral Sir George J. S. Warrender. On 27 November Jellicoe, who was shortly to take charge of the Admiralty as First Sea Lord in David Lloyd George's coalition government, invited Rear Admiral Alexander Duff, second in command of the 4th Battle Squadron, to head up the new Anti-Submarine Division (ASD) of the Naval Staff.[112] The ASD was formally constituted on 18 December, with Captain F. C. Dreyer as Duff's Assistant Director.[113] Two days after Jellicoe's promotion to First Sea Lord on 7 December, Rear Admiral Alexander Bethell, an

---

[108] William N. Still, *Crisis at Sea: The United States Navy in European Waters in World War I* (Gainesville: University Press of Florida, 2006), pp. 91–110, 446; Geoffrey L. Rossano, *Stalking the U-Boat, U.S. Naval Aviation in Europe during World War I* (Gainesville: University Press of Florida, 2010), p. 208 et seq.; Sims, *The Victory at Sea*, pp. 118–22, 320.

[109] Webb, 'Trade Defence in War', p. 38. See also, Seligmann, *The Royal Navy and the German Threat, 1901–1914*, p. 110.

[110] Norman Leslie, 'The System of Convoys for Merchant Shipping in 1917 and 1918', *Naval Review* 5, no. 1 (1917): 42–95, p. 43.

[111] Jones, *WIA*, IV, p. 45. Interestingly, this had been essentially Admiral Sir Arthur Wilson's prediction regarding the scheme when it had been discussed in 1905: see, Seligmann, *The Royal Navy and the German Threat*, p. 111.

[112] Copy of Jellicoe to Duff letter, 27 November 1916, National Maritime Museum, Greenwich, DUFF 1.

[113] Admiralty Memorandum, 16 December 1916, Anti-Submarine Division papers: Volume I, Organisation and Personnel, TNA ADM 137/2715.

experienced blockade theorist with Naval War College connections, and formerly the Director of Naval Intelligence, was instructed to replace Warrender, who suffered from deafness and who Jellicoe, as a result of Warrender's performance during the 16 December 1914 Scarborough raid, believed was 'absent-minded', as SNO Plymouth.[114]

Resource scarcity meant that in February 1917 there were only 14 destroyers available at Devonport (Jellicoe transferred ten more from the Grand Fleet) in addition to a paltry 12 sloops stationed at Queenstown.[115] Aircraft and airship bases had not yet been constructed to cover these approaches.[116] Before the introduction of convoys it was hoped that arming merchant vessels and deploying Q-ships would usefully deter and potentially destroy German submarines in the Channel. One of these vessels that scored an important victory in the Plymouth district was HMS *Privet*, previously the 800-ton London and Channel Islands ferry *Island Queen*.[117] Requisitioned by the Admiralty in December 1916 and given the designation *Q19*, on 12 March 1917 this specialized A/S vessel seriously damaged a U-boat 20 miles southeast of Start Point, although *Privet* was heavily damaged in the encounter and sank while being towed into Plymouth Sound.[118] The U-boat encountered was initially believed to have been *U85* but was more likely *UC68*, which had been laying a minefield south of Plymouth before the encounter, although the exact fate of neither boat has been ascertained.[119]

Clearly, more comprehensive A/S and trade protection measures were required. As early as 15 December 1916 Duff had drafted a letter to Jellicoe stating his intention to expand surface and RNAS patrols around the British Isles, including in the English Channel.[120] Given the scarcity of patrol craft Duff proposed that the outgoing DAS, Rear Admiral Vaughan-Lee, should

[114] Service record of Alexander Edward Bethell, TNA ADM 196/19/332. *The Naval Who's Who, 1917*, p. 23. See also, Nicholas Lambert, *Planning Armageddon, British Economic Warfare and the First World War* (Cambridge, MA: Harvard University Press, 2012), pp. 217–18; Marder, *FDSF*, II, pp. 134–47, 441; Paul G. Halpern, 'Warrender, Sir George John Scott, of Lochend, Seventh Baronet (1860–1917)', in *The Oxford Dictionary of National Biography* (Oxford University Press, 2012). Warrender died shortly thereafter on 8 January 1917.

[115] Gibson and Prendergast, *German Submarine War*, p. 160; Jellicoe, *The Submarine Peril*, pp. 17–18.

[116] Howlett, 'The Royal Naval Air Service', pp. 125–9.

[117] Alan G. Jamieson, *A People of the Sea: The Maritime History of the Channel Islands* (Slingsby, York: Methuen, 1986), p. 463.

[118] E. Keble Chatterton, *Q-Ships and Their Story*, Kindle ebook (London: Sidgwick and Jackson, 1922), chapter 12, loc. 2807, pp. 170–1; Messimer, *Verschollen*, p. 104.

[119] McCartney, 'The Maritime Archaeology of a Modern Conflict', p. 160; Termote, *Krieg Unter Wasser*, UC-Boote, loc. 6922; Messimer, *Verschollen*, p. 306.

[120] Abbatiello, *Anti-Submarine Warfare*, p. 88.

prepare an air patrol scheme for the Atlantic approaches, including bases in Ireland, at Falmouth or the Scilly Isles, plus a base at Plymouth (established at Cattewater) and Newyln (Land's End), to cover traffic approaching the Channel.[121] The coasts of these contested waters at the Channel entrance were dangerous for U-boats to approach; the Bishops Rock and Western Rocks formations near the Scillies, the Manacles off the Lizard, the Chaussee de Sein reefs off Finistère, the Casquets reef west of Alderney and the Minquiers reef south of Jersey had all plagued mariners for centuries, but now provided some degree of protection for merchant trade in the Plymouth district, compounded by the U-boat commanders' inherent fear of detection from the air.[122]

On 13 March Wing Captain Eugene L. Gerrard, RNAS arrived to take command of the naval aviation squadrons in Bethell's district, which on 3 April were constituted together under Gerrard's command as the RNAS South West Group.[123] On 17 April Gerrard and Bethell adopted the scheme proposed by Squadron Commander R. B. B. Colmore, of Naval Air Station (NAS) Mullion.[124] Colmore's report, forwarded on 23 April by Gerrard to the new DAS (and Fifth Sea Lord), Commodore Godfrey Paine,[125] described a combination of routine, emergency and contact (destroyer plus seaplane) patrols, arranged so that at least one machine was always kept in readiness to launch and respond to U-boat reports at short notice.

In February three H12 flying boats under Squadron Commander Ralph Hope-Vere were flown out to the Scillies, where the Royal Navy was represented by Commander William Oliver, to begin patrolling the Cornwall approaches.[126] Initially based on the same 'Spider Web' octagonal patrols utilized by NAS Felixstowe, by August the patrol system had evolved to include specified area patrols for emergency response.[127] Bethell also arranged

[121] Jones, *WIA*, IV, pp. 45–6.

[122] See for example, Rodger, *The Command of the Ocean*, p. 172; Jamieson, *A People of the Sea*, p. 418.

[123] Service record for Eugene Louis Gerrard, DSO, TNA ADM 273/2/42. After 1 April 1918 Gerard became Brigadier-General in command of the RAF's No. 9 Group.

[124] RNAS Station Index, 31 March 1918, TNA AIR 1/670, in Stephen Roskill, ed., *Documents Relating to the Naval Air Service, 1908–1918* (London: Spottiswoode, Ballantyne, 1969), Appendix II, p. 750. See also, Abbatiello, *Anti-Submarine Warfare*, Appendix 2, p. 176.

[125] Wing Captain South West Group to Director Air Services, 23 April 1917, TNA AIR 1/644. See also, Peter London, *U-Boat Hunters: Cornwall's Air War, 1916–1919* (Truro: Dyllansow Truran, 1999), p. 55.

[126] Jones, *WIA*, IV, p. 47; Abbatiello, *Anti-Submarine Warfare*, p. 119; Richard Larn, *The Isles of Scilly in the Great War* (Barnsley: Pen & Sword, 2017), p. 92; C-in-C Plymouth to 4th Sea Lord, Application for additional trawlers for HM Naval Sub-Base, Scilly Isles, 4 April 1917, TNA ADM 137/1299, p. 31.

[127] Jones, *WIA*, IV, p. 48; Wing Captain E. L. Gerrard, 'South-West Group-Patrol

patrol zones for the trawler and auxiliary flotillas in the Plymouth area,[128] and the entire system was networked together by telephone and telegraph cables. W/T stations were established at the Scillies, Land's End, Falmouth, Plymouth and Portland.[129] In addition to French naval aviation forces operating from the coast of Brittany, after June 1917 the Americans began to develop their naval aviation forces in France, which ultimately would have included eight seaplane stations, four non-rigid airship bases and three kite-balloon facilities, although only a few of these planned bases were operational when the war ended.[130]

Convoy escorts were arranged starting on 26 May 1917, with the first convoy running from Gibraltar escorted by HMS *Hardy*, flagship of the Senior Officer of the TB escorts, and supported by one of the H12 flying boats from the Scillies.[131] The commander of the *Hardy* had interesting comments on convoy tactics: in a 6½ knot convoy only one ship in the convoy would use running lights, with the lights of all other ships extinguished. Destroyers should be spread out as far as was possible, with six destroyers used to escort a 15-merchant ship convoy.[132] Early in June Admiral Bethell arranged for designated shipping arriving in the Plymouth district area to be met by destroyers and then escorted either to their destination or to Falmouth for further routing.[133] The need for additional destroyers for escort duty was real, as the inbound convoys and independent merchants made tempting targets unless well escorted, as was demonstrated on 29 June when a U-boat attempted to attack a convoy 50 miles west of Guernsey but was driven off by the escorts.[134]

The introduction of inbound convoys on the Atlantic routes forced the U-boats to adjust their tactics, and by August the U-boat commanders had switched from the vital inbound to the less significant and unescorted outbound shipping.[135] By November Bethell advocated that all Channel traffic should be organized into convoys, effectively endorsing coastal convoys, a measure the Naval Staff had not then determined was necessary.[136] By the summer of

---

Orders' 1 September 1917, TNA AIR 1/305. See also Wing Captain Gerrard to C-in-C Plymouth, 19 September 1917, TNA AIR 1/644.

[128] Newbolt, *Naval Operations*, V, p. 197.

[129] Ibid., p. 197.

[130] Rossano, *Stalking the U-Boat*, p. 81.

[131] ACNS Duff to C-in-C Devonport, Rear Admiral Bethell, 'Gibraltar Merchant Ship Convoy Report from Escort', 26 May 1917, TNA ADM 137/1323; Abbatiello, *Anti-Submarine Warfare*, p. 119.

[132] CO HMS *Hardy*, 4th Destroyer Flotilla, to C-in-C Devonport, 5 June 1917, TNA ADM 137/1323.

[133] Admiral Bethell, Devonport General Orders, 5 June 1917, TNA ADM 137/1299.

[134] War Cabinet minutes, WC 172, 29 June 1917, TNA CAB 23/3/20, p. 4.

[135] Marder, *FDSF*, IV, p. 260.

[136] Abbatiello, *Anti-Submarine Warfare*, p. 118. See Bethell to Admiralty, 5 November 1917, ADM 137/1324.

1918 aircraft and D/F were playing a major role in the Plymouth district. As Bethell reported in May, it was now routine for D/F intercepts to locate and triangulate the position of U-boats, against which seaplanes could then be directed.[137] The U-boats, even hobbled, could still score individual success as we have seen.

In the case of August 1918 there were at least eight U-boats operating in the Plymouth district (*U107, U113, UB86, UB88, UB92, UB109, UB125, UC49*). Kapitanleutnant Reinhard von Rabenau in *UB88* was the most successful, sinking three ships worth a total of 6,488 tons and damaging another (in the Portsmouth district) of 4,090 tons. Kapitanleutnant Hans Trenk in *UB86* sank a pair of merchants worth collectively 3,048 tons and damaged the *Charity* of 1,735 tons. Notably, both von Rabenau and Trenk survived the war.[138]

There were 11 boats operating in the Plymouth area in September (*U53, U54, U82, UB87, UB88, UB91, UB104, UB112, UB113, UB117, UB125*). U-boat 'ace' Kapitanleutnant Erwin Wassner, with over 100,000 tons to his name, between 16 and 18 September in *UB117* sank five ships worth 9,342 tons.[139] Neither *UB104* nor *UB113* returned from their patrols.[140] U-boat veteran Kapitanleutnant Wilhelm Rhein in *UB112* had the distinction of closing out the submarine campaign in the Channel when he destroyed seven ships worth a total of 8,397 tons during the first four days of October and damaged another 1,960-ton merchant, shortly before the conclusion of the U-boat campaign itself.

Conclusions

The experience of unrestricted submarine warfare in the English Channel during the First World War suggests several conclusions. First, the cross-Channel convoys from 1914 onwards indicated the correct model for protecting merchant shipping, a model that was gradually adopted by the Naval Staff after May 1917. Although losses in the dense Channel traffic continued, the small tonnage being sunk was not substantial enough to impact Britain's war effort, despite representing a significant portion of the total merchant tonnage destroyed during the war. Second, the introduction of coastal convoys in May 1918, combined with further tightening of the Dover barrage, finally reduced Channel losses to a negligible level, while simultaneously raising the risk to U-boats attempting the Channel transit.[141] The ASD believed, in its post-war analysis, that 37 U-boats had been sunk in the Channel, of which 22 have

---

[137] Admiral Bethell A/S report, 15 May 1918, TNA ADM 137/1486.

[138] Michelsen, *Submarine Warfare*, pp. 207–8.

[139] Michelsen, *Submarine Warfare*, p. 218.

[140] Messimer, *Verschollen*, pp. 215, 224.

[141] Waters and Barley, *Defeat of the Enemy Attack on Shipping*, table 2.

since been confirmed or rediscovered, out of the 203 lost to all causes during the war.[142]

Critically, the relative scale of tonnage lost in the Channel has been overlooked. Data compiled for this study demonstrates that losses in the Channel were comparable to the entire Mediterranean theatre in terms of tonnage damaged or sunk. This reflects the astonishing lack of any detailed investigation of the Plymouth district, where the majority of the Channel losses occurred, which was one of the most vital naval districts during the entire war. There is no study of the Plymouth district or Admiral Alexander Bethell, who commanded there during the submarine crisis.

At Plymouth, the dispersal method and approach zones kept losses from scattered U-boats and merchant raiders to a marginal level, but the introduction of unrestricted submarine warfare in 1917 changed the calculus.[143] Material improvements in A/S weapons, mines and detectors, combined with comprehensive convoys, eventually turned the tables on the U-boats, which by the end of the war were being sunk in increasingly significant numbers by deep minefields, aerial bombs and depth-charge equipped escorts. The Dover command faced unprecedented aerial and destroyer attack and was tasked with the complex and difficult task of blocking the Dover Strait. From the outset Portsmouth was involved in escorting troopships and convoys, providing the model for the Atlantic and coastal convoy network that eventually secured Britain's seaborne trade.

[142] McCartney, 'The Archaeology of First World War U-Boat Losses in the English Channel', p. 186, Messimer, *Verschollen*, p. 13.

[143] Webb, 'Trade Defence in War', 36.

AFTERWORD: ALDERNEY, THE CHANNEL ISLANDS, AND THE STUDY OF HISTORY[1]

ALAN JAMES

'On its own, the history of these communities or island republics is of only modest, local interest, whilst its significance expands and takes on a brilliant radiance under the bright light of the histories of France and of England'.[2] So claimed the French writer and intellectual, Eugène Pégot-Ogier, who was among Victor Hugo's circle during his exile on the Channel Islands, in his lengthy *Histoire des isles de la Manche* of 1881. As if to confirm the truth of this observation, the contributors to the present volume have directed the spotlight of international history onto the islands and uncovered the richness of their history as it played out on the stage of centuries of nearly permanent Anglo-French rivalry. Yet, by portraying the islands as passive objects of insight and meaning in this way, Pégot-Ogier arguably underestimated the value of the history of his temporary home. Situated between the two states, not just geographically but politically, economically, and culturally, the islands are more than just supporting actors to be brought out of the shadows. They cast a certain light of their own into previously unseen corners of the stage. Paradoxically, perhaps, it is precisely because they defy easy categorisation and seem to stand aloof from familiar political trends that the history of the Channel Islands can be employed to illuminate that of their more powerful neighbours. Indeed, the very smallness, isolation, and exceptional nature of the islands, which has traditionally shielded them from the critical gaze of historians, can be usefully held up like a conceptual mirror to put even some of

[1] I would like to thank Dr Eric Barré, Université de Caen, Normandie, for generously sharing with me his considerable knowledge and the fruits of his extensive research into the islands and the Channel.

[2] 'Isolée, l'histoire des bailliages ou républiques insulaires n'offre qu'un médiocre intérêt local, tandis qu'elle se généralise et brille d'un éclat réel sous la vive lumière de l'histoire de France et d'Angleterre', Eugène Pégot-Ogier, *Histoire des isles de la Manche* (Paris: E. Plon, 1881), v.

our most cherished expectations and common assumptions about international history to greater scrutiny. It seems certain, therefore, that the academic interest in the history of these beguiling islands which has been sparked by the chapters in this volume will continue to grow in the future, shaping our understanding, not only of the naval and political relations of France and Britain, but of the nature of the very international system in which they operated.

War is the common theme that runs throughout the entire history of these islands. This is best illustrated by the naval history offered here by Colin Partridge. The focus on Alderney, in particular, and the key role of its harbour, however, not only uncovers an essential feature of this military competition. It also demonstrates the value to historians of distinguishing between the islands and of digging into their individual circumstances and particularities. At the same time, however, Jean de Préneuf reminds us that the study of war in and around the Channel Islands is also the study of global war, for the Anglo-French rivalry that unfolded there was, of course, what largely drove naval warfare globally. He demonstrates how Alderney's proximity to and threatening influence on the key Channel port of Cherbourg make it an ideal vantage point from which to evaluate the evolution of French strategic priorities. A largely defensive posture, traditionally pursued through dissuasion, was adopted by France in the Channel in order to protect the autonomy of its navy and create the freedom to confront threats or to pursue interests elsewhere. Eventually, de Préneuf reminds us, by the years leading up to the First World War, this same need took the form of a difficult cooperation with Britain. In this way, he demonstrates how a focus on the French preoccupation with the islands can help to reveal the broad contours of this evolving, national strategic outlook.

As Andrew Lambert has described it elsewhere, French interest in the islands had always been 'negative' like this. In contrast, he provides a study of British strategy in the nineteenth century that was more purposeful. For Britain, defence of the islands and of Alderney, in particular, was needed in the age of steam to maintain an offensive footing and control of the Channel in the event of war. Other 'harbours of refuge' were part of the same strategic ambition. Despite whatever else can be said about the need to provide protection for civilian shipping, William Allsop's detailed study of the sheer magnitude, cost, and complexity of these port works and fortifications confirms this overriding and very pressing military priority. In this respect, as Jean de Préneuf also reminds us, Alderney's position offered Britain certain, clear strategic opportunities, functioning as 'l'avant-garde britannique contre la France'. Thus, international tension inevitably drew attention to the islands, and the study of both the French and British perspectives together in the same volume reinforces how a pair of complementary, national outlooks developed and interacted to shape each other and the wider strategic context of the Channel. This dynamic was perhaps most clearly, and openly, expressed during that relatively rare period of naval co-operation between Britain and France during the First World War. Yet, for all periods, the nature of this interaction is a precious key with which to unlock the workings of cross-Channel relations.

Inevitably, each power's relations with the islands themselves also shaped the long history of this international tension. The Channel Islands reaffirmed their allegiance to the English crown in 1204, despite the loss to France of the rest of Normandy and other Angevin lands confirmed by the defeat at the Battle of Bouvines ten years later. Thereafter, they remained a particular source of royal pride and a tangible, legal expression of the English monarchy's lingering, extensive claims to French territory. The influence of the crown on the islands grew notably, however, when the unprecedented threat to the international order posed by Louis XIV in the seventeenth century elevated them to the status of key strategic assets. In order to take advantage, in 1689 William III formally ended the Bull of Neutrality of 1483 that had been allowing the islands to trade freely with France. The aim was to exploit the islands as a privateering base with which to attack French trade and disrupt their navy. According to Richard Harding, the islands became vital forward 'outposts' in the eighteenth century. In addition to privateering, they offered opportunities for intelligence gathering, precious contacts, and a source of local expertise in pilotage, for example. Yet the very real and growing danger of French invasion made providing effective defences a serious challenge. This imperative not only shaped British strategic thought but inevitably also affected the islands themselves, physically and politically. As Harding points out, more balanced land and sea defences were needed, and this required greater acceptance of a British presence more generally by the islanders, however reluctant they might have been. This insight into the pressures that drove the evolution of the relationship between the islands and Britain is an important reminder of a central theme of the history of the Channel Islands. It was always conditioned by the careful management and negotiation of a distinct political distance from Britain and by a mutually defining tension. The close study of the islands, then, not only illuminates the complementary strategic outlooks driving Anglo-French relations but the key role the islands themselves played in the different symbiotic relationships and tensions that shaped the broader diplomatic and military context of the Channel.

Victor Hugo famously described the Channel Islands as 'little pieces of France fallen into the sea and scooped up by England'.[3] This is potentially

---

[3] 'Les îles de la Manche sont des morceaux de France tombés dans la mer et ramassés par l'Angleterre'. From 'L'Archipel de la Manche' which was intended to be a preface to his 1866 novel, *Les Travailleurs de la mer*, but was first published on its own in 1883 and in later editions published with the novel. Victor Hugo, 'L'archipel de la mer', in *Les travailleurs de la mer, Vol. 1*, Oeuvres Complètes. Roman. X. (Paris: Émile Testard, 1891), 36.

misleading, however. In her description of the attempt to harness and direct privateering from the islands in the mid-eighteenth century, Anna Brinkman-Schwartz exposes some of the limits of British political influence and this centrifugal tendency that shaped the islands' dealings with Britain. Not just a potential force that could be unleashed at will, British interests at times required attempts to impose restrictions and to curtail the islanders' activity. This sense that the islands were considered an asset to be managed, and one that posed unique challenges because of their own agency, reminds us that we cannot think of them simply as strategic assets or as a contested prize. War and direct competition may well have been the principal drivers of their history, but this history was marked by many ambiguities and uncertain relationships. It is far more accurate to describe the islands as a constantly contested, negotiated space. This complexity is captured by the many papers in this volume that address another, related theme: the competitive pursuit from both sides of the Channel of intelligence and hydrographical knowledge.

From at least as early as the sixteenth century, when French Huguenots used the islands as a refuge and a staging post in international intrigue, they remained an active stage for spies and a conduit for the exchange of information.[4] This was not a minor, secondary issue. For both France and Britain, intelligence was a key aspect of coastal defence, sitting right alongside such priorities as fortifications, harbour works, shipbuilding, recruitment, and so on. In their own ways, then, the islands were essential to the interests of both states. Work on the different means by which they pursued these interests is needed, therefore, such as an assessment of the Channel Islands that was undertaken in the eighteenth century by the French navy and engineering corps, for example. This would provide an important complement to Richard Harding's study of more direct British involvement on the islands.[5] Yet, all the studies collected here that touch on competitive intelligence gathering feed the sense that the Channel Islands have always been quite distant, resistant, and difficult to govern, protect, or exploit and that this, too, shaped the wider history of the region.

Frédéric Saffroy provides a very clear warning against over-estimating the role of the British or French state in his detailed coverage of the legal complexities of the notion of sovereignty, or ownership, as it applied over the ages to the islands and to formal influence at sea. Although he argues that contested sovereignty was not an especially problematic issue for the two monarchies until the nineteenth century, it became so with rising tension

---

    [4] Alain Landurant, *Montgommery le régicide* (Paris: Tallandier, 1988), 61, 216–17.
    [5] There is important work being done on this by Sylviane Llinarès and Edern Olivier-Jégat. See also Sylviane Llinarès, Benjamin Égasse, and Katherine Dana, *De L'estran à la digue: histoire des aménagements portuaires et littoraux, XVIe-XXe siècle*, Histoire (Rennes: Presses Universitaires de Rennes, 2018).

over fishing rights and, particularly, oyster beds. The very clear implication is that the difficult legal ambiguities and complications that have largely come to define the islands were not initially all that unusual. Thus, far from some lingering medieval relic, the constitutional complexities we commonly associate with the Channel Islands grew with time, an idea that is supported by the contested boundary between Guernsey and France that exists still in the twenty-first century. Indeed, Isabelle Delumeau's discussion of the growing French obsession with hydrography in the nineteenth century, particularly around the Minquiers in the 1880s, shows that this was linked not just to the evolving needs of coastal defence but more widely to competing claims of sovereignty. Yet this growing competition was not straightforward, as is also borne out by Michael Barritt's complementary study. The dangerous, difficult, and determined pursuit of hydrographical knowledge is revealed by the two papers from both the French and British perspectives respectively, and similar imperatives and fears applied. The civil relationship between Beautemps-Beaupré and Martin White, for example, which was described in both, is itself an illustration of an important idea. We see cooperation at the personal level, a shared human interest in charting and navigation, at the same time that they each advanced the competitive political and military interests of their respective states.

There is nothing new in highlighting the unique identity and the peculiar nature of the Channel Islands' association with Britain and with France, of course. This is a key theme in traditional histories of the islands. As Richard Harding notes, the earliest history of Jersey by Philip Falle in 1694, for example, was an act of self-preservation in the face of Louis XIV's menacing strength. It was an attempt to demonstrate the importance of the islands to England, to strengthen the association, and to enumerate to the islanders the privileges that it brought.[6] Abraham Mourant expressed similar pride in the islands' status as the oldest possessions of the English crown in the preface to his 1868 re-edition of the influential *Chroniques de Jersey*, originally compiled in 1585 from earlier manuscripts. In this case, Mourant marvels at the strength of French military might to fully justify his celebration of the steadfast loyalty of the islands to the British crown that protected them.[7] Such histories were clear attempts to insist upon and to celebrate exceptionalism and thereby to cement this relationship. Thus, in all of them there is the unmistakable quali-fication that the enthusiasm for the crown depended upon Britain's relatively limited authority, the lack of parliamentary jurisdiction, and the respect for their customs and traditions that the islands were able to command. In many ways, then, the relationship was never distorted or threatened by the many tensions and strains that were always in evidence but defined by them.

[6] Philip Falle, *An Account of the Island of Jersey* (London: John Newton, 1694).

[7] Abraham Mourant, ed. *Chroniques de Jersey* (Jersey: Philippe Falle, 1868), iii.

French-speaking, and very consciously not part of the machinery of the British state, the islands professed loyalty to the crown only due to their lingering claim to the duchy of Normandy and, crucially, only insofar as this would provide political and economic privileges and exemptions.

There were other political purposes for older histories of the islands. By 1904, in one of a number of travel accounts or general interest books that were appearing in French, Henri Boland recognised Alderney's position as Britain's 'Gibraltar de la Manche' and bemoaned what he saw as an increasing cultural and linguistic turn on the islands towards the English. The reasons for this were clear. According to Boland, earlier French attempts to reconquer the islands lingered there in the popular memory. Equally, all the leading families had built their fortunes by attacking French shipping during the dangerous First Empire in France and had enjoyed British protection doing so. Although he insisted that the islanders remained culturally French, at least historically, he regretted that they were currently more likely to 'fear' France. [8] What concerned them, according to Boland, was the prospect of the intrusive French system with their 'gendarmes' and their restrictive and costly customs and regulations. Nevertheless, although they saw the revolutionary ideas that emanated from France as threatening, Boland closed with the observation that there were storm clouds on the horizon. A 'rebellious wind was blowing' on the islands. There was a thirst for modern ideas, and the time was fast approaching when the people would rise against the oligarchs.[9]

Pégot-Ogier's much more substantial, academic history developed this idea. His was an open celebration of republican France and its potential influence. The distant relationship with Britain that the Channel Islands had long sustained simply confirmed that, from their earliest beginnings, the islands embodied the virtue of liberty. These culturally French people had always valiantly defended their autonomy. Regrettably, however, he claimed that by the nineteenth century this spirit had started to wane. The islands had fallen into torpor and indolence due to the unedifying pursuit of money, but also to their inwardness and the lack of any classical education. Pégot-Ogier's call, therefore, was to let the light of France redeem the islands and allow them to reach their historical destiny. He was using history for this very clear purpose, to educate and to energise the islands toward revolutionary reform. They were to shake off their parochial isolation and embrace liberal progress of the sort begun by William III and which blossomed in the American and French Revolutions. Without such redemption, the lesson that seemed to emerge from the long history of the Channel Islands was that they risked irrelevance or, worse, the very serious danger of closer integration into the British state.

---

[8]   Henri Boland, *Les îles de la Manche* (Paris: Hachette, 1904), 56, 266.
[9]   'Un vent de fronde souffle'. Ibid., 278–9.

Again, however, it is clear that in this contest over their allegiance and identity, the islands themselves were key actors and not just political footballs in some sort of competition involving international league tables. In this respect, the islands embody Renaud Morieux's vision in his magisterial study of 2008, *Une mer pour deux royaumes: la Manche, frontière franco-anglaise (XVIIe–XVIIIe siècles).*[10] In this important work, Morieux sets out to overturn the idea of the history of the Channel as an extension of Franco-British rivalry. In his hands, the Channel takes on a more shared and politically fluid character. Different, often competing, conceptions of what defines a 'maritime frontier' created a complex environment of varied, overlapping interests. He explores the commonalities across the water, the shared interests of maritime communities, and the economic and social ties or the conflicts that do not necessarily fit the neat, binary national boundaries that we often impose upon the past.[11] Although Morieux's study does not extend to the First World War, arguably it is then that his notion of a shared yet contested sea is most apt. Thus, like some other contributors to this volume, Thomas Vaisset evokes Morieux in his description of the shared responsibility for the Channel between Britain and France during the war. More than ever before, the Channel had become a Franco-British lake of sorts, and the Channel Islands were at the heart of French naval efforts to protect crucial shipping, not least as bases for French seaplanes which sought out German submarines. In Alexander Howlett's complementary study of the British perspective on operations, the islands are recognised as a French zone of influence. Taking a broader perspective of the command of operations in the Channel, he shows how they fit into a fully comprehensive and ultimately successful anti-submarine and trade defence system that was able to meet the German challenge.

For all periods of history, however, the Channel Islands could be held up in a similar way as a perfect illustration of Morieux's view of the unsettled, subjective nature of the Channel. From his largely eighteenth-century perspective, Morieux describes the legal ambiguity of the islands in the context of a discussion of smuggling. Any advantage to Britain of holding the Channel Islands, he says, depended upon accepting and tolerating the illicit smuggling and contraband that was rife there and recognising the limits

---

[10] Renaud Morieux, *Une mer pour deux royaumes: la Manche, frontière franco-anglaise XVIIe-XVIIIe siècles* (Rennes: Presses Universitaires de Rennes, 2008). Also available in English translation; *The Channel: England, France and the Construction of a Maritime Border in the Eighteenth Century* (Cambridge: Cambridge University Press, 2016).

[11] See also, André Lespagnol, 'Les îles Anglo-Normandes et la France de l'Ouest : une relation particulière', in Frédéric Chauvaud and Jacques Péret, eds *Terres marines : études en hommage à Dominique Guillemet* (Rennes : Presses Universitaires de Rennes, 2006), 85–90.

of its own authority. The islanders' connections with France meant that their loyalty and cooperation were far from guaranteed. It was a relationship that was carefully managed, and largely by the islanders themselves. Naturally, they mostly professed their attachment to the British crown in unproblematic terms, referring to the greater good, a shared history and religion, and a common hatred of the French. Yet, there was a clear economic interest, and they knew how to play their unique position to their advantage. The case for exemption from fiscal regulation by the British or from any restrictions to their activity was built upon their insistence that they were not actually smugglers themselves. The islands were merely 'entrepots', they claimed. According to their mercantilist logic, this was not only lucrative but it protected the wider economy because bullion from England that was spent at the islands on French goods did not actually leave the kingdom. The richer the islands were allowed to become, in other words, the better it would be for Britain. Were they to be regulated more closely, the smuggling trade would simply go to other French ports with disastrous effects. Indeed, nearby Cherbourg, watching with interest the British attempt to regulate the islands from the 1760s, hoped to take advantage by becoming a free port itself or even by proposing a joint venture with the islands. This was a prospect that was taken seriously in Britain. As it happens, the British state backed down. In this case, it was better to tolerate almost unrestricted smuggling through the islands than to risk pushing them into the arms of the French, moving the trade elsewhere to French advantage, and losing the privateering and spying opportunities that came with this.[12]

In this way, Morieux demonstrates how the islands capitalised on their unique constitutional position to deflect attention and protect their privileges and their relative freedom of action. He quotes from petitions to the crown of 1766 against a plan to establish customs officers on the islands that reasserted this exceptional status. Their rights and freedoms, the islanders insisted, were the formal, legal, and just recompense for their long history of extraordinary fidelity and bravery in protecting British possessions and defending them against French attack at great cost to themselves.[13] Elsewhere, Morieux reminds us that the Channel Islands had always been important remnants of England's ongoing, tenuous claim to the French throne and a means of justifying sovereignty of the Channel itself.[14] Thus, it is striking that Morieux is otherwise largely silent about the islands. He takes few opportunities to discuss their agency or to employ them to develop his theme of contested boundaries and subjective, shifting jurisdictional ambiguities in the Channel. Indeed, the whole history of the Channel Islands was conditioned by the

---

[12] *Une mer pour deux royaumes : la Manche, frontière franco-anglaise XVIIe–XVIIIe Siècles*, 244–51.

[13] Ibid., 248–9.

[14] Ibid., 114–15.

cultivation of their distinct legal position in this way which is significant not only for future research into the history of the islands themselves but more broadly. As Morieux acknowledges, declarations of this sort were actually a common refrain.[15] Elsewhere, equivalent declarations of particular local circumstances, of histories of loyal service, and of corresponding legal privileges and exemptions were a widely employed device by maritime communities. Far from making the Channel Islands peripheral or unrepresentative, their particularly obscure constitutional position and carefully crafted reputation for 'uniqueness', makes them an especially useful, rarefied embodiment of early modern maritime and naval history itself.

Much recent naval history highlights the agency of coastal communities and independent actors. Naval power, on both sides of the Channel, was as much as anything else the outcome of constant constitutional negotiation and management of the tension between the aims of central government and local interests. Indeed, in many ways, the countless formal declarations of loyalty to the crown, which often contained equally strident claims to immunity from it, became the very currency of exchange in the political economy of early modern maritime government. In ports and harbours of early modern France, in particular, royal authority was often very distant or only notionally recognised. The maritime periphery of the realm was an astonishingly intricate pattern of entrenched medieval traditions. Indeed, among the greatest challenges France faced as a naval power was penetrating this dense patchwork of competing, overlapping, even contradictory, claims to countless different local privileges and exemptions. Virtually every community held dearly to its own constitutional traditions, and any major operations at sea or initiatives to build French naval power were necessarily accompanied by a flurry of legislation that attempted, often mostly in vain, to make the authority of the King and the admiral of France felt. The findings of a comprehensive survey of all the ports and harbours of France by Cardinal de Richelieu of 1631, for example, revealed the full extent of the constitutional challenge that the crown then faced.[16] There was only a notional system of admiralty courts in place. The right to raise anchorage fees and other harbour dues, salvage rights, authority over coastal militias, or the right to distribute 'congés' or passports, all such privileges, it was reported, were so widely contested and dispersed amongst a bewildering number of claimants that plans to expand the navy had to be restricted to ports and to provinces over which Richelieu could exert personal authority in his own right as a local governor. Though every port and every province claimed to be honouring legal traditions as loyal servants of the king, they defended their privileges tenaciously and resisted any royal incursions.

---

[15] Ibid., 252.

[16] Alan James, 'Voyage et inspection maritime de M. D'infreville sur les côtes françaises de l'océan, 1631', *French History* 15, no. 4 (2001).

The Channel Islands, therefore, are more generally representative than their reputation as constitutional outliers would suggest. The way they played their status and negotiated their place within the wider maritime or naval strategy of the British state to their own advantage whilst maintaining active links with France has echoes everywhere, in all aspects of early modern life. Indeed, their declaration of fealty and devotion to the crown in their petitions of 1766 evokes the plea of virtually every rebellious noble whose loyalty was ever questioned, every petition by a beleaguered Huguenot community in the sixteenth century, every municipality facing increased taxation or billeting in wartime. All such protests were accompanied by earnest promises of undying devotion to the crown, illustrated with a claim of exemplary, usually military, service in the past, and an assertion of the legality of their special status on this basis. Historians, therefore, have many opportunities to reassess these and other patterns by exploring, not just what makes the Channel Islands exceptional, but what they have in common with other communities and the interactions and relationships between them as part of a genuinely comparative and regional history.

Anna Brinkman-Schwartz has demonstrated the value of the Channel Islands as a laboratory in which to study privateering and the challenges of distance, both political and geographical, that all powers faced directing naval power. Yet Michel Aumont's study of nearby Granville raises many interesting parallels. Granville was also integrated into trading networks in the Channel and subject to the capricious effect of international tensions, and there was a range of motivations for participating in privateering, just as there was on the islands. In times of war, Aumont argues, when the French monarchy tried to direct a *guerre de course*, only the most daring, or those in a position to gamble on a windfall prize, put to sea on behalf of the state. Otherwise, it appears, many there preferred to wait until peace could allow them to return to their main commercial activity, smuggling. This hints at strained and distant relations with Paris that recall those between the Channel Islands and the English crown. It also raises the possibility of some routine cooperation with the islands and the idea that, for citizens of Granville, conducting a war against their neighbours off the coast was simply not considered to be as profitable or welcome as colluding with them in the contraband trade. Of course, more work would be needed on these and other relationships to draw any firm conclusions. Yet, privateering was not just an instrument of the state nor an economic necessity created by war. There was a broader, more complex, but still regional, picture that Anglo-French competition complicated but did not entirely define.

It would appear from the chapters gathered together in this volume, therefore, that the Channel Islands have a bright future as the object of further historical research. The many complementary studies offered here demonstrate the explanatory power the islands hold as a common focus for the exploration of both French and British perspectives in the long history of their competition at sea. A fuller picture emerges of how the two powers influenced each other and, together, shaped the wider strategic environment in which they competed. In this sense, not only is the contested history of the Channel Islands brought to life by the study of Anglo-French relations, but the deeper study of the islands themselves has been shown to be equally illuminating. Indeed, the particular constitutional status and tensions that governed relations between the islands and the two great powers provide a model of local maritime governance. This presents more than just an opportunity to revisit traditional, state-centred debates about the long historical struggle between powerful political centres and declining maritime peripheries. In many ways, the Channel Islands allow us to transcend such debates altogether and to step out from the long conceptual shadow of the notion of the rising, nation state which has dominated the field of international history since its foundations in the nineteenth century. A similarly transcendent potential of the islands was identified by Victor Hugo over a century ago. 'Let us admire them, and let us venerate them,' he said. 'These microcosms reveal in miniature, in all its stages, the very formation of humanity. Jersey, Guernsey, Alderney; former dens for bandits, now workshops; former navigational hazards, now safe ports.'[17] For him, their transformation from their lawless, piratical beginnings to lawful and industrious citizenship embodied progress itself and inspired hope for the future of civilisation. As historians, we do not have to embrace with the same enthusiasm this nineteenth-century faith in human progress in order to share some of Hugo's optimism. The continued study of the shifting political, commercial, and cultural relations of the islands with each other and with their powerful neighbours as well as of their wider regional and long-distance trading networks promises a great deal.[18] Indeed, in many respects, the Channel Islands provide an elevated platform with an unobstructed view from which we may survey the future direction of maritime and naval history itself.

Alan James
King's College London

---

[17] 'Ces espèces de petites nations-là font la preuve de la civilisation. Aimons-les, et vénérons-les. Ces microcosmes reflètent en petit, dans toutes ses phases, la grande formation humaine. Jersey, Guernesey, Aurigny ; anciens repaires, ateliers à présent. Anciens écueils, ports maintenant'. Hugo, 'L'archipel de la mer', 86.

[18] On the vibrant activity and reach of the Guernsey merchants, see Gregory Stevens Cox, *The Guernsey Merchants and Their World in the Georgian Era* (Guernsey: Toucan Press, 2009).

BIBLIOGRAPHY

Primary Sources

Archival collections

Great Britain

Alderney Society Museum
Alnwick Castle
Devon Record Office (DRO)
Durham University Library
Hartley Library Southampton University
Hull Record Office (HRO)
Island Archives Guernsey
National Maritime Museum, Greenwich (NMM)
Naval Historical Branch and Admiralty Library, Portsmouth (NHB)
Royal Archives, Windsor Castle RA
Scottish Record Office (SRO)
The British Library (BL)
The National Archives on the United Kingdom (TNA)
Admiralty. ADM
Air Ministry AIR
Cabinet CAB
High Court of Admiralty: HCA
Home Office HO
Maps MPH
Ministry of Transport MT
State Papers SP
War Office WO
The Parliament Archives
The United Kingdom Hydrographic Office (UKHO)

France

Archives départementales d'Ille-et-Vilaine, Rennes
Archives du ministère des Affaires étrangères (MAE)
Archives nationales (AN)
Administrations financières et spéciales (Conseil des prises), AN, G5
Fonds Marine, AN, Marine

Archives du Service hydrographique et océanographique de la Marine, Brest, (SHOM)
Médiathèque de Granville
Musée d'Art et d'Histoire de Granville
Service historique de la Défense (SHD)
Archives de l'armée de Terre, Vincennes, SHD-TV
Archives de la Marine, Brest, SHD-MB
Archives de la Marine, Cherbourg, SHD-MC
Archives de la Marine, Vincennes, SHD-MV

Contemporary books and articles

Anonymous, *La Prise de Cherbourg. (30 avril 1889)* (unknown, 1889).
Armor (pseudonym of Maxime Laubeuf), *Les sous-marins et la guerre contre l'Angleterre* (Paris, 1899).
Aube, Théophile, *La guerre maritime et les ports militaires de la France* (Paris-Nancy, 1882).
Bourchier, Lady, *Memoir of the Life of Admiral Sir Edward Codrington: with Selections from his Public and Private Correspondence* (London, 1873).
Bourgois, Siméon, *Les torpilleurs, la guerre navale et la défense des côtes* (Paris, 1888).
Bowles, William, *Naval Administration* (London, 1854).
Bruce, Henry A., *Life of General Sir William Napier* (London, 1864).
Cabart-Danneville, Charles, *La défense de nos côtes* (Paris, 1895).
Chesney, George Tomkyns , *The Battle of Dorking* (London, 1871).
Cobbett, W, *The Parliamentary History of England from the Earliest Period to the Year 1803* (London, 1806), vol. 1.
Collins, Greenville, *Great Britain's Coasting Pilot* (London, 1686).
Corbett, Julian S., *England in the Seven Years War a Study in Combined Strategy*, vol. I. (2 vols, London, 1907).
——, 'The Capture of Private Property at Sea: The Nineteenth Century and After' in Alfred T. Mahan, *Some Neglected Aspects of War* (London, 1907), pp. 115–54.
Courthille, Edgar de and Hédouin, F., *Pilote de la Manche. Côtes nord de France, par E. de Courthille, ... avec le concours de F. Hédouin, ...* (2 vols, Paris, 1880).
Dawson, *Memoirs of Hydrography, Including Brief Biographies of the Principal Officers Who Have Served in H.M. Naval Surveying Service Between the Years 1750 and 1885* (Eastbourne, 1883).
De Guerin, T. W. M., 'The English Garrison of Guernsey from Early Times', *Transactions of the Guernsey Society of Natural Science and Local Research*, vol. 5 (1905), 66–81.
Dufriches-Foulaines, François-Nicolas, *Code des prises et du commerce de terre et de mer* (Paris, 1804).
Dumouriez, Charles François Du Périer, François Barrière and Saint-Albin Berville, *La Vie et les Mémoires du Général Dumouriez*, vol. I (3 vols, Paris, 1822).
Falle, Philip, *An Account of the Island of Jersey* (Jersey, 1837, 4th ed.).
Fournier, François-Ernest, *La flotte nécessaire. Ses avantages stratégiques, tactiques et économiques* (Paris-Nancy, 1896).

Grasset, Albert , *La défense des côtes* (Paris-Nancy, 1899).

Harcourt, L. F. V. 'Account of the Construction and Maintenance of the Harbour at Braye, Alderney', *Minutes of the Proceedings of the Institution of Civil Engineers*, vol. 37, no. 1874, 60–83.

Hesseln, Robert de, *Dictionnaire universel de la France* (Paris, 1771).

Holland Rose, John, and Broadley, A. M., *Dumouriez and the Defence of England against Napoleon* (London, 1908).

Houette, Alfred, *Les Courants de la Manche* (Paris, 1894).

Lacourt Gayet, George, *La Marine Militaire de la France sous le Règne de Louis XV* (Paris, 1902).

Lanessan, Jean-Louis de, *Notre défense maritime* (Paris, 1914).

Leslie, Norman, 'The System of Convoys for Merchant Shipping in 1917 and 1918', *Naval Review* 5, 1 (1917), 42–95.

Lockroy, Edouard, *La défense navale* (Paris-Nancy, 1899).

Meadows, Philip, *Observations Concerning the Dominion and Sovereignty of the Seas* (London, 1689).

Moore-Smith, G. C., 'Letters from Colonel William Napier to Sir John Colborne, Chiefly in Connexion with His "History of the War in the Peninsula" ', *English Historical Review*, 18, 72 (October 1903), 725–53.

O'Byrne, W. R., *A Naval Biographical Dictionary* (London, 1849).

Parker, Charles S., *Sir Robert Peel: from his Private Papers* (3 vols, London 1889–99), vol. 3.

Rollin, Henri, *Marine de guerre et défense nationale* (Paris, 1912).

Ross, Captain John, *A Treatise on Navigation by Steam, comprising a history of the steam engine, and an essay towards a system of the naval tactics peculiar to steam navigation as applicable to commerce and maritime warfare, including a comparison of its advantages as related to other systems in the circumstances of Speed, Safety and Economy, but more particularly in that of National Defence.* (London, 1828).

Tupper, Ferdinand Brock. *History of Guernsey and Its Bailiwick, with Occasional Notes of Jersey.* (Guernsey, 1854).

Vauban, Sébastien Le Prestre de, *Projet d'une dixme royale* (Rouen, 1707).

Welwod, William, *An Abridgement of All Sea-Lawes* (London, 1613).

Newspapers and periodicals

British

Colburn's United Service Magazine
Guernsey Almanack 1850 (H. Brouard)
Industry Illustrated
Lloyd's Evening Post
Proceedings of the Royal Geographical Society
The Comet, Guernsey
The Illustrated London News
The London Chronicle
The Star, Guernsey

French

L'Avranchin
La Vigie de Cherbourg
Le Gaulois
Le Matin
Le Petit Parisien

Official documents and publications

*Annales hydrographiques (*Service hydrographique de la Marine ed., Paris, 1838–1914).
Annales maritimes et coloniales (Ministère de la Marine et des Colonies, Paris, 1816–47).
Census of England and Wales 1901, Alderney, HMSO (1903).
Darrieux, Gabriel, *Stratégie et tactique. La doctrine* (Paris, 1906).
Degouy, Jean-Baptiste, *Marines étrangères. Marines anglais, allemande et italienne*, vol. 2 (Paris, 1897–8).
Dufriches-Foulaines, François-Nicolas, *Code des prises et du commerce de terre et de mer* (Paris, 1804).
Givry, Pierre, *Pilote français, Instructions nautiques...* (3 vols, Paris, 1842–51).
Hamelin Ferdinand, *Rapport de son excellence M. le ministre de la Marine à l'Empereur sur la transformation de la flotte* (Paris, 1857).
International Court of Justice, 'The Minquiers and Ecrehos case', Judgment of 17 November 1953, *I.C.J. Reports* (The Hague, 1953).
Journal officiel de la République française. Débats parlementaires. Chambre des députés (Paris, 1875–1918).
Kerros, Charles-Marie, *Manuel du pilote-côtier, par Ch. Kerros,...* (Paris, 1869).
Nove-Josserand, André, *Organisation du commandement en Manche et Océan* (Paris 1921).
Pothuau, Marie, *Communications en Manche et mer du Nord* (Paris, 1929).
Revue maritime et coloniale (Ministère de la Marine et des Colonies, Paris, 1848–1914).
Statistique des pêches maritimes (Ministère de la Marine et des Colonies, Paris, 1866–1914).
Thomassin, Charles Athanase, *Pilote de la Manche, côtes nord de la France, par M. Thomassin,...* (3 vols, Paris, 1871–5).
Toulouse Lautrec, Guillaume de, *Le transport en France du Corps expéditionnaire britannique. Août-septembre 1914* (Paris, 1935–6).
White, Captain Martin RN, *Sailing Directions for the English Channel* (Hydrographic Office, London, 1835).

Personal papers and correspondence

Barnes, G. R. and Owen, J. H. eds, *The Private Papers of John, Earl of Sandwich, First Lord of the Admiralty, 1771–1782* (London, 1936).
Benson, A. C. and Viscount Esher, *The Letters of Queen Victoria* (London, 1908).

Gooch, George P. ed., *The Later Correspondence of Lord John Russell* (London, 1925).

Stevens, Joan, *Victorian Voices: An Introduction to the Papers of Sir John le Couteur* (St Helier, 1969).

Temple Patterson, A. ed., *The Jellicoe Papers, 1916–1935*, II (2 vols, London, 1968).

Secondary Sources

Published

Abbatiello, John J., *Anti-Submarine Warfare in World War I: British Naval Aviation and the Defeat of the U-Boats* (New York, 2006).

A. Nelson Seaforth (pseud. Sir G. Sydenham Clarke), *The Last Great Naval War* (repr. Forgotten Books, 2015).

Aspinall-Oglander, Cecil, *Roger Keyes* (London, 1951).

Aubrey, Philip, *The Defeat of James Stuart's Armada* (Leicester, 1979).

Audoin-Rouzeau, Stéphane, *Combattre* (Paris, 2008).

Aumont, Michel, 'Les armateurs granvillais et la guerre de course: d'une activité de compensation à la tentation du risque', *Annales de Normandie* 2 (July–December 2011), 81–99.

——, *Les corsaires granvillais. Une culture du risque maritime, 1688–1815* (Rennes, 2013).

——, 'Jean Lévesque, sieur de Beaubriand, dit "Beaubriand-Lévesque", bourgeois granvillais et corsaire de Sa Majesté Louis XIV', in *Capitaines corsaires. Audaces, fortunes et infortunes*, ADCC (ed.) (Saint-Malo, 2014), pp. 139–50.

Bacon, Reginald, *The Dover Patrol, 1915–1917* (New York, 1919).

Barré, Éric, 'L'organisation défensive de Cherbourg et de la presqu'île du Cotentin de la fin du XIXᵉ au début du XXᵉ siècle', *Revue de la Manche* (1996), 150–71.

Battesti, Michèle, *La marine de Napoléon III. Une politique navale* (Vincennes, 1996).

Baugh, Daniel A., 'Why Did Britain Lose Command of the Sea During the War for America?', in *The British Navy and the Uses of Naval Power in the Eighteenth Century*, Black, Jeremy and Woodfine, Philip (eds) (Leicester, 1988), pp. 149–70.

——, *The Global Seven Years War, 1754–1763* (London, 2011).

Baumber, Michael *General-at-Sea: Robert Blake and the Seventeenth Century Revolution in Naval Warfare* (London, 1989).

Becker, Jean-Jacques, *1917 en Europe. L'année impossible* (Brussels, 1997).

Bellairs, R. M., 'Historical Survey of Trade Defence since 1914', *Royal United Services Institution Journal* 99, 595 (1954), 359.

Bellamy, Martin, *Christian IV and his Navy: A Political and Administrative History of the Danish Navy, 1596–1648* (Leiden, 2006).

Benson, Joel D., 'England, Holland, and the Fishing Wars', *Philosophy Study*, 5, 9 (September 2015), 447–52.

Benton, Lauren and Ford, Lisa, *Rage for Order: The British Empire and the Origins of International Law 1800–1850* (Cambridge, MA, 2016).

Benton, Lauren and Ross, Richard J. (eds), *Legal Pluralism and Empires, 1500–1850* (New York, 2014).

Black, Jeremy, *Parliament and Foreign Policy in the Eighteenth Century* (Cambridge, 2004).

Black, Nicholas, *The British Naval Staff in The First World War* (Woodbridge, 2011).

Borde, Christian, 'Le Comité central des armateurs de France face aux enjeux de la guerre maritime', *Revue d'histoire maritime*, 20 (2015), 91–102.

Brinkman, Anna, 'The *Antigallican* Affair: Public and Ministerial Responses to Anglo-Spanish Maritime Conflict in the Seven Years War 1756–1758', *The English Historical Review* (to be published in December 2020).

Carter, Alice Clare, *The Dutch Republic in Europe in the Seven Years War* (London, 1971).

——, *Neutrality or Commitment: The Evolution of Dutch Foreign Policy 1667–1795* (Bath, 1975).

Chamberlain, Muriel E. *Lord Aberdeen: a Political Biography* (London, 1983).

Chapuis, Olivier, *A la mer comme au ciel: Beautemps-Beaupré & la naissance de l'hydrographie moderne, 1700–1850 : l'émergence de la précision en navigation et dans la cartographie marine* (Paris, 1999).

Charpentier, Emmanuelle, 'Incertitude et stratégies de survie: le quotidien des femmes de "partis en voyage sur mer" des côtes nord de la Bretagne au XVIIIème siècle', *Annales de Bretagne et des Pays de l'Ouest*, 117, 3 (2010), 39–54.

——, *Le peuple du rivage: Le littoral nord de la Bretagne au XVIIIème siècle* (Rennes, 2013).

Chatelle, Albert, *La base du Havre et la guerre sous-marine secrète en Manche (1914–1918)* (Paris, 1949).

Clayton, Anthony, *Three Republics One Navy: A Naval History of France, 1870–1999* (Solihull, 2014).

Clements, Bill, *Martello Towers Worldwide* (Barnsley, 2011).

Cobb, Stephen, *Preparing for Blockade, 1885–1914: Naval Contingency for Economic Warfare* (Farnham, 2013).

Corbett, Julian S. and Newbolt, Henry, *Naval Operations*, 5 vols, reprint (Uckfield, 1920–31).

Coysh, Victor, 'Admiral Lefebvre and HMS *Dasher*', *Transactions of La Société Guernesiaise* 18, 1 (1966), 49–63.

Danckwerts, V. H., '1807–1917: A Comparison', *Naval Review Journal* 8, no. 1 (1919), 14–30.

Davenport, Trevor and Partridge, Colin, *The Fortifications of Alderney* (Alderney, 1993).

Davies, W., *The Harbour that Failed* (Alderney, 1983).

Dear, Ian, *The Royal Yacht Squadron 1815–1985* (London, 1985).

Dunn, Steve, *Blockade: Cruiser Warfare and the Starvation of Germany in World War One* (Barnsley, 2016).

——, *Securing The Narrow Sea: The Dover Patrol, 1914–1918* (Barnsley, 2017).

——, *Bayly's War: The Battle for the Western Approaches in the First World War* (Annapolis, 2018).

Duroselle, Jean-Baptiste, *La Grande Guerre des Français, 1914–1918. L'incompréhensible* (Paris, 2002).

Ehrman, John. *The Navy in the War of William III, 1689–1697: Its State and Direction* (Cambridge, MA, 1953).

Elleman, Bruce and Paine, S. C. M. (eds), *Naval Blockades and Sea Power: Strategies and Counter-Strategies, 1805–2005* (London-New York, 2005).

Evans, David, *Building the Steam Navy: Dockyards, Technology and the Creation of the Victorian Battlefleet, 1830–1906* (London, 2004).

Faulkner, Marcus and Lambert, Andrew, *The Great War At Sea, A Naval Atlas, 1914–1919* (Barnsley, 2015).

Fayle, C. E., *Seaborne Trade: Submarine Campaign* (3 vols, London, 1920–4), vol. 2.

Fisher, S., 'Captain Thomas Hurd's Survey of the Bay of Brest during the Blockade in the Napoleonic Wars', *The Mariner's Mirror* 79, 3 (1993), 293–304.

Fleury, Christian, 'Jersey and Guernsey: Two Distinct Approaches to Cross-Border Fishery Management', *Shima: The International Journal of Research into Island Cultures*, 5, 1 (2011), 24–43.

Gardiner, Robert (ed.), *Conway's All the World's Fighting Ships. 1860–1905* (London, 1979).

Gash, Norman, *Sir Robert Peel: the Life of Sir Robert Peel after 1830* (London, 1972).

Gat, Azar, *War in Human Civilisation* (Oxford, 2006).

Gauci, Perry, *William Beckford: First Prime Minister of the London Empire* (New Haven, CO, 2013).

Gibson R. H. and Prendergast, Maurice, *The German Submarine War, 1914–1918* (London, 1931).

Glover, Richard *Britain at Bay: Defence against Bonaparte, 1803–14* (London, 1973).

Goldrick, James, *After Jutland: The Naval War in North European Waters, June 1916–November 1918* (Barnsley, 2018).

Gosset, W. P., *The Lost Ships of the Royal Navy 1793-1900* (London, 1986).

Hackmann, Willem, *Seek & Strike: Sonar, Anti-Submarine Warfare and the Royal Navy, 1914–54* (London, 1984).

Haggerty, Sheryllynne, 'Risk, Networks and Privateering in Liverpool During the Seven Years War, 1756–1763', *The International Journal of Maritime History*, 30, 1 (2018), 30–51.

Halpern, Paul G., *The Mediterranean Naval Situation 1908–1914* (Cambridge, MA, 1971).

——, *A Naval History of World War I* (London, 1995).

Hamilton, Charles Iain, *Anglo-French Naval Rivalry 1840–1870* (Oxford, 1993).

Hasenson, Alec, *The History of Dover Harbour* (London, 1980).

Heathcote, Tony A., *British Admirals of the Fleet: 1734–1995* (Pen & Sword, Barnsley 2012).

Hobbs, David, *The Royal Navy's Air Service in the Great War* (Barnsley, 2017).

Hurd, Archibald, *The Merchant Navy* (3 vols, London, 1921–9), vol. 3.

Ingrao, Christian, *Les chasseurs noirs. La brigade Dirlewanger* (Paris, 2006).

Jamieson, Alan. G., *A People of the Sea: The Maritime History of the Channel Islands* (London, 1986).

Jellicoe, Lord, *The Submarine Peril* (London, 1934).

Jones, H. A., *The War in the Air* (6 vols, Oxford, 1922–37).

Keble Chatterton, E., *Q-Ships and Their Story* (London, 1922).

Kennedy, Paul M., *The Rise and Fall of British Naval Mastery* (London, 1976).

——, 'The War at Sea', in *The Cambridge History of The First World War*, Jay Winter ed. (3 vols, Cambridge, 2014), vol. 1, pp. 321–48.

Kinkel, Sarah, *Disciplining the Empire: Politics, Governance, and the Rise of the British Navy* (Cambridge, MA, 2018).

Kirkwood, Patrick M., 'The Impact of Fiction on Public Debate in Late Victorian Britain: The Battle of Dorking and the "Lost Career" of Sir George Tomkyns Chesney', *The Graduate History Review*, 4, 1 (2012), 1–16.

Knight, Roger, *Britain Against Napoleon: The Organization of Victory, 1793–1815* (London, 2014).

Kulsrud, Carl, *Maritime Neutrality to 1780* (Boston, 1936).

Lambert, Andrew, 'The Royal Navy and the Defence of Empire, 1856–1918', in *Imperial Defence: The Old World Order 1856–1956*, Greg Kennedy (ed.) (London, 2008), pp. 111–32.

——, *The Crimean War; British Grand Strategy against Russia 1853–1856* (Ashgate, 2011).

——, 'The Wellington system and national strategy, 1814–1852'. Unpub conference paper. Wellington Congress Southampton University, April 2019.

Lambert, Nicholas, *Planning Armageddon, British Economic Warfare and the First World War* (Cambridge, MA, 2012).

La Morandière, Charles de, 'Grandeur et décadence de la pêche des huîtres dans la région granvillaise', *Études Normandes* 96 (1958), 85–111.

——, *Histoire de la pêche française de la morue dans l'Amérique septentrionale* (Paris, 1962–4).

Larn, Richard, *The Isles of Scilly in the Great War* (Barnsley, 2017).

La Ronciere, Charles de, *Histoire de la Marine Francaise VI : Le crépuscule du Grand Règne. L'apogée de la Guerre de la Corse* (Paris, 1932).

Laurens, Adolphe, *Introduction à l'étude de la guerre sous-marine* (Paris, 1921).

——, *La guerre sous-marine. La protection de la navigation commerciale* (Paris, date unknown).

Le Masson, Henri, *Propos maritimes* (Paris, 1970).

Lempriere, Raoul, *History of The Channel Islands* (London, 1974).

Le Pelley, John, 'The Privateers of the Channel Islands, 1688–1713', *The Mariner's Mirror* 30, 1 (1944), 22–37.

——, 'Channel Island Seamen in the Wars of William III and Anne', *Transactions of the Société Guernesiaise* 14, 1 (1946), 35–47.

Lespagnol, André, *Messieurs de Saint-Malo: Une élite négociante au temps de Louis XIV* (Rennes, 1997).

——, 'Les îles anglo-normandes et la France de l'Ouest: une relation particulière', in *Terres marines. Études en hommage à Dominique Guillemet*, Frédéric Chauvaud and Jacques Péret (eds) (Rennes, 2005), pp. 85–90.

London, Peter, *U-Boat Hunters: Cornwall's Air War, 1916–1919* (Truro, 1999).

Ludendorff, Erich, *Ludendorff's Own Story, August 1914–November 1918* (2 vols, London, 1919).

McCartney, Innes, 'The Archaeology of First World War U-Boat Losses in the English Channel and Its Impact on the Historical Record', *The Mariner's Mirror* 105, 2 (May 2019), 183–201.

Marder, Arthur, *From The Dreadnought to Scapa Flow* [hereafter *FDSF*] II, 5 vols (Oxford, 1960–70).

Marder, Arthur (ed.), *Portrait of an Admiral, The Life And Papers Of Herbert Richmond* (London, 1952).

Marnot, Bruno, *Les grands ports de commerce français et la mondialisation au XIXe siècle* (Paris, 2011).

Mayne, Richard. *The Battle of Jersey* (London, 1981).

Messimer, Dwight, *Verschollen: World War I U-Boat Losses* (Annapolis, 2002).

——, *Find and Destroy: Antisubmarine Warfare in World War I* (Annapolis, 2003).

Meyer, Jean, 'La course: romantisme, exutoire social, réalité économique. Essai de méthodologie', *Annales de Bretagne* 78, 2 (June 1971), 307–44.

Michelsen, Andreas, *Submarine Warfare, 1914–1918* (Miami, 2017).

Minca, Claudio and Rowan, Rory, *On Schmitt and Space* (Abingdon, 2016).

Morgan-Owen, David, *The Fear of Invasion: Strategy, Politics, and British War Planning, 1880–1914* (Oxford, 2017).

Morieux, Renaud, *Une mer pour deux royaumes: La Manche, frontière franco-anglaise (XVIIe–XVIIIe siècles)* (Rennes, 2008). English edition: *The Channel: England, France and the Construction of a Maritime Border in the Eighteenth Century* (Cambridge 2016).

Morriss, Roger, and Saxby, David, eds, *The Channel Fleet and the Blockade of Brest, 1793–1801* (London, 2001).

Motte, Martin, *Une éducation géostratégique. La pensée navale française de la Jeune Ecole à 1914* (Paris, 2004).

Motte, Martin and Préneuf, Jean de, 'L'écriture de l'histoire navale française à l'époque contemporaine: un modèle national ?', *Revue historique des armées* 257 (2009), 27–43.

Moulin, Jean, 'France: La Marine Nationale', in *To Crown the Waves: The Great Navies of the First World War*, Vincent P. O'Hara, W. David Dickson and Richard Worth (eds) (Annapolis, 2013).

Muir, Rory, *Wellington Waterloo and the Fortunes of Peace 1814–1852* (London, 2015).

Murie, Yves, *La digue qui a fait Cherbourg* (Cherbourg-Octeville, 2006).

The Naval Who's Who, 1917 (Polstead, 1981).

O'Brien, F. T., *Early Solent Steamers: A History of Local Steam Navigation* (Newton Abbott, 1973).

Osborne, Eric, *Britain's Economic Blockade of Germany, 1914–1919* (London, 2004).

The Oxford Dictionary of National Biography (Oxford, 2008).

Pares, Richard, *Colonial Blockade and Neutral Rights 1739–1763* (Philadelphia, 1975).

Partridge, Colin, *Harbours of Refuge in the Channel Islands 1775–1904*, unpub. MS (Alderney, 2012).

Partridge, Colin W. and Davenport, Trevor G., *The Harbour and Fortifications of Alderney* (Alderney, 1993).

Partridge, Michael S., *Military Planning for the Defence of the United Kingdom 1814–1870* (London, 1989).

Pedroncini, Guy, *La défense sous la Troisième République* (2 vols, Vincennes, 1986), vol. 2.

Poussou, Jean-Pierre, *Bordeaux et le Sud-Ouest au XVIIIe siècle: croissance économique et attraction urbaine* (Paris, 1983).

Préneuf, Jean Martinant de, 'Entre Londres, Rome et Berlin. Les marins français et la figure mouvante de l'ennemi 1871–1914' in *Ennemi juré, ennemi naturel, ennemi héréditaire. Construction et instrumentalisation de la figure de l'ennemi. La France et ses adversaires (XVIe–XXe siècles)*, J. Ülbert (ed.) (Hamburg, 2011), pp. 289–302.

——, 'L'évacuation par voie maritime des réfugiés belges des ports du Nord et du Pas-de-Calais: octobre 1914–février 1915', *Revue du Nord*, 404–5 (2014), 85–109.

—— and Vaisset, Thomas, 'Le Parlement, la Marine et la création de la Direction de la guerre sous-marine, 1914–1917', *Revue d'histoire maritime* 20 (2015), 67–89.

——, Vaisset Thomas and Vial, Philippe (eds), 'La Marine nationale et la Première Guerre mondiale: une histoire à redécouvrir', *Revue d'histoire maritime* 20 (2015), 14–191.

Raban, Peter, 'Channel Island Privateering 1739–1763', *International Journal of Maritime Research* 1, 2 (December 1989), 287–99.

——, 'The Profits of Privateering: A Guernsey Fleet, 1756–1762', *The Mariners Mirror*, 80, 3 (1994), 298–311.

Reinert, Sophus, 'Rivalry: Greatness in Early Modern Political Economy', in *Mercantilism Reimagined: Political Economy in Early Modern Britain and its Empire*, Stern, Philip J. and Wennerlind, Carl (eds) (Oxford, 2014), pp. 348–70.

Rodger, N. A. M., *The Safeguard of the Sea* (London, 1997).

——, *The Command of the Ocean* (New York, 2006).

Rohl, John C. G., *Wilhelm II: Into the Abyss of War and Exile, 1900–1941* (Cambridge, 2014).

Røksund Arne, *The Jeune Ecole: The Strategy of the Weak* (Leiden, 2007).

Rollet de l'Isle, Charles-Dominique-Maurice, *Étude historique sur les ingénieurs hydrographes et le Service hydrographique de la marine, 1814–1914* (Paris, 1951).

Ropp, Theodore, *The Development of a Modern Navy, 1871–1904* (Annapolis, 1987, orig. 1937).

Roskill, Stephen (ed.), *Documents Relating to the Naval Air Service, 1908–1918* (London, 1969).

Rossano, Geoffrey L., *Stalking the U-Boat, U.S. Naval Aviation in Europe during World War I* (Gainesville, FLO, 2010).

Rossano, Geoffrey L. and Wildenberg, Thomas, *Striking the Hornets' Nest* (Annapolis, 2015).

Saffroy, Frédéric, *Le bouclier de Neptune. La politique de défense des bases françaises en Méditerranée (1912–1931)* (Rennes, 2015).

Saint-Denis, Guy de, 'Le bateau-feu Les Minquiers (1865–1891)', *Revue de la Manche* 163 (juillet 1999).

——, 'La station navale de Granville sous la deuxième République', *Revue de la Manche* 183 (juillet 2004).

Salter, J. A., *Allied Shipping Control, An Experiment in International Administration* (Oxford, 1921).

Scheer, Reinhard, *Germany's High Sea Fleet in the World War* (Kindle ebook, 2013, orig. 1920).

Schmitt, Carl, *The Nomos of the Earth in the International Law of the Jus Publicum Europeanum*, trans. G. L. Ulmen [first German edition 1950] (New York, 2003).

Scott, H. M., 'The Importance of Bourbon Naval Reconstruction to the Strategy of Choiseul after the Seven Years War', *International History Review* 1, 1 (January 1979), 17–35.

Seligmann, Matthew, *The Royal Navy and the German Threat, 1901–1914* (Oxford, 2012).

Sims, William, *The Victory at Sea* (Annapolis, 2016).

Sinsoilliez, Robert, *Histoire des Minquiers et des Écréhou* (Saint-Malo, 1995).

Somos, Mark, 'Selden's Mare Clausum: the secularisation of international law and the rise of soft imperialism', *Journal of the History of International Law* 14, 2 (2012), 287–330.

Sondhaus, Lawrence, *German Submarine Warfare in World War I: The Onset of Total War at Sea* (New York, 2017).

Spindler, Arno, *Der Handelskrieg Mit U-Booten* (5 vols, Berlin, 1933–66).

Starkey, David J. *British Privateering Enterprise in the Eighteenth Century* (Exeter, 1990).

Still, William N., *Crisis at Sea: The United States Navy in European Waters in World War I* (Gainesville, FLO, 2006).

Strachan, Hew, *From Waterloo to Balaklava: Tactics, Technology and the British Army 1815–1854* (Cambridge, 1985).

Studd, R. G. '"The Dover Patrol 1915–1917" By Admiral Sir Reginald Bacon', *Naval Review Journal* 8, 3 (1920), 423–4.

Sturtivant, Roy and Page, Gordon, *Royal Navy Aircraft Serials and Units, 1911–1919* (Tonbridge, 1992).

Syrett, David. *Admiral Lord Howe: A Biography* (Annapolis, 2006).

Temple Patterson, A., *The Other Armada: The Franco-Spanish Attempt to Invade Britain in 1779* (Manchester, 1960).

Tennent, A. J., *British Merchant Ships Sunk by U-Boats in World War One* (Cornwall, 2006).

Termote, Tomas, *Krieg Unter Wasser: Unterseebootflotille Flandern, 1915–1918* (Hamburg, 2015).

Terraine, John, *Business in Great Waters: The U-Boat Wars, 1916–1945* (Kindle ebook, 2009).

Thomazi, Auguste, *La Marine Française Pendant La Grande Guerre (1914–1918)*, (5 vols, Paris, 1925),
vol. 1.

——, *La guerre navale dans la Zone des armées du Nord* (Paris, 1925).

Thornton, Tim. *The Channel Islands, 1370–1640: Between England and Normandy* (Woodbridge, 2012).

Treadwell, Terry, *The First Naval Air War* (Stroud, 2010).

Villiers, Patrick, *Marine royale, corsaires et trafics dans l'Atlantique de Louis XIV à Louis XVI* (Dunkirk, 1991).

Virol, Michèle, *Vauban: De la gloire du roi au service de l'État* (Paris, 2003).

Webb, Richard, 'Trade Defence in War', *Royal United Services Institution Journal* 70, no. 477 (1925), 31–55.

Williamson, James A., *The English Channel. A History* (London, 1961).

Williamson, Samuel, *The Politics of Grand Strategy, Britain and France Prepare for War 1904–1914* (Cambridge, MA, 1969).

Winfield, Rif, *British Warships in the Age of Sail. Vol. IV* (Seaforth, 2014).

Zysberg, André, La monarchie des Lumières (Paris, 2002).

Unpublished MA and PhD Theses

Abbatiello, John J., 'British Naval Aviation and the Anti-Submarine Campaign, 1917–1918' (PhD thesis, King's College London, 2004).

Black, Nicholas, 'The Admiralty War Staff and Its Influence on the Conduct of the Naval War between 1914 and 1918' (PhD thesis, University College London, 2005).

Boulard, Emmanuel, 'La défense des côtes. Une histoire interarmées (1815–1973)' (PhD thesis, Sorbonne University, 2013).

Brinkman, Anna, 'The Court of Prize Appeal as an Agent of British Wartime Foreign Policy: The Maintenance of Dutch and Spanish Neutrality During the Seven Years War' (King's College London, DPhil thesis, 2017).

Chancerel, Pierre, 'Le marché du charbon en France pendant la Première Guerre mondiale (1914–1921)' (PhD thesis, Université Paris Ouest-Nanterre, 2012).

Chatelain, Sébastien , 'La place de Cherbourg dans la guerre franco-allemande de 1870–1871. Etude du rôle stratégique d'une place forte maritime' (MA thesis, EPHE, 2007).

Everard, Cyril Ernest, 'The Isles of Scilly and the Channel Islands: "bench-mark" hydrographic and geodetic surveys, 1689–1980' (PhD thesis, University of London, 2004).

Howlett, Alexander L. N., 'The Royal Naval Air Service and the Evolution of Naval Aviation in Britain, 1914–1918' (PhD thesis, King's College London, 2019).

Martin-Deidier, Annick, 'La guerre de course à Saint-Malo de 1681 à 1814' (PhD thesis, Sorbonne University, 1976).

Masson, Renée, 'La marine française lors de la crise de Fachoda (1898–1899)' (PhD dissertation, Sorbonne University, 1955).

Moucheboeuf, Daniel, 'L'œuvre navale de Delcassé de 1907 à 1913: Élément d'une politique de puissance' (MA thesis, Sciences Po Paris, 2001).

Née, Marlène, 'Arsenal et activités associées : les industries militaires à Cherbourg 1900–1939' (PhD thesis, University of Caen, 2008).

Nofficial, Sébastien, 'Le Parlement et la marine de guerre en France (1871–1914)' (PhD thesis, Université de Bretagne Sud, 2015).

Walser, John R., 'France's Search for a Battlefleet. French Naval Policy, 1898–1914' (PhD thesis, University of North Carolina, 1976).

Webb, Adrian J. 'The Expansion of British Naval Hydrographic Administration, 1808–1829' (PhD thesis, University of Exeter, 2010).

Online resources

https://gallica.bnf.fr

https://uboat.net

https://www.gov.gg

https://www.historyofparliamentonline.org

https://www.servicehistorique.sga.defense.gouv.fr

https://www.unicaen.fr/recherche/mrsh/maritime (bibliography of the Guernsey maritime history available online) : *Bibliographie provisoire de l'histoire maritime du baillage de Guernesey (des origines à 1939)* <https://www.unicaen.fr/recherche/mrsh/sites/default/files/public/maritime/Bibliographie%20guernesey%202022.pdf> [accessed 18 July 2023].

Ralph Mollet, 'Jersey's oyster fishing industry', *Annual Bulletin of La Société Jersiaise*, 1935 <https://www.theislandwiki.org/index.php/Jersey%27s_oyster_fishing_industry> [accessed 25 March 2020].

State of Guernsey, 'Extending the Bailiwick of Guernsey's Territorial Seas', P.2019/5, Billet d'Etat, II – 2019, Wednesday, 30th, 2019 <https://www.gov.gg/article/172632/Bailiwick-of-Guernseys-territorial-seas-will-be-extended-on-23-July-2019> [accessed 25 March 2020].

Widener, Michael, *Freedom of the Seas, 1609: Grotius and the Emergence of International Law. An exhibit marking the 400th anniversary of Hugo Grotius's Mare Liberum* (Part 8), October 2009, Lillian Goldman Law Library (Yale Law School) <https://library.law.yale.edu/news/freedom-seas-part-8> [accessed 25 March 2020].

INDEX